Social Engineering and the Social Sciences in China, 1919–1949

China's introduction to and development of Western social sciences in the late 1920s and 1930s grew from a larger intellectual movement in Europe and the United States emphasizing the empirical study of society. The idea of applying scientific methods to better understand and control social, political, and economic forces was timely for a country still emerging from its long imperial past and struggling to modernize. The empirical approach offered the hope of engineering Chinese society to eradicate such problems as poverty, illiteracy, and corruption and to promote education and industrial development.

In this book, Yung-chen Chiang tells the story of the origins, hopes and visions, and achievements of the social science movement in China during the first half of the twentieth century. Chiang focuses in particular on the efforts of social scientists at three institutions – Yanjing Sociology Department, Nankai Institute of Economics, and Chen Hansheng's Marxist agrarian research enterprise – to relate their disciplines to the needs of Chinese society. Because all three groups received funding from the Rockefeller Foundation, their stories constitute a unique window onto Sino-American interactions, revealing how the social sciences became a *lingua franca* of the cultural frontier as patron and clients negotiated through the medium of social science agendas and methodologies.

Drawing on an impressive variety of archival materials used here for the first time, this study corrects and enriches current scholarship, offering simultaneously a more detailed account and a panoramic view. Chiang does more than relate an extraordinary phase in the history of the social sciences in modern China; by focusing on the three most dynamic social science enterprises, he engages the complex issues of the transfer, indigenization, and international patronage of social science disciplines. Chiang's study of China's experience with Western social science, driven in large part by Sino-American intellectual and cultural exchanges, offers important lessons for contemporary social science development and education in China.

Yung-chen Chiang is Associate Professor of History at DePauw University, Indiana.

Cambridge Modern China Series

Edited by William Kirby, Harvard University

Other Books in the Series

Social Engineering and the Social Sciences in China, 1919–1949

YUNG-CHEN CHIANG

DePauw University

CAMBRIDGE
UNIVERSITY PRESS

PUBLISHED BY THE PRESS SYNDICATE OF THE UNIVERSITY OF CAMBRIDGE
The Pitt Building, Trumpington Street, Cambridge, United Kingdom

CAMBRIDGE UNIVERSITY PRESS
The Edinburgh Building, Cambridge CB2 2RU, UK
40 West 20th Street, New York, NY 10011-4211, USA
10 Stamford Road, Oakleigh, VIC 3166, Australia
Ruiz de Alarcón 13, 28014 Madrid, Spain
Dock House, The Waterfront, Cape Town, 8001, South Africa

http://www.cambridge.org

First published 2001

Printed in the United States of America

Typeface Times New Roman 10/13 pt.   *System* QuarkXPress [BTS]

A catalog record for this book is available from the British Library.

Library of Congress Cataloging in Publication Data
Chiang, Yung-chen.
Social engineering and the social sciences in China, 1919–1949 / Yung-chen Chiang.
p.   cm. – (Cambridge modern China series)
Includes bibliographical references.
ISBN 0-521-77014 9 (hb)
1. Social engineering – China – History – 20th century.   2. Social sciences – China
– History – 20th century.   3. Social change – China.   I. Title.   II. Series.
HN733.C439   2000
300′.951′0904 – dc21
99-056830

ISBN   0 521 77014 9   hardback

For Li-feng and Carolyn
Jishi shi "bizhou zizhen," haishi
yao xiexie nimen dui wo de xinxin

Contents

Contents

Contents

Photo section follows page 158.

Acknowledgments

During the long years stretching from my graduate student days that began in Taiwan to the completion of this book, I have accumulated a considerable amount of indebtedness to a number of individuals. I would like first to mention Chang P'eng-yuan, my teacher at Taiwan Normal University and a member of the Institute of Modern History at the Academia Sinica. Over the years he has been most generous in giving me encouragement and support. To Philip A. Kuhn, my adviser at Harvard, I owe first of all for his suggestion that I work on the development of the social sciences in China. His support and guidance were indispensable for the completion of the thesis and its development into this book. To the late John King Fairbank, I owe for the special care and interest he gave me concerning my personal well-being and intellectual growth. To Carsun Chang's daughter, Diana, I owe my gratitude for the 1977 Carsun Chang Memorial Scholarship for Study Abroad that she set up and administered. I am indebted to the following friends who gave me editorial help at different stages of the writing: Christena Biggs, Mei-lan Chin-Bing, Allen Chun, Sally Church, William Haas, Wing Yee Hom, Mary Mazur, Anne Thurston, and David Wank. In addition, Frederic Wakeman, Jr., and Paul Trescott read my thesis and gave me many helpful comments.

Much of the work for this book was a shoestring operation. As a foreign student pursuing graduate work during the lean years of the 1980s when American citizenship was a prerequisite to most fellowships, I was fortunate to have received two National Cash Register Foundation East Asian Scholarship travel grants, in 1983 and 1985, which enabled me to collect valuable materials for this book. A Rockefeller Archives Center travel grant in 1984 enabled me to spend a week using its professional facilities in North Tarrytown, New York. A postdoctoral fellowship from the Center for Chinese Studies at the University of California, Berkeley, from 1986 to 1987 enabled me to expand the scope of my work beyond the Anglo-American–oriented social scientists to include the Marxists. I am grateful for the help given by Joyce Kallgren, director of the Center at the time of my fellowship term. During the last stage of writing, I was fortunate to have received a Fisher Fellowship from DePauw University in the fall of 1990, which gave me the luxury of a semester's time of concentration.

Finally, I would like to express my gratitude to my wife, Li-feng, whose dedication and love have sustained my work and well-being; and to our daughter, Carolyn, whose sweetness, sparkling spirit, and music playing have brought great joy and enrichment to our lives. Their love and companionship have taught me that there is life, after all, beyond academia. At long last, I, too, can present to them something I have thoroughly enjoyed working on for as long as Carolyn can remember. To them, I dedicate this book.

Note on Names and Romanization

This study adopts the pinyin romanization system, with two exceptions. First, out of respect for their own choice and to facilitate corroboration and future research using multilingual sources, those who adopted English names and used them consistently and those who completed their careers in the United States are identified accordingly. Thus, it is H. D. Fong rather than Fang Xianting; Franklin Ho instead of He Lian; Leonard Hsu and not Xu Shilian; and James Yen in place of Yan Yangchu. Second, it retains personal names and place names that are long familiar in the West. Thus, it is Sun Yat-sen rather than Sun Zhongshan; Chiang Kai-shek instead of Jiang Jieshi; Peking rather than Beijing; and Canton rather than Guangzhou.

1

Introduction

When it comes to learning, sociology is the foundation. Only when sociology is understood will the cause of peace or disorder, prosperity or decline, be known, and will objectives from self-cultivation, ordering one's family, pacifying a nation, to bringing peace to the world be achieved. Truly this is a great learning!

Yan Fu (1896)[1]

Social science research in China during the 1930s constituted part of a larger phenomenon that occurred simultaneously in the United States and Western Europe. It was a movement toward an empirical study of society in order to control the social, political, and economic forces at work. The origins of this social science movement are diverse due to the differences in the academic and cultural traditions of these countries.[2] However, when the movement came to represent a new approach in the early twentieth century, it exhibited not only a strikingly uniform tendency toward empirical research, but a belief in the technocratic potentials of the social sciences.[3]

1. Yan Fu, "Yuan qiang" (On Strength), *Yan Fu sixiang zhitan* (Themes of Yan Fu's Thought) (Hong Kong, 1980), p. 16.
2. For a bird's-eye view of this phenomenon, especially in connection with sociology, see Martin Bulmer, Kevin Bales, and Kathryn Kish Sklar, eds., *The Social Survey in Historical Perspective, 1880–1940* (Cambridge, 1991) and Edward Shils, *The Calling of Sociology and Other Essays on the Pursuit of Learning* (Chicago, 1980), especially "The Confluence of Sociological Traditions," pp. 134–64 and "Tradition, Ecology, and Institution," pp. 165–256.
3. For studies of the technocratic claims and American social sciences, see William E. Akin, *Technocracy and the American Dream: The Technocrat Movement, 1900–1941* (Berkeley, 1977); John McClymer, *War and Welfare: Social Engineering in America, 1890–1925* (Westport, CT, 1980); and Guy Alchon, *The Invisible Hand of Planning: Capitalism, Social Science, and the State in the 1920s* (Princeton, 1985).

One major factor that contributed to the rise of this empirical approach was the patronage of social science research by philanthropic foundations, particularly the Rockefeller Foundation. The Laura Spelman Rockefeller Memorial appropriated about $21 million for the social sciences from 1923 to 1928 when it was reorganized into the Division of the Social Sciences of the Rockefeller Foundation. Besides exerting a powerful influence on the development of the social sciences in the United States, the Memorial set the prototype for patronage of social science research on a large scale. Through concentrated funding to selected institutions, the Memorial contributed to the ascendance of several social science centers in the United States, such as Chicago, the Brookings Institution, Columbia, Harvard, Minnesota, Yale, Berkeley, Stanford, Cornell, Pennsylvania, and the National Bureau of Economic Research.[4]

This strategic targeting for support of premier social science centers was an attempt to address the lack of scientific rigor of the social sciences, which the Memorial attributed to the old scholastic traditions that were "largely deductive and speculative, on the basis of secondhand observations, documentary evidence and anecdotal material."[5] According to a report commissioned by the Memorial in 1923, almost all the Ph.D. dissertations in the social sciences written in the United States from 1919 to 1922 belonged to library research – 86 percent at Chicago and 95 percent at Columbia, for example.[6] In order to foster empirical approaches, the Memorial deployed its resources for a two-pronged attack on economics, sociology, political science, psychology, anthropology, and history: provisions of institutional grants for research and a fellowship program to train a new generation of elite social scientists.[7]

That the Memorial could not have fostered something that had not already emerged within the social science disciplines is obvious. It is, however, beyond dispute that money from the Memorial contributed to

4. Martin and Joan Bulmer, "Philanthropy and Social Science in the 1920s: Beardsley Ruml and the Laura Spelman Rockefeller Memorial, 1922–29," *Minerva*, XIX.3 (autumn 1981), pp. 347–407; Martin Bulmer, "Support for Sociology in the 1920s: The Laura Spelman Rockefeller Memorial and the Beginnings of Modern, Large-Scale, Sociological Research in the University," *The American Sociologist*, 17 (November 1982), pp. 185–92.
5. Ramond Fosdick, *The Story of the Rockefeller Foundation* (New York: Harper & Brothers, 1952), p. 194.
6. Martin and Joan Bulmer, "Philanthropy and Social Science in the 1920s: Beardsley Ruml and the Laura Spelman Rockefeller Memorial, 1922–29," p. 373.
7. Fosdick, *The Story of the Rockefeller Foundation*, p. 195.

the ascendance of the institutions that responded to the Memorial's new initiatives in the social sciences. This is certainly the case with research institutes, such as the Brookings Institution and the National Bureau of Economic Research, that depended for their endowments, administrative expenditures, and project funds on the Memorial and, later, the Rockefeller Foundation, in addition to the Carnegie Corporation.[8] More subtle but no less definitive is the connection between foundation support and the university social science programs that achieved national prominence. The University of Chicago, which received close to three and a half million dollars from the Memorial, is perhaps the most illustrious example of this linkage. In essence, what the Memorial pursued was a policy of building on strength, or as Wickliffe Rose, president of the Rockefeller International Education Board and General Education Board, put it, of "making the peaks higher." It is noteworthy that more than half of the $21 million that the Memorial appropriated for the social sciences went to five major centers – Chicago, Columbia, the Brookings Institution, the London School of Economics, and Harvard.[9] Moreover, the four universities that the Memorial supported – Columbia, Chicago, Harvard, and Pennsylvania – produced, together with Wisconsin, more than 80 percent of the Ph.D.'s in the social sciences in the United States from 1919 to 1922.[10]

Direct funding to universities, however, did not fully illustrate the Memorial's policy of "making the peaks higher." For in addition to institutional grants, the Memorial also funded research through the Social Science Research Council. Created in 1923, the Social Science Research Council was an operating arm for the Memorial and, later, the Rockefeller Foundation, which contributed more than 92 percent of the Council's $6.25 million budget from 1924 to 1940.[11] Like the National

8. Dorothy Ross, *The Origins of American Social Science* (Cambridge: Cambridge University Press, 1991), pp. 400–4; and Ellen Lagemann, *The Politics of Knowledge: The Carnegie Corporation, Philanthropy, and Public Policy* (Middletown, CT: Wesleyan University Press, 1989), pp. 57–70.
9. Martin and Joan Bulmer, "Philanthropy and Social Science in the 1920s: Beardsley Ruml and the Laura Spelman Rockefeller Memorial, 1922–29," p. 386.
10. Lawrence Frank, "The Status of Social Science in the United States," p. 5, Laura Spelman Rockefeller Memorial Archives deposited at the Rockefeller Archives Center (hereafter cited as RAC LSRM) III 63.679. Note that Martin Bulmer has mistakenly reported that these five institutions produced three-quarters of the Ph.D.'s in the social sciences. See his "Support for Sociology in the 1920s: The Laura Spelman Rockefeller Memorial and the Beginnings of Modern, Large-Scale, Sociological Research in the University," p. 187.
11. The discussion in the following two paragraphs, unless indicated otherwise, is based on Donald Fisher, *Fundamental Development of the Social Sciences: Rockefeller Philan-*

Research Council of the National Academy of Sciences,[12] the Social Science Research Council promoted and coordinated interdisciplinary empirical social science research through committees, conferences, fellowships, and grants-in-aid. One cannot overemphasize the impact the Social Science Research Council's programs had on the social sciences in the United States. Consider, for example, the Council's fellowship program, which consumed 26.3 percent of its budget from 1924 to 1940. Of the 519 fellowships the Social Science Research Council awarded between 1923 and 1940, 240 were postdoctoral. As of 1951, 75 percent of these postdoctoral fellows whose employment status was known worked in academia, spreading across North America in fifty-six universities. Some of them became the most famous social scientists in the United States: Herbert Blumer, Crane Brinton, John Kenneth Galbraith, Simon Kuznets, Harold Lasswell, Charles Loomis, Margaret Mead, Robert Redfield, and Louis Wirth.

The national scope and posture of the Social Science Research Council, however, belied the fact that the Council's programs, like the Memorial's, disproportionately benefited elite institutions. Take, for example, the Council's postdoctoral fellowship program. While a total of thirty-two universities were represented, more than 70 percent of the fellows during the interwar years came from eleven universities. To be more precise, 49 percent were graduates of Chicago, Harvard, Columbia, Stanford, Yale, and Berkeley, and another 22.5 percent were from Wisconsin, Minnesota, Pennsylvania, Michigan, and Cornell. These institutions, furthermore, benefited from the infusion of these fellows to their faculty. While most universities had one ex-fellow, Chicago, Pennsylvania, Columbia, Berkeley, Stanford, Yale, Michigan, Illinois, and Cornell each had six or more ex-fellows on their faculty.

The Memorial's policy of "making the peaks higher" was not limited to the United States, but was global in its intent. In the words of the Memorial's director, Beardsley Ruml, "the development of social science requires that there should be in the world a dozen, fifteen, twenty, well-rounded and effective research institutions."[13] In practice, however, the

thropy and the United States Social Science Research Council (Ann Arbor: University of Michigan Press, 1993), pp. 199–211.

12. For an analysis of the National Research Council, see Robert Kohler, "Science, Foundations, and American Universities in the 1920s," *OSIRIS*, 2nd series, 1987, 3:135–64.

13. Quoted in Donald Fisher, "The Role of Philanthropic Foundations in the Reproduction and Production of Hegemony: Rockefeller Foundation and the Social Sciences," *Sociology*, 17.2 (May 1983), p. 212.

Memorial's power was much more circumscribed globally than domestically. Instead of cooperating with the existing peaks within the national systems, the Memorial often found itself having to foster fledgling new centers. In Great Britain, for example, due to the lukewarm response by Cambridge University to the Memorial's overtures, it was the London School of Economics, an empirically oriented institution founded in 1895 by Sidney and Beatrice Webb and George Bernard Shaw, that became the major beneficiary of the Memorial. As the fifth largest grant recipient of the Memorial, the London School of Economics was transformed from a small institution, providing mainly part-time courses, to become the principal social science center in Great Britain.[14] Elsewhere in Europe, the concern about the "speculative inertia" and strife among professors kept the Memorial from committing itself in France, Austria, and Germany, even though the social sciences were relatively advanced there. Instead, the Memorial concentrated on three major centers where interdisciplinary work in economics flourished: the Institute of International Studies in Geneva, the Institute of Social Science at the University of Stockholm, and the Institute of Economics and History at the University of Copenhagen.[15] Given its brief history, the Memorial could not extend much beyond the United States and Europe and only made a scant beginning in Asia in 1928, when it made a seven-year grant totaling $140,000 to Yanjing (Yenching) University in China. Nevertheless, in China too it was not the established premier universities but rather the keen and resourceful private institutions analyzed in this book that rose to become prominent social science centers by responding to the Rockefeller patronage.

This first Rockefeller grant to Yanjing was significant in that not only did it link Chinese social sciences to the empirical social science movement in the United States and Western Europe, but it incorporated China into the patronage network of American philanthropies. From this modest beginning, the Rockefeller support of the social sciences in China would by the early 1930s evolve into an ambitious program mobilizing Chinese social scientists for a concerted attack on China's rural poverty. That modern Chinese social sciences constituted part of a Western social science movement with technocratic aspirations raises an intriguing issue

---

14. Martin and Joan Bulmer, "Philanthropy and Social Science in the 1920s: Beardsley Ruml and the Laura Spelman Rockefeller Memorial, 1922–29," p. 396.
15. Earlene Craver, "Patronage and the Directions of Research in Economics: the Rockefeller Foundation in Europe, 1924–1938," *Minerva*, XXIV.2–3 (1986), pp. 208–9.

concerning a possible convergence of traditions, particularly in view of the fact that there had existed in China the Confucian ideal of using knowledge to govern society and the examination system that recruited men of letters into the governing process. Might this perennial Chinese ideal of governing society through knowledge have rendered a certain kind of Western social science knowledge particularly congenial to the Chinese? And to what extent was the development of the social sciences in modern China shaped by the convergence of this Chinese ideal and the modern Western notion of social engineering?

Equally intriguing is the issue concerning the incorporation of Chinese social scientists into the patronage network of American philanthropies. The Rockefeller support of social science research in China followed the patterns it had developed in the United States and Western Europe. Whether it was through funding directly from the Foundation itself or through its subsidiary funding agencies, it was a practice of "making the peaks higher." Here the issue transcends the field of Chinese studies and joins that of the study of philanthropy, on which a vast literature exists, though China is underrepresented in it.[16] A detailed study of the interactions between Chinese social scientists and American philanthropies would provide some documented data in a cross-cultural context to enrich the discussion of some of the highly contested issues in this literature: namely, the role of philanthropy in perpetuating a conservative ideology as well as in determining the research agenda and methodology.

Taking the involvement of American philanthropies in empirical social science research in China as the focal point, this study argues that the development of the social sciences in modern China was shaped by the convergence of ideas and aspirations at two different levels: first, the convergence of the traditional Chinese ideal of governing society through knowledge and the modern Western notion of social engineering, a convergence that led Chinese social scientists to see their work as a means to steer China's modernization; and second, the convergence of Chinese

---

16. This literature is too vast to cite here. For a convenient compendium from a critical perspective, see Robert Arnove, ed., *Philanthropy and Cultural Imperialism: Foundations at Home and Abroad* (Boston, 1980). For more recent discussions and debates, see the following articles: Donald Fisher, "The Role of Philanthropic Foundations in the Reproduction and Production of Hegemony: Rockefeller Foundation and the Social Sciences," *Sociology*, 17.2 (May 1983), pp. 206–33; Martin Bulmer and Donald Fisher, "Debate," *Sociology*, 18.4 (November 1984), pp. 572–87; and Barry Karl and Stanley Katz, "Foundations and Ruling Class Elites," *Daedalus* (winter 1987), pp. 1–40.

social scientists' aspiration in social engineering and the Rockefeller Foundation's ambition to guide China's modernization.

Three cases illustrate the central theme of this study. The first two were social science enterprises in the academic setting: the sociology department at Yanjing University in Peking and the Institute of Economics at Nankai University in Tianjin – the most prominent social science centers in modern China in their respective fields. The third case study involves a competing social science enterprise, led by the Marxist agrarian economist Chen Hansheng, which, significantly, also received funding from the Rockefeller Foundation through its subsidiary funding agency, the Institute of Pacific Relations. While Yanjing and Nankai represented the Anglo-American oriented social science establishment, Chen Hansheng's enterprise was rooted in the intellectual and ideological universe that stretched from Moscow in the west to Tokyo in the east.

Evolved from the YMCA movement in Peking sponsored by Princeton University graduates in 1906, the Yanjing Sociology Department, the subject of Chapters 2 and 3, metamorphosed from a vehicle for social betterment into a premier sociological center in China by the late 1920s. The trajectory of its history followed some of the broader trends in early twentieth-century American sociology. The legacy of the department in social service reflected the influence of the American social survey movement, particularly the Pittsburgh Survey of 1906–9. When a competing paradigm emerged within the department in the early 1930s, it mirrored what had happened a few years earlier with the social survey movement in the United States. Of the factors that contributed to the decline of the American social survey movement,[17] two are pertinent to the development of the Yanjing Sociology Department: the rise of empirical sociology, particularly the Chicago school of sociology; and the entry of the Rockefeller Foundation in the patronage of social science research.

This paradigm shift at Yanjing reflected an accurate, though slightly belated, reading of a realignment of power within American sociology. A crude and yet unmistakable indicator of Chinese cognizance of the American academic scene is their changing perceptions of the premier graduate program in sociology in the United States. Columbia University was the mecca for Chinese students in sociology until the late 1920s, when it had long been outshone by the University of Chicago. A major

---

17. Bulmer, Bales, and Sklar, eds., *The Social Survey in Historical Perspective, 1880–1940*, pp. 299–311.

shift toward Chicago did not occur until the early 1930s,[18] when Chicago had in turn passed its prime.[19] Not only did Chicago remain the most preferred institution well into the 1940s, but the Chicago methodology helped provoke a paradigm crisis at Yanjing.[20]

A new funding policy of the Rockefeller Foundation, altogether unrelated to the debate at Yanjing, delayed the resolution of this crisis, however. Instead of contributing to the ascendance of the new rising paradigm, as it had with Chicago sociology, the Rockefeller Foundation helped neutralize its impact at Yanjing. After having supported the department's social service mainstream since 1928, the Foundation bolstered its power again by incorporating its advocates into an ambitious rural reconstruction scheme in north China in 1935. Two years later, the war with Japan broke out. The resultant retreat of the Rockefeller Foundation wreaked havoc at Yanjing. The rebels from the prewar era thrived. Working in a war-torn economy in China's southwest and fusing the insights and approaches from sociology and social anthropology, they set up field stations, tested Western theories against the field, and strove to relate their disciplines to the nation's needs. In its reenactment of paradigm shifts within American sociology, Yanjing typified, albeit in a dramatic way, the powerful influence the United States had on knowledge transfer in modern China. Where Yanjing was unique was in its efforts and success in obtaining external funding.

The Nankai Institute of Economics – the jewel of Nankai University, the only private institution to have achieved national prominence in modern China – was the only other institution that, in addition to responding to the new empirical social science movement from abroad, thrived on funding from the United States. As analyzed in Chapters 4 and 5, the Nankai Institute of Economics embodied twenty years of brilliant collaborative work in academic entrepreneurship between two economists who received their training at Yale University: Franklin Ho (He Lian) and H. D. Fong (Fang Xianting). This premier center of

18. Robert MacIver, who joined the sociology department at Columbia in 1927, reminisced that at first nearly one-third of his graduate students were Asians, most of them Chinese. He was a little mystified why "[i]n later years these Chinese students vanished." See his *As a Tale That Is Told* (Chicago 1968), p. 98.
19. The decline of Chicago sociology began with the departure of Robert Park, who was on leave traveling around the world for much of 1931 and 1932, and eventually retired in 1934. See Martin Bulmer, *The Chicago School of Sociology: Institutionalization, Diversity, and the Rise of Sociological Research* (Chicago, 1984), pp. 122–3, 205–7.
20. The other major source of inspiration, as is discussed in Chapter 3, was Bronislaw Malinowski's functionalism in social anthropology.

economic research in modern China began with a simple adaptation in the Chinese context of a Western economic research tool: the compilation of index numbers. Emulating the work of Irving Fisher, his mentor and teacher at Yale, Franklin Ho set out in 1926 to compile index numbers on wholesale prices and money markets in Tianjin, where Nankai was located. The first breakthrough occurred in 1929, when Nankai received a grant from the Institute of Pacific Relations to study industrialization in Tianjin, which helped transform Ho's hitherto one-man enterprise into the Nankai Institute of Economics, with a grandiose scheme to measure the extent and effect of industrialization in China as a whole.

No sooner had this research program crystallized, however, than Nankai was under pressure to reinvent itself. As the Rockefeller Foundation's funding policy in China underwent a major shift toward rural reconstruction in the early 1930s, Nankai moved swiftly to position itself for inclusion into the patronage network of the Rockefeller Foundation. In addition to discarding its earlier macroeconomic concern about China as a whole in favor of a microeconomic focus on north China, it made a dramatic shift from urban to rural by proposing to study county government and rural industries in Hebei. In 1935, like Yanjing, Nankai was incorporated into the Rockefeller scheme for social engineering in north China.

Unlike Yanjing, however, Nankai did not suffer a near collapse following the outbreak of the war with Japan. Although it had to weather, as did Yanjing, the near withdrawal of Rockefeller support and the departure of key personnel, Nankai carried on its work in China's southwest by seeking funding from the business community. Along with the retreat of the Rockefeller Foundation, however, came an attenuation of its influence, which manifested itself in the reversion at Nankai to a research focus on macroeconomics. Whatever field work there remained, it was once again connected with index numbers. Nankai thus returned to where it had started two decades before. Nevertheless, whether it was macroeconomics or microeconomics, whether it was urban or rural, Nankai remained remarkably consistent in its endeavor to relate economics to the needs of the nation.

As unique and distinct as Yanjing and Nankai each was, both operated in academia and within the Anglo-American social science tradition. Whether it was through social service or social engineering, both envisioned social and economic change in terms of management and control. It came perhaps as no surprise that in China during the 1920s, when the fledgling Chinese Communist movement was spreading its wings, Marxism should have inspired a contending social science that envisioned nothing short of a revolution.

Like mainstream social sciences at Yanjing and Nankai, Marxist social sciences in China developed in stages and along different paths. Chapter 6 analyzes two such early endeavors. The first concerns Shanghai University, a radical institution founded in 1922 with a mission to train its students in Marxist social sciences for making revolution. At the core of this experiment was its sociology department, which, in sharp contrast to its counterparts in mainstream academic institutions, propounded Marxist and Soviet sociology as it existed at the time. This radical endeavor did not last long, however. Having being swept into the vortex of revolutionary politics of the early 1920s and situated at the eye of its storm, Shanghai University became a casualty in the coup against the Communists in 1927. Given its history and the way it ended, student activism and revolutionary politics understandably became the much celebrated legacies of Shanghai University. What has hitherto been overlooked, however, was one characteristic that the experiment at Shanghai University epitomized about the early Chinese Communist movement: a preoccupation with the universal truth of Marxism while ignoring the need to study the situation in China.

The other early endeavor in the Marxist social sciences involved a solitary effort in agrarian surveys by Mao Zedong. Beginning from his celebrated report on the peasant movement in Hunan in 1927, Mao sprang into a brief spurt of survey activities during a most trying period of his revolutionary career, between his retreat to the Jinggang mountains in late 1927 and his further retreat to southern Jiangxi in 1930. He was a tenacious worker, braving adverse conditions, as in one case, when the survey had to be hastily concluded because the pursuing enemy troops had caught up with him. Although most of his surveys were small in scale and his method crude, relying primarily on informants whom he cross-examined in group sessions, he was versatile in his experimentation with a variety of approaches. He was unique in that he alone among the early Chinese Communist leaders perceived the need to gain a thorough understanding of the field in order to make revolution. Most important perhaps was the powerful legacy his surveys bequeathed. His vision and approach would dictate the way social investigations were to be conducted in the People's Republic.

Political circumstances explain much but not all of the limitations of these two early endeavors in the Marxist social sciences. Neither

10

the theoretical orientation at Shanghai University nor the solitary effort by Mao in agrarian surveys was conducive to the development of a discipline. The one sustained effort that brought the Marxist social sciences to the level attained by Yanjing and Nankai was the agrarian research group led by Chen Hansheng, the subject of Chapters 7 and 8.

Educated in the United States and Germany, Chen Hansheng was a historian by training, a Comintern agent by avocation, and an agrarian researcher by commitment. In contrast to Yanjing and Nankai, which had to adapt to the funding preferences from without, Chen remained singularly successful in bringing philanthropies to terms with his research agenda. His agrarian research was from the very beginning devoted to promoting the Comintern as well as the Chinese Communist Party's thesis on how the semifeudal and semicolonial nature of the Chinese society was the root cause of the nation's deepening agrarian crisis.

With shrewd political and organizational skills, he built his radical enterprise by exploiting resources within the establishment. The most dramatic illustration was his use of the Academia Sinica – the highest research institution of the Guomindang government, which had outlawed Marxism – as his institutional base from 1929 to 1933. After the government caught up with him and forced his departure, he moved on to utilize host institutions. By placing himself in an advisory position and his key assistants in research organizations, he went on to propagate his Marxist diagnosis of China's agrarian crisis.

The most fascinating chapter of Chen's career was perhaps his association beginning in 1934 with the Institute of Pacific Relations, which supported him with project grants and twice brought him to the United States as a staff member in its New York office from 1936 to 1939 and as a sponsored guest in political exile from 1946 to 1950. While his sojourns in the United States enabled him to engage in agent activities for the Chinese Communist Party, the Institute of Pacific Relations benefited from the research as well as from inside political information and keen observations by Chen. This working relationship ended in 1950 when Chen departed from the United States for fear of political persecution then brewing in the United States Senate.

Despite its radical persuasion and combative posture toward the Anglo-American–inspired inquiries, Chen Hansheng's Marxist group was as much a part of the empirical social science movement as were Yanjing and Nankai. The most eloquent proof that linked Chen's group to Yanjing and Nankai on the one hand, and all three together to the movement in the Western world on the other, was their common bond to the Rockefeller Foundation – the subject of Chapter 9.

Although China was a peripheral concern in its global priorities when the Rockefeller Foundation entered the field of the social sciences during the 1920s, it was in fact more closely drawn into the Foundation's patronage network than direct appropriation figures indicated. This was because the Foundation made appropriations to other organizations that in turn distributed funds for research. During the 1930s, the Institute of Pacific Relations expended more research funds in China than in all other countries combined.

Then entered the Rockefeller Foundation itself. What began as an effort to broaden the Foundation's narrow focus on medicine culminated in the middle of the 1930s in a multifaceted program in rural reconstruction, surpassing anything the Foundation had ever attempted at home, particularly with its ambitious goal in social engineering that had heretofore been judiciously eschewed by the Foundation. This new Rockefeller program in rural reconstruction was never intended to advance the social science disciplines, but rather to steer Chinese social scientists toward applying their knowledge to direct China's modernization. Thus, in pushing Yanjing and Nankai to turn rural in their respective research programs and then incorporating both into its rural reconstruction program, the Rockefeller Foundation in turn stimulated the passion for social engineering at both institutions.

Like Yanjing, Nankai, and the architects of the Rockefeller rural program, Chen Hansheng's Marxist group too was committed to the notion of social engineering. As social scientists who professed to understand society, both the Anglo-American-oriented and Marxist social scientists, each in their own ways, perceived themselves as social engineers to plan and guide China's modernization process. For the social scientists at Yanjing and Nankai, research was a rational, scientific process through which to guide China's modernization. For Chen Hansheng, the purpose of agrarian research was to demonstrate how China's semifeudal and semicolonial production relations obstructed the nation's productive forces and how revolution was the only recourse to release the productive forces that hitherto remained shackled. For both sides, the blueprint was available and its efficacy proven, as demonstrated respectively by the technocracy model of the New Deal in the United States and the five-year plans in the Soviet Union. As far apart as technocracy and revolution were, both embodied the same aspiration shared by the social scientists in all three enterprises: to act as social engineers to guide China's modernization, whether capitalist or socialist.

That a convergence of interests in social engineering existed between Chinese social scientists and American philanthropies by no means affected the asymmetrical nature of the power relations between them. That both Yanjing and Nankai formulated their research programs in response to the funding preferences of the patrons suggests that the research agenda and methodology in China were indeed set by the Institute of Pacific Relations and the Rockefeller Foundation. More complicated, however, was the case of Chen Hansheng, who had an uncanny ability to subvert philanthropies with his own social vision, methodology, and agenda. This cross-cultural setting thus highlights an intriguing question about the complex relationship between patrons and clients. Chen Hansheng's may have been a rare case, a striking example of a client – and a Comintern agent to boot – fashioning the game of patronage to serve his interests as well as those of his patrons. Nor were the leaders at Yanjing and Nankai passive players. In this unique chapter of Sino-American cultural interactions, the social sciences became a kind of *lingua franca* of the cultural frontier. The patron and clients negotiated through the medium of social science agendas and methodologies. While Chinese social scientists were co-opted into the American academic culture, their American patrons were being manipulated by them as well.

Yanjing, Nankai, and Chen Hansheng's cases were by no means typical of the social sciences in China during the first half of the twentieth century. Nor were the sociology, economics, and Marxist agrarian economics they each represented any more important intrinsically than other social science disciplines. Least of all were the empirical bent and social engineering they espoused representative of Chinese social scientists of the day. Among the social science disciplines in China during the first half of the twentieth century, political science, for example, was perhaps the least inclined toward empirical approach. Furthermore, except for the few political scientists at Yanjing and Nankai who were inducted by their entrepreneurial colleagues in sociology and economics respectively, no Chinese political scientists played a role in seeking funding from American philanthropies.

An empirical approach, social engineering, and academic entrepreneurship constitute the criteria that determine not only which social science disciplines, but which institution within a social science discipline that this study analyzes. To be sure, Yanjing, Nankai, and the Chen Hansheng enterprise each was unique in its history, leadership, and institutional setup, which in turn was reflected in the materials each of them left behind. While the extended working relationship Yanjing and Nankai had with the Rockefeller Foundation and its subsidiary funding agencies left behind extensive records on the institutional and financial issues related to both institutions, the same was not true with Chen Hansheng's Marxist enterprise, which only clandestinely tapped into the Rockefeller largess. Furthermore, the scholarly output and the impact of the three social science enterprises were uneven, with Yanjing's being the thinnest, Nankai's at the middle, and Chen Hansheng's the most substantial, which partially explains the progression in the degree and scope of the analysis in this book of the scholarly production from Yanjing, to Nankai, and, finally, to Chen Hansheng.

The approach adopted in this book appears narrow when compared with recent literature on the history of Chinese social sciences that generally takes on the history of a discipline as its scope of analysis.[21] Yet it offers a unique angle to bring into sharp relief a host of broad issues. The distinct institutional focus enables this study to remedy the lack of specificity and precision characteristic of encyclopedic surveys. It differs from current scholarship in that it offers a tapestried narrative that is at once more detailed and panoramic than individual portrayals of them combined. By drawing on a variety of archival materials never utilized before,[22] this study corrects and enriches current scholarship by offering fuller and more calibrated analyses of Yanjing, Nankai, and Chen Hansheng's agrarian research enterprise. At the same time, by conceptualizing their rhetoric and research in terms of the notion of social engineering, whether technocratic or revolutionary, it transcends the institutional and disciplinary focuses embedded in current scholarship. More than simply offering a history of these institutions, or of the social

---

21. The following four works deal with the discipline of sociology: Han Minghan [mo], *Zhongguo shehuixueshi* (A History of Chinese Sociology) (Tianjin, 1987); Yang Yabin, *Zhongguo shehuixueshi* (A History of Chinese Sociology) (Jinan, 1987); Bettina Gransow, *Geschichte der chinesischen Soziologie* (Frankfurt/Main, 1992); Georges-Marie Schmutz, *La sociologie de la Chine Matériaux pour une histoire 1748–1989* (Berne, 1993). Sun Chung-hsing, "The Development of the Social Sciences in China before 1949," Ph.D. dissertation, Columbia University, 1987, deals with the entire spectrum of the social sciences. Finally, Leo Douw, "The Representation of China's Rural Backwardness, 1932–1937," Ph.D. dissertation, University of Leiden, 1991, which though not specifically about the social sciences, analyzes Chen Hansheng's group.
22. The exception is the dissertation by Sun Chung-hsing, which used the Rockefeller archives.

science disciplines they represented, or of the extraordinary academic entrepreneurs who built these research enterprises, this study at once broadens and sharpens our understanding of their endeavor to bring these disciplines to bear on Chinese society. Furthermore, by focusing on these three most dynamic and best documented social science enterprises in modern China, this study engages the complex issues of the transfer, indigenization, and international patronage of social science disciplines, where the most spectacular of the drama was enacted.

What makes the achievements of the Yanjing, Nankai, and Chen Hansheng enterprises all the more impressive was the fact that they took place at a time when the institutional and financial constraints, together with the prevailing academic cultures and traditions, all conspired to hinder the development of empirical social science research in China. To begin with, there was little or no empirical research tradition or institutional structure for it in modern China's emerging universities and government agencies. That Yanjing, as an American missionary enterprise, was one of the pioneering empirical social science centers in China is significant. More enduring efforts by the Chinese themselves to collect social science data, particularly economic information, began only in the early 1920s. In Peking, the Government Bureau of Economic Information, established in 1921 with William Donald as the director and Liu Dajun (D. K. Lieu) as the codirector, maintained a journal that published articles based largely on information collected from newspaper clippings.[23] In Shanghai and Canton, the Bureau of Markets and Bureau of Agriculture and Industry were also established in the early 1920s. Both bureaus were the first in China to compile index numbers of wholesale prices.

The early attempts by government agencies to collect social science data were sporadic and unsystematic; however, in universities where the social sciences were strictly subjects of instruction, the situation was even worse. In the case of economics, students began their concentration in the first year, and proceeded to take increasingly specialized economics courses without having to study any other subjects. In most cases, only one textbook was used. As this was invariably written in English, stu-

---

23. In addition to *Chinese Economic Bulletin*, which appeared in 1921, the Bureau in 1923 began publishing *The Chinese Economic Monthly*, which was in 1927 expanded and renamed *The Chinese Economic Journal* and continued the publication into the 1930s. See Earl Albert Selle, *Donald of China* (New York, 1948), pp. 223–5, 253–4.

dents had to struggle with the language before they learned the subject. Professors were burdened with too many teaching responsibilities, which left them little time to do research. Most of them were students who had returned from the United States and tended to repeat what they had learned while abroad. Their lectures and textbooks were almost entirely related to conditions in the West, especially in the United States, and had little relevance to China.

For instance, while "securities analysis" and the "business cycle," fashionable subjects at the time in the United States, were taught in many Chinese universities, neither subject bore any relevance to Chinese conditions.[24] There was no securities market in China, and given the state of the economy at the time, the "business cycle" was simply nonexistent. Many professors were experts on particular aspects of the American economy, such as Ma Yinchu on the municipal finance of New York City, and Franklin Ho on the U.S. federal income tax system. Few, if any, knew anything about Chinese county government financing or traditional land taxation. It is not surprising that upon graduation students could not even read the financial page of a Chinese newspaper because they had not been taught the specialized terms commonly used in such publications.

Many factors contributed to this uncritical adoption of the American social science curriculum. An important factor was a heavy teaching load, which left the professors neither time nor energy to prepare for class or engage in research. The political turmoil in the 1920s resulted in serious salary arrears for teachers. In order to make ends meet, many teachers were forced to teach long hours, ranging from twelve to thirty hours a week. Some of them taught in more than one institution, or even in institutions in two different cities, for example, in Peking and Tianjin, or in Shanghai and Nanjing. Franklin Ho of Nankai gave the following vivid description of how this was done.

> My friend Li Ch'üan-shih [Li Quanshi], who received his Ph.D. at Columbia [1922], ... taught courses in economics, history of economic doctrines, public finance, and money and banking in four different universities in Shanghai. ... [H]e went from one university to another on a rickshaw from morning till late afternoon. The results

---

24. The discussion in this paragraph is based on Franklin Ho, "The Reminiscences of Ho Lien (Franklin Ho)" (New York: East Asian Institute, Columbia University, 1972), pp. 73–5.

were disastrous; like other teachers, he did not have time to prepare for the courses he taught. He repeated the same lectures from year to year. He had no time or funds for research, no time to update the material he used, and no time for his students.[25]

In an apt use of an economic concept, Ho concluded that "the value of a teacher would depreciate in proportion to the time he stayed in his profession."[26]

American influence was not limited to the adoption of American curricula and textbooks. These repatriated students brought home with them the issues and methodologies that they had studied. The academic disciplines thus transmitted reflected no conscious design or systematic adoption on the part of Chinese social scientists. Fortuitous factors such as the institutions and teachers they happened to come into contact with in the United States often determined the approaches they used or even the disciplines in which they specialized.

Since a sizable number of Chinese students during the Republican period gravitated toward a few major universities in the United States, such as Columbia, Harvard, and Chicago, major schools or approaches in the American social sciences have in varying degrees exerted influence on the Chinese academic community. For instance, until the late 1920s, a high proportion of Chinese students chose Columbia for graduate work. From 1908 to 1929, of the ninety-one students who are known to have studied economics in the United States, forty-nine or 53.8 percent of them enrolled at Columbia.[27] Because many of them became professors upon their return, they brought back to the Chinese university curriculum the "business cycle" theory, a then fashionable subject in the United States, of which the main proponent was the Columbia economist Wesley Mitchell.[28] Furthermore, largely through the influence of Mitchell and Irving Fisher, the econometrician at Yale mentioned earlier, statistical work on prices and standard of living became a fashionable undertaking in China in the late 1920s. Most revealing, both of the influence of the teacher and of the enterprising spirit of the student, was Franklin Ho's imitation of Irving Fisher in compiling and publishing in a newspaper in Tianjin weekly index numbers

25. Ibid., pp. 72–3.
26. Ibid., p. 73.
27. Figures adopted from Paul Trescott, Jian-Ye Wang, and Yan Zhi-Jie, "The Introduction of Western Economic Ideas into China," (unpublished paper, April 1985), Table 2.
28. Ho, "Reminiscences," p. 73.

on wholesale prices as well as foreign and domestic exchanges and bond markets.[29]

Actual teacher–student interaction was not the only channel through which dominant trends in American social sciences were transmitted to the Chinese academic community. Always keen on watching the American academic scene, Chinese social scientists were constantly searching for what they viewed as the latest trends or approaches. There might have been a time lag between the rise of these trends or approaches in the United States and their vogue in China. This time lag often manifested itself in the rise and fall of a given institution as a favorite place for Chinese students to pursue graduate studies. A case in point was the changing Chinese perceptions of Columbia, then Chicago, as the most prominent sociology center during the 1920s and the 1930s. Due to the reputation of Franklin Giddings at Columbia, his home institution was the mecca for Chinese students in sociology until the late 1920s, when it had long been outshone by Chicago. Robert MacIver, who joined the sociology department at Columbia in 1927, reminisced:

> My class of graduates . . . was at first of very moderate size and nearly a third of the students were Orientals, largely Chinese. The latter were avid learners but poorly trained, and they frequently did not understand English well enough to grasp much of what I tried to teach. Some of the others were really able, but the majority lacked the capacity to express themselves effectively. I came to the conclusion that most schools gave a poor training in English. In later years these Chinese students vanished.[30]

In the mid-1930s, when Chicago had passed its prime, a group of dedicated sociology professors and students at Yanjing began passionately promoting "community studies," an approach that was influenced by both the Chicago school of sociology and functionalism in social anthropology.[31]

The ramifications of American dominance of higher education in China went beyond the adoption of American textbooks and curricula. In the social sciences, the use of American textbooks perpetuated the situation in which the social sciences in China remained subjects concerned

---

29. For more discussion of this venture à la Fisher, see Chapter 4.
30. Robert MacIver, *As a Tale That Is Told* (Chicago, 1968), p. 98.
31. The decline of Chicago sociology began with the departure of Robert Park, as indicated in footnote 19.

with the West and had little bearing on Chinese society. Little had changed in the conception of Western knowledge dating from the turn of the twentieth century, when a major influx began that saw ideas from the West as embodying the secrets behind Western success rather than as a means to understanding Chinese society.

There was one problem unique to social scientists who went abroad to study during the first two decades of this century, particularly those who went to secondary schools in China, where the primary language of instruction was English. Most of them had no prior exposure to the subjects in which they would specialize while abroad. They learned the terminologies and specialized concepts only in English and rarely had to expound their specialties in Chinese until they returned to China to teach. After a prolonged education in English, both in China and in the United States, it is only natural that they would find English rather than Chinese a preferable medium through which to discuss the subjects they had learned in the United States. To make the situation worse, terminologies had not yet been translated or standardized. Chinese translations on subjects of their specialties were generally nonexistent.

Thus the problem was not just an undue reliance on American textbooks. Some Chinese social scientists experienced a reverse language barrier. Efforts at overcoming this reverse language barrier were arduous, especially if the returnees did not already have a solid background in Chinese before they left China. Some of them left before they had finished secondary education and spent their formative years in the United States for a decade or more. Upon their return, they found themselves unable to lecture and write in Chinese. Jiang Tingfu (Tsiang T'ingfu, B.A., Oberlin, 1918; Ph.D., Columbia, 1923), the Qinghua historian, who later became an important government official, was one such example. At age eleven, he switched to a Presbyterian missionary school in Xiangtan, Hunan, in order to receive an English education and, at seventeen, went on to study in the United States.[32] He recounted in his "Reminiscences" how he regained his command of Chinese.

> I began exactly the way I did when I was six years old in the country, namely, by reviewing the Four Books and Five Classics of Confucianism. I did not try to re-memorize these classics, but by repeatedly reading them aloud, most of the passages came back to me.

---

32. Howard Boorman and Richard Howard, eds., *Biographical Dictionary of Republican China* (New York, 1967), I:354–8.

From the basic texts, I went on to study the essays and poems usually selected for secondary school education. From that point, I went on to read such books as seemed proper.[33]

H. D. Fong of Nankai went through a similar process to regain his ability to lecture and write in Chinese. His early publications were all written in English first and then translated into Chinese by his assistant. He would then check for accuracy himself. The final touch was given by his ablest assistant, Li Rui. By thus repeating this process several times with all of his early publications, Fong learned to write in academic Chinese again.[34]

In addition to their conscientious efforts to re-educate themselves in order to function in Chinese, Jiang and Fong were pioneers in their attempt to indigenize the social sciences in China. Yet they were by no means representative of the repatriates. The majority of the returnees in the 1920s seem to have had no qualms about repeating what they had learned while abroad. The eagerness to demonstrate one's access to "the latest trend from the West" remained a powerful motivation for a social science professor to lecture on subjects that were fashionable in America but had no relevance to China.

The most obstinate obstacle was perhaps the traditional elitist bias of Chinese intellectuals. Modern empirical social science research embodied a radically different approach to scholarship from that of the Chinese tradition. The field work approach in particular posed a special challenge to the traditional image of a scholar, which was invariably framed in a study or a landscape painting but never on the street or in the field.

A classic example of the clash of values could be found in the person of Li Jinghan (Franklin Lee), Sidney Gamble's most valuable collaborator, discussed later in this book. Returning from the United States with a M.A. degree in sociology, Li Jinghan enraged his relatives and bewildered his friends by engaging in a study of rickshaw pullers in Peking. A relative scolded him with the following words: "You did not become a professor. Nor have you tried to get a lucrative job in the government. Instead, you associate yourself with the dirty and rude laborers. You are really out of your mind!"[35] An intellectual friend, poking fun at his work

---

33. Jiang Tingfu, "The Reminiscences of Tsiang T'ing-fu (1895–1965)" (New York: East Asian Institute, Columbia University, 1974), pp. 99–100.
34. H. D. Fong, *Reminiscences of a Chinese Economist at 70* (Singapore, 1975), p. 43.
35. Li Jinghan, "Beijing wuchanjieji de shenghuo" (Lives of the Proletariat in Peking), *Shenghuo* (Life Weekly), I.37 (July 4, 1926), p. 218.

on the street, presented him with a couplet playfully adopted from a Tang dynasty poem:

Among those you chat and laugh with, none is known as a scholar;
But there are lots of illiterates with whom you mingle.[36]

These scandalous remarks to Li Jinghan reveal more than resistance to the undignified nature of the field work approach. Equally mystifying to those imbued with traditional elitism was the subject of investigation. From their elitist perspective, work among rickshaw pullers, peddlers, or shop owners was not only an activity unfitting for an educated man, but was also a misguided effort. In the words of one intellectual: "To educate one hundred rickshaw pullers would not be as useful as to educate a rickshaw customer. Similarly, a donation from a rich man would certainly be larger than what can be raised from one hundred shop owners."[37]

This deeply entrenched elitism and tendency to treat the social sciences as abstract theories rather than methods and categories for the study of society formed the background against which the three social science enterprises analyzed in this study emerged. The story of the Yanjing Sociology Department, the Nankai Institute of Economics, and Chen Hansheng's agrarian research enterprise constituted a unique and extraordinary chapter in the history of the social sciences in modern China. Elitism, to be sure, permeated all these three social science enterprises. That the social scientists in all three enterprises perceived themselves as social engineers bespeaks an elitism that stemmed from the Confucian elitist tradition and reinforced by the modern technocratic ethos embodied either in the New Deal in the United States or state planning in the Soviet Union.

No less conspicuous was the element of careerism, the exception being members of Chen Hansheng's group who, owing to their commitment to revolution, rejected the idea of serving the existing government. Many Yanjing and Nankai social scientists, by contrast, had no qualms in giving up teaching for a government career. While they viewed government service as an avenue toward social engineering, their critics derided their behavior a mockery of the Confucian dictum: "Having excelled in study,

36. Li Jinghan, "Shenru minjian de yixie jingyan yu ganxiang" (Some Experience and Thoughts from My Efforts to Immerse Myself with the Masses), *Duli pinglun* (Independent Review), 179 (12/1/1935), p. 8. This couplet is adopted from Liu Yuxi's (772–842) "Loushi ming" (Song from a Shed), with the meaning purposely reversed.
37. Li Jinghan, "Beijing wuchanjieji de shenghuo."

one should enter government service."[38] The truth lay perhaps in between, for many of these social scientists genuinely believed that their personal interest in government service coincided with the ideal of social engineering. What enabled the Yanjing and Nankai social scientists to link government service – and, revolution, in the case of Chen Han-sheng's radical group – with social engineering was their new approach to the social sciences. No longer were the social sciences abstract theories from the West, as had been the case with the previous generation, but rather analytic tools for the study of Chinese society. Their endeavors to make the social sciences relevant to Chinese society and thus useful for the nation's modernization or revolution at the same time made them truly the first generation of empirical social scientists in China. This study attempts to reconstruct their story by focusing on the leading spirits involved in these three social science enterprises – their visions and aspirations, their leadership roles and entrepreneurial skills, and their research and analyses of their society.

38. *The Analects*, 19.13; my translation.

2

The Yanjing Sociology Department: The Social Service Phase, 1919–1925

LIKE medical care and famine or disaster relief, education had been an integral part of the missionary enterprise in China since the turn of the twentieth century. Although generally weak in their offerings of social science courses, the Christian colleges were particularly strong in sociology.[1] This special emphasis on sociology reflected the complementary nature of the aims of evangelism and social service of the Christian colleges. It is because activities in social service generated a need for more information about the communities to be served that the Christian colleges pioneered field research in China.

More significantly, it was the Americans in these colleges who pioneered the work. In fact, the individuals enshrined in the early history of the social sciences in China were all Americans: C. G. Dittmer of Qinghua College, H. S. Bucklin and Daniel Kulp of Shanghai College, John Stewart Burgess and Sidney Gamble of Yanjing University, and J. Lossing Buck of the University of Nanking. These exclusively American undertakings of early empirical social research in China bespoke a much larger pattern of influence through which the United States would dominate the development of the social sciences in China until the Communist Revolution of 1949.

Among these early field research centers, the one that best illustrated American influence and, later, Chinese adaptations and participation was the sociology department at Yanjing University – the most ambitious and successful of all Protestant missionary institutions of higher educa-

---

1. In 1926, for instance, while Chinese institutions on the average provided three times as much instruction in political science and economics as did Christian colleges, they offered only about half of the sociology courses. Herbert Cressy, *Christian Higher Education in China* (Shanghai, 1928), p. 58.

tion in modern China.[2] In 1925, at the height of missionary colleges' dominance in the teaching of sociology, the Yanjing Sociology Department offered about 40 percent of all the sociology courses given by the ten leading Christian colleges put together. If the statistics on Chinese institutions are included, Yanjing alone offered roughly one fourth of all the sociology courses offered in China in the mid-1920s.[3] Yanjing's dominant position in sociology was particularly conspicuous, for as late as 1925 no reputable Chinese institution of higher education had a department of sociology.[4]

In addition to being the foremost sociological center in China, the Yanjing Sociology Department was unique in the aspiration of its members and their participation in work that aimed at effecting changes in society. The period from the late 1920s to the early 1930s was characterized by a surge of activity in social reform. The fascination with the social benefits of science and democracy popular during the May Fourth period gave way to a recognition of the need for concrete programs to attack specific problems that had been plaguing China.

At the local level, spontaneous efforts in reform proliferated. By the mid-1930s, these local activities, collectively known as the rural reconstruction movement, had spread nationwide in twenty-two provinces ranging from literacy campaigns, cooperatives, and agricultural extension work to comprehensive programs for the reconstruction of entire counties.[5] By becoming involved in national affairs as well as regional experimental work, the Yanjing Sociology Department ventured into the arena of social engineering. Whether serving in the government, directing work at the department's experiment station, or teaching primarily in the classrooms, all members of the department were convinced of the absolute importance of sociology in charting the course for China's modernization.

Their belief in social engineering and in the crucial role played by

2. For a pioneering study of Yanjing University, see Philip West, *Yenching University and Sino-Western Relations, 1916–1952* (Harvard, 1976).
3. These figures are only approximations. The 40 percent figure is derived from a survey made by J. Stewart Burgess. See Leonard Hsu, "The Teaching of Sociology in China," 374, chart. This figure is then used to compare with the analysis given in Herbert Cressy, *Christian Higher Education in China* (Shanghai, 1928), p. 58.
4. The short-lived National University of Political Science (1923–1927) at Wusong, Jiangsu had a department of sociology. See Leonard Hsu, "The Teaching of Sociology in China," *Chinese Social and Political Science Review*, 11.3 (1927), pp. 373–5.
5. Xu Yinglian, et al., *Quanguo xiangcun jianshe yundong gaikuang* (A General Account of the Nationwide Rural Reconstruction Movement) (Zouping, 1935), Appendices.

sociology echoed the perennial Chinese ideal of using knowledge to govern society. At the same time, this claim of the supremacy of sociology in guiding China's modernization represented a far more ambitious vision than the ameliorative nature of social service commonly conceived by sociology departments at missionary colleges. The reincorporation of scholarship into the governing process can be traced by following the transformation of the Yanjing Sociology Department from one that focused on social service into one that aspired to social engineering.

PRINCETON-IN-PEKING AND COMMUNITY SOCIAL SERVICE

The emphasis on social service at the Yanjing Sociology Department is a legacy of the YMCA movement in Peking. In 1905, the Philadelphian Society, a student YMCA at Princeton University, accepted the invitation from the International Committee of the YMCA to sponsor and staff an association in Peking. Officially launched in 1906, the organization was called Princeton-in-Peking and, eventually, the Princeton Yenching Foundation in 1930. Robert Gailey (M.A., 1896), who had been the YMCA secretary in Tianjin since 1897, was chosen as the first Princeton representative. Dwight Edwards (B.A., 1904), transferred from Japan, became the first and immediate reinforcement for Gailey. By the end of 1909, when John Stewart Burgess (B.A., 1905) reached Peking, Gailey's original one-man team had grown to a membership of five.[6]

These Princeton secretaries concentrated their effort among three groups of young men in Peking: students in Christian as well as government institutions, young men in general, and the foreign legation guards. Of particular importance was the emphasis Princeton-in-Peking attached to its student work. It reflected a strategic choice calculated to conquer the empire by capturing its leaders. As its promotional literature put it: "From their ranks [the student class] come all the officials and leaders."[7]

Students at missionary schools were the most amenable to the Princeton workers. Since many of these students were already believers, they could use summer conferences and Bible institutes – the familiar YMCA formats in the United States – to inspire a few souls to pledge themselves to evangelical work. Students at government institutions, however, posed

---

6. They were Gailey, Dwight Edwards, John Stewart Burgess, L. D. Froelick, 1906, and J. W. Chambers, 1909.
7. "The Princeton Work in Peking," p. 2.

problems. Most challenging for Princeton-in-Peking was to find an avenue of communication to the mind of these students. Education had proven the best means of entry to the literati class, as was borne out by Gailey's success with the Tianjin elite through their collaborative efforts in education.[8] To Christianity, however, students in government institutions remained as resistant as had been their literati predecessors. A breakthrough was finally made by Burgess, who found in the social gospel a link between Christianity and national rejuvenation that had an immense appeal to the Chinese students.

After his graduation from Princeton in 1905, Burgess became an English teacher and a volunteer YMCA worker in Kyoto. In 1907, he returned to the United States to study theology and then went to Columbia University, where he received an M.A. degree in sociology in 1909. Thereafter he was sent to Peking to join the Princeton team there.[9]

Burgess spent six months studying Chinese before he began teaching at government colleges: first in the College of Languages for six weeks, then in the Higher Normal College and the Customs College. He set out to work among these students, who responded enthusiastically. For example, at the College of Languages, he helped twenty students form a club, which held study sessions at the school, at the YMCA, and at his house. Where he encountered difficulty was to get the students interested in Christianity. While his club discussed a variety of topics, ranging from the social sciences, to politics and student life in America, and to hygiene, none touched directly on Christianity.[10] In an attempt to relate Christianity to the interest of the Chinese students, he decided to find out what issues preoccupied them.

His approach to this question was to find out what Chinese students were reading. In early 1911, he sent out a questionnaire to a number of Chinese educators and a few foreigners who were in close contact with students.[11] The respondents to this survey generally agreed that students were most interested in the social sciences – economics, politics, and

---

8. Shirley Garrett, *Social Reformers in Urban China: The Chinese Y.M.C.A., 1895–1926* (Harvard, 1970), pp. 45–100.

9. *The National Cyclopaedia of American Biography* (New York, 1954), 39: 423–4.

10. Burgess, "Annual Report, September 30, 1910 to January 1, 1911," p. 5, the YMCA Archives deposited at the University of Minnesota (hereafter cited as YMCA) Princeton-in-Peking Box, 1906–1912 Folder. The only topic that may have lent itself to discussion on Christianity was "Evolution and its Significance."

11. Burgess, "What Chinese Students Are Reading?" *The Intercollegian* (November 1911), pp. 31–7.

sociology. Yan Fu's translations and Liang Qichao's writings were particularly singled out as the most important sources of information for the students. In fact, the list of the most widely read books in the social sciences reads like a resumé of Yan Fu's translations.[12]

What transpired in Burgess's survey was an intense desire among China's youth to understand modern Western science. While he was convinced that no evangelical tracts written with conventional theology would appeal to the Chinese, he believed that the same preoccupation that prompted the Chinese to embrace social Darwinism would make them receptive to the message of the social gospel.

Burgess's little survey in fact did not unearth anything that he had not already known. It confirmed what he had known all along about the aspiration of the Chinese students. Whatever he had learnt from the survey, he applied to his student work. In 1911, he organized the first summer conference for students from government schools in North China at Wofosi (Sleeping Buddha Temple) in the scenic Western Hills fourteen miles north of Peking, where four such conferences for missionary school students had been sponsored by Princeton-in-Peking since 1908. The theme of the first conference for government school students was: "Christianity and Present Day Problems."[13] Now with the findings of the survey in hand, Burgess planned his second conference around the theme of "Christianity and National Progress," with stirring lecture titles such as "The Factors That Make a Nation Strong," "Individual Regeneration and National Progress," and "The Social Responsibility of Students."[14] The conference was a success. Of the forty-nine student delegates,[15] twenty-eight were non-Christians. Among them nine decided to become Christians at the conference, fifteen pledged themselves to study Christianity, and only four recorded no decision.[16]

Since his main task was to organize YMCA branches in government schools, Burgess came into contact with a large number of students. He was impressed by their consuming desire to save China, being constantly inundated with questions concerning governmental systems, currency reform, and army training. He was, however, at the same time struck

---

12. Ibid., p. 32.
13. S. B. Collins, "A Conference for Government School Students of North China," *The Intercollegian* (November 1912), p. 31.
14. Ibid., p. 32.
15. Qinghua sent the largest delegation, numbering twenty-four. The schools and colleges in Peking sent sixteen, Tianjin seven, and Baoding and Wuchang one each. Ibid.
16. Ibid., p. 33.

by the fact that although young people were trying to lay plans for the political, financial, and educational reconstruction for China, none of them had any real knowledge of the society they set out to rejuvenate.

It was not the students alone who were groping in the dark. Their teachers, too, lacked knowledge about Chinese society. Burgess recalled that he once heard an American college president, then an adviser to the Chinese government, discussing with a group of Chinese who had studied in the West about whether there really was much surplus wealth in China, but no one knew the answer.[17] Implied in these remarks was a critique of what he characterized as "a most impractical idealism" among China's intellectuals.[18]

As if to correct the most impractical idealism among the Chinese students, Burgess set out to channel their energy into practical social service. In the 1912 summer conference that he organized for government school students, "social service" constituted one of the major lecture series and was reported to be the most popular session.[19] In October, under Burgess's guidance, thirty students from six Peking colleges – three government and three missionary institutions – formed the Peking Students' Social Service Club (Beijing shehui shijinhui).[20] The Club membership grew to well over six hundred by 1915. It opened the first public playgrounds in China, started free night schools, and sent teams to lecture people on citizenship, hygiene, and household sanitation. In 1915, the Club made a plan to establish a settlement house near the YMCA headquarters. This settlement house would have occupied the front rooms in a house the Club had rented for lectures and night schools. According to the plan, this settlement house would be a workman's club, where they would come to hear lectures and play games. Hyperbolically hailed by Burgess as the first social settlement house in China, this planned settlement house was in fact not quite like Toynbee Hall in England, for Club members would not have lived there.[21]

---

17. Burgess, "China's Social Challenge: II, Beginnings of Social Investigation," *The Survey* (October 13, 1917), p. 41.
18. Burgess attributed this remark to Gardner Harding in the latter's *Present-Day China* (New York, 1916). I am, however, not able to locate this remark in Harding's book, which in fact described in favorable terms the aspiration of the Chinese intellectuals.
19. Collins, "A Conference for Government School Students of North China," p. 32.
20. Garrett, *Social Reformers in Urban China*, p. 133.
21. The plan was suspended when a heavy rain in early summer partially destroyed the ceiling of the club house and forced the Club to look for a new headquarters. Burgess, "Annual Report, October 1, 1914–September 30, 1915," p. 18 YMCA Annual and Quarterly Reports 1914 (M)–1915 Box 5 (A–B) 1915 Folder.

There was another brief undertaking the Club launched a few years later that never appeared in Burgess's or any YMCA reports. In November 1919, the Club began publishing a thrice-monthly magazine, the *New Society* (*Xin shehui*). On the editorial board of this magazine were a number of individuals who were destined to play important roles in various social, cultural, and political movements in the future: Zheng Zhenduo, a student then at the Railroad College who was to become a famous literary critic and historian; Xu Dishan, a student at Yanjing University who later went on to receive an M.A. degree from Columbia in 1925 and who would become a writer of national stature; Qu Shiying (alias Qu Junong), a student also at Yanjing who would receive his Ed.D. from Harvard in 1926 and then join James Yen's Mass Education Movement as head of the education department; and Qu Qiubai, a student then at the Russian Language College who would become secretary-general of the Chinese Communist Party from 1927 to 1928.

As the official organ of the Club, the *New Society* was a forum for service, surveys, critiques, and theories of society. Reflecting the YMCA credos, the magazine advocated a gradualist approach, through surveys, reform, and education, to bring about a free, classless democratic society.[22] This utopian vision, informed primarily by Leo Tolstoy, reflected unmistakably the ethos of the May Fourth New Culture Movement. Most of the essays in the magazine were written in the same spirit that permeated much of the May Fourth literature in their call for enlightenment, humanitarianism, and the liberation of the individual from the fetters of tradition.[23] However, as Marxism began to exert influence among the New Culture intellectuals, the *New Society* too began to reveal some radical edges. Qu Qiubai, who published altogether twenty-two essays in the magazine, for example, began to portray socialism in a positive light as early as January 1920.[24] Then in April two special issues on labor appeared. When the third special issue came out on May 1, the ever-vigilant police arrested the manager and shut down the magazine. Three months later, the indignant editorial board put out the first issue of a successor magazine, *Rendao*, with a French title *L'Humanité*.

22. [Zheng] Zhenduo, "Fakan ci" (Inaugural Editorial), *Xin shehui* (The New Society) (November 1, 1919), p. 1.
23. The most detailed discussion to date of the *New Society* with a particular focus on Qu Qiubai is in Chen Tiejian, *Qu Qiubai zhuan* (A Biography of Qu Qiubai) (Shanghai, 1986), pp. 68–91. See also Charles Hayford, *To the People: James Yen and Village China* (Columbia, 1990), pp. 121–2, and Paul Pickowicz, *Marxist Literary Thought in China: The Influence of Ch'ü Ch'iu-pai* (Berkeley, 1981), pp. 21–5.
24. Chen Tiejian, *Qu Qiubai zhuan*, pp. 83–5.

Although this new magazine, as suggested by its name, had not departed from the original utopian reformist vision, the wary YMCA decided to withdraw its financial support, bringing to a close its participation in the production of the New Culture Movement. This episode, together with the fact that the YMCA secretaries chose to expunge it from the record, showed that the YMCA drew the limits at social ameliorism and was unwilling to be connected to radical social programs.

Among the various activities to which the Peking Students' Social Service Club devoted itself, most significant was the experiment in social investigation that the Club conducted. In November 1912, Burgess persuaded four of its members to conduct a small experiment to acquaint themselves with the life of rickshaw pullers, who provided the most important means of transportation in Peking.[25] They used a house on an alley away from a main street as a station for what Burgess called the first "social clinic" in China. The gate man of the house was dispatched to the street to summon one rickshaw puller for an interview in the house. After the interview, the process of randomly picking a rickshaw puller from the street was repeated. Twenty-seven rickshaw pullers went through the "clinic," where the students asked them questions on health, education, religion, and the history of China.[26]

It was the consciousness of the students that was raised; they learned much about the impoverished life of the rickshaw pullers. The Club became so interested in the problems of the rickshaw pullers that in the winter of 1914, they conducted a survey with questionnaires of the lives of 302 rickshaw pullers selected from every part of the city.

This investigation was calculated to arouse public indignation at the plight of the rickshaw pullers and thereby public effort to ameliorate the situation. The Club entrusted the analysis of the data to Tao Menghe, sociology professor at Peking University and one of the future leaders of the May Fourth Movement. As expected, Tao passionately condemned the entire system of man-pullers and proposed a program for reform.[27]

As a piece of social research this investigation left much to be desired.

25. The following discussion on this experiment is based on Garrett, p. 134; and Burgess, "China's Social Challenge: II," pp. 42–4.
26. A report based on the results of the interview was later published, but I have not been able to locate it.
27. Tao published a Chinese version ten years later. See "Beijing renli chefu zhi shenghuo qingxing" (Lives of Rickshaw Pullers in Peking) in *Menghe wencun* (A Collection of Tao Menghe's Essays) (Shanghai, 1926), *juan* II, pp. 101–21.

First, the sample of rickshaw pullers investigated was statistically insignificant.[28] It constituted only 1.45 percent of the estimated total of 20,859 in Peking in 1915. Nor was this a random survey; the rickshaw pullers were picked up in a hit-or-miss fashion. Second, the questionnaires used in the investigation required the interviewees to volunteer information concerning themselves and their families. This format made it impossible to control the quality and comparability of the responses. The investigators varied in their conscientiousness and skills. The rickshaw pullers made the matter worse by injecting into their responses their conceptions and criteria, which were often different from those of the investigators. These problems were reflected in the poor quality of the responses concerning the rickshaw pullers' living conditions, health, living expenses, income, and savings.

Under Burgess's guidance, the Club conducted other, larger investigations that included a survey of forty social institutions – poor houses, orphanages, industrial workshops, hospitals, and government institutions.[29] Their success emboldened Burgess. In 1917, when Sidney Gamble (B.A., Princeton, 1912), an heir of the founder of Procter & Gamble Co., went to Peking, Burgess persuaded him to undertake, and perhaps finance, a comprehensive survey of the city of Peking. This joint effort resulted in *Peking: A Social Survey*, which was published in 1921.

The survey kindled local interest in having the community surveyed and social work organized. To meet the demand, the YMCA, the YWCA, and Yanjing University united to supply personnel to conduct investigations, plan new enterprises, and render technical advice in social service. For its part, Yanjing University took advantage of this staff to develop vocational courses in social service with practical work in community service.

A CLASH OF VISIONS

Just as Princeton-in-Peking began to branch out into the sphere of higher education while at the same time maintaining YMCA programs in Peking, conditions emerged that required it to redefine its mission. First, there was a controversy concerning whether the Princeton group should reduce its staff in order to encourage a native leadership within the

28. See ibid., p. 106 for Tao's critique of this survey.
29. Burgess, "Princeton's World Outlook: The Achievements and Future of the Princeton Center in China," *The Princeton Alumni Weekly*, XVI.34 (May 31, 1916), "Supplement," p. 6.

Peking YMCA. The Philadelphian Society of Princeton University sent out annually two or three recent graduates for a two-year term of service in Peking. By the late 1910s, Princeton-in-Peking had grown into an enterprise that supported ten or more staff members.[30]

The Princeton group was informed by D. W. Lyon of the Chinese YMCA in 1921 that Yu Rizhang (David Yui), general secretary of the National Committee of the Chinese YMCA, would like to see a reduction in the number of foreign secretaries in Peking in order to encourage the development of Chinese initiative and leadership.[31] However, one month later, Fletcher Brockman, who was John Mott's close associate for both home and foreign divisions and was therefore Lyon's superior, passed through Peking and gave the Princeton group an exactly opposite advice; he challenged Princeton-in-Peking to commit whatever it could muster to meet the needs of the field. To add to the confusion, Yu Rizhang, who supposedly had conveyed this idea to Lyon while attending the Washington Conference (1921–22) in the United States, denied that it was ever the attitude of the Chinese YMCA.

Lyon may not have misrepresented the Chinese sentiment, given the fact that it occurred in the context of the Washington Conference, a poignant occasion when China's national pride was at stake amidst discussions on the territorial integrity of China and the reversion of the Shandong concession by Japan to China. The Chinese YMCA may have requested the reduction of foreign secretaries at first, but retracted when confronted with the reality of inadequate native sources of funding. Thomas Blaisdell, who had a one-year stint with Princeton-in-Peking in 1922 after his graduation from the New York School of Social Work, argued that the low salary for Chinese secretaries could not get men of high caliber for YMCA work. The disposition to lead on the part of some foreign secretaries, he further charged, worked to discourage Chinese leadership.[32]

Because it originated from a request of the Chinese YMCA, this controversy precipitated a debate among members of Princeton-in-Peking. By the early 1920s, by virtue of Burgess's collaboration with Yanjing

---

30. That is, six permanent and three to six short-term members, with the latter teaching at the Peking School of Commerce and Finance that Princeton-in-Peking had established in 1914.
31. Olin Wannamaker to Ambrose Todd, June 5, 1925, YMCA Princeton-in-Peking Box 1923–1925 Folder.
32. "Administrative Report for 1923," YMCA Annual and Quarterly Reports, 1923–1931, Box 12 (A–M) 1923 Folder.

University, Princeton-in-Peking had entered the field of higher education. Burgess's affiliation with Yanjing began in 1918, when he volunteered to give a course on social investigation to students at the university. Both Burgess and Gamble were listed as special lecturers in social studies in the university's report in 1918. In these capacities, they mobilized their students to help with their Peking survey. With the schedules provided by them, the students collected data related to social welfare institutions in the capital.[33]

Burgess began to conceive of a plan for a closer cooperation between Princeton and Yanjing in 1919. He proposed that Princeton-in-Peking enlarge its work by sending out a number of social workers, who would teach at Yanjing in addition to giving their time to community work in Peking. Burgess envisioned that this collaborative enterprise would eventually lead to the establishment of a Princeton School of Social Science at Yanjing. As anticipated, Yanjing responded favorably to Burgess's proposal because it would bring in additional teaching staff without any financial obligation to the University. To facilitate the plan, Yanjing nominated Burgess as professor and head of the department of social science.

Such enthusiasm from Yanjing prompted the Princeton group to recommend in 1923 that Princeton see as its mission in China the development of the YMCA work and the establishment of the Princeton School of Political and Social Sciences at Yanjing University. Obviously with the Chinese wish for the reduction of foreign YMCA secretaries in mind, the trustees responded by adopting a five-year plan through which Princeton-in-Peking would gradually reduce its commitment to the YMCA work in Peking and would transfer the resources thus released to the support of a social science program at Yanjing.[34]

The trustees' plan to concentrate on higher education at the expense of the YMCA work stunned most members of Princeton-in-Peking, who viewed the YMCA work as their raison d'être in Peking. Dwight Edwards, the executive secretary, for example, was greatly alarmed by the proposed cut in the YMCA area. In a letter to Yu Rizhang, he

---

33. Burgess, "Where East Meets West," *The Princeton Alumni Weekly*, XXVIII.12 (December 1927), p. 339.
34. The trustees' plan would reduce the YMCA share of the budget from 70% in 1923 to just below 17% in 1927 and, by contrast, would increase the Yanjing share of the budget from less than 16% to over 60% during the same period. See enclosure, Dwight Edwards to David Yui, July 13, 1923, YMCA Princeton-in-Peking Box, 1923–1925 Folder.

prodded Yu to take note of the serious consequence that "at the end of five years there will be need of only two foreign secretaries in Peking doing YMCA work."[35]

Burgess, by contrast, saw in the trustees' plan a rapid expansion of the work he had already started at Yanjing. Obviously intending to pique the institutional pride of the trustees, he noted that some American institutions had entered the field of education – the Shanghai College with its urban social work in Shanghai under Daniel Kulp and the University of Nanking with its agricultural extension program, but declared that "in the field of organized philanthropy we have practically no competition."[36]

Meanwhile, Gailey, the pioneering member and chair of the Princeton group, decided to resign. The question of how to allocate this extra position vacated by Gailey forced into the open a clash of visions among members of the Princeton group. While the majority faction fought hard to keep this position as a YMCA slot, Burgess and Blaisdell argued that the budget saved from this position should be used for work at Yanjing. At the last open session in June 1925, with wives participating as voting members, the majority faction won with a vote of fourteen to six.[37] The resolution called for the trustees to maintain Princeton-in-Peking's commitment to the YMCA until 1930 and, only then, to begin appropriating any income beyond this commitment to social science work at Yanjing.

Burgess failed in his attempt to reinvent Princeton-in-Peking. While the majority clung to the conventional notion of performing social service in the city of Peking, Burgess had passed them by with an endeavor on training for social service. He envisioned his social science program at Yanjing with a three-part goal of bringing to China modern scientific approaches to social betterment: the training of professional social workers, the introduction of modern social welfare concepts and administration, and the planning and execution of social surveys.

Burgess embodied the convergence of several broad trends within the progressive movement in the United States. His survey work bore the hallmark of the American social survey movement, particularly the Pittsburgh Survey of 1906–9: the social survey as a means for mobilizing the

---

35. Ibid.
36. Burgess's report, n.d., YMCA Princeton-in-Peking Box, 1923–1925 Folder.
37. It is noteworthy that Sidney Gamble, Burgess's collaborator in social surveys in Peking, and his wife voted to keep the fifth YMCA position. See the attached "Statement of the Vote on Alternative," ibid.

community toward social reform. All of his surveys in Peking, from the small survey of rickshaw pullers, to the medium surveys of social institutions, and to the comprehensive study of Peking that he conducted with Sidney Gamble, reflected the quintessentially Progressive beliefs that social research and social planning inform each other and that the community, when sufficiently informed, would arouse itself to strive for its own betterment.[38]

Intricately related to the survey movement were the charity organization movement and the social settlement movement, both originated in England in the latter half of the nineteenth century. In his attempt to introduce into China modern social welfare concepts and administration, Burgess advocated the same tenets that had characterized the charity organization movement: the pooling of resources and coordination of efforts, the dispensation of relief based on need, and, most important of all, vigilance against pauperism among the poor.[39]

While the charity organization movement provided Burgess with working assumptions and operational principles in his call for modernizing charity institutions in China, the social settlement movement inspired him to launch community social service in Peking. Originated in England in 1884 with the founding of Toynbee Hall and spread to the United States immediately afterwards, the social settlement movement was powered by reform-minded young men and women who used their settlement houses in working class neighborhoods as bases to provide community service and instigate reforms.[40] Like the social settlement movement in the United States, Burgess's Peking Students' Social Service Club opened and operated a public playground, sponsored lectures on hygiene and household sanitation, and conducted social surveys. Where Burgess's adaptation deviated from the American model was the absence of a settlement house where the students would come to live and serve the community. While the settlement house constituted the heart of the social settlement movement, the elitism on the part of the students – as evidenced by the failed attempt mentioned earlier to establish a settlement house in 1915 – made its adoption difficult, if not impossible.

38. Bulmer, Bales, and Sklar, eds., *The Social Survey in Historical Perspective, 1880–1940*, pp. 1–48, 245–68, 291–315; also Jean Converse, *Survey Research in the United States: Roots and Emergence 1890–1960* (Berkeley, 1987), pp. 22–38.
39. Roy Lubove, *The Professional Altruist: The Emergence of Social Work as a Career, 1880–1930* (Harvard, 1965), pp. 7–10.
40. Allen Davis, *Spearheads for Reform: The Social Settlements and the Progressive Movement, 1890–1914* (Oxford, 1967), pp. 3–25.

Fundamental differences distinguished the charity organization movement from the social settlement movement. The two movements differed in their views on what produced poverty. While the charity organization movement emphasized the individual causes of poverty, the social settlement movement stressed the social and economic conditions that crushed the poor. Their approaches were also different. In its attempt to elevate philanthropy to scientific status, the charity organization movement focused on the technique over the cause of social welfare work. The social settlement movement, by contrast, was committed to social reform.[41]

Despite these differences in assumptions and approaches, the relationship between these two movements had by the early 1900s been transformed from earlier open hostility to that of close cooperation. It is, therefore, not surprising to observe how Burgess would draw inspiration from these two movements wherever he deemed appropriate. Whether or not he was aware of the inherently conflicting premises of the two movements, he must have viewed the two as essentially complementing each other for his efforts to direct community social service in Peking. The charity organization movement and the settlement movement converged upon one common focal point that Burgess came to appreciate: the emphasis on investigation, even though each saw "investigation" from its own perspective, with the former focusing on the individual and the latter on the society.

Intricately linked to the settlement movement during the Progressive era was the social gospel movement, which sought to infuse humanitarianism and social concern into the teaching and practice of the Protestant church. Burgess believed in the social gospel. In this sense, he was not a typical YMCA secretary of his time, for the YMCA did not formally endorse the idea of the social gospel until the late 1920s. As a movement that aimed at the uplifting of Christian young men, body and mind, the YMCA took the individual, but not society, as the focal point of emphasis, not unlike the charity organization movement. Moreover, because the YMCA thrived on the strong financial backing of the business community, it was understandably hesitant to venture into controversial areas lest it antagonize the mainstay of the movement.[42]

Burgess thus embodied the coalescence of the four broad trends of the

41. Ibid., pp. 17–22.
42. C. Howard Hopkins, *History of the Y.M.C.A. in North America* (New York, 1951), pp. 532–8.

Progressive era: the social survey movement, charity organization movement, the settlement movement, and the social gospel. His keen concern both with the uplifting of the individual and the planning of community action for social reforms made him impatient with the missionaries who refused to modify their approaches in order to reach the Chinese. His interest in social investigation, the common denominator of all the four movements mentioned above, enabled him not only to identify the aspirations of the Chinese students, but to channel their idealism into practical social service. The Peking Students' Social Service Club, with the kind of community services it performed and social surveys it conducted, was admittedly minuscule in comparison with similar community organizations in the United States. The Club, which had some six hundred members by 1915, was nevertheless a remarkable success when measured against the elitist tradition within which these students had been reared.

THE INCEPTION OF A SOCIAL SCIENCE PROGRAM

The success Burgess had in introducing modern social service ideas and survey techniques to students and community groups in Peking was a strong impetus that led him to see Yanjing as both a social service clearing-house and training ground for social workers. One major obstacle he continued to face, however, was the small budget that Princeton-in-Peking slated for his work at Yanjing. The clash of visions and his defeat mentioned earlier explained why Yanjing's share of the budget increased little despite the fact that Princeton-in-Peking had been able to increase its annual budget steadily, as is illustrated by the figures in Table 2.1 from 1906 to 1928. From the meager beginning in 1906 that went for the support of Gailey, the sustained growth in the contributions received at its peak in 1926 enabled the Princeton group in Peking to operate on a budget that was fourteen times larger than when it first started.

Nonetheless, the Chinese YMCA could not have sustained its work in Peking had Princeton-in-Peking reduced its support as the trustees had planned. As a large portion of the local contributions to the Peking YMCA came from government officials, the chronic salary arrears in the early 1920s had a detrimental effect on the income of the YMCA. However, continued financial commitment to the Peking YMCA took away resources that could have been used for the educational work of Princeton-in-Peking. The agreement of collaboration that Princeton-in-Peking and Yanjing reached in 1921 amounted to little. As an example, the newly created department of sociology did not have a single full-time

37

Table 2.1. *Princeton-in-Peking Annual Budget,*
1906–1928, Selected Years, in U.S. dollars

1906	4,393.50
1913	9,251.39
1918	21,400.00
1920	25,000.00
1921	46,995.00
1924	50,040.00
1926	58,700.00
1927	50,802.00
1928	53,115.00

Sources: "The Princeton Work in Peking," *The Princeton Alumni Weekly*, XIV.18 (February 11, 1914), 384; "Princeton in World Service," (n.p., n.d. [1916]); "Princeton-in-Peking, January 1924, Annual Report of the Board of Trustees for 1923," (New York, n.d.), p. 6; 'Activities in America,' in C. A. Evans, comp., "Princeton in China," 7.

faculty member.[43] Burgess himself had to split his time between teaching at Yanjing and working for the Peking YMCA. It became obvious that the department could develop only by relying upon part-time teachers.

In 1923, Princeton-in-Peking appointed Xu Shuxi (Ph.D., Columbia, 1925) to be the first political science faculty member at Yanjing. Even though this constituted at best a nominal beginning of what they hyperbolically referred to as the Princeton School of Political and Social Science, the appointment of Xu Shuxi to head his one-man department of political science stretched the resources of Princeton-in-Peking. In 1924, the Princeton group found itself unable to proceed with the plan to offer a position in sociology to Leonard Hsu (Xu Shilian, Ph.D., Iowa, 1923). Only after Sidney Gamble personally put up the funds did Princeton-in-Peking succeed in appointing Leonard Hsu to the sociology department a year later.[44]

The two social science departments at Yanjing continued to claim an

43. Although the first official reference to the Yanjing Sociology Department appeared only in April 1923, the Yanjing administrators had begun in 1919 to use "the head" of "the department of sociology" to refer to Burgess.
44. *Princeton Peking Gazette*, I.1 (February 1925), p. 7. See next chapter for more about Leonard Hsu.

insignificant share of the total expenditure of Princeton-in-Peking.[45] The two departments were, furthermore, advised that no dramatic increase in the budget could be expected for 1929, which as it turned out coincided with the onset of the depression. Fortunately, by means of special lecture funds provided largely by Yanjing, Princeton-in-Peking secured part-time service of experts from other institutions in Peking.[46] As a product of community social service, it was natural that the Department drew its faculty from the YMCA and the YWCA. In fact, the YWCA for many years provided the Department with two teachers from its staff. In 1920–21 when Burgess returned to the United States, Lily Haass of the YWCA became the acting head of the department. The Peking Union Medical College was another major cooperating institution. Ida Pruitt of the Hospital Social Service and John B. Grant, professor of public health at the college, contributed to the development of a specialized field in the department.

The use of part-time teachers was an efficient way of utilizing the resources available for the new enterprise. The problem is that this arrangement remained a permanent feature of the department well into the mid-1920s. Despite its dependence on borrowed teachers, Yanjing thrived, however. In 1925, for instance, it alone offered over one-fourth of the total number of all the sociology courses taught in China although the department only had one newly appointed full-time member – Leonard Hsu – out of a faculty of eleven.[47] This predominant position Yanjing achieved in the mid-1920s thus reflected the resourcefulness of the department in maximizing the limited resources at its disposal and, at the same time, the general underdeveloped state of sociology in China's higher education.

Financial stringency was not the only major problem that beset Princeton-in-Peking. Its difficult financial conditions were aggravated by the hostile attitude of the Princeton administrators. The use of the name "Princeton" in an organization that received no official sanction from the

---

45. For instance, out of a budget of $50,802 for 1927, only $7,000 was allocated to the two departments. Even the larger budget for 1928 amounted to only $12,800 out of a total Princeton-in-Peking budget of $53,115 – $5,150 for the department of political science and $7,650 for the sociology department. See Wannamaker to Xu Shuxi, February 25, 1928, The United Board for Christian Higher Education in Asia files (hereafter cited as UB), RG11 337.5148, deposited at Yale Divinity School.
46. *Princeton Peking Gazette*, II.2 (January 1927), p. 3.
47. One bulletin of "Announcement of Courses" for 1924–5 listed fourteen faculty members.

university irritated the administrators who guarded jealously the use of the university's name. The Princeton administrators had an understandable concern that Princeton-in-Peking might take advantage of the name and take away some contributions that should have been given to the university itself. Even though the trustees in 1930 approved the use of the name "Princeton School of Public Affairs in Yenching University," the administration, in response to an inquiry of an alumnus, stated that "Princeton has no organic connection with, or share in control of any department of Yenching University, at Peking."[48]

THE TURN TO FOUNDATIONS

Princeton's hostile attitude forced Princeton-in-Peking to explore alternative sources of funding. In 1921, Burgess submitted an application to the Commonwealth Fund of New York. The program for which support was requested envisioned the creation of local community service groups and that of a community service council for the entire city of Peking. These service groups and the service council would sponsor community programs in the following areas: social relationships, extension education, playgrounds and recreation, poor relief and industrial workshops, public health, moral reform, and industrial welfare. The YMCA, the YWCA, and the local church would control these community service bodies and would be empowered to co-opt other interested organizations and individuals.[49]

This program on community service was a continuation, on a larger scale, of the work that Princeton-in-Peking had initiated, beginning with the formation in 1912 of the Peking Students' Social Service Club and culminating in the creation in November 1919 of a Community Service Group in the Dengshikou district in Peking. The Peking Students' Social Service Club represented an external force impinging upon a community that accepted a certain degree of poverty, dislocation, and disease as normal social phenomena. The Dengshikou project, on the other hand, presupposed a radically different social vision. It viewed all these traditionally tolerated social phenomena as symptoms of social dysfunction that could and should be eradicated.

---

48. Collins to W. H. Daub, May 3, 1930, Princeton-in-Asia files.
49. Burgess, "The Program of Community Work and Social and Civic Education of the Princeton University Center in China" (n.d.), enclosure in a letter dated June 21, 1921, Princeton-in-Asia files.

The Community Service Group in the Dengshikou district became the model from which Burgess formulated his community-based social service plan in Peking. In the Dengshikou project, the controlling body was constituted of members of the YMCA, the YWCA, and the local church of the American Board of Commissioners for Foreign Missions. This organizational structure was what Burgess suggested in his proposal to the Commonwealth Fund. The social programs sponsored by the Dengshikou group were likewise adopted with only minor changes of wording in the proposal.[50]

Burgess's proposal to the Commonwealth Fund reflected a realization on his part that Princeton-in-Peking was no longer capable of meeting the growing demand for modern social service in Peking. The limitation, however, was not so much caused by lack of funding as it was created by want of trained personnel.[51] More serious were problems in the organization and actual implementation of the various programs. The only programs that showed modest success were playgrounds, public lectures and night schools, and the women's industrial workshop. Yet there were problems with these successful programs as well. The Community Service Group found it impossible to secure the consent of the guild leaders and shopkeepers to allow their apprentices to attend night schools – their most successful program. In addition, great care had to be taken to screen out the students who attended government schools during the day and were sent to these free night schools by their parents. The most serious problem occurred, however, at the poorhouse for men. The broker who provided the initial funds to start the project decided to withdraw his support upon learning that the inmates were given industrial work, which he deemed improper because it did not conform to the conventional practice.[52]

These problems in organization and implementation of community service were by no means unique to the Dengshikou district and reflected a phenomenon that occurred when the reform force collided with the vested interests and accepted practices. What made the Dengshikou situation particularly critical was the lack of trained personnel. The situation was best illustrated by Burgess's own description of the

---

50. Gamble, *Peking: A Social Survey*, p. 393.
51. For instance, although the controlling body of the Dengshikou Community Service Group contributed the initial budget of $600, the residents of the community soon raised another $700. A rich broker, moreover, pledged $350 to start a poorhouse. Ibid., pp. 394, 395.   52. Ibid., pp. 395–400.

superintendent of the poorhouse for men: "Since there were no trained Chinese social workers for such positions, we first obtained, as superintendent, a former pastor whose large heart and sympathetic knowledge of human nature were greater than his knowledge of how constructively to help the poor."[53] The Dengshikou district alone had proved too big a field for Princeton-in-Peking to handle. The dilemma was that three new districts had since requested similar assistance. It was with this perception that community social service would soon become a citywide movement that Burgess appealed to the Commonwealth Fund to assist.

Because Burgess was confident that local contributions would be sufficient to cover the operating budget of his community service programs, all he requested were a small social settlement and a well-equipped playground.[54] The focus of his request concentrated on what he deemed most lacking in the field: trained social workers, Western as well as Chinese. He appealed for funding in support of the social science program at Yanjing as a way to train social leaders and workers. His specific requests were: a recitation hall and support of a full faculty with one professor in each of the fields of sociology, political science, economics, and history.

Burgess's request was, however, rejected by the Commonwealth Fund, which concentrated its work in child and community health programs and confined its field of operation to the United States and Europe.[55] In 1923, Princeton-in-Peking approached the Laura Spelman Rockefeller Memorial, a philanthropic trust established in 1918 by John D. Rockefeller Sr. in memory of his wife. The application promoted the same theme that had been presented to the Commonwealth Fund two years earlier: an integrated program that correlated training in applied social sciences with objectives in community social service.[56] This emphasis on social betterment would have been in accordance with the Memorial's funding preference had it been presented just a year or two earlier when the Memorial had still focused on work among women and children with which Mrs. Rockefeller had been associated. The YMCA and the

53. Ibid., p. 395. The passage quoted here is taken from a slightly abridged version of the chapter that Burgess published separately. See his "Community Organization in the Orient," *The Survey* (June 25, 1921), p. 434.
54. The discussion in this paragraph is based on Burgess, "The Program of Community Work and Social and Civic Education of the Princeton University Center in China," pp. 9–10.
55. For a brief account of the history of the Commonwealth Fund, see *The Commonwealth Fund: Historical Sketch, 1918–1962* (New York, 1963).
56. Wannamaker, "Princeton-in-Peking: Application for Financial Aid," February 14, 1923, RAC LSRM 80.834.

YWCA had in fact been the major beneficiaries of the Memorial. With the appointment of Beardsley Ruml as its director in 1922, however, the Memorial had shifted its emphasis to basic social science research at the major academic centers.[57]

Princeton-in-Peking on its part quickly took note of the Memorial's new funding preference. With a copy of Gamble's *Peking: A Social Survey* presented for Ruml's perusal, Princeton-in-Peking began to underscore its achievement and commitment to social research. However, because sociology had clearly been the hand-maiden of community social service, Princeton-in-Peking was unable to formulate a clearly defined research program. In early 1923, Leighton Stuart, president of Yanjing, tried a different approach, suggesting that the Memorial help establish an Institute of Social and Economic Research at Yanjing.[58] He requested that the Memorial send a scholar to study the needs, the location, and the necessary equipment and personnel for establishing such an Institute.[59]

The Memorial did not approve Stuart's request for reconnaissance. If this request had been granted, it would have created the impression that the Memorial was directly involved in the project, which was what the trustees had specifically instructed the officers to avoid.[60] In February 1924, nearly a year had elapsed, Princeton-in-Peking in desperation scaled down its request to a sum of $3,000 to release to J. B. Tayler, an economics professor at Yanjing, to investigate for a year problems surrounding the establishment of the proposed Institute.[61]

57. Martin and Joan Bulmer, "Philanthropy and Social Sciences in the 1920s: Beardsley Ruml and the Laura Spelman Rockefeller Memorial, 1922–29," *Minerva*, XIX.3 (autumn 1981), pp. 347–407.
58. This suggestion was taken from a similar recommendation that the China Educational Commission had made in 1922. The Commission recommended the establishment of an Institute of Social and Economic Research to give postgraduate training and to serve as a central clearing-house for social science information collected in the field by the various Christian institutions. See *Christian Education in China: The Report of the China Educational Commission of 1921–1922* (Shanghai, 1922), pp. 205–8.
59. "Request of Peking University for the Establishment and Maintenance by the Laura Spelman Rockefeller Memorial of a Bureau, or an Institute of Social Research in Connection with the University in Peking, China," March 29, 1923, RAC LSRM 80.834.
60. In 1924, the trustees laid down twelve principles altogether – six negative and six positive. The principle that would have been applied to the consideration of Yanjing's request would be the fourth of the six negative principles: "Not to carry on investigation and research directly under the Memorial, except for the guidance of the Memorial." For a discussion of the origin and process that led to the formulation of these six negative principles, see Fosdick, *The Story of the Rockefeller Foundation* (New York, 1952), pp. 200–1.
61. Wannamaker to Ruml, February 29, 1924, RAC LSRM 80.834. Incidentally, this proposal would have served a dual purpose for Yanjing if it were funded. In addition to

When Galen Fisher of the Institute of Social and Religious Research in New York, who was supported by John D. Rockefeller Jr., contemplated sending a commission to China to determine the need for establishing the proposed Institute, Ruml decided not to finance the Tayler proposal and to leave the matter to Fisher.[62] Fisher's Commission of Social Research in China, of which Tayler was a major member, recommended the establishment of an Institute of Social and Economic Research.[63] It suggested, however, that the Institute should exist primarily for research rather than for teaching, which was precisely what Yanjing had tried to use to its advantage in its application to the Memorial. When the Institute of Social and Religious Research acted on the Commission's recommendations, Yanjing was not the beneficiary. Instead, the Institute chose the China Foundation for the Promotion of Education and Culture, providing the latter with a three-year grant beginning in 1926 to establish a Department of Social Research.[64]

The failure of Princeton-in-Peking to formulate a research program reflected not so much a weakness on its part as the backward state of field research in China. The field was simply too vast and too little traversed. Princeton-in-Peking had pioneered modern social service and social investigation in Peking. To a large extent, it was its very success that created the problem. By the middle of the 1920s, the enterprise it had launched and fostered for nearly two decades had outgrown the resources under its disposal. In order to tap the new sources of funding from the newly institutionalized philanthropies, Princeton-in-Peking would have had to be able to articulate a clearly defined program. And it was here that lay the crux of the problem. It had created a program, fostered its growth, and came to a point when it could not decide on its future course. In early 1925, almost six years after Princeton-in-Peking had decided to develop the social science program at Yanjing, Burgess sent out a circular letter to solicit opinions on the desirability and best

providing Tayler with traveling expenses in connection with his proposed study trip, this sum of $3,000 would have also enabled Yanjing to employ Leonard Hsu as Tayler's substitute, whom, as indicated above, the university had not been able to hire due to lack of funding.

62. Roger Greene's Memo on Galen Fisher, April 23, 1924, RAC RG4 48.1105.
63. "Suggestions for the Organization of an Institute of Social and Economic Research," prepared by the Commission of Social Research in China, *Shehuixue zazhi* (The Chinese Journal of Sociology), II.5–6 (June–August 1925), pp. 19–42.
64. For more discussion on the China Foundation and its Department of Social Research, see Chapter 9.

approach for such a program.[65] Princeton-in-Peking was lost in a quandary; it was never to succeed in redefining its own identity and its mission. Although it would continue to contribute financially to the social science program at Yanjing, Princeton-in-Peking would see the leadership role transferred to the Chinese on the faculty. Symbolic of the profound change that was to take place in the Yanjing Sociology Department, Burgess took an extended leave in 1926 to complete his Ph.D. work at Columbia and eventually severed his affiliation in 1929 when he joined Temple University in Philadelphia.

65. Burgess, "Statement Regarding Proposed Princeton School of Political and Social Science in connection with Yenching University," *Shehuixue zazhi* (The Chinese Journal of Sociology), II.5–6 (June–August 1925), pp. 42–3.

3

The Yanjing Sociology Department: From Social Service to Social Engineering, 1925–1945

THE departure of Stewart Burgess in 1926 ushered in a new era within the Yanjing Sociology Department. With Princeton-in-Peking having retreated to the sideline to play the fund-raising role in the United States, the department embarked on a course toward recruiting Chinese faculty and fostering Chinese leadership – part of a growing trend in missionary institutions in China in the late 1920s. Like all institutions of higher education in China at the time, Yanjing benefited from a steady supply of Chinese with Ph.D. degrees from American universities. In a matter of a few years, Yanjing's entrepreneurial young arrivals would redefine the mission and intellectual orientation of the department. Two competing wings emerged within the department in the early 1930s.[1] The social service wing, which carried on Princeton-in-Peking's YMCA legacy, was to develop the notion of social engineering by participating in an ambitious rural reconstruction program funded by the Rockefeller Foundation. Challenging the establishment within the department was the rebel sociology wing, which maintained the primacy of empirical research and chided their reform-minded colleagues for plunging into action without having adequate knowledge about the field. Through their competition, these two wings made the department the most exciting sociological center in China during the 1930s.

---

1. My characterization of the two competing wings is inspired by Fei Xiaotong. See his "Liu Ying ji" (Remembering My Journey to England to Study), *Wenshi ziliao xuanji*, No. 31 (October 1962), pp. 31–65. While Bettina Gransow renames my "Sociology Wing" as the "Social Anthropology Wing" (Sozialanthropologie-Flügel), I submit that it is anachronistic both because of the unmistakably sociological focus in the contemporary writings of the members of the wing and of the fact that Fei himself and Lin Yaohua only moved into anthropology after they had left Yanjing. See Bettina Gransow, *Geschichte der chinesischen Soziologie*, pp. 116, 215 (28n).

THE CONSOLIDATION OF THE SOCIAL SERVICE WING

By the mid-1920s, the YMCA and the YWCA were no longer the only organizations that drew social workers. In Peking, the Rockefeller Foundation-financed Peking Union Medical College had a social service department. From the government side, a variety of social agencies also demanded trained personnel. The Mass Education Movement under James Yen, which was launched in 1923 and was moved to Ding Xian in 1926, also drew upon social workers.[2] In 1925, Yanjing added certificate programs and correspondence courses to the sociology department, and changed the name of the department to that of the department of sociology and social work.

The creation of a social service wing within the department reflected better the work that had been done at the department. The social service wing clearly represented the mainstream of the department. The founder of the department, Stewart Burgess, was no ordinary urban reformer. As a YMCA secretary and a sociologist by training, he was deeply struck by the stark contrast between the industrialized West and China; he and the missionaries as well as many Chinese intellectuals themselves likened China to the medieval West. His surveys of Peking and its guilds were underlined by a belief that China, having been forced into the modern age by the West, could "make the greatest amount of progress with the least number of mistakes"[3] if fundamental conditions of the society were ascertained and knowledge about the mistakes as well as the successes of the West were utilized. In defining the social science programs at Yanjing, Burgess expressed the hope that the "school will train not only students proficient in social and political theory, but men capable of taking positions in municipal and national government affairs, positions in the economic and business world and the field of social work."[4]

This confidence in the possibility of both effecting desired social change and working within the system were characteristic tenets of the YMCA. At the same time, they could be easily translated into the political aspirations of Chinese intellectuals – whether in the sense of serving

---

2. Charles Hayford, *To the People: James Yen and Village China* (Columbia, 1990); Wu Xiangxiang, *Yan Yangchu zhuan* (A Biography of Yan Yangchu) (Taipei, 1981).
3. Gamble and Burgess, *Peking: A Social Survey*, p. 28.
4. Burgess and others, "Statement Regarding Proposed Princeton School of Political and Social Science in Connection with Yenching University," *Shehuixue zazhi* (The Chinese Journal of Sociology), II.5–6 (June–Aug. 1925), p. 43.

or ruling society. In this regard, the career of Leonard Hsu, the first Chinese appointee of the department and the leader of the social service wing, serves as a classic example. Born in 1901 in a high elite family in Xiangtan, Hunan, Leonard Hsu went to the United States in 1918 for his college education. His was an extremely fast track; after having graduated from Stanford with a B.A. degree in 1921, he went on to receive his M.A. in 1922 and Ph.D. in 1923, both from the University of Iowa. He taught for one year at Iowa after graduation as a lecturing fellow on Oriental politics and government. An offer of a history position from Yanjing for the following year fell through when the potential benefactor in Chicago retracted his offer.[5] Hsu had no choice but to bring his American wife, Ruth, back to China for a position at Wuchang Normal University. Fortunately for both Yanjing and Hsu, Sidney Gamble put up the funds to enable Yanjing to appoint Hsu to a position in the sociology department. A year later in 1925 Princeton-in-Peking put Leonard Hsu on its payroll and thus regularized his position at Yanjing.

Handsome, smart, and adroit in wheeling and dealing, Leonard Hsu was a real specimen of a tiny thoroughly Americanized elite of the Republican period who preferred the American way of life and the use of English in both professional and social circles.[6] A daughter of a Yanjing colleague of his who became his goddaughter in 1947 sketched the following most vivid portrait of a middle-aged Hsu, who had returned from the United States to Shanghai as a representative of Reynolds Metal Corporation:

> I was surprised to see how short he was. But he was a good-looking man in his prime: smooth-complexioned, strong of build, slightly balding, and possessed of a warm, ingratiating smile. In his blue double-breasted suit and gold silk tie, he looked to me like a model in a fashion magazine. His shoes were of lustrous brown leather and wing-tipped. A spanking white handkerchief was sticking out of his jacket pocket, showing the initials "L.H." in gold embroidery.[7]

A sleek businessman occupying a four-room suite at the plush Park Hotel and throwing weekly Saturday dinner and dance parties for the business and political leaders in Shanghai, Hsu emerged in this rare

5. Leighton Stuart to Leonard Hsu, January 18, 1924, UB RG11 337.5147.
6. Interview with Lin Yaohua in Framingham, MA, on May 7, 1982.
7. Katherine Wei and Terry Quinn, *Second Daughter: Growing Up in China, 1930–1949* (Boston, 1984), p. 200. Katherine Wei is Yang Kaidao's daughter.

portrait also as a political insider who had at his disposal all sorts of information ranging from the patronage network at the very top down to intelligence reports on Communist sympathizers.[8]

Much of the flair and political instinct so vividly captured in this portrait was already evident in the young Leonard Hsu. Soon after his arrival at Yanjing, he became involved in the administration of the department and in planning for its development. Hsu proved to be a most enterprising administrator. His strategy for expansion called for a close cooperation between the department and the various social welfare organizations, such as the YMCA, the YWCA, the Mass Education Movement, and the China International Famine Relief Commission. He proposed that the department design its program to suit the needs of these organizations. This policy, he believed, would serve a dual purpose. It would enhance the opportunity for the students to be employed by these organizations upon graduation and, at the same time, raise the professional standard of these organizations with trained personnel.[9]

Leonard Hsu soon outgrew this narrow vision of the goal of the department. In early 1928, he presented an ambitious developmental plan for the department. It was a three-staged expansion plan leading toward the establishment of a Yanjing School of Social Work and Social Research that would offer more than a dozen degrees and diplomas, including a Ph.D. degree program in sociology and another in social administration.[10] In addition to making this developmental plan for the sociology department, Leonard Hsu since the end of 1927 had been pushing for a School of the Social Sciences to facilitate cooperation among the university's three social science departments – sociology, political science, and economics.[11]

The idea of a closely coordinated school of the social sciences was the theme that Yanjing stressed in its second appeal to the Laura Spelman Rockefeller Memorial. In June 1928, the trustees of the Memorial voted the sum of $140,000 over a period of seven years beginning from 1928 to strengthen the social science program at Yanjing. This grant from the Memorial enabled Yanjing to adopt Hsu's proposal. Prior to the award

8. Ibid., pp. 211–23.
9. Hsu to Burgess, December 8, 1927, UB RG11 317.4842.
10. Leonard Hsu to Wannamaker, Stuart, and Burgess, February 4, 1928, UB RG11 317.4843, and the enclosure, 317.4842.
11. Hsu, "Report of an Informal Meeting Among Major Teachers in the Department of Sociology, Political Science, and Economics Held on December 10th [1927]," UB RG11 314.4813.

of this grant, the diversity of funding had hampered the coordination of the three social science departments. Princeton-in-Peking had confined its financial commitment to the maintenance of the departments of sociology and political science. The economics department had been maintained by Yanjing and the London Missionary Society, which was responsible for the salary of its representative at the department, J. B. Tayler. The grant from the Memorial at last created a fiscal basis to subsume these departments under one large administrative unit. A College of Applied Social Sciences was inaugurated in 1929. Leonard Hsu, in addition to being the chairman of the sociology department, was elected dean of the college.[12]

Hsu's personal ambitions were in politics. When he first began his career as a professor, he merely advocated that sociology professors should be made to head local social research and welfare institutions.[13] When he had solidified his position within the university and begun to extend his connections into the political arena, he became more ambitious. In December 1926, the Communists and left-wing Guomindang members organized a national government at Wuhan after the tri-city was taken by the Northern Expedition forces under the overall command of Chiang Kai-shek. Hsu had previously befriended Eugene Chen (Chen Youren), the Trinidad-born liberal-turned-leftist who was foreign minister of the Wuhan regime. Perhaps through Eugene Chen's recommendation, Hsu was invited by the Wuhan regime to act as an expert observer in regard to a program of social education and betterment in Hankou.[14]

Although nothing is known about his visit to Hankou, judging from the ideological position of the Wuhan regime and its increasingly radicalized politics, it is doubtful that Hsu would have found Hankou receptive to his expert assistance. As a "man in touch with everything and everyone worth knowing" and a "light-footed traveler whom neither war nor revolution would ever catch out of position,"[15] he must have returned to the sheltered Yanjing before factional and ideological conflicts led to the bloody coup in Shanghai in April and the purge of Communists at Wuhan in July.

12. In its effort to standardize the educational system nationwide, the Ministry of Education refused to recognize the College of Applied Social Sciences. Yanjing was forced to retract the name and place the sociology department in the College of Arts.
13. Xu Shilian, "Duiyu shehuixue jiaocheng de yanjiu" (A Study of the Curriculum of Sociology), *Shehuixue zazhi* (The Chinese Journal of Sociology), II.4 (April 1925), p. 4.
14. Wannamaker to Edmund Day, April 10, 1928, RAC LSRM 80.834.
15. Katherine Wei and Terry Quinn, *Second Daughter*, p. 223.

This ill-starred venture was only one of Hsu's many attempts to enter the political arena. At the time he accepted the invitation to go to Hankou, he was senior secretary of the ministry of foreign affairs of the Peking government, which his host, the Wuhan regime, was trying to overthrow. This courting of competing political factions was a wise strategy for aspiring politicians; the fluid political scene in the 1920s made it shrewd to bet simultaneously on different factions. His acceptance of the invitation of the Wuhan regime represented his attempt to gain entry to a political and military force that by the end of 1926 was on the verge of conquering the nation. He did not seem to have experienced difficulty when he turned to cultivate the victorious Guomindang regime. By 1930, he had succeeded in securing a firm footing in politics by acting as a part-time adviser to the Nanjing government.

Academia was another arena in which Hsu was keen on cultivating connections. In 1930, he finalized an agreement with the Institute of the Social Sciences of the Academia Sinica to conduct a crime survey on its behalf. The Institute offered four scholarships to enable the department to employ students for a four-month survey of prisons in the provinces of Shanxi, Hebei, Hunan, and Hubei.[16]

Hsu's effort to cultivate academic connections and thereby enhance the prestige of the department culminated in his attempt to bring about a collaborative project between Yanjing and the University of Chicago. In 1931, he was awarded a Rockefeller fellowship for a year-long study tour in the major academic centers in the United States, London, Paris, Geneva, and Moscow. During his two visits to the University of Chicago, he succeeded in arousing the interest of several Chicago administrators and social scientists in his proposal to establish a Social Science Research Institute at Yanjing University.[17]

The idea of a Chicago-Yanjing project may have originally been conceived by Yanjing's president, Leighton Stuart.[18] Yet Hsu's success in

16. This project was directed by Yan Jingyao (Class of 1928), then an assistant in the department and who had written a thesis on a model prison in Peking. Three sociology majors participated in this project: Xu Yongshun (Class of 1932), C. K. Yang (Yang Qingkun, Class of 1933), and Dong Wentian (Class of 1933).
17. The Chicago people whom he approached included Robert Hutchins, the president; Donald Slesinger, the associate dean of the Division of Social Sciences; Robert Park, Leonard White, and Harold Lasswell.
18. In his letter dated December 22, 1930 to Wannamaker, Stuart stated: "The idea has occurred to me it might be possible to take advantage of Leonard's presence to induce the University of Chicago to undertake . . . these [social science] departments as their contribution towards University service in China." UB RG11 356.5491.

Chicago must have exceeded what Stuart had anticipated. Not only was Hsu able to arouse the interest of the Chicago people, but he persuaded them to make a joint request for assistance to the Rockefeller Foundation. This proposal was, however, turned down by the Rockefeller Foundation. It was a weak proposal without a genuine research focus. Hsu outlined a four-pronged approach, each purporting to deal with one of the four aspects of the Chinese society that he respectively labeled as "familial organization," "the village community," "social economy," and "politics."[19] Yet these categories were ill-defined. The last two categories could have subsumed the first two and thus made them superfluous. Moreover, the proposed Institute had no institutionalized arrangement to handle the exchange between Yanjing and Chicago. Faculty at each of these two institutions would have had to have been invited to join the Institute on the basis of their interest and credentials, making the proposed Institute look more like a club than a research center.

Though he was a great promoter, Hsu does not seem to have been an institution builder. A case in point was the administration of the department's sociological laboratory in Qinghe. A market town located three miles northeast of the campus, Qinghe was adopted as a sociological field station in fall 1928. While Hsu was the chairman of the survey committee, Yang Kaidao (Cato Young, Ph.D., Michigan, 1927), who joined the department in 1928, was the director of field work. In 1930, because Yang Kaidao returned to his alma mater, the National Central University in Nanjing, to organize a department of rural administration, the Qinghe station was placed under the supervision of Zhang Hongjun (Class of 1925; M.A., Chicago, 1929) who had joined the department in 1929.

Despite the funding from the Rockefeller Foundation and the fanfare created by the parties concerned, the department did not seem to have accomplished much at the Qinghe station beyond maintaining and staffing it and having a number of students writing theses on some aspects of the town.[20] Yang Maochun (Martin Yang, B.A., Cheeloo, 1931; Ph.D., Cornell, 1942) remembered that the university's Qinghe station was nothing more than a trapping. Perhaps partly reflecting Cheeloo's

19. Hsu to Edmund Day, July 20, 1931, RAC RG1.1 601.22.200.
20. "Study of a Typical Chinese Town" that Leonard Hsu read at the formal opening of Yanjing University in 1929 was based on a preliminary survey, under the direction of Yang Kaidao, of Qinghe by three sociology majors.

(Shantung Christian University) hostile attitude to Yanjing, he asserted that even the professor who taught rural sociology – an obvious reference to Yang Kaidao – seldom visited the station.[21]

In a Rockefeller Foundation staff conference in 1934, Selskar Gunn, who was to engineer the China Program funded by the Foundation, pointed out that Yanjing was "not very inspiring in terms of China's future."[22] Furthermore, in 1933, in enlisting Leighton Stuart's help to persuade the Rockefeller Foundation to permit Zhang Hongjun to use the Foundation's fellowship for a Javanese-India-European study tour instead of for a Ph.D. degree at the University of Chicago, Leonard Hsu warned the Yanjing president that the Qinghe station would practically have to close if Zhang were to leave Yanjing for more than a year.[23] Given the department's emphasis on social service and the fact that Hsu had by then been with the department for nearly a decade, this was an astonishing statement for two reasons: first, because the parties concerned, Zhang Hongjun himself included, valued a study tour over a Ph.D. that would, in turn, strengthen the department's work in social service; and second, because Leonard Hsu could not find a substitute within the department to direct the field work.

Far more serious, the Qinghe station did not address the real needs of the village. In spring 1930, the department announced the decision to open a community center in Qinghe. The plan was to outfit this center with a lecture room, where people could gather and listen to specialists' advice on topics ranging from improved methods of farming, crop and animal improvement, cooperative marketing, to health and hygiene. In addition, because "[l]ike all small towns Ching Ho [Qinghe] is very deficient in cultural materials," it was decided that the new community center should have a reading room. Fully aware of the fact that only half of the adult male population and 4 percent of the adult female population in Qinghe were literate, the department nonetheless planned to "have a reading room where those who can read can find out for themselves how to make the most of their job, and read what other people are doing."

---

21. Yang Maochun, *Jindai Zhongguo nongcun shehui zhi yanbian* (The Transformation of Modern Chinese Rural Society) (Taipei, 1980), p. 107. Yang enrolled in the graduate division of the Yanjing Sociology Department in fall 1930. He left without having completed the program in the summer of 1931 to join Liang Shuming's rural reconstruction work in Shandong.
22. Staff conference, April 30, 1934, RAC RG1.1 601.22.201.
23. Hsu to Stuart, April 25, 1933, UB RG11 322.4925.

The department announced that it only had a Victrola and some records and appealed for donations to outfit this reading room.[24]

Whether or not Yanjing's record in Qinghe was mediocre, by the mid-1930s the department found itself drawn into the rural reconstruction movement. The department, which originated from the YMCA movement, had been urban-oriented. Now by adopting Qinghe as a sociological laboratory, the department could claim to be participating in the rural reconstruction movement. Many among the faculty, Leonard Hsu in particular, became involved in the movement in a variety of capacities. His cultivation of connections in government was finally rewarded. In 1933, he was granted a special leave from Yanjing to become an official in Nanjing.

THE RISE OF THE SOCIOLOGY WING

During the early 1930s, the sociology wing began to emerge under the leadership of Wu Wenzao (Qinghua, Class of 1923; B.A., Dartmouth, 1925; Ph.D., Columbia, 1929). Wu was born in Jiangyin county in Jiangsu province in 1901.[25] His father was in the rice retailing business. He transferred from the middle school he had enrolled in Jiangsu to Qinghua College in Peking in 1917. His seven years at Qinghua coincided with the New Culture Movement (1915–23) and the celebrated event of the May Fourth Movement in 1919. The exposure he had to the intellectual currents steered his interest toward Western social and political theories. Indicative both of his keen interest in gaining access to the available literature and his entrepreneurial instinct, he and two fellow students opened a bookstore at Qinghua that proved to be popular among the students and profitable to themselves.[26]

Like other Qinghua graduates, Wu Wenzao proceeded to enroll as an upperclass student in an American college with support from the American Indemnity Funds. He chose Dartmouth, where he received a B.A. degree in 1925. He then went to Columbia for graduate study in sociology. Both his M.A. and Ph.D. theses were products of library research; the former was an analysis of Sun Yat-sen's Three Principles

---

24. *Yenching Faculty Bulletin*, May 1, 1930, pp. 1–2.
25. Unless otherwise noted, the discussion in the following three paragraphs is based on Wu Wenzao, "Wu Wenzao zizhuan" (Wu Wenzao's Autobiography), 20 pages, reprint of the article originally published in *Jinyang xuekan* (Jinyang Bimonthly), 1982.6.
26. Zhang Zhongfu, *Miwang ji* (A Record about Perplexity: An Autobiography) (Hong Kong: 1968), pp. 28–9.

of the People and the latter of British opinion and action toward the opium question in China.

Wu had gone to Columbia on the advice of Qinghua's demographer and labor expert, Chen Da (Qinghua, Class of 1916; Ph.D., Columbia, 1923), with the understanding that he would eventually assume a teaching position at Qinghua. However, toward the end of his graduate studies at Columbia, an alternative position presented itself, a result of the expansion of the social science program at Yanjing.

Following the award of the grant from the Laura Spelman Rockefeller Memorial, Yanjing launched an intensive search for new social science faculty. In the sociology department, Yang Kaidao became the new appointee for the position in rural sociology that the department had slated for priority appointment. The second priority position was in social work, which went to Zhang Hongjun in 1929. Wu Wenzao became one of the candidates for the third position in the department. The department in fact had two strong candidates for this third position, the other being Wu Jingchao (Qinghua, Class of 1923; Ph.D., Chicago, 1928) whom Robert Park considered one of the best students he had ever had.[27] Wu Wenzao, however, had the advantage of being a known quantity, both as a person and as a scholar. As a fellow graduate student of Wu's at Columbia, Burgess knew first hand that Wu was "especially good in social philosophy, social theory and history."[28]

A far more important factor to Burgess was his personal knowledge of Wu Wenzao as a person. Wu Jingchao, though "good in social research" and knowing "the Chicago technique thoroughly," was not a Christian. In concluding his summary for Stuart of these two candidates, the two Wu's who were Qinghua classmates and good friends, Burgess attached the following remark:

> I want to express at this time my hesitation to load up our depart-
> ment or any other department with a majority of men whom we are
> not sure of as to their Christian motives. I feel more strongly than
> ever after studying at Columbia and Chicago that mere social tech-
> nique is not sufficient for the solution of China's problems. There
> must be the religious dynamics there also.[29]

Not surprisingly, the position went to Wu Wenzao, who duly accepted the offer. This was not a difficult decision for Wu, given Yanjing's prominent

27. Burgess to Stuart, June 25, 1928, UB RG11 355.5475.
28. Ibid.   29. Ibid.

lead in sociology in China. There was, however, a personal reason as well. Wu's fiancée, Xie Wanying (pen name Bingxin), had joined Yanjing in 1926 after having graduated from Wellesley.

Wu Wenzao soon attracted a group of followers at Yanjing. Together they constituted the small yet dynamic sociology wing within the department. Its membership, including the faculty, could not have exceeded a dozen even at its peak. It was a closely knit group. The core of this group was all students whom Wu Wenzao actually taught: they were Huang Di (Class of 1931; M.A., 1933), Lin Yaohua (Lin Yueh-hua, Class of 1932; Ph.D., Harvard, 1940), Xu Yongshun (Class of 1932; Ph.D., Minnesota, 1943), Fei Xiaotong (Class of 1933; Ph.D., London School of Economics, 1938), C. K. Yang (Yang Qingkun, Class of 1933; Ph.D., Michigan, 1940), and Li Youyi (Class of 1936; M.A., 1939).

Under Wu Wenzao's guidance, members of the sociology wing moved toward a theoretical perspective informed by both British social anthropology and the Chicago school of sociology. In concrete terms, they adopted a functionalist approach to the study of any local settlement that they could define as a community. They labeled their approach "community studies" (*shequ yanjiu*). Their enthusiasm in the search for scientific rigor and social relevance of their discipline enabled them to attract like-minded individuals from within and without the department.

Among these allies, most notable were: Yan Jingyao (Class of 1928; Ph.D., Chicago, 1934), Li Anzhai (Li An-che, Class of 1929), and Zhao Chengxin (Class of 1930; Ph.D., Michigan, 1933), who went to Yanjing when the social service wing was the dominant force but had since come to a different theoretical position from their former teachers. To propagate their functionalist approach, they edited a newspaper supplement, "social research," which lasted, with one brief interruption, from 1933 to 1937, when the war with Japan broke out. In addition, they engaged in field work in villages in north and southeastern China.

The visits to Yanjing by Robert Park and Alfred Radcliffe-Brown, both from the University of Chicago, in 1932 and 1935, respectively, expanded Wu Wenzao's network. With his connections, he was able to obtain for his students advanced training abroad. In a hyperbolic language, Fei Xiaotong thus described Wu's academic entrepreneurship:

He had a master plan in his mind to groom his disciples. He would use every opportunity to send them to different major centers in anthropology in England and in the United States. He had it all planned, and, as it turned out, gradually realized who should go where and study with whom.[30]

As for himself and his journey to the London School of Economics, Fei gave a vivid, if also overblown, description of a fairly complicated plan:

When I was a student at Yanjing, I was an active supporter of the "community studies" group. However, the power of the department then lay in the hands of the Social Service Faction. I therefore could not expect the department authorities to send me abroad to study upon graduation. My teacher Wu Wenzao not only came up with the idea, but worked it out for me to get into the graduate school at Qinghua. It would not only give me some training in anthropology, but would enable me, after graduation from the graduate school, to secure a Qinghua scholarship to go to England to study with the master of functionalism [Malinowski].[31]

TWO COMPETING PARADIGMS

There was a marked difference in methodology between the two competing wings within the department. While members of the sociology wing agreed with members of the social service wing about the need for social reforms, they questioned the validity of the work that came from them. Assuming a posture virtually identical to that of the Chicago school's with regards to its stand on the social survey movement in the United States, these rebels charged the department's social service mainstream as being unscientific. The fundamental mistake of the social survey method, they argued, lay in its overriding concern for social reforms; so much so that they had in fact formed their conclusions before they embarked on research.[32] While these rebels were not averse to social reforms per se, they believed their task as sociologists was to study society as detached as they would be with a rock, an animal, or a specimen in the laboratory and, regardless of their own social philosophy, let the findings thus obtained guide social reforms.

Here was a competition between two paradigms: the dominating

30. Fei Xiaotong, "Liu Ying ji," *Wenshi ziliao xuanji*, No. 31 (Oct. 1962), pp. 43–4.
31. Ibid., p. 42.
32. For a standard Chicago critique of the social survey method, see Vivien Palmer, *Field Studies in Sociology: A Student's Manual* (Chicago, 1928), pp. 48–50.

social survey method, on the one hand, and the emerging "community studies" approach, on the other. The period from the late 1920s to the early 1930s witnessed the surge of a social survey movement in China. According to one estimate, there were over nine thousand surveys conducted between 1927 and 1935, averaging one thousand per year.[33] Two broad trends could be discerned in these nine thousand surveys. One was a decided shift of focus from the coastal to the hinterland provinces. Surveys on coastal provinces dropped from a yearly total of 82 percent in 1927 to 43 percent in 1935. The other trend was a turn toward rural areas. While of all the surveys conducted in 1927, 78.6 percent were urban, 6.5 percent rural, and 24.8 percent provincial,[34] the same relative percentage in 1933 to 1935 changed to 23.8 percent urban, 37.8 percent rural, and 38.4 percent provincial. The percentage of rural surveys was, in fact, higher than these figures suggest because the provincial surveys were largely rural surveys.

The dramatic increase of rural surveys reflected the rise of the rural reconstruction movement, and, more important, revealed unequivocally that social surveys were really aimed at social reforms. And herein lay the fundamental flaw of the social survey method. From the perspective of the sociology wing, most social surveys ended up begging the questions that had prompted the surveys in the first place. To illustrate their case, they referred to a social survey of Ding Xian that the Mass Education Movement had produced in 1933.[35] While they did not question the accuracy of the data presented in this survey, they argued that the data were collected to prove what the Mass Education Movement had found wrong with China – the "four culprits": ignorance, poverty, infirmity, and the lack of a civic spirit. If diagnosis preceded survey, were the data collected "naked facts" as the Mass Education Movement claimed? And had not the remedy, too, been prescribed before the survey? After all, had not the Mass Education Movement proposed to "cure ignorance with literacy campaigns, poverty with economic reconstruction, infirmity with public health, and the lack of a civic spirit with civics education." In short, the sequence that should have begun with research and concluded with a diagnosis and remedy was completely reversed. As such, social

33. Zhao Chengxin, "Shehui diaocha yu shequ yanjiu" (Social Surveys and Community Studies), *Shehuixue jie* (Sociological World), Vol. 9 (August 1936), pp. 157–9.
34. The total of 99.9 percent is in the source.
35. Li Jinghan, *Ding Xian shehui gaikuang diaocha* (Ding Xian: A Social Survey) (Beiping, 1933).

surveys were not so much scientific undertakings as endeavors to mobilize opinion and resources for social reforms.[36]

There were serious methodological implications for the reform orientation of social surveys. Most social surveys relied upon questionnaires and presented statistics without much analysis, supposedly to let facts speak for themselves. As a competing paradigm, the "community studies" approach relied instead on participant observation. From the perspective of the sociology wing, not only did the social survey method rely too much on the ability of survey workers and the cooperation of the interviewees, but it determined what issues were to be researched before entering the field.

There was one point of convergence between the two paradigms, however. Despite their criticisms of the social survey method, members of the sociology wing, too, were inductionists. They cautioned each other not to indulge in value judgments and maintained that their task as objective sociologists was to "discover facts." Fei Xiaotong confessed later that they had believed that the field worker "should not carry any theory to the countryside, but rather let himself be a roll of film automatically photographing the facts of the outside world."[37]

Beyond this inductionist approach, however, these two paradigms had little in common. There was no agreement even on the definition and interpretation of a social problem. From a functionalist vantage point, members of the sociology wing argued that the problem-oriented social survey approach failed to take into account that society is an intricately connected mechanism. Their functionalist perspective on society was best illustrated by two studies produced by two of its best known members: Fei Xiaotong and Lin Yaohua. Fei Xiaotong's *Peasant Life in China*, the better known of the two, was based on field work conducted in summer 1936 in Kaixiangong, a village in his native Wujiang county in Jiangsu.[38] His primary goal in this study was to elucidate the social "functions" major customs and institutions played in Kaixiangong, or, as Fei himself put it, to analyze "the functions of the social institutions, in relation to the need that they purport to satisfy and in relation to other institutions on which their working depends."[39]

36. Zhao Chengxin, "Shehui diaocha yu shequ yanjiu," pp. 159–62.
37. David Arkush, *Fei Xiaotong and Sociology in Revolutionary China* (Harvard, 1981), p. 91.
38. Fei Xiaotong, *Peasant Life in China: A Field Study of Country Life in the Yangtze Valley* (London, 1939).
39. Ibid., p. 4; Arkush, *Fei Xiaotong and Sociology in Revolutionary China*; pp. 68–79.

While Fei Xiaotong dwelled on functions, Lin Yaohua expounded on equilibrium, which he believed characterized the working of both the individual and society. In *The Golden Wing*, an autobiographical family history written in the form of a novel and with himself appearing as the "Little Brother,"[40] Lin Yaohua portrayed the families of two brothers-in-law and traced the vicissitudes that brought prosperity to one and decline to the other.[41] He argued that the system of human relations was "in a constant state of balance," that is, equilibrium. The state of equilibrium, to be sure, could not last forever, being constantly disturbed by changes in the environment, technology, personnel, and the international setting. However, he maintained that no matter how great the disturbing force was, a new equilibrium, which might be qualitatively different from the one in the previous cycle, would eventually reestablish itself.[42]

From this functionalist perspective, an approach that isolated an institution from its larger societal context could not show whether an institution had outlived its usefulness in the social organism, and therefore would be unable to render an accurate diagnosis for effective social reforms. The social survey method was, in short, a tunnel-vision approach to society. As Fei Xiaotong put it, "There is no so-called 'population problem' or 'family problem.' Our questions are: 'What is the population in a given area? Its social organizations? And their relations with the family structure, etc."[43]

Since a culture was the sum total of its various components, Fei argued that any social reform involved a process of dismantling and reconstituting this sum total. Because the various components of a culture formed an organic whole, it was imperative to examine what function each played in order to determine whether the old ones could be discarded and the new ones would mesh with the rest. Any social reforms that ignored this organic nature of culture would fail. As Fei cautioned: "Swift as a steamship is, it can be a most difficult thing to move when beached."[44]

Explicit in Fei's functionalist perspective was his criticism of the ways

40. Confirmed by Lin himself in an interview with him in Framingham, MA, on May 7, 1982.
41. Lin Yueh-hua, *The Golden Wing: A Sociological Study of Chinese Familism* (London, 1947).
42. Ibid., pp. 224–9.
43. Fei Xiaotong, "Lunshi jiyan: iii, guanyu shidi yanjiu" (The London Letters: 3, On Field Work), "Shehui yanjiu," *Yishi bao*, n.s., No. 44, March 10, 1937.
44. Fei Xiaotong, "Gui xing tongxun weisheng" (Epilogue of Letters from a Journey to Guangxi), "Shehui yanjiu," *Yishi bao*, n.s., No. 5, June 3, 1936.

reforms were carried out both by the government and by the rural reconstruction organizations. One classic example that he and his comrades in the sociology wing frequently referred to was the government's effort to suppress the "old-fashioned" schools (*sishu*). Although Fei touched upon the failure of the modern school system to meet the needs of the rural populace in his letters from the field in Kaixiangong in 1936, it was Liao Taichu (Class of 1932; M.A., 1935), the closest ally of the sociology wing from the department of education, who furnished the detailed documentation.

Based on his field work in Wenshang county, Shandong, in 1935–6, Liao Taichu's field reports were the best illustration of the functionalist viewpoint promoted by the sociology wing. In his series of reports, Liao pointed out that the old-fashioned schools in Wenshang, far from being obsolete institutions anachronistically clinging to an irrelevant past, were vibrant centers of activities in the villages. The sponsors of the schools were powerful local gentry, and, sometimes, village or township heads. The teachers, being the only literate persons in the villages and, in some cases, retired officials, were the indispensable advisers to the villagers in matters concerning the government, lawsuits, contracts, and anything that required an ability to compose with neat calligraphy.

In contrast to this, the teachers in the government schools were local graduates of primary schools, or, at best, of short-term teachers' training courses. They were invariably young, inexperienced, ill-paid, and ill-educated – particularly in the traditional literary skills that the villagers respected the most. On a more practical level, the fixed schedule based on the academic calendar determined by the Ministry of Education in Nanjing did not coincide with the agricultural cycle of the rural populace.

Even more striking was the adaptability of the old-fashioned schools in Wenshang. The graduates from government primary schools faced the dilemma of either going to junior high schools located outside the county – a burden beyond the financial capability of the peasant – or remaining in their home villages and becoming useless because the education they received, being general in nature, did not fit them for a life in the countryside. In contrast, the old-fashioned schools, by developing a system mimicking the modern system of offering a continuous elementary, secondary, and college education, proved to be a more attractive alternative for the rural populace.[45]

45. Liao Taichu, "Wenshang xian de sishu zuzhi, xu wan" (Old-fashioned Schools in Wenshang, Continued), "Shehui yanjiu," *Yishi bao*, n.s., No. 19, September 9, 1936. An

The message was clear: effective social reforms presuppose functional studies of the institutions targeted for intervention. Mere imposition of an alien substitute, no matter how modern or desirable it may be, is doomed to fail. However, even though the sociology wing criticized the well-meaning yet ill-advised reforms, they were not opposed to the idea of reform per se. As Fei Xiaotong argued, when reviling at the "American school of sociology" – his code name for the problem-oriented social surveys in general and the social service wing in particular: "Society . . . can be . . . observed, analyzed, and explained with generalizations. These generalizations . . . can then be used beneficially for the control of future phenomena."[46]

However, members of the sociology wing chose to play the role of detached sociologists. Their bold claim of the social benefits that could be derived from their scholarship thus stood in sharp contrast to the unpretentious self-image of how they, as sociologists, did their work. This self-image, in turn, led them to see themselves as producers, rather than consumers, of sociological knowledge. Whereas their competitors in the social service wing were always ready to assume government positions, members of the sociology wing believed that scholars and administrators could best benefit from each other if a division of labor between them were properly arranged.

The sociology wing's passionate plea for detached objectivity may have been reinforced by Robert Park, who taught one lecture course and led a seminar at Yanjing in fall 1932. Park once told some of his American students who wanted to be civil rights activists that the "world was full of crusaders."[47] His advice to them was to be "the calm, detached scientist who investigates race relations with the same objectivity and detachment with which the zoologist dissects the potato bug." Park did not mince his words when questioned about his lack of passion for social issues. He declared that he did not "belong to the evangelical school of sociology." And his answer to the question about what he did for the people was a gruff: "Not a damn thing!"

English version of these field reports, including Liao's field work in Chengdu, Sichuan, in 1945–1946, was published in 1949. See his "Rural Education in Transition: A Study of the Old-Fashioned Chinese Schools (Ssu-shu) in Shantung and Szechuan," in *The Yenching Journal of Social Studies*, IV.2 (February 1949), pp. 19–67.

46. Fei Xiaotong, "Xie zai 'Wenshang xian de sishu zuzhi' zhi qian" (Preface to "The Old-Fashioned Schools in Wenshang County"), *Yishi bao*, n.s., No. 15, August 12, 1936.

47. All the direct quotes of Park's in this paragraph are from Fred H. Matthews, *Quest for an American Sociology: Robert E. Park and the Chicago School* (Montreal, 1977), p. 116.

It should be pointed out that although functionalism has since been criticized in the West for perpetuating a conservative ideology opposing social change, it is clear from the above discussion that this was not the case with members of the sociology wing. In China in the 1930s, when there was a strong consensus on the need for change, functionalism was perceived by its followers as a more scientific agent for change. On the other hand, it was clear that while they were critical of social workers who were not able to bring to the field a functionalist perspective, they were equally scandalized by practices which forced facts to fit into pre-conceived theories. Their belief in the need to go into the field without being a crusader made them equally suspicious of Marxist generalizations. In Wu Wenzao's words: "In recent years . . . college students often consider it fashionable to apply dialectic materialism and think it respectable to participate in the Debates on the Social History of China. How formulaic, how mechanical this kind of training in thinking is!"[48]

ENTRY OF THE SOCIAL SERVICE WING
INTO THE FIELD OF SOCIAL ENGINEERING

The Rockefeller Foundation's involvement in China had been primarily in medicine, as manifested in its heavily funded model institution, the Peking Union Medical College, and in the area of premedical education. In the early 1930s, however, a major change occurred in the Foundation's programs in China. The Rockefeller Foundation in an attempt to develop practical applications of the social sciences in China gave the edge to the social service wing.

The prime mover behind this policy change was Selskar Gunn, the Foundation's vice-president in Europe. In summer 1931, Gunn visited China while returning from his post in Paris to the United States to review the Foundation's programs in China. During his seven-week trip, Gunn visited eight cities, toured forty-eight institutions, and interviewed more than one hundred people.[49] Staggered by the complexity of China which he observed, Gunn was nevertheless intrigued by the opportunities for the Foundation to mold a nation that had "become plastic after centuries of rigid conventionalism."[50] As a public health expert who had

---

48. Wu Wenzao, "Xiandai shequ shidi yanjiu de yiyi he gongyong" (The Meaning and Function of Modern Community Studies), in *Shehui yanjiu*, Nos. 51–100 (bound volume) (No. 66, January 9, 1935), p. 128.
49. Gunn, "Report on Visit to China, June 9th to July 30th, 1931," RAC RG1.1 601.12.129.
50. Gunn to Max Mason, September 8, 1931, RAC RG 1.1 601.12.129.

had extensive experience in Eastern Europe, he was most impressed by James Yen's Mass Education Movement, which struck him as similar to the work Andrija Stampar had suggested for Yugoslavia. He was especially moved by Yen's idealism, his multifaceted approach to the rural problems, and his demand for the economic feasibility and replication of his program at the village level.[51]

Before his visit to Ding Xian, Gunn had heard widespread criticisms about China's uncritical acceptance of Western ideas and methods from Chinese and foreigners with whom he came into contact. James Yen's Mass Education Movement, whose leadership was composed mainly of Chinese who had been educated in the West, thus represented to Gunn a most stimulating social experiment that challenged the privileged intellectuals to tackle China's rural problems instead of dwelling on the high-sounding Western theories they had learned while abroad. He was convinced that the key to China's most urgent need lay in the rural reconstruction movement, especially in James Yen's Mass Education Movement. In his report on his China trip, Gunn recommended that the Foundation study the situation in order to consolidate the Foundation's work in China.[52]

The Foundation acted upon Gunn's recommendation by appointing none other than Gunn himself to study and propose a new program in China. Thereupon Gunn returned to China and stayed for an extended period of time from October 1932 to February 1934. During his residency in China, Gunn began to formulate his program around the central theme of rural reconstruction. From his frequent visitations to the existing rural reconstruction centers and exchanges of ideas with people, he came to be convinced of the importance of a close coordination of efforts between academic institutions and rural reconstruction centers. He believed that academic institutions could provide training of personnel and research for rural reconstruction centers, which, in return, would serve as laboratories for the testing and the application of ideas or theories formulated by the former.

As Gunn's program began to crystallize, it became clear that he was embarking on a drastically different course of action than what the Rockefeller Foundation had hitherto pursued. In his attempt to make the academics contribute to rural reconstruction work, he advocated that

---

51. Gunn, "Report on visit to China, June 9th to July 30th, 1931," pp. 85–7.
52. James Thomson, Jr., *While China Faced West: American Reformers in Nationalist China, 1928–1937* (Harvard, 1969), Ch. 6.

they reorient their disciplines toward a more practical focus. In addition, he espoused a multidisciplinary approach that would bring together experts from the various fields of the social sciences, public health, agronomy, and engineering. Of these experts, he accorded social scientists a special role in the overall planning and coordination of a comprehensive program in rural reconstruction.

Word that the Rockefeller Foundation had decided to support the social sciences and would be in favor of work in rural reconstruction quickly spread. Suddenly, everyone talked about rural reconstruction in his grant application to the Rockefeller Foundation. In this scramble for grants, the performance of the social service wing of the Yanjing Sociology Department was astounding. Yanjing's campaign to win Gunn's support began even before he had visited the campus in 1931. N. G. Gee, who had been Rockefeller Foundation's premedical education adviser before he became Yanjing's vice-president in New York, had alerted Yanjing that Gunn was more interested in reviewing its social science rather than natural science programs.[53] Being already a beneficiary of the Rockefeller patronage of the social sciences, Yanjing fully anticipated that Gunn's visit would bring additional support for its social science programs.

Unfortunately for Yanjing, Gunn became critical of the Yanjing programs when he returned in 1932 to formulate his new program for China. Whereas Gunn's interest was directed to rural reconstruction, particularly as it was represented by James Yen's Mass Education Movement, he came away from his visit to Yanjing with the impression that the Yanjing Sociology Department was primarily engaged in research in theoretical sociology.[54] His opinion about Qinghe, the department's laboratory, was less than enthusiastic.[55]

Gunn's negative evaluation was a shock to Stuart and his social science faculty. Like many other institutions, Yanjing awaited the final presentation to the Foundation of Gunn's program with great expectation and anxiety. All concerned expected that his program would be liberally funded by the Foundation; the figure generally quoted was

---

53. For an excellent biography of Gee, see William Haas, *China Voyager: Gist Gee's Life in Science* (Armonk, New York: M. E. Sharpe, 1996).
54. Gunn, "Report on visit to China, June 9th to July 30th, 1931," p. 55.
55. Interview with Dr. C. C. Chen (Chen Zhiqian), a public health expert trained at the Peking Union Medical College who was involved in the Rockefeller-supported rural reconstruction projects, November 15, 1985, Berkeley, California.

$1,000,000 annually.[56] The stakes were high and Yanjing was determined to win a place in Gunn's program.

In early 1933, Yanjing began an aggressive campaign to prove to Gunn that it was committed to rural reconstruction. In his letter to Gunn that requested an annual grant of $30,000 for three years, Stuart apologetically acknowledged Yanjing's belated recognition of the need to organize its programs for rural reconstruction. He contended, nonetheless, that public service and rural reconstruction had always figured prominently in the activities among the social science faculty. To illustrate his point, he referred to the faculty members who served as advisers or officials in the government and to J. B. Tayler, who founded the North China Industrial Service Union that attempted to revive and improve rural, small-scale industries.[57]

Through their constant conferences with Gunn and John B. Grant, Gunn's assistant and professor of public health at the Peking Union Medical College, Stuart and Leonard Hsu came to grasp two principles that were of tremendous appeal to Gunn: "coordinated effort" and "university standard for rural reconstruction work." In early fall of 1933, Yanjing made its first breakthrough. Knowing that Gunn was most enthusiastic about the Nankai Institute of Economics and James Yen's Mass Education Movement, Yanjing adopted a strategy that called for limited cooperation and coordination with the two favored institutions. In what would turn out to be a prelude to a shrewd battle for funding to be described fully in Chapter 9, Yanjing worked out an agreement with Nankai to present a joint proposal to Gunn whereby the two institutions would take over J. B. Tayler's North China Industrial Service Union. At the same time, Stuart submitted a separate request to Gunn to enable Yanjing to establish an Institute of Rural Administration. In his request, Stuart dwelled on the importance of formulating a well-integrated program in rural reconstruction to avoid unnecessary duplication of efforts by individual institutions.[58]

Yanjing's proposal for joint Yanjing-Nankai sponsorship of Tayler's North China Industrial Service Union was a brilliant move to reverse the embarrassing and critical situation created by Tayler's resignation from

56. The actual figure was in fact much smaller. Gunn's own estimate given to the trustees was $300,000 annually. See "Report of the Committee on Appraisal and Plan," December 11, 1934, RAC RG3 900 22.170, p. 106.
57. Stuart to Gunn, January 23, 1933, RAC RG1.1 601.22.201.
58. Stuart to Gunn, undated [received by Gunn in Shanghai in September 1933], RAC RG1.1 601.22.201.

Yanjing and his decision to join Nankai. By proposing a joint enterprise, not only could Yanjing demonstrate its willingness to cooperate with other institutions, but it could enhance its chances of getting support by virtue of Gunn's deep interest in both Nankai and Tayler.

The request for the establishment of an Institute of Rural Administration was an equally astute move. The only complication was that it was perceived as an encroachment upon the sphere in which Cheeloo University was supposed to have specialized. As if to test Yanjing's determination to turn rural-minded, Gunn requested an endorsement from Yanjing's trustees in New York. The Yanjing trustees were hesitant. First, there was a procedural problem. Both the initiative and the final presentation for the establishment of the Institute were done entirely in the field, without any prior consultation with the trustees. The field officers had never sought the approval of the trustees, who, in fact, only learnt it from Gunn.[59] Second, there was the issue of finance. Knowing that the grant to inaugurate a new enterprise rarely covers the whole expense, the trustees were concerned that they would have to assume the financial responsibility of the proposed Institute.[60]

More serious was the problem of encroachment upon Cheeloo's territory. Christian colleges in China had since 1922 begun a protracted and futile search for a "correlated program." The objective of this "correlated program" was to achieve a division of labor among Christian colleges in order to eliminate unnecessary competition and duplication of programs among themselves. According to this plan, Yanjing was designated as the institution to concentrate on the social sciences while Cheeloo was assigned to develop a rural program. The Yanjing trustees had reasons not to antagonize the Associated Boards for Christian Colleges in China, to which the Yanjing board was a member.

The Yanjing field officers had in 1934 unilaterally announced Yanjing's withdrawal from further discussion of the Correlated Program on the grounds that some Christian colleges were hampering the creation of a "correlated program" by their continued resistance to be either reconstituted or amalgamated.[61] When the field learnt that the trustees were hesitant to give their endorsement to the proposed Institute, they sent

59. B. A. Garside to Stuart, May 16, 1934, UB RG11 357.5509.
60. Garside to Stuart, March 19, 1934, UB RG11 357.5508.
61. "The Attitude of Yenching University to the Proposed Correlation of the Christian Colleges of China," "Minutes of China Christian Educational Association, Council of Higher Education, January 19–20, 1934," pp. 5–6, UB RG11 449.6014.

strongly worded memoranda to the trustees in a desperate effort to secure the necessary endorsement.[62] Fortunately for the field officers, both the Associated Boards and the Yanjing trustees granted their endorsement with a proviso that Yanjing's program would not interfere with any rural program that Cheeloo might develop.

As an outsider, Gunn could hardly have cared less about the internal politics and denominational squabbling among different mission boards. His overriding concern was his own correlated program, to which Yanjing's proposed Institute of Rural Administration could form a natural unit. From his perspective, Cheeloo's conception of a rural program was dated and inadequate to meet China's need.[63] At any rate, through brilliant maneuvers, Yanjing had finally won Gunn's confidence. Even though Gunn continued to have doubt about Yanjing and "wondered just how far the rural swing was motivated by the hope of getting money,"[64] he included Yanjing in his China Program, which was approved at the trustees' meeting in December 1934.

In January 1935, Gunn returned to China to initiate his China Program. He and John B. Grant were more than ever convinced by the necessity to coordinate the rural reconstruction programs of the three institutions that were being included in his China Program, for example, Yanjing, Nankai, and the Mass Education Movement. Through a combination of pressure and cajolery, they finally succeeded in April 1936 in forming a North China Council for Rural Reconstruction that consisted of the participating members of Yanjing, Nankai, Qinghua, the University of Nanking, the Peking Union Medical College, and the Mass Education Movement.

With much imagination, the North China Council for Rural Reconstruction elected into the Council Liang Zhonghua, the administrative supervisor of Jining and its thirteen surrounding counties, which the Shandong provincial government had designated as an experimental district in 1935. Liang Zhonghua was a colleague of the latter-day Confucian sage Liang Shuming, whose rural reconstruction program at Zouping in Shandong – and, by extension, Jining – represented a conservative alternative to James Yen's American approach in Ding Xian.[65]

62. Stuart to Garside, April 18, 1934, UB RG11 357.5508; Garside to Stuart, May 16, 1934, UB RG11 357.5509.
63. See Chapter 9 for more discussion on Cheeloo's failure to develop a rural program.
64. Gunn to Max Mason, April 11, 1935, RAC RG1.1 601.22.201.
65. Guy Alitto, *The Last Confucian: Liang Shu-ming and the Chinese Dilemma of Modernity* (Berkeley, 1979).

The election of Liang Zhonghua into the Council brought about something quite unexpected. In fall 1936, Liang Zhonghua invited the Council for a collaborative rural reconstruction work at Jining. The Council was empowered to nominate its personnel to official positions. As unlikely as this alliance was, this event enabled the Council to acquire a second base of operation in addition to the Ding Xian station that had been the base of the Mass Education Movement. Thus, at the inauguration of Gunn's China Program, the participating member institutions were individually responsible for different fields of training and research in the two stations, namely, with economics, civil administration, and social administration in Jining and public health and education in Ding Xian. Each member institution would appoint faculty who would live and teach in the station. Students on their part received in-field training and fellowships provided by the Rockefeller Foundation. The involvement of the Yanjing Sociology Department culminated in the appointment of Zhang Hongjun as the magistrate of Wenshang county, north of Jining. It was truly a triumphant moment for the social service wing. In addition to contributing Zhang Hongjun as magistrate, the social service wing supplied personnel for a Department of Social Administration in Jining with Zhang as the chairman. Other teaching staff included Yang Kaidao, Wang Hechen (Class of 1925; M.A., New York University, 1930), and Wu Yuzhen (Class of 1929; M.A., 1932 C.S.W., 1936, New York School of Social Work).

The collaboration between the Rockefeller-funded North China Council for Rural Reconstruction and the Confucian-inspired Zouping-Jining was not as improbable as it appeared. Critics of the two experiments argued that both erred in their diagnoses of and proposed remedies to the problems that had been plaguing Chinese society.[66] The four culprits of ignorance, poverty, weakness, and lack of a civic spirit that the Mass Education Movement – the mainstay of the Council – singled out for attack reflected, in the critics' view, merely symptoms rather than the root causes. Zouping was similarly at fault in its attempt to rejuvenate a sociomoral order, or to recreate a *Gemeinschaft*. If their diagnoses were off the mark, their remedies would simply serve to perpetuate or even accelerate a total breakdown. In short, despite the dif-

---

66. Note that not all of the critics of the movement were Marxists; they represented all shades in the entire ideological spectrum of the day. Among them, most articulate were Qian Jiaju, a prominent member of Chen Hansheng's Agrarian China Society (discussed in Chapter 8), and Wu Bannong, a member of Tao Menghe's Institute of the Social Sciences at the Academia Sinica.

ference in their outlooks, both essentially operated under the existing power structure and thus worked toward the preservation of the status quo.[67] There is much truth in the critics' contention that both Ding Xian and Zouping deliberately steered clear of issues they deemed dangerous and lost sight of the fact that real progress would be impossible unless these issues were first solved.

The question of ideological leaning is by no means merely radical rhetoric. It was symptomatic of an ultimate flaw of the Rockefeller-financed rural reconstruction program, and, for that matter, of most rural reconstruction programs in the 1930s; that is, it had to seek the support and collaboration of those who were in power. It takes little insight to understand why of the whatever little amount of work the Mass Education Movement was able to achieve, it was in the areas of public health and education, but not local finance or administration, where the established order had its vital interests.

Despite its social engineering rhetoric, the North China Council for Rural Reconstruction fared no better. Although it managed to fit into the Jining field, the Council failed in its negotiation with the authorities of Hebei for a modest control of local administration in Ding Xian. Council members held several special sessions in fall 1936 to discuss proper approaches for negotiation, their viable options, and what they ought to demand as their minimum share of power. In the end, however, it was the Council that had to make the compromise. In order to secure permission to engage in experiments in local administration in Ding Xian, the Council had to promise that under no circumstances would its policies come into conflict with the existing laws as well as the wishes of the gentry and the "people."[68]

The war with Japan that broke out in July 1937 renders it moot as to whether or not this Rockefeller-instigated and -financed rural reconstruction program could have succeeded. Yet it seems clear that a program would stand a better chance to succeed if it were limited in scope and particularly if it were not to disturb the existing power structure. Literacy and public health campaigns fell into this category. Once

---

67. See the articles written by Wu Bannong and Qian Jiaju and reprinted in Qian Jiaju, ed., *Zhongguo nongcun jingji lunwen ji* (A Collection of Essays on Agrarian Economy in China) (Shanghai, 1936).
68. *Huabei nongcun jianshe xiejinhui xunlian yanjiu weiyuanhui jilu* (Minutes of the Committee on Training and Research of the North China Council for Rural Reconstruction) (n.p., n.d.), pp. 151–85. I am indebted to Charles Hayford for bringing this document to my attention.

the program seemed to lose its innocuous nature, as when the Foundation redirected the work toward social engineering, it encountered difficulties and resistance. While many of these difficulties and much of the resistance were embedded in the existing structure and its practices, as documented by the Nankai participants analyzed in Chapter 5, ultimately they were symptomatic of a power structure that was impervious to the best social engineering intentions of the professors. As neither the Foundation nor the professors had any intention to take on the system, they chose to compromise; their program would have been destined to falter whether or not the war had intervened.

THE DEPARTMENT DURING THE WAR

While the social service wing was riding the tide of social engineering and was clearly in the spotlight of the day, the sociology wing had reached its all-time low in terms of personnel. Some of its members were abroad: Fei Xiaotong was in England and C. K. Yang in the United States. Still others were away doing field work. More important, its leader, Wu Wenzao, was abroad on sabbatical leave during 1936–7, first attending the Harvard Tercentenary Ceremony and then visiting major social science centers in the United States and in Europe.

However, being away did not prevent Wu Wenzao from contemplating plans for his sociology wing. In April 1937 while he was still abroad, he presented a proposal to the Rockefeller Foundation that called on the Foundation to support an Institute for Research in the Social Sciences at Yanjing. It was an ambitious proposal that envisioned international cooperation in establishing a training center in sociology and social anthropology to train Chinese students to conduct research on Chinese society. Wu Wenzao pushed for this proposal after he had returned to Peking and continued to do so under Japanese occupation.

However, the war changed many things. The social service wing never regained its strength. Through its participation in the Rockefeller Foundation's China Program, it had reached its peak just before the war. Almost all of its senior members joined the government. Leonard Hsu himself left China for the United States as soon as the war had started.[69] His departure greatly annoyed Grant, who viewed Hsu's sudden depart-

---

69. Hsu stayed in the United States during the war years with his American wife and two daughters. After the war, he joined the Reynolds Metal Corporation as Coordinator of Foreign Operations.

ure as a desertion from the field work that the North China Council for Rural Reconstruction had maintained in Jining since 1936.[70]

The departure for government service of senior members of the social service wing was not a phenomenon unique to Yanjing. The war with Japan precipitated a new wave of movement from academia to government. Few among those who made this career change, however, would have portrayed their move in terms of social engineering. A sense of duty to the nation fighting a war of survival notwithstanding, a senior government position was a much more attractive alternative in an economy and society ravaged by the war. Not until toward the end of the war when postwar reconstruction was put on the agenda, could these academics-turned-bureaucrats entertain once again the idea of putting their expertise to use in charting the course of development for the nation.

The department was able to carry on its work during the first few years of the war. However, the situation worsened when Wu Wenzao left for the southwest, and especially when the university was reopened in Chengdu following Pearl Harbor and the occupation of the Peking campus by the Japanese. There were simply no senior professors left on the faculty. In an unusual move, the Rockefeller Foundation entrusted grants from the China Program funds to Wu Wenzao and empowered him to use his own discretion in distributing these funds for sociological research. In the past, the Foundation had consistently given money to institutions rather than to individuals. This move amounted to a recognition of Wu Wenzao's ability as a teacher and a research supervisor. However, it had some very interesting repercussions that the Foundation did not anticipate.

It was unusual because Wu Wenzao was no longer on the Yanjing faculty; he had left academia and was serving on the Supreme National Defense Council in Chongqing. By placing grants at Wu's disposal for sociological research, the Foundation in effect created a competing academic power center to the Yanjing Sociology Department which was also funded by the same China Program. This by itself was not necessarily an undesirable phenomenon. However, if one considers the factionalism and the competition in academic patronage, by giving Wu Wenzao the resources to maintain and to extend his academic patronage, the Foundation was undermining the very vitality of the department.

70. Grant to Gunn, August 27, 1937, RAC RG1.1 601.14.147.

The Foundation was aware of the problem. Its field officer had tried to urge Wu Wenzao and Yang Kaidao to rejoin the department by arguing that the Foundation could not justify its support of a program as weak as the department was.[71] In contrast, the Yanjing-Yunnan Station, which was supported by the funds under Wu Wenzao's disposal, was thriving. This station was staffed by Wu Wenzao's protégés: Fei Xiaotong as director, and Li Youyi, Zhang Ziyi, Shi Guoheng, Tian Rukang (T'ien Ju-k'ang, Qinghua, Class of 1940; Ph.D., London School of Economics, 1948), and others. Francis Hsu (Xu Langguang, B.A., Shanghai University, 1933; Ph.D., London School of Economics, 1940), an outsider who was not one of Wu Wenzao's students and who was the acting director of the station while Fei was visiting the United States in 1943–4, was a concrete example of Wu Wenzao's extending his patronage network.

This anomalous position of Wu Wenzao vis-à-vis Yanjing gave rise to factionalism at yet another level. The university administration complained that because of the personal animosity between Wu Wenzao and Mei Yibao (Mei Yi-pao, Qinghua, Class of 1922; B.A., Oberlin, 1924; Ph.D., Chicago, 1927), who became the wartime president of the university, Wu Wenzao purposely held back his men from joining or rejoining the faculty.[72]

During the war, Fei Xiaotong's Yanjing-Yunnan Station became a most thriving center of research in social anthropology.[73] Returning from England where, under Malinowski's supervision, he wrote up his field work in Kaixiangong for his Ph.D. thesis *Peasant Life in China* (published in 1939), Fei Xiaotong was as eager to do field work as before but had become more sophisticated in methodology. He had shed all remnants of inductionism in his thinking and had begun advocating that field workers should bring theories to be tested and refined in the field.[74]

Despite the difficult wartime situation, through his own research and his direction of the station, Fei Xiaotong established himself as a leading sociologist. True to his conviction that sociological knowledge was beneficial to the control of the society, he began writing essays commenting on current events by drawing insight from his research. His advocacy of small-scale rural industry – a position that Nankai had adopted and then

---

71. Marshall Balfour to Wu Wenzao, November 19, 1943, RAC RG1.1 601.22.204.
72. Roger Evans' interview with Mei Yibao, May 14, 1945, RAC RG1.1 601.23.218. See Chapter 9 for more discussion of factionalism at Yanjing.
73. David Arkush, *Fei Xiaotong and Sociology in Revolutionary China*, pp. 79–103.
74. For a different interpretation of this point, which fails to follow Fei's intellectual development through different phases of his academic life, see ibid., pp. 90–1.

abandoned during the war[75] – and his concern for the "conservation" of the rural society whose talents and resources, he argued, were relentlessly siphoned off by large urban centers made him a provocative columnist.[76] He became the best-known sociologist both at home and abroad and even outshone his teacher Wu Wenzao. And like Wu, he knew how to cultivate connections abroad and consolidate his influence at home.[77]

Factionalism prevented members of the sociology wing from building a solid base within the department, not to mention a network that would extend beyond the university, thereby providing sociology in China with a more viable institutional base. Nor were there any indications that efforts were made to renew the camaraderie with the former allies in the sociology wing. Liao Taichu, the closest ally before the war, was teaching at Yanjing and was concurrently its field station director at Chongyiqiao. The feud between Mei Yibao and Wu Wenzao may have prevented any possibility of collaboration, especially when they had to compete for funding from the same donor. At its worse, factionalism tended to fragment prematurely the efforts of the individual sociologists and to freeze any ongoing dialogue among them. Before a school could be created, recurrent factionalism would divide its members. It is as if before a house could be created, it was already divided.[78]

Amid this seemingly frivolous personal animosity, nevertheless, something positive was germinating – a growing specialization during the war in the southwest among members of the original sociology wing and their allies. To a certain extent, the lack of collaboration among them reflected a situation in which each of them was busy in carving out a sphere of specialization. Fei Xiaotong, for example, was definitely thriving in the field of social anthropology. Lin Yaohua, on the other hand, was moving into cultural anthropology.

Another fascinating example was Li Anzhai, one of the prewar allies, who went with his wife to Labrang in Gansu. Intrigued by the close link

---

75. See Chapter 5.
76. Arkush, *Fei Xiaotong and Sociology in Revolutionary China*, pp. 137–73. For a translation of Fei's brilliant and best-known analysis of Chinese society, see Gary Hamilton and Wang Zheng, trs., *From the Soil: The Foundations of Chinese Society* (California, 1992).
77. See Chapter 9.
78. See Chapter 9 for a discussion on factionalism and how it erodes patronage networks within China.

between British social anthropology and colonial administration, he viewed his work among the Tibetans there as his personal crusade that recreated his vision of what functionalist anthropologists had done for Africa.[79] Like an ideal functionalist anthropologist who, according to Malinowski, would act as the defender of African rights and desires, Li did not see Sinicization as the answer in Labrang or Tibet – his dream location for field work where he finally entered in 1956, ironically, with the People's Liberation Army. Although China was no longer an empire – nor could it aspire to be a colonial power – to Li Anzhai, Labrang, and the then still unreachable Tibet, were his Africa.[80]

Just as sociology in China seemed to be coming into its own, the civil war of 1946 to 1949 intervened. Concerns about violence, demoralization, and an impending general breakdown took precedence over academic issues. Fei Xiaotong, for example, became better known in China as a political columnist and essayist than as the sociologist he was trained to be, writing prolifically on issues of political corruption, the question of U.S. aid to the Nationalists, and the sole reliance on military solutions by both sides. Wu Wenzao was on the staff of the allied occupation in Japan until 1951 when he returned to China, after frantic efforts by his American friends first failed to secure him a teaching position at the University of Tokyo and then succeeded in doing so at Yale with funding from the Rockefeller Foundation only to be thwarted by an American consul in Tokyo who refused to issue visas to Wu and his wife, Bingxin.[81] In this tense and highly politicized atmosphere, sociological research in China came virtually to a halt. The final blow came in 1952. Determined to follow the Soviet models in academic affairs, the new socialist government restructured tertiary institutions in China into three types: comprehensive universities of sciences and humanities; polytechnics; and

---

79. Not all anthropologists who worked in Africa during the interwar period were functionalists. Nor did British colonial officials welcome them as Li assumed. The British colonial government relied upon government anthropologists. See Henrika Kuklick, "The Sins of the Fathers: British Anthropology and African Colonial Administration," Robert Jones, ed., *Research in Sociology of Knowledge, Sciences, and Art* (Greenwich, CT, 1978), pp. 93–119.
80. See Chapter 9 for more discussion on Li Anzhai.
81. David Rowe of Yale was the most active among Wu's American friends who tried to bring Wu and Bingxin to the United States. Apparently caught by some snags in the security clearance process, they were deemed persons "prejudicial to the interests of the United States" and were denied their visas. It is a testimony to the integrity of the Wu's that before they went back to China, they returned the $2,000 travel advance given to them by the Rockefeller Foundation. RAC 200s.419.4990.

specialized colleges. For ideological discipline and the purpose of serving the needs of the nation's economic development, applied science and technology towered over the humanities and the social sciences.[82] Whereas economics, finance, politics, and law were reincarnated in the Soviet mode, sociology, which had been suspended in the Soviet Union for decades, was abolished.[83]

Tragic would have been too mild a word to describe the end of this fascinating story of the Yanjing Sociology Department. The little over forty years of its existence is a record of idealism, dedication, failures, and triumphs against a background of poverty and violence, a background drastically worsened by Japanese invasion from 1937 to 1945 and the civil war that immediately followed. From its initial focus on social service, the department had by the early 1930s transformed itself into a center of sociological research extolling the virtue of social engineering. The Yanjing enterprise thrived on American largess; it would not have become what it was had it not benefited from the vision and support of Princeton-in-Peking and, later, the patronage of the Rockefeller philanthropy. In methodology, too, the Yanjing enterprise depended largely on intellectual guidance from the West. Both its YMCA legacy and the functionalism-inspired "community studies" approach of the sociology wing were foreign models.

The war with Japan disrupted the department's work and dispersed its highly talented faculty and graduates. In the backward and isolated southwest, cut off from easy reach of Western patronage and influence, sociological research started anew. Although the Yanjing enterprise declined, it witnessed some of its most talented and resourceful former members setting up field stations, entering new fields, and making bold and new attempts to use their disciplines to answer the needs of Chinese society. In this sense, the 1952 decision to abolish sociology occurred just at a time when the discipline was on its way to becoming an empirical science with a Chinese data base. It was not until 1979 that sociology was rehabilitated.

The nearly thirty years' hiatus was, however, too wide a gap to be easily

---

82. See Ruth Hayhoe, *China's Universities, 1895–1995: A Century of Cultural Conflict* (New York: Garland Publishing, 1996), pp. 77–83 and Suzanne Pepper, *Radicalism and Education Reform in 20th Century China: The Search for an Ideal Development Model* (Cambridge: Cambridge University Press, 1996), pp. 164–79.

83. Siu-lun Wong, *Sociology and Socialism in Contemporary China*, pp. 37–44 and Han Minghan [mo], *Zhongguo shehuixueshi* (A History of Chinese Sociology) (Tianjin: Tianjin renmin chubanshe, 1987), pp. 169–72.

bridged. Gingerly treading the lines sanctioned by the Communist Party, Chinese sociologists are careful in their evaluation of the pre-1949 legacy. As late as 1987, nearly a decade after the nation had embarked on an outward-looking open-door policy, the two books published that year on the history of Chinese sociology continued to insist on a teleological evaluation of this legacy, emphasizing its failure in comprehending the fundamental social, political, and economic crises in Chinese society whose successful resolution came only with the victory of the Chinese Communist Party.[84] Both authors discussed the development of sociology of the pre-1949 era in the context of China's search for modernity and modern nationhood, contrasting the academic establishment with the various endeavors – Marxist and otherwise. Yang Yabin's survey placed more emphasis on the academic establishment. By contrast, Han Mingmo's foregrounded the Marxist endeavors. Moreover, while Yang took pains to vindicate the achievements of the pre-1949 academic sociological establishment, Han was less charitable with this legacy. "Sociology in China has a history of more than ninety years," granted he, "but the data it has produced is not abundant." More astounding was his quip that the subject has elicited the interest of foreign scholars only because "it has taken place in the most populous country in the world."[85] While he called for an objective evaluation of the sociology under the *ancien régime*, his was a teleological interpretation. Academic sociology of the pre-1949 era represented, for him, part of a larger movement that began with the protosociological philosophizing at the turn of the twentieth century and culminated with the victory of the Chinese Communist Party. In this teleological scheme, academic sociology was as misguided and superficial as the rural reconstruction movement. By contrast, it was the glorious contributions of the Marxist sociological endeavors, particularly that of Mao Zedong's agrarian surveys, that helped inscribe "the towering monument that is the People's Republic of China."[86]

---

84. Han Minghan [mo], *Zhongguo shehuixueshi* and Yang Yabin, *Zhongguo shehuixueshi* (A History of Chinese Sociology) (Jinan: Shandong renmin chubanshe, 1987).
85. Han Minghan [mo], *Zhongguo shehuixueshi*, "Preface."
86. Ibid., p. 3.

4

The Nankai Institute of Economics: The Germinating Stage, 1927–1931

IF the Yanjing Sociology Department was the preeminent sociological center in China during the Republican period, the Nankai Institute of Economics had virtually no rivals and stood in a class by itself in the field of economic research. As part of Nankai University, a private Chinese institution, it would have had little prospect for growth, let alone expansion, had it depended solely on university appropriations. Nor could it rely, as did Yanjing, upon a missionary board in New York to raise funds. Nonetheless, the Nankai Institute of Economics rivaled Yanjing in its ability to raise funds from the United States, particularly from the Rockefeller Foundation. And to measure up to Yanjing's foremost position in sociological research, the Institute pioneered empirical studies of Chinese industries, local government and finance, and compiled the most authoritative and complete series of index numbers on prices. These achievements bear testimony to the individuals whose vision, leadership, and entrepreneurial skills created the Nankai Institute of Economics.

Nankai University was the only private Chinese university to achieve national prominence during the Republican period. It was the crowning achievement of a school system that began in 1898 in Tianjin, as a family school with five students. Zhang Boling, who first served as the tutor at this small family school, was the moving spirit behind this educational enterprise. Largely due to Zhang's belief in expansion and his perseverance in raising funds, in little more than thirty years the small family school was transformed into a comprehensive school system that offered instruction from the primary to graduate levels.[1]

1. *Nankai daxue xiaoshi: 1919–1949* (A History of Nankai University: 1919–1949) (Tianjin, 1989); Hu Shi, "Chang Po-ling: Educator," *There Is Another China* (New York, 1948), pp. 4–14; and E-tu Zen Sun, "The Growth of the Academic Community 1912–1949," in

In 1907, when the middle school, which grew out of the little family school three years earlier, moved into its permanent site outside the old south gate of the city, Nankai was a tiny school on two acres. Yet, in 1922, when the land two miles outside the city was acquired for the newly established university,[2] it was more than eighty acres, while the original middle school compound grew to nearly eighteen.[3] Before the war with Japan broke out in 1937, the Nankai school had become an enterprise on over one hundred and thirty acres.

This was truly a remarkable achievement considering that Nankai's rapid growth, especially in the 1920s, occurred against a background, at government universities, of chronic financial crises and misappropriations of educational funds that resulted in salary arrears for teachers. Many professors were forced to seek alternative employment or teaching positions, where salary income was regular and employment more certain. Noticeable was the migration of teachers, generally toward the south. Peking, the citadel of learning, to which not a few clung under great hardship, lost many of its best teachers. Those who stayed on often had to take part-time jobs in addition to their full-time positions – a strategy they sardonically caricatured as "pulling rickshaws for three companies."[4]

THE FINANCIAL BASE

Nankai's financial situation was no less precarious than that of governmental institutions. The only advantage it had was that it did not solely depend on government appropriations. However, numerous as the sources of its funding may have been – local gentry, bankers, industrialists, warlords, and government – they were likewise unreliable and were easily cut off by constant realignment of political and military forces, which was typical during the early Republican period. One major factor that sustained the growth of the university during the first part of the 1920s was the much discussed yet hitherto little understood bequest of

John K. Fairbank and Albert Feuerwerker, eds., *The Cambridge History of China*, Vol. 13, pp. 372–4.

2. According to *Nankai daxue xiaoshi*, this land, located in Balitai, was part of a larger tract of land designated permanently for rental purposes. The university paid only a nominal annual rent on the land it rented. See *op. cit.*, pp. 90–1.

3. Roger Greene, "Visit to the Nankai School, Tientsin," (September 14, 1916), p. 1, RAC RG4 26.549; N. Gist Gee, "Nankai College," December 1922, p. 1, RAC RG4 62.1524.

4. *Qinghua daxue xiaoshi gao* (A Draft History of Qinghua University), p. 64.

half a million Mexican dollars (about a quarter of a million American dollars) willed to the University by Li Chun, Jiangsu military governor and a native of Tianjin, who had committed suicide in October 1920, following a nervous breakdown.[5]

The bequest was given by Li's brother in the form of first-year bonds of the Republic at the face value of $2,170,000 Mexican dollars, though their market value amounted to only $412,300 Mexican dollars.[6] The fate of these bonds was extremely uncertain. A few months after the transfer of the ownership, they were reorganized at a 60 percent loss of face value. Later, they did not even have a market quotation. Nevertheless, the interest income from these bonds, which fluctuated between seventy and a hundred thousand Mexican dollars, continued to come in from the Peking government and formed the mainstay of the university's budget until 1926, when the former lost control over the salt revenue from the provinces, from which the interest payment of these bonds was made. This is testimony to Zhang Boling's ingenuity in keeping himself free from any political alliance lest his Nankai should suffer the consequences of any political realignment.[7]

The whole episode of the Li Chun bequest illustrates the precarious nature of financial pledges that were not channeled through more institutionalized arrangements. Yet under the conditions prevailing at the time, Nankai had to accept any contributions, small or large, however they were given and whoever they were from. Warlords and politicians were Nankai's most conspicuous benefactors. In addition to Li Chun, the warlord benefactors included Yuan Shikai, Xu Shichang, Yan Xishan, Wang Zhanyuan, military governor of Hubei, and Chen Guangyuan, military governor of Jiangxi.[8]

---

5. This half a million Mexican dollars constituted one-fourth of Li Chun's bequest. According to his will, another fourth of his bequest was for famine relief in Hebei and the remainder, that is, half of his bequest, would go to his surviving wife and his younger brother. See Tao Juyin, *Beiyang junfa tongzhi shiqi shihua* (An Anecdotal History of the Period under the Northern Warlords) (Beijing, 1958), Vol. 5, p. 193.
6. The following account is based on Gee's several reports on Nankai (December 1922), p. 5; (April 9, 1924), RAC RG4 62.1526, (March 18, 1925), p. 1; RAC RG4 62.1527, and Gee's letter to Roger Greene dated January 10, 1927, RAC RG4 62.1527. Note that according to *Nankai daxue xiaoshi*, its face value was $2,180,800 and market value was $500,006 (in Mexican dollars). See *Nankai daxue xiaoshi*, p. 88. For a short and cynical account of the Li Chun bequest, see Dou Shouyong and Su Yumei, "Li Chun yisheng de julian" (Li Chun's Lifelong Plunder), *Tianjin wenshi ziliao xuanji* (A Selection of Literary and Historical Materials Related to Tianjin), No.1 (Tianjin, 1978), p. 117n.
7. Gee's March 18, 1925 report, ibid.
8. *Nankai daxue xiaoshi*, pp. 5, 87, 89.

Following the standard American practice in philanthropy, Nankai helped these warlords, along with other benefactors, achieve some measure of immortality by leaving behind their namesakes in the form of buildings on campus. For example, the Weiting auditorium of the middle school was built by utilizing a 5,000 silver tael contribution from Yuan Shikai – Weiting being his courtesy name. Li Chun's namesake was the Xiushan Hall, a classroom building that was built in 1923 and destroyed by Japanese bombs in 1937. Nankai's politician benefactors were equally well known. They included Li Yuanhong, Liang Shiyi, then chairman of the board of the Bank of Communications, Zhou Ziqi, then director of the Currency Bureau, and Cao Rulin, one of the infamous trio who were the public enemies of the student demonstrators of the May Fourth Movement.[9]

In the highly charged atmosphere immediately after the May Fourth Movement, Nankai's practice of accepting "tainted money" became an embarrassment. Nankai's alumni who were students in Japan at the time initiated a campaign to remove Cao Rulin from the board of trustees. Zhang Boling defended Nankai's practice by arguing that the use of manure could not tarnish the beauty of the flower.[10] Nevertheless, Nankai had to become more discreet in its subsequent fund-raising campaigns. Even though Nankai would continue to accept contributions from warlords and politicians,[11] the university would never again invite a warlord or an infamous politician to serve on its board of trustees.

That Nankai turned to warlords and politicians, but not industrialists or bankers, revealed not only the state of the economy in China at the time, but also the sad truth contained in the conventional wisdom that associated official posts with the accumulation of wealth. Nankai's only major venture with an industrialist ended in failure. A mining school was established in 1921.[12] But five years later, the university was forced to close it because the benefactor was unable to continue his annual pledge, due to business failure. Zhang Boling was constantly under pressure to raise more funds in order to support his vastly expanding

9. Cao Rulin, in addition to being a benefactor, was also a member of the trustees of the university.
10. *Nankai daxue xiaoshi*, p. 89.
11. For example, Cai Huchen, military governor of Suiyuan, contributed $5,000 Mexican dollars in 1920; Xu Shichang $80,000 Mexican dollars in 1922; and Jin Yunpeng, $10,000 Mexican dollars in 1923.
12. The money was given by Li Zushen, a Henan mining industrialist. *Nankai daxue xiaoshi*, p. 88.

enterprise and to replace the contributions that had ceased. A well-informed American visitor reported in 1923 that Nankai had accumulated a deficit of a quarter of a million Mexican dollars, primarily a result of overexpansion.[13]

Although Zhang Boling believed in expanding with a deficit,[14] Nankai's success ultimately depended upon its ability to reach for stable and institutionalized sources of funding. When income from the Li Chun bequest ceased, two funding agencies came to the rescue. The first was the Rockefeller Foundation. As part of an effort to assure a pool of quality students for its newly established Peking Union Medical College, the Rockefeller Foundation began in the late 1910s to strengthen science education in selected colleges.[15] Nankai's relationship with the Rockefeller Foundation began in 1922 with a matching grant of a hundred thousand Mexican dollars for the construction of a science building and another twenty-five thousand for the equipment. During the 1920s, the Rockefeller Foundation's aid to Nankai amounted to about one hundred eighty thousand Mexican dollars. The second agency was the China Foundation for the Promotion of Education and Culture. Established in 1925 with the Boxer Indemnity funds remitted by the United States, the China Foundation set out with a pronounced policy of strengthening science education and research.[16] Nankai's share of the China Foundation grant totaled one hundred sixty-five thousand Mexican dollars, voted in 1926 and 1929, respectively.[17]

THE FOREIGN-EDUCATED FACULTY AND THE ADMINISTRATORS

The success in financial campaigns and academic excellence reinforced each other, as evidenced by Nankai's ability to attract to its faculty Chinese with a Western education. Chinese students who had gone to the West for advanced studies started to return in increasing numbers beginning in the early 1920s. Nankai's terms of employment were not particularly attractive. While the monthly salary at Qinghua University was in

---

13. Gee to Roger Greene, April 19, 1923, RAC RG4 62.1525.
14. Hu Shi, "Chang Po-ling: Educator," pp. 9–10.
15. For information concerning the Peking Union Medical College, see Mary Ferguson, *China Medical Board and the Peking Union Medical College* (New York, 1970).
16. For more discussion of the China Foundation, see Chapter 9.
17. Being a member of the board of the trustees of the Foundation, Zhang Boling was naturally criticized for taking advantage of his position to benefit Nankai. See Gee's 1927 report.

the range of $300 Mexican dollars, the monthly salary of an entry-level professor at Nankai was only $180 Mexican dollars.[18] Where Nankai was superior to most other Chinese universities, government or private, was in its solvent finances, a marked contrast to most institutions of higher education. Franklin Ho, for example, chose a monthly $180 Mexican dollars position at Nankai over an offer from Jinan University in Shanghai as the dean of its school of commerce with a monthly salary of $300 Mexican dollars.[19] Thus, despite its lower than average salary scales, Nankai was able to adopt a policy that offered positions primarily to students returned from the West. In 1930, for instance, thirty-one of its forty-one faculty members had an advanced degree from the United States.[20]

The financial factor aside, Nankai's ability to attract a continuous flow of repatriated students from America throughout the 1920s was also a result of academic talent scouting. Following a common practice at that time, Nankai offered positions to Chinese who had received doctorates in the United States. The existence of fraternity organizations among Chinese students in American universities provided a convenient network for this recruitment practice. For instance, Nankai apparently made good use of the Chengzhi hui (Society for the Fulfillment of Life's Ambitions), one of the best-known of these fraternities and of which Zhang Boling was a member. The famous historian and future diplomat, Jiang Tingfu (Chiang T'ing-fu, Ph.D. Columbia, 1923); the economists: Franklin Ho (He Lian, B.A. Pomona, 1922, Ph.D. Yale, 1926), H. D. Fong (Fang Xianting, Ph.D. Yale, 1928), Li Choh-ming (Li Zhuomin, Ph.D. Berkeley, 1936), and Rockwood Chin (Chen Guoping, Ph.D. Yale, 1937); and the political scientists: Ling Bing (Ph.D. Clark, 1919), Hsiao Kung-ch'üan (Xiao Gongquan, Ph.D. Cornell, 1926), and Zhang Chunming (Ph.D. Yale, 1931), who joined Nankai and taught there for varying lengths of time, were all Chengzhi hui members.[21]

At Nankai, these young professors lived in the Western-style faculty residence in Baishu cun (Village of a Hundred Trees), which was furnished with a club house. With an electric percolator, they served them-

---

18. Franklin Ho, "The Reminiscences of Ho Lien (Franklin Ho)" (New York: East Asian Institute, Columbia University, 1972; hereafter cited as Ho, "Reminiscences"), p. 51; *Nankai daxue xiaoshi*, p. 121.
19. Note that Ho explained that he decided on Nankai because the "Peking-Tientsin [Peking-Tianjin] area constituted the intellectual center of China." See Ho, "Reminiscences," p. 51.
20. *Nankai daxue xiaoshi*, p. 119.
21. H. D. Fong, *Reminiscences of a Chinese Economist at 70* (Singapore, 1975), pp. 23–5.

selves and foreign visitors M.J.B. coffee imported from the United States.[22] Over the coffee, they exchanged news and gossip, and played various Chinese and Western games, including miniature billiards on a small square table with wooden balls.[23] There was also a grass tennis court for outdoor recreation.[24] Because many of them "had been friends when they were students in the United States,"[25] a sense of camaraderie prevailed.

Their relationship with Zhang Boling, though cordial and bound by mutual respect, was not without tension. As a naval officer turned educator, Zhang Boling appeared impatient with abstract ideas and intellectual pursuits that he considered impractical or merely pedantic. For instance, it was simply beyond his comprehension why Franklin Ho should be full of enthusiasm for statistical work on the fluctuation of commodity prices at wholesale and retail as well as in domestic and international markets. Zhang Boling must have been so baffled by the idea of interpreting the simple and seemingly mundane market reality with mind-boggling strings of numbers that he took Franklin Ho to task.

"What do you need all these figures for? What are you trying to find out?"

"Well, my statistical studies can prepare us for the scientific reconstruction of China," Ho replied.

"Well, your procedure often reminds me of a man who tries to locate an elephant with a microscope. If you want to know what we can do in China, why, there are all sorts of things that we can do without going into all this elaborate compilation of data. For example, do we need to have a statistical survey before we put in a highway from the city to the university campus?"[26]

Li Ji (Li Chi), the famous Harvard-trained archeologist (Ph.D., 1923), who was enthusiastic about making anthropometrical head measurements all over China, was similarly taken to task. He was questioned one

22. N. Gist Gee, "Report on Nankai University, Tientsin, China," April 2, 1928, RAC RG4 CMB 62.1527.
23. H. D. Fong, *Reminiscences of a Chinese Economist at 70*, p. 39; Gee, "Report on Nankai University, Tientsin, China," (April 2, 1928), pp. 1–2, RAC RG4 62.1527.
24. *Nankai daxue xiaoshi*, p. 123.
25. Ho, "Reminiscences," p. 53; see also Charles Lilley, "Tsiang T'ing-fu: Between Two Worlds, 1895–1935," Ph.D. thesis, University of Maryland, 1979, p. 225.
26. Tsiang T'ing-fu, "The Reminiscences of Tsiang T'ing-fu (1895–1965)" (New York: East Asian Institute, Columbia University, 1974), p. 91.

day by Zhang Boling as to the usefulness of anthropology. Offended, Li replied that anthropology was completely useless, and left Nankai the next year.[27] Years later one professor recalled that he and other American-trained Ph.D.'s on the faculty had "moments of rebellion" against Zhang's indifference to the higher intellectual life they had been accustomed to while abroad.[28]

If tension between them and Zhang Boling was subdued, discontent with the university's top administrators was explicit. The registrar, the bursar, the business manager, and the dean – nicknamed the "Four Guardians" (*sida jingang*) – were the mainstay of Zhang Boling's Nankai system.[29] Their shrewd management and stringent conservation measures, which had helped bring Nankai to what it was, incurred strong resentment from the faculty. H. D. Fong, who worked with Franklin Ho to build up the Nankai Institute of Economics, felt the urge in his *Reminiscences* to castigate them in the following words: "They suffered, in front of the faculty members, a kind of inferiority complex which was offset only by the security of their tenure and the President's trust in their integrity."[30]

Zhang Boling's vision may indeed, as the professors seemed to imply, have been circumscribed by his narrow utilitarian approach, and that of his administrative lieutenants by their preoccupation with efficiency and conservation. However, their irritation with Zhang may have been a symptom of a defense mechanism that masked some deep-seated frustration and disappointment on the part of the professors themselves for their having to settle on a position at Nankai. For one thing, Nankai had neither the elite aura of Peking University, nor the carefully cultivated American atmosphere of Qinghua College. In the 1920s, many of the Nankai professors were Qinghua graduates, and virtually all had been upperclassmen in American colleges before they went on to graduate schools. All the grandeur and urbane amenities to which they had grown

---

27. Ibid.   28. Ibid., p. 93.
29. Yu Chuanjian, the Dean, was graduated from the Nankai Middle School in 1906. He had a B.A. degree (1920) in economics from National Peking University and a Master of Education (1932) from the Teachers College of Columbia University. The business manager, Meng Qinxiang, was another Nankai product, who graduated from Nankai's teachers' training program in 1906. Hua Wuqing, the bursar, whose educational background, though unknown, but definitely not an architect, designed and built all of Nankai's buildings before 1937. The registrar was Kang Nairu, who was graduated from Zhili Higher Technical School and taught chemistry in the Nankai Middle School. See *Nankai daxue xiaoshi*, pp. 12–13.
30. H. D. Fong, *Reminiscences of a Chinese Economist at 70*, p. 39.

accustomed suddenly disappeared when they returned and started teaching at Nankai. Not only did Nankai have no glorious tradition nor illustrious chancellor, but during the first four years of its existence, the university had to share the same campus with the middle school. The professors may have viewed their affiliation with Nankai a mere temporary sojourn, and as soon as opportunity arose elsewhere, they would be ready for the leap. Most indicative of this sojourner mentality among the professors was the way their contract was signed. After the first one-year contract expired, the university would ordinarily offer a three-to-five-year renewal contract. However, in 1922, every single one of the twenty-five professors opted for an annually renewed contract.[31]

In 1929, one such occasion arose when not one, but many professors left Nankai. Following the completion of the Northern Expedition in 1928, government institutions began to receive regular appropriations from the treasury.[32] Qinghua University, which was nationalized in 1928, began to bolster the strength of its faculty by raiding other universities. With its unique source of income from the portion of the Boxer Indemnity returned by the United States, Qinghua was able to offer very attractive terms of employment, including ample provision of funds for library and laboratory facilities, a lighter teaching load, higher salaries, and, above all, a one-in-every-five-year sabbatical leave for professors to go abroad for intellectual refreshment.[33] Nankai appeared to bear the brunt of this aggressive recruitment offensive. In 1929, Jiang Tingfu, Xiao Ju, and Li Jitong left Nankai en masse for Qinghua.[34]

This exodus of key faculty members to Qinghua was a serious blow to Nankai; neither in terms of its prestige nor in terms of its financial resources was Nankai able to fill the vacated positions with professors of equal caliber. Zhang Boling was greatly irritated by Qinghua's recruitment strategy, which he viewed as highly unethical. However, after the initial shock and anger had subsided, it became clear to him that Nankai, after all, could not hope to compete with universities like Qinghua or Peking in every field. This realization in turn led to a reassessment of the university's resources and a redefinition of its developmental goals.

---

31. N. Gist Gee, "Nankai College: Report (December 1922)," RAC RG4 62.1524.
32. The discussion in the following two paragraphs is based on Ho, "Reminiscences," pp. 63–4.
33. According to Ho, the sabbatical leave at Qinghua was once every seven years. Here I follow the information given in *Qinghua daxue xiaoshi gao*, p. 107.
34. Included in this list given by Ho, there was also Hsiao Kung-ch'üan, who, though he also left Nankai in 1929, did not join the Qinghua faculty until 1932.

During this period of crisis, Franklin Ho emerged as the faculty member most trusted and most frequently consulted by Zhang Boling.

FRANKLIN HO AND THE ORIGIN OF
THE NANKAI INSTITUTE OF ECONOMICS

Born into a wealthy and influential landlord family in rural Hunan in 1895, Franklin Ho began his education in traditional style, attending family and lineage schools. His family's financial status, however, had enabled him to seek a modern education away from home. His journey took him to Guilin and Changsha, where he finally enrolled in the Yale-in-China Academy, and eventually to the United States. From 1919 to 1926, he studied first at Pomona and then at Yale Graduate School. Although these were turbulent May Fourth years, which sent shock waves to Chinese student communities in the United States, they did not seem to have any impact on him. For one thing, there were very few Chinese students at either of the universities he attended – six at Pomona and twenty at Yale.[35] However, a more important reason may have been that he simply did not subscribe to student activism.[36] It should be noted that Ho had become a Christian in 1918, during his last year at the Yale-in-China Academy. During his seven years in the United States, he was fully absorbed in his studies. He had an outstanding academic record at Yale,[37] where he wrote his thesis under T. S. Adams on a comparative study of income taxation in the United States and Great Britain.

His most valuable experience at Yale was the research he did for Irving Fisher, a famous expert on econometrics. At the office quarters that Fisher attached to the back of his stately mansion on 460 Prospect Street,[38] Ho began working, along with a large research staff that Fisher

---

35. Ho recalled that Chinese students at Yale numbered less than a dozen while he was there. But according to one account, they numbered around twenty in 1924. See *Chinese Students' Monthly*, XX.4 (February 1925), p. 66.
36. He recalled that he attended only two Chinese student gatherings while he was in the United States: one in Berkeley in 1919, with Wu Chaoshu as the speaker about the Paris Conference; the other in New York in 1922, with Lo Jialun as the speaker. But the most indicative of his indifference to student activism is the complete silence in his "Reminiscences" of his reaction to the May Fourth Movement, considering the fact that he was in Changsha and Shanghai to prepare for his trip to America from May to July 1919, when the Movement was at its height in both cities.
37. He was awarded a Sterling Scholarship for his academic achievement in 1924. See *Chinese Students' Monthly*, XIX.8 (June 1924), p. 73.
38. Irving Norton Fisher, *My Father Irving Fisher* (New York, 1956), pp. 158, 224–5.

had assembled, on a part-time basis from 1923 and then on a full-time basis from 1925 to 1926 when he returned to China. In addition to helping Fisher compile his weekly index numbers on wholesale and stock prices, he was put in charge of the project, "An Encyclopedia of Index Numbers."[39] As a gesture of good will and appreciation of his good work at his office, Fisher presented Ho a check for $500 as a parting gift when Ho came to the office for the last time to bid the professor goodbye.

The experience and interest of his work with Fisher determined Ho's own research work upon his return to China. At Nankai, where he began teaching in 1926, he set out to conduct a critical inventory of statistical research on prices in China up to 1926. Emulating Fisher, he turned his four-room house in the faculty compound into a workshop and living quarters for his family and his assistants.[40] It was a private project financed with his own money and his own statistical equipment, which he brought back from Yale.

While Zhang Boling must have first thought that the project was nothing more than pedantic academicism, the situation began to change. In spring 1927, Franklin Ho declined the offer of a remunerative position as research director of the Department of Social Research of the China Foundation. In what obviously amounted to a deal, Zhang Boling agreed to allocate some funds in the university budget for Ho's research and accepted Ho's proposal that an independent University Committee on Social and Economic Research be established to engage in compiling statistics bearing upon social, economic, and industrial problems in China.[41]

With excellent planning, he made full use of a 1927 grant from the China Foundation for an inquiry into the family budgets of the working classes in Tianjin. He assembled for the committee a staff of sixteen full-time members – eleven field investigators, four computing clerks, and Ho himself. Eight investigators were assigned to the family budget inquiry and one to a separate project on the carpet industry in Tianjin. The main line of research remained his favorite work on index numbers, which he now – as had his teacher Fisher at Yale begun in 1923 – turned into a service for the business communities and research institutions in China and abroad. His "Weekly Statistical Service," which began publication on January 1, 1928 as a supplement to the famous Tianjin newspaper,

39. Ho, "Reminiscences," p. 49.   40. Ibid., p. 95.   41. Ibid., pp. 57–8.

Dagong bao (*L'Impartial*), included indices on foreign and domestic exchange rates and bond markets.[42] This line of work brought much desired publicity for the committee, and yet took up only a fraction of its resources – a couple of investigators and computing clerks. As an example of his resourcefulness, Ho made a side project out of the family budget inquiry – "An Index of Numbers of the Cost of Living of the Working Classes in Tianjin."

The committee, furthermore, provided Ho with an initial organizational base, tiny as it was, to build up his own research team. As the committee began conducting research on industries in Tianjin, he convinced Zhang Boling of the need to add an industrial economist to the faculty and to have him concurrently serve as director of research of the committee. For this position, he recommended H. D. Fong (Fang Xianting), his close friend and Chengzhi hui fraternity brother at Yale, who had written a thesis on the structure of British factory systems around the 1850s. From 1929 to 1948, for twenty years, Franklin Ho and H. D. Fong formed a highly dedicated and coordinated team that brought the Nankai social science group into prominence both in China and abroad.

The initial success of the committee reflected Franklin Ho's ingenuity in planning and enthusiasm in research. Impressive as the name may have sounded, the University Committee on Social and Economic Research was a one-man committee. The most vulnerable was its budget. The appropriation from the university was a puny $1,500 Mexican dollars. The critical situation arose in early 1928, when the China Foundation refused the committee's application for further assistance. Desperate, Franklin Ho tried the Commonwealth Fund in New York, enlisting the help of his former Yale teachers and utilizing his Yale connections.[43] This attempt, however, failed as well. Without a choice, he discontinued all of the committee's research except the statistical work, which incurred only the expenses of a field investigator and two computing clerks.

---

42. Indices on commodity prices at wholesale, bar silver prices, and rates for dollars were soon incorporated into this publication. See *Nankai University Committee on Social and Economic Research: Work and Project* (November 1928), p. 2; see also "Board of Trustees Minutes of May 26, 1928," Institute of Pacific Relations, p. 141, James Shotwell Papers, Box 29, deposited at Columbia University.
43. E. B. Reed, formerly of Yale, was then director of the division of education of the Commonwealth Fund.

THE ENTRY OF THE INSTITUTE OF PACIFIC RELATIONS

The situation dramatically changed by the involvement of the Institute of Pacific Relations in sponsoring social science research in China. Organized in Honolulu in 1925, the Institute of Pacific Relations was conceived by its founders to be a vehicle for leaders of opinion in the Pacific countries to exchange ideas on how to improve mutual relations.[44] This idea had its background in the Hawaiian YMCA method of bringing leaders of different racial communities together for free and frank discussions.[45] However, the Institute quickly cast aside this approach. First of all, the YMCA, though the organizing force behind all the national groups that attended the Honolulu conference, from the outset gave in to the pressure for broader representation and a secular approach.[46] More important was the leadership shift. The first chairman of the Institute was Ray Lyman Wilbur, president of Stanford, who was not enthusiastic about the YMCA dominance nor its formalistic conference method.[47] Although he soon resigned to become the secretary of interior under Hoover, the increasing participation of academic leaders from the various membership countries continued to attenuate the YMCA influence. When Edward Carter, the secretary of the American Council, emerged to become the most powerful man in the Institute in the late 1920s, he steered the Institute to become a sponsor of research on Asia.

The Institute learned the importance of research almost from the very beginning. Experience from the first Honolulu conference made it clear that while good will and eagerness to solve problems were evident, the conferees simply did not have adequate and accurate information with which to work. The lesson learned from this experience was to devise long-term research projects that would form the basis for discussions at the Institute's biennial conferences. In order to promote and coordinate research of the various national councils, the Institute added a research

---

44. John B. Condliffe, *Reminiscences of the Institute of Pacific Relations* (Vancouver, 1981), p. 2.
45. Ibid., p. 3; see also John Thomas, *The Institute of Pacific Relations: Asian Scholars and American Politics* (Seattle, 1974), p. 1.
46. Edward Carter, "A Personal View of the Institute of Pacific Relations, 1925–1952," *Hearings on the Institute of Pacific Relations*, 82nd Cong., 2nd sess., Pt. 14, p. 5318.
47. He intercepted the move to make the YMCA responsible for organizing the New Zealand Council of the Institute of Pacific Relations. It was also reported that he had little patience for the YMCA discussion method developed by William Kilpatrick of Teachers College, Columbia. See Condliffe, *Reminiscences of the Institute of Pacific Relations*, pp. 5, 7.

secretary in 1927. A New Zealander, John B. Condliffe, was chosen for this position. Amicable, perceptive, and, above all, appreciative of the ability and judgment of Asian scholars, Condliffe brought with him an open-minded attitude that stressed close consultations among the different national groups toward the formulation of the Institute's research programs. Confronting him, however, was the domineering and opinionated Carter, who envisioned a centralized international research program with American scholars controlling the formulation and execution of projects.

The inevitable clashes between these two approaches occurred during Condliffe's reconnaissance trip to Japan and China in late 1927 and early 1928. With a $10,000 budget at his disposal, Condliffe set out to look for researchers to carry out projects adopted at the Honolulu conference, and, at the same time, to solicit projects formulated locally. However, even before Condliffe began his journey, Carter had already revealed his view that the purpose of the mission was nothing more than to gather information concerning personnel and resources in China on the basis of which a research program could then be developed by the Institute's International Research Committee in New York.[48]

While in China, Condliffe learned the International Research Committee had decided in New York every single project that he was asked to investigate in the field. Worse than that, the International Research Committee even began corresponding with an expert in the field whom Condliffe had interviewed for an entirely different project,[49] which not only made his trip superfluous, but undercut his position as a project coordinator and dispenser of funds. With tact, patience, and reason, he was able to demonstrate that this kind of academic arrogance was misplaced. First of all, the projects suggested at the conference and formulated in New York were more often than not unworkable in the field. Second, it completely ignored research that had developed independently in China and Japan. As it turned out, the research program that emerged from Condliffe's trip was a compromise of these two opposite approaches. The two largest projects, "Land Utilization in China" under J. Lossing Buck and "Food and Population in Japan" under Shiroshi Nasu, were part of a land utilization project formulated in New York. Yet, they in fact arose from the work that had already begun in China and Japan; the International Research Committee quietly with-

48. Condliffe to Merle Davis, February 4, 1928, IPR Box 108, Condliffe Folder I.
49. Ibid.

drew its original project.[50] The only project suggested and adopted at the conference was the Manchurian studies, of which Zhang Boling of Nankai had the largest share of the research funds allocated for this project in China.[51]

It was not accidental that Nankai was chosen to be entrusted with a major Manchurian project. As a grant recipient of the Rockefeller Foundation and the China Foundation, Nankai had become an internationally accredited institution and, as a result, a major stop on the itinerary of almost any foreign visitor to China. Condliffe was no exception. In Tianjin, he was instantly impressed by Zhang Boling and the social scientists he gathered around him. With a Manchurian project in his hand, he could not but notice the existence at Nankai of a committee on Manchurian studies that Zhang Boling had organized a few months before his visit to arouse Chinese awareness through research, forum discussions, and publications of Japanese aggression in the area. Over dinner at Nankai, he, together with Zhang Boling's star social science faculty, worked out a proposal to the Institute of Pacific Relations.[52] But the most important factor that brought about Condliffe's favorable action perhaps was his decision not to entrust this project in China to the recognized Manchurian expert at Yanjing University, Xu Shuxi (Ph.D., Columbia, 1925), a decision based entirely on personality differences.[53]

NANKAI UNDER THE AEGIS OF
THE INSTITUTE OF PACIFIC RELATIONS

The Manchurian project did not benefit Franklin Ho and his University Committee on Social and Economic Research. Yet Condliffe's visit was to mark a turning point for Ho's career. Condliffe conducted his talent scouting by interviews and small group meetings. Franklin Ho, who had been in correspondence with him and who had impressed many Western

---

50. "Minutes of Research Committee Meeting, American Council, Institute of Pacific Relations," May 25, 1928, p. 89, Shotwell papers, Box 29.
51. He was granted $2,000 of the $3,000 allocated.
52. Condliffe, "Travel Notes, October 1927–February 1928," p. 126, Condliffe Papers, Carton 36, deposited at Bancroft Library, the University of California, Berkeley. Originally known as the Committee on Manchuria and Mongolia Studies (ManMeng yanjiuhui), it was renamed the Committee on the Studies of the Northeastern Provinces (Dongbei yanjiuhui) in October 1928. See *Nankai daxue xiaoshi*, pp. 194–7.
53. Ibid., p. 113.

scholars and specialists in China,[54] naturally received his special attention. He ranked Ho at the top of his list of five best economists in China.[55] Being an economist himself, and one who wrote a doctoral thesis on "The Industrial Revolution in the Far East,"[56] Condliffe took great interest in Ho's work on index numbers and the carpet industry in Tianjin. Even though he was well aware of Ho's financial difficulty, a number of factors combined to delay Condliffe's making a recommendation for financial assistance. First, it was difficult to fit Ho's work into the research program Condliffe was recommending, especially as the land utilization and Manchurian projects had come to define the China program. Second, all projects, according to the normal procedure, were supposed to be submitted through the national councils. However, the China Council was still dominated by the YMCA, which seemed to place emphasis on political issues. Franklin Ho's junior status, furthermore, would not have put him in a strong position to claim a share of the research funds. For the time being, all that Condliffe could do was to request the Institute to send a supporting letter on Ho's behalf to the Commonwealth Fund, to which the latter was applying for assistance.[57]

This was a very trying period for Ho. The Social Research Department of the China Foundation was the only organization in China from which he could hope to solicit funds. Yet the Social Research Department of the China Foundation itself was financially unstable; it owed its very existence to a three-year grant beginning in 1926 from the Institute of Social and Religious Research in New York.[58] Ho's application for continuing assistance in 1928 thus coincided with the Social Research Department's own financial crisis. When the Commonwealth Fund likewise turned down his application, Ho faced a critical situation.

It happened that Carl Alsberg, director of the Food Research Institute

---

54. In his interview with J. B. Tayler, Roger Greene of the China Medical Board of the Rockefeller Foundation was told that Ho would make a better research director than Tao Menghe for the Institute of Social Research of the China Foundation. See Roger Greene's interview with L. K. Haass and J. B. Tayler, March 10, 1928, RAC RG4 38.846.
55. By order of rank, they were Liu Dajun (D. K. Lieu, B.A. Michigan, 1915), Franklin Ho, Zhao Renjun (Jen-Tsun Chao, Ph.D. Harvard, 1928), Xiao Ju, and Shou Jingwei (Kinn-Wei Shaw, Ph.D. Columbia, 1926). See Condliffe to Carter, April 10, 1928, IPR Box 108, Condliffe Folder I.
56. See *Economic Record* (Melbourne), II.3 (November 1926), pp. 180–209, II.4 (May 1927), pp. 82–101.
57. In addition, Condliffe took the initiative to explore the possibility of assistance from the Institute of Social and Religious Research in New York.
58. See Chapter 9.

at Stanford University, requested that the China Council recommend two junior faculty members to take charge of two projects under his supervision. As an indication of how desperate the situation was, Ho applied for one of these projects, "The Trend of Pacific Agriculture from Subsistence Farming to Cash Crop Farming."[59]

In the application, which was transmitted through Ding Wenjiang (V. K. Ting), another member of the board of trustees of the China Foundation, Ho made a moving appeal to have the project placed under his university committee rather than to him personally.[60] It was indeed a heartening effort to save the little enterprise of his creation as he poignantly quoted Alsberg's own words that preference would be given to "young Chinese already in academic life, who may be hard pushed financially to remain in the academic career because of the temporary disturbed conditions."[61] In July 1928, Ho briefly resigned from Nankai and became the head of the economics section of the Institute of the Social Sciences of the Academia Sinica in Nanjing.[62] Although this remains a very obscure episode in Ho's career, the bleak future of the university committee must have been its major cause.

The situation turned dramatically in Ho's favor, however. In July, Alsberg wrote to offer Ho the project for which he had applied. Ho wrote to accept the offer in September. At about the same time, using the argument that Ho's work was the closest to the project suggested by the influential Paul Monroe of Columbia's Teachers College, "Village Handicraft Industries in North China," Condliffe successfully incorporated the work Ho had started on the Tianjin carpet industry into a much-expanded project supported by the Institute of Pacific Relations. Under the title, "Industrialization in Tianjin," Ho was given a grant in the amount of $15,000 for three years: $3,000 for 1928, $8,000 for 1929, and $4,000 for 1930.

The award of the grant complicated the situation. Now Ho had to delay his research trip to the United States as required of him by the Alsberg project. In summer 1929, another totally unexpected event

59. Ho himself gave a rather different account of this episode. See Ho, "Reminiscences," p. 61.
60. Ho to Ting [Wen-chiang; Ding Wenjiang], April 22, 1928, IPR Box 108 Condliffe Folder I.
61. Alsberg to David Yui, March 7, 1928, IPR Box 105 Alsberg Folder ('27–'31) II.
62. See Kuo Ting-yee [Kuo T'ing-i], "He Cuilian xiansheng nianbiao" (A chronological table of Mr. He Lian's life), incomplete manuscript, n.d. I am indebted to Mrs. Franklin Ho for allowing me to use this manuscript.

happened. Ho was persuaded to head an Industrial Research Institute, which was established in Tianjin in July. With an endowment of $230,000 Chinese dollars, the Institute planned to work, through industrial and economic research, on the improvement of industrial and commercial products and the promotion of new industries based on the natural resources of North China. This large endowment was a result of a "patriotic tariff" imposed by student leaders of a boycott movement in Tianjin upon merchants who carried Japanese goods after the Jinan Incident of May 3, 1928, in which the Japanese military tried to block the advance of the Northern Expedition.[63]

In a complete reversal of the situation, Ho now faced the problem of having too many projects on his hands. He made the obvious decision to resign from the Alsberg project so that he could stay in China to administer the Industrial Research Institute and to supervise the project on "Industrialization in Tianjin." Resourceful as he was, Ho planned to pool his Tianjin project fund with that of the Institute in order to make a concerted effort to investigate all the major industries in Tianjin and, eventually, in the major industrial centers in North China.[64] Unfortunately, only two months after the Institute began its work when its first project on "Retail Grain Trade and Milling in Tianjin" was barely begun, the Institute was forced to close by the Guomindang authorities in Tianjin, who ruled that the endowment fund of the Institute should be used instead to start a woolen factory – a sad case that underscored how undependable native sources of funding were.[65]

Yet the difficult time had passed. Ho was married to Shwen Dji Yu (Yu Shunzhi, B.A., Pomona, 1925), a fellow Hunanese, whom he met while they were both students at Pomona. In September, before the biennial conference convened in Kyoto, two powerful men from the Institute of Pacific Relations, Edward Carter and James Shotwell, chairman of the International Research Committee, visited Tianjin. One of the results of their visit was another project for Ho – "Population Movement from Shandong and Hebei to Manchuria." This project was officially approved at the Institute of Pacific Relations' Kyoto conference of 1929. A grant of $7,500 for two years was awarded beginning from 1930.

---

63. H. D. Fong, *Grain Trade and Milling in Tientsin* (Tianjin, 1934), p. 367n. According to Jiang Tingfu, it was he who came up with this idea of a patriotic tariff and a research institute. See, Tsiang T'ing-fu, "The Reminiscences of Tsiang T'ing-fu," pp. 106–8.
64. Ho to Alsberg, July 15, 1929, IPR Box 116, Shotwell Folder 8.
65. Tsiang T'ing-fu, "Reminiscences," pp. 106–8; Fong, *Grain Trade and Milling in Tientsin*, p. 367n.

All of a sudden, the university committee found itself engaged simultaneously in three different lines of research – the compilation of index numbers, survey of industries in Tianjin, and population movement. These three lines of work reflected academic interest as well as national or international concerns of the time. Efforts in compiling index numbers had proliferated in China since the mid-1920s, presumably because of the claim that it could provide a scientific basis for the socioeconomic reconstruction of the nation. According to an estimate, fifty series of index numbers had been compiled and published by 1932.[66] Although the quality of these works varied greatly, the interest stimulated academic discussion and scrutiny, which, in turn, raised the level of sophistication of the work.[67]

The project on "Population Movement from Shandong and Hebei to Manchuria," on the other hand, touched upon the highly charged issue concerning Japanese aggressions there. For obvious reasons, the China Council had singled out Manchuria as a top priority research topic. The New York group of the Institute of Pacific Relations was no less keen in promoting research on Manchuria. In fact the International Research Committee laid down at the Kyoto conference a policy to give priority to research on situations from which "international controversy, especially in the political field, may arise."[68] This was incidentally a sure sign of the definite break with the earlier non-controversial YMCA approach.[69] At the Institute's Kyoto conference, five papers on Manchuria were presented, two by Chinese, another two by Japanese, and one by an American.

The project on population movement from North China to Manchuria was, however, conceived by the Institute as not so much a continuation of the Manchurian research but as a part of the Institute's grand project on food and population in the Pacific. The main objective was determination of the socioeconomic conditions and consequences of migration

---

66. Among them, twenty-two were still being continued. See Feng Huanian, "Zhongguo zhi zhishu" (Index Numbers in China), *Jingji tongji jikan* (Quarterly Journal of Economics and Statistics), I.4 (December 1932), pp. 664–7.

67. In his "Reminiscences," Ho said that the Bureau of Markets in Shanghai adopted his suggestions for revising its index after 1926. See his "Reminiscences," p. 96.

68. "Report of the International Research Committee to the Board of Trustees of the American Council of the Institute of Pacific Relations," February 12, 1930, Shotwell papers, Box 29.

69. Merle Davis resigned from his post as secretary-general to protest this shift toward tackling politically controversial issues. See Thomas, *The Institute of Pacific Relations*, p. 6.

at both ends of the population movement. Ho began his field work in northern Manchuria with twenty investigators in spring 1930. By August 1931, when the field work was completed, they covered 2,274 settlers' families in sixty-five villages. The work on the emigration side in Shandong began in late 1931 and was completed in December 1932. Altogether 5,500 families and 425 villages were investigated.[70] In both northern Manchuria and Shandong, two kinds of schedules were used: one for a comprehensive survey of the socioeconomic conditions in villages, the other for an intensive investigation of individual farm families.[71]

In accordance with a proposal submitted by Ho, the Institute approved at the biennial conference in Shanghai in 1931 an extension of the population movement project for two more years with an annual grant of $5,000. The Japanese occupation of Manchuria following the Mukden Incident of September 18, 1931, however, made it difficult to conduct further field investigation. Ho therefore recommended an early conclusion of the project in December 1932 on the ground that the information already collected was sufficient for a satisfactory report. Indeed, judging from the progress reports submitted by him and by William Holland, then the assistant to Condliffe, the project must have yielded a wealth of information from the field.[72]

The published result of the project was a disappointment, however. The initial reports, which Ho published in 1930 and 1931, were essentially library research based on materials collected by the South Manchurian Railway Company and, to a much lesser extent, by E. E. Yashnov of the Chinese Eastern Railway.[73] The only publications based on field data were the five articles written by Wang Yaoyu, who had participated in the field investigation in both Shandong and Manchuria.[74]

70. Holland to Condliffe, December 24, 1930, IPR Box 129, Holland Folder; "Research: Special Research Conference in Tokyo," *I.P.R. Notes*, No.2 (February 1935), pp. 25–7.

71. Ho, "Progress Report on Population Movement from North China to Manchuria," December 4, 1932, IPR Box 285 China Institute of Pacific Relations, 1933–1934 Folder.

72. In June 1937, Holland urged Ho to bring out a report on the project. He indicated that A. J. Grajdanzev had worked on the data for two years at Nankai. Holland to Ho, June 17, 1937, IPR Box 287 Franklin Ho, 1933–1935 Folder.

73. These reports are: "Dong sansheng beibu jianglai yimin kenzhi liang guji" (An Estimate of the Capacity for Colonialization in Northern Manchuria), in "Jingji yanjiu zhoukan" (Economic Research Weekly Supplement) of *Dagong bao*, No. 15 (June 8, 1930); "Minguo yilai Dong sansheng nongye zhi fazhan" (The Development of Agriculture in Manchuria since the Founding of the Republic), ibid. (August 17, 1930); and *Population Movement to the Eastern Frontier in China*, 1931.

74. They are: "Dong sansheng zudian zhidu" (The System of Land Tenure in Manchuria),

Among the three projects that Franklin Ho and his university committee were working on in 1929, the "Tianjin Industrialization Project" was the most important, both in terms of its bearing on the thinking of economists of the time and Nankai's future research. Following the conclusion of the Northern Expedition, the Nationalist government in Nanjing, in line with Sun Yat-sen's plans for national reconstruction, singled out industrialization as a priority. Although debates on the appropriate strategies to bring about industrialization or modernization in China did not arise until the early 1930s, economists in general did not question the notion that China should develop large urban industries based on Western models. With the "Tianjin Industrialization Project," Franklin Ho and H. D. Fong intended to discover how industrialization had affected the city's manufacturers. Four industries were chosen for case studies: carpet weaving, hosiery knitting, rayon, and cotton industries.

The publications that resulted from research into these four industries were well-received. H. D. Fong, the project director, and his investigators were praised for the rigor of their methodology and for their objective presentation of field data. It should be pointed out, however, that the industries chosen for investigation were not the best examples for illustrating how industrialization had affected the city's manufacturing process. With the exception of the cotton industry, carpet weaving, hosiery knitting, and rayon were all handicraft industries, which, according to them, had not been significantly affected by the process of industrialization.[75] The reason for this obvious flaw in sampling was simple; there happened to exist some data, though incomplete, which had been collected by the Tianjin city government just a year earlier. In fact, H. D. Fong's research team was mainly recruited from investigators who had formerly conducted the survey for the city.[76]

Zhengzhi jingji xuebao (The Quarterly Journal of Economics and Political Science), III.1 (October, 1934), pp. 80–108; "Jin ershinian lai Shandong Yidu xian wushi ge nongcun de nonghu he gendi suoyouquan zhi bianqian" (The Changes in Peasant Households and Land Ownership in the Fifty Villages in Yidu County in Shandong in the Past Twenty Years), in "Jingji yanjiu zhoukan," No. 115 (May 29, 1935); and the following three articles reprinted in H. D. Fong, ed., *Zhongguo jingji yanjiu* (Studies in Chinese Economy) (Changsha, 1938): "Shandong nongmin licun de yige jiantao" (An Analysis of the Reason Why Peasants in Shandong Left Their Villages), pp. 178–87; "Dongbei nongcun de 'maiqing' zhidu" (The System of "Sale before the Harvest" in Manchuria), pp. 262–72; and "Dong sansheng 'xiang' de chayi" (The Variation of Size in Manchuria), pp. 406–10.

75. *Industrialization in China: A Study of Conditions in Tientsin*, 1929, p. 1.
76. Ibid.

All four industries were evaluated against the yardsticks from the study of the Industrial Revolution in England, on which Fong had written a Ph.D. dissertation. As such, the "Tianjin Industrialization Project" intended to answer why industrialization had not occurred in China and presented policy recommendations for China to hasten its advent. Out of these studies emerged Nankai's diagnosis of China's underdevelopment. According to this diagnosis, both internal and external problems plagued Chinese industries: the external problems were political, and the internal, economic.[77] The political problems, of which the most serious at the time were civil wars, disrupted the transportation, closed off markets, and increased the tax burden for the manufacturers. In the economic arena, the problems were the lack of capital, poor management and marketing, and low labor productivity. While acknowledging that the problems that confronted native Chinese industries were serious and deep-seated, Fong was nonetheless optimistic. If peace and order could be restored, a good dose of sound economic planning should revive the industries. In essence, Fong called for the government to assist the industries to achieve the economies of scale by helping them form cartels to assure quality, labor productivity, and, if necessary, to fix the prices. With the cartels conducting research and providing market information, the manufacturer should "be able to run his business on a scientific basis, and bring new hopes to the already declining industry."[78]

The "Tianjin Industrialization Project" reflected the scope of research that Ho and Fong envisioned for themselves. The regional character of the Tianjin project was necessitated by the limited resources Ho and Fong had at hand. As the titles of their preliminary reports to the Institute of Pacific Relations clearly suggest, the ultimate goal of their research was an overall estimate of the extent and effect of industrialization in China as a whole. However, at the same time, they were fully aware that the industrial sector of China constituted many regional economic zones, each capped by a large industrial city. The major industries in these different economic zones, furthermore, differed in their nature and varied in the extent of their industrialization. Therefore, in-depth investigation of the industries in these regional economic zones had to be carried out before the extent of industrialization in China could be measured accurately.

---

77. The following discussion is based on Fong, *Hosiery Knitting in Tientsin* (Tianjin, 1930), pp. 72–6.
78. Ibid., p. 76.

Because Ho now knew the Institute of Pacific Relations's research projects were primarily financed by the Rockefeller Foundation, he began to entertain the hope that the latter or any other philanthropic foundations might be induced to support Nankai's industrialization project in a much-expanded version. In the same preliminary reports to the Institute of Pacific Relations, Franklin Ho and H. D. Fong called for assistance from foundations to enable Nankai to canvass the entire industrial sector of the nation, region by region, for the purpose of reaching an ultimate and accurate measurement of industrialization in China.

This obsession with measuring the extent of China's industrialization gradually subsided. First, no research funds were secured. Furthermore, this project was too ambitious and too impractical by any criteria. To carry it out, the Nankai group would have had to become a mobile research team, moving from one region to another as the project progressed. Moreover, even Ho and Fong themselves acknowledged that statistics on China's industrialization derived from investigations on the nation's industrial sectors alone had little relevance to the economy of the nation as a whole – which they referred to as "a land of economic medievalism," "barely touched by the revolutionary change of industrialization."[79] Among the industrial centers they proposed to study, except for Mukden in Manchuria and Wuhan on the Yangtze river, Shanghai, Wuxi, Qingdao, Tianjin, and Canton were all coastal cities.

Nevertheless, leaving aside the questions of methodological and sampling flaws, these series of studies on Tianjin industries were in themselves good and useful reports on the individual industries surveyed. They were furthermore important landmarks for Ho. First was the pattern of the division of labor that Ho worked out with his colleagues. Although the project on the Tianjin industries was awarded to Ho by the Institute of Pacific Relations, H. D. Fong was the actual project director. Except for the population movement project that Ho personally directed, this was to become a pattern of collaboration among the growing Nankai social science team. Ho essentially became an academic entrepreneur who concentrated his effort in getting grants for his colleagues who then set out to execute the projects in the field.

The significance of these Tianjin industry surveys lay in the financial and institutional implications for Ho. To begin with, funding for these surveys was the crucial factor that kept his university committee from being dissolved. With the successful conclusion of a project, Ho was

79. *Industrialization in China*, p. 3.

in a strong position to receive more research grants. The project on population movement was merely the first example. More important, however, was the recognition and status accorded him as a consequence. Prior to the completion of any of these surveys, Ho was only a junior professor whose ability was recognized but not proven. His attendance at the 1929 Kyoto conference of the Institute of Pacific Relations had to be arranged by Zhang Boling in connection with the Alsberg project. Yet, in less than two years, he rose to a position to edit the Chinese papers for the Institute's 1931 Shanghai conference. Soon afterward, he became the research secretary of the China Council through whose office passed all project proposals from China and authorization of grants from New York.

The success with the Institute of Pacific Relations in turn helped Ho to solidify and expand his institutional base at Nankai. This was in part contributed by the nature of the grants. The Institute required Nankai to match its grants on a dollar-for-dollar basis, as was stipulated by the Laura Spelman Rockefeller Memorial, the Institute's largest source of support. This funding policy became a very effective argument for Ho to claim a larger share of the university's budget. Thus, the appropriation for Ho's university committee rose from the negligible $1,500 in 1928 to $10,000 in 1929 and $20,000 (all in Mexican dollars) in 1931.[80]

This meteoric increase of appropriations to the university committee no doubt reflected Ho's ability in financing and supervising his projects. Yet in an unexpected way, Ho was benefited by a crisis Nankai University faced in 1929. As noted earlier, Nankai lost many of its star faculty members to Qinghua in 1929 as a result of the latter's faculty recruitment offensive. During the crisis, Zhang Boling frequently consulted with Ho, who had several times declined tempting offers from other institutions. The conclusion that came out of their numerous meetings was that Nankai could not hope to compete with universities such as Qinghua and National Peking and thus should concentrate its efforts on fields that were not then covered by the latter two institutions. Given Nankai's resources, business was the logical choice. As an economics professor who had demonstrated his dedication to teaching and research, his resourcefulness in formulating plans and soliciting funds for research, and, above all, his loyalty to the university, it was natural that Ho would have been chosen by Zhang Boling to direct the business program at Nankai. In late spring 1930, Zhang Boling offered Ho the deanship of

---

80. Holland to Condliffe, December 20, 1930, IPR Box 116, Holland Folder.

the College of Commerce and the chairmanship of the department of economics in the College of Arts, in addition to the chairmanship of the University Committee on Social and Economic Research which he had created in 1927. Ho accepted the offer and recommended that all three be amalgamated into an Institute of Economics.

5

The Nankai Institute of Economics: Academic Entrepreneurship and Social Engineering, 1931–1947

THE creation of the Nankai Institute of Economics in 1931 marked the conclusion of Franklin Ho's apprenticeship in academic entrepreneurship. His association with the Institute of Pacific Relations was a rite of passage that opened up for him a new world of possibilities, particularly the connections that would facilitate his access to the Rockefeller philanthropy. The story of the Nankai Institute of Economics is one of triumphs and innovations. Under Ho's leadership, the Institute would steer economics in China from its theoretical emphasis to an empirical approach, thus bringing China into the data base of the discipline of economics. This effort to indigenize economics prompted Nankai to tackle problems confronting China's rural industries and local government finance, which, along with the funding interest of the Rockefeller Foundation, would lead Nankai to enter the field of social engineering.

THE GENESIS OF A RESEARCH PROGRAM

In December 1930, the British economic historian, R. H. Tawney, visited Nankai in connection with his study on China's agriculture and industry commissioned by the Institute of Pacific Relations.[1] In contrast to the eager and often obtrusive requests for lectures showered upon Tawney elsewhere, he was welcomed in a subdued manner by Nankai. They proffered him and his company a comfortable house with servants, plus an invitation to stay indefinitely for quiet writing.[2] During Tawney's sojourn, Franklin Ho put at Tawney's disposal his staff as well as his collection of literature and data on the Chinese economy. This service facilitated

---

1. Ross Terrill, *R. H. Tawney and His Times* (Harvard, 1973), pp. 67–71.
2. Holland to Condliffe, December 20, 1930, IPR Box 129, Holland Folder.

Tawney's work, which was presented as a data paper at the 1931 Shanghai Conference of the Institute of Pacific Relations and eventually was published in 1932 under the title *Land and Labour in China*.

Just as his experience was most pleasant, Tawney's opinion about Nankai was most favorable. He considered Nankai, together with James Yen's Ding Xian experiment, the two most "fruitful things" that had happened in China at the time.[3] Franklin Ho did not miss this opportunity presented by the presence of this world-renowned scholar. He produced a draft proposal for the establishment of the Nankai Institute of Economics and asked for Tawney's suggestions. Thereafter, he sent a copy of the revised proposal through Holland to Condliffe for the latter's use with the Rockefeller Foundation.

In late May, Edward Carter of the Institute of Pacific Relations arranged an interview for Zhang Pengchun (Ph.D., Columbia, 1922), Zhang Boling's brother, with the Rockefeller Foundation. This preliminary discussion with Edmund Day was a success, for the director of the social sciences division telegraphed Selskar Gunn, the Foundation's vice-president in Europe, for a conference with the Nankai authorities. It happened that Gunn was opportunely on his way to China from Paris.[4] The conference between Ho and Gunn took place at Nankai in July.

Just as they had accomplished with Tawney a few months earlier, Nankai made a favorable impression on Gunn. Riding on the momentum, Ho decided to act swiftly by presenting to Gunn a formal application for assistance. As anticipated, the Foundation voted a grant of $75,000 to be disbursed over a period of five years beginning in 1932 toward the support of the Nankai Institute of Economics.

One of the objectives of the Nankai Institute of Economics was to rectify the predominantly foreign-based and theoretical approach to the social sciences prevailing in China at the time. To address this widely criticized and yet seldom tackled problem, the Institute proposed "to teach economics with special reference to Chinese problems and to vitalize teaching by means of research."[5] In order to accomplish these two goals, the Institute adopted a policy that coordinated teaching with research. Each professor would conduct research in the field of his specialty and teaching. The research, whether field investigation or

---

3. Holland to Condliffe, January 29, 1931, IPR Box 129, Holland Folder.
4. For more discussion on Gunn and his China Program, see Chapters 3 and 9.
5. "Memorandum on the Programme of Work: Nankai Institute of Economics, Nankai University, 1932–1933," p. 1, RAC RG1.1 601.51.432.

library research, would, in turn, provide materials for classroom instruction and, eventually, for textbook compilation – a much needed undertaking given the common practice of using textbooks imported from the United States.

Despite its ideal to "vitalize teaching" through research, the Institute must have found it difficult to coordinate undergraduate teaching with the research it was attempting. The only major innovation the Institute introduced into its undergraduate education was the deferment of specialization from the sophomore year to the junior year in order to provide the students with a broader humanistic background. Eventually, undergraduate teaching was discontinued in 1934 by an ordinance of the Ministry of Education that ruled the Nankai Institute of Economics incompatible with the University Organization Law the former had promulgated. Undergraduate teaching in economics was transferred to the original but re-created department of economics in the College of Commerce. The Institute of Economics became essentially a research institution with a small graduate program, which was introduced in fall 1933.[6]

By emphasizing teaching and research on Chinese economics, Nankai advocated the indigenization of economics in China. This attempt reflected a genuine desire to bring China into the data base of the discipline of economics. At the same time, it manifested an unswerving conviction that economics provided an indispensable guidance to steer China through the most profound transformation the nation had yet experienced. In an ardent, if also bald, display of the technocratic rhetoric, it touted its effort as one "guided by scientific knowledge and by men of trained intelligence, who look at the problem as one of social engineering for the common good"; unlike the ideological left and right – the "revolutionary enthusiasts" and the reactionaries – who operated "in an atmosphere of ignorance, prejudice and passion."[7]

Before Nankai started its graduate program, this aspiration for social engineering could only have been expressed through research. The Institute decided to limit its work to North China, with special emphasis on the areas surrounding Tianjin and Peking. This narrower scope of research represented a major retrenchment of the vision

6. Ho did not mention these institutional changes in his reports to the Rockefeller Foundation.
7. "Prospectus of the Nankai Institute of Economics" (June 1931), p. 3, RAC RG1.1 601.52.439.

compared to Ho's idea two years before of making Nankai a mobile research team around the nation. The research topics, geared to the new emphasis on policy implications, were so chosen that upon completion their results would help "furnish a scientific basis for practical solution."[8]

In presenting his application to the Rockefeller Foundation, Ho outlined eight projects that the Institute planned to study. They were surveys of agricultural economy, industries, fatigue and efficiency in industries, commodity production and distribution, currency and inflation, usury, and local government finance, and the administration of the land tax.[9] All these projects had either broad or specific policy implications. The "Fatigue and Efficiency in Industries" project, for instance, was intended to determine the optimum hours of work rather than accept the supposedly mindless imitation of the eight-hour work day legislation in the West – a revealing statement about Nankai's probusiness stance.

At the time when Franklin Ho drew up these projects, the proposed Nankai Institute of Economics comprised Ho himself and H. D. Fong, whose combined expertise was statistics, income taxation in the United States and England, and British economic history. They were by no means treading on unfamiliar territories. Ho himself had done some work in agricultural economy in conjunction with his population movement project, and Fong had directed the "Tianjin Industrialization" project, which he had just completed. Nevertheless, the diversity of the projects and the implications for social engineering were clearly calculated to appeal to the Rockefeller Foundation's interest.

Most significant, however, was the emergence at the Institute of a coherent program of research. Broadly classified, these eight projects fell into three categories: agricultural economy, industries, and local government finance. These three fields in themselves formed a well-coordinated program of research on various aspects of the society in North China. However, there are reasons to believe that Ho may not have realized the emergence of such a program nor recognized its full implications.

It is not clear, for instance, whether Ho's emphasis on the "regional scope" of research marked any real departure from his earlier methodological position. Despite his comment that national surveys would only vitiate the results because of the co-existence of a "medieval and modern economy" in China,[10] it did not occur to him that similar conditions

8. Ibid., p. 5.   9. Ibid., pp. 5–7.   10. Ibid., p. 5.

existed in the regional economy in North China as well. This regional emphasis probably reflected his more realistic assessment of the resources at his disposal and of the "scope" of the program that was more likely to convince the Foundation about its manageability.

Since a regional approach in Ho's notion merely reflected a simple contraction of the scope from the entire nation to North China, there were no changes in assumptions and methodology in his program for the new Nankai Institute of Economics. For instance, his industry surveys under the new program were a mere continuation of Fong's earlier Tianjin project except for a change of location. Indeed, there is no indication in Ho's outline of the new program that suggested a new departure in his thinking. Before the various projects on agricultural economy, industries, and local government finance could form a coherent program at the Institute, a more distinct focus would have to emerge to replace this conceptually nonspecific "regional" notion.

THE SHIFT TOWARD A RURAL FOCUS

A new focus for the program emerged rapidly, a result of a major reorientation of the Rockefeller Foundation's policy engineered by Selskar Gunn. As indicated earlier, Gunn's fortuitous visit in summer 1931 was a major factor in Nankai's success in its first application to the Rockefeller Foundation. To be sure, Ho and Fong had established their reputation as excellent social scientists. Gunn was reported to have made the grant to Nankai on the basis of the strong endorsement of the Institute of Pacific Relations. Nevertheless, it was also clear that Nankai happened to fulfill Gunn's vision of how the Foundation should function in China. In addition to proposing funding for social science work in China, Gunn believed the Foundation should support national universities instead of missionary colleges because the former, in his opinion, were "the institutions of the future."[11] However, national universities in general were beset by political and ideological interference from the government and by demonstrations from the students. As a private Chinese university with an excellent academic record, Nankai became the logical choice for the Foundation.

Ultimately, however, Nankai's success depended on its ability to fashion its program to conform to the new Rockefeller program that

---

11. Gunn, "Report on Visit to China," p. 21.

Gunn was developing in China. As a testimony to his observance, Franklin Ho was quick to detect Gunn's enthusiasm with James Yen's Mass Education Movement. Although he did not have the advantage Yanjing had in having a board in New York to provide advance intelligence work and guidance, Ho responded to the changing Rockefeller funding policy far more swiftly and imaginatively than Yanjing did. Shortly after Gunn's visit to Nankai, a rural tinge began to appear in the research program that Ho reformulated for the Institute. All the marginal projects, which were included in its grant application merely to impress the Foundation, were expunged.[12] The result was a much more clearly defined research program centered around the following three fields: agricultural economy, county government, and rural industries. In the fall of 1931, he presented two grant proposals to the Institute of Pacific Relations: "District [County] Government in North China" and "Rural Industries in North China."[13]

Ho was, however, still one step short of coming to realize that his research program could have constituted a well-coordinated attack on the political and economic aspects of rural society in North China. The final push came from Gunn, who returned to China in October 1932 to review the Foundation's program. Gunn stayed in China for more than a year until February 1934 and put together an ambitious program toward rural reconstruction work. Just a few months after Gunn began his residence in China, Ho started to stress the rural focus of his research program.[14]

FINANCE AND PERSONNEL TO 1937

Nankai's shift toward a rural focus in the early 1930s reflected the rising tide of the rural reconstruction movement, the same pressure that pushed Yanjing toward the same path. At the same time, this rural swing illustrates the power philanthropic foundations had upon their grant recipients. This eagerness to take the cue from Gunn reflected Nankai's dependence on Rockefeller funding. Nankai never developed a viable financial base. Ho was able to raise enough local contributions to claim

12. See "Memorandum on the Programme of Work: Nankai Institute of Economics, Nankai University, 1932–1933," p. 1, RAC RG1.1 601.51.432.
13. The Institute of Pacific Relations approved in 1931 a two-year grant to the district government project under the direction of Zhang Chunming, and appropriated funding the following year for the rural industries project.
14. See "Program of Work of the Institute for 1933–1934," enclosure, Selskar Gunn to Edmund Day, June 12, 1933, RAC RG 1.1 601.51.432.

only slightly more than two-thirds of the first annual Rockefeller funding of $15,000. Besides, as shown in Table 5.1, nearly half of these so-called "local contributions" in the early years was, in fact, composed of grants from the Institute of Pacific Relations, which was funded by the Rockefeller Foundation.

Rockefeller funding was given on a dollar-per-dollar matching basis. Supposedly it constituted no more than half of the total budget of the Nankai Institute of Economics. However, the financial reports of the Institute were extremely dubious. One suspects Ho's budgetary reports were largely accounting manipulations to satisfy the terms of the Rockefeller funding. Local contributions may never have actually matched the grants from the Rockefeller Foundation. The most questionable item was the one listed under the Tianjin Industrial Research Institute. The Institute was reported to have contributed to the budget for the years of 1932–3 and 1933–4, whereas it had been defunct since late 1929, after only a few months of existence.[15]

Another irregular item was the grants from the Institute of Pacific Relations. These grants were treated as local contributions without ever being questioned by the Foundation, even though these funds of the Institute of Pacific Relations came from none other than the Rockefeller Foundation itself and which also required a dollar-per-dollar local matching contributions. In other words, the same "local contribution" was used by Nankai to match the Rockefeller funding twice: first with the Rockefeller grants through the Institute of Pacific Relations, then together with the latter, with the Rockefeller funding for Nankai.

Whether or not the Rockefeller funding in fact represented a much larger factor than is indicated here will perhaps never be known. It is, however, clear that an irregularity as striking as this could not have escaped the scrutiny of the Rockefeller Foundation had it not been for the sympathetic tolerance of its vice-president, Gunn. Having decided that Nankai was the best center in China and that the quality of its work compared "favorably with similar institutions elsewhere in the world,"[16] Gunn was determined to help Ho as best as he could.[17]

It is beyond any doubt that Nankai was built on Rockefeller money.

15. See Chapter 4.
16. Gunn to Mason, February 9, 1936, RAC RG1.1 601.52.433.
17. In 1934, he recommended a special appropriation of $7,500 to help Nankai offset losses in exchange due to the inflation of the dollar. Then, with the inauguration of the China Program, he brought additional appropriations to Nankai – $18,750 and $15,000 in 1935 and 1936, respectively.

Table 5.1. *Finances of the Nankai Institute of Economics, 1932–37, in Mexican dollars*

	Budget (%)	RF[a] (%)	IPR[b] (%)	U[c] (%)	LC[d] (%)
1932-33	103,648.48 (100)	51,824.24 (50)	22,487.50 (21.7)	19,936.74 (19.2)	9,400.00 (9.1)
1933-34	122,398.42 (100)	50,000.00 (40.9)[e]	15,447.50 (12.6)	25,611.82 (20.9)	31,339.10 (25.6)
1934-35	154,361.00 (100)[e]	64,125.00 (41.5)[e]	7,125.00 (4.6)[e]	41,911.00 (27.2)	41,200.00 (26.7)
1935-36	135,060.48 (100)	75,716.56 (56.1)	4,201.87 (3.1)	34,298.63 (25.4)	20,843.42 (15.4)
1936-37	151,869.00 (100)	94,435.00 (62)	0 (0)	33,334.00 (22)	24,100.00 (16)

[a] the Rockefeller Foundation.
[b] the Institute of Pacific Relations.
[c] university appropriations.
[d] local contributions.
[e] estimate.

Sources: compiled from the Nankai Institute of Economics' reports (1932–37) to the Rockefeller Foundation, in RAC RG 1.1 601.51.432 and 52.433.

Table 5.2. *Distribution of Staff Members, 1928–37*[a]

	Professors	Lecturers	Instructors	Research assistants	Total
1928–29	1			1	2
1929–30	2			2	4
1930–31	2			5	7
1931–32	3	1	2	2	8
1932–33	9	3	5	8	25
1933–34	11	2	9	10	32
1934–35	11	2	9	10	32
1935–36	9	8	5	8	30
1936–37[b]	12	10	6	5	33

[a] Not including investigators, computing assistants, and clerks.
[b] First term only.
Source: *Nankai Institute of Economics: Its History and Work, 1927–36* (Tianjin, 1937), 27.

The statistics on staff members as summarized in Table 5.2 illustrate the decisive role played by the Rockefeller funding in the development of the Nankai Institute of Economics. Note that the real watershed in the history of the Institute came in the period of 1932–3 when the Rockefeller funding started, not in the period 1931–2, when the Institute formally began its work.

In the first year of its existence (1931–2), the Institute was only able to add a political scientist, Zhang Chunming, to its original team of two. However, in the following academic year, when the Rockefeller funding became available, the number of the faculty dramatically increased to nine. Until 1937, when the war with Japan broke out, the faculty positions were mostly filled by students returned from the West, most with doctoral degrees;[18] their fields of specialty were as varied as economics,

18. They were: from Yale – Franklin Ho (Ph.D., 1926), H. D. Fong (Ph.D., 1928), and Zhang Chunming (Ph.D., 1931); from Harvard – Wang Ganyu (M.A., 1930), Ding Ji (Leonard G. Ting, M.B.A., 1932), and Zhang Mengling (Ph.D., 1934); from Columbia – Ren Zongji (M.A., 1924), Wang Guozhong (M.S., 1931), and Lin Weiying (Ph.D., 1936); from Illinois – Chen Xujing (Su-ching Chen, Ph.D., 1928) and Li Qinglin (Shison Li, Ph.D., 1933); from New York University – Yuan Wenbo (Ph.D., 1930) and Huang Bangzhen (Ph.D., 1935); from California – Lin Tongji (Ph.D., 1934) and Li Choh-ming (Li Zhuomin, Ph.D., 1936); from Stanford – Zhang Jinjian (M.A., 1935); from Cornell – Wu Huabao (M.A.); and from Ohio State – Dong Chengxian (M.A., 1932).

economic history, political science, statistics, accounting, money and banking, agricultural economy, and sociology.

As most of them were economists whose expertise was highly sought after by the business community, many left for more lucrative positions in banking or industries. Some were even lured into government careers. In fact, Franklin Ho himself was on leave for government service from 1936 to 1945, though he remained the director of the Institute very much in fact as in name. The core of the faculty was composed of Ho, Fong, Zhang Chunming, Chen Xujing, Li Choh-ming, and Ding Ji (Leonard Ting).[19]

While students returned from the West dominated the ranks of professors, graduates of the university, and later of the Institute, staffed the lower echelons of the Institute. A striking fact is that in its twenty years of history, few Nankai graduates ever reached the rank of professor. It was perhaps more economical and efficient to simply tap the steady influx of students returned from the West than to groom its own graduates. There were only four Nankai graduates who attained the status of professorship: Wu Daye (B.A., 1930), Li Rui (B.A., 1930), and Feng Huade (B.A., 1932), who had served the Institute faithfully and meritoriously; and Chen Zhenhan (B.A., 1935), who owed his rapid advancement to a Qinghua scholarship that enabled him to earn a Ph.D. degree from Harvard (1940).

Nankai's poor record in this regard was closely related to its inability to send its students abroad for advanced training. This was partially due to the Rockefeller Foundation's policy. The Foundation did make provision for fellowships in its support of the Nankai program. However, it chose a very narrow criterion for granting its fellowships. The stipulations enabled the recipients to go abroad to seek information short of qualifying them as candidates for a higher degree. In all, only four junior members participated in the fellowship program: They were three of the best Nankai graduates – Wu Daye to Harvard, and Li Rui and Feng Huade to the London School of Economics – and one junior faculty – Ye Qianji to Cornell. None of them was given the opportunity to secure an advanced degree. Virtually every single member, whether it be a Nankai graduate or faculty, who obtained an advanced degree from abroad did so on his own, mostly with scholarships earned through competitive examinations.[20]

---

19. Ding was drowned while swimming in a lake in Kunming on October 4, 1940.
20. They were: through a Qinghua Scholarship for Study in the United States – Song Zuonan (Ph.D., Pennsylvania), Chen Zhenhan, and Wu Baoan (M.A., 1941; Ph.D.,

COUNTY GOVERNMENT AND FINANCE IN HEBEI

Few Nankai professors were actually involved in the field investigation for which the Institute was famous. The well-coordinated research program on agricultural economy, rural industries, and county government that Franklin Ho had put together involved only two faculty members – H. D. Fong and Zhang Chunming.

Zhang Chunming's project on county government in North China was a pioneering work. The project was divided into three parts, each focused on a different level of the local society. At the highest level was the county government. The focus of research was the structure and functions of county government, especially its system of taxation and the administration of justice, education, and public works. At the intermediate level was the ward (*qu*), which was created by the Nanjing government in 1927 supposedly to introduce local self-government. The purpose was to study the impact of this new unit of administration on local society. Finally, at the bottom was the village study, which intended to examine village leadership and its various institutions, including voluntary associations, such as the crop-watching societies and irrigation societies; and secret societies, such as the Red Spears.

The problem was where and how to begin; no one had any idea as to how it could be conducted except for the vague notion of the need for sampling and for consulting the county archives. It was perhaps because of this difficulty in devising approaches to the project, the field investigation did not begin until January 1933, more than a year after funding for this project had been approved in 1931 by the Institute of Pacific Relations.

Little is known about the field work, and virtually nothing as to how and why the counties were chosen.[21] The field was simply too wide. The eleven counties surveyed form three clusters,[22] scattered far apart. Zhuo Xian, the northernmost county surveyed, was almost six hundred miles from Daming, the southernmost county in the study. Yet the project had only three field investigators: Feng Huade and a fellow Nankai gradu-

Harvard, 1945); through a Sino-British Boxer Indemnity Fund Scholarship – Bao Juemin (faculty, Ph.D., London, 1940); and through a Ministry of Education Scholarship – Sang Hengkang (M.A., 1943; Ph.D., Harvard, 1947), Song Xia (Song Zejiu, M.A., 1943), Yang Jingnian (graduate student, 1936–7).

21. They were Xian Xian, Xingtai, Daming, Handan, Zhuo Xian, Nanpi, Dongguang, Qing Xian, Gaoyang, Nanhe, and Mancheng.

22. The exception is Zhuo Xian which was farther to the north in the vicinity of Peking.

ate, Yue Yongqing, and Wang Yaoyu, who had worked with Ho on the Manchurian project. Even with discriminating use of their time, they could not have spent more than one month in each county.

Most serious was the impractical research design, that is, the use of schedules. Much of the field investigation involved visits to county government offices for interviews with clerks. Because the clerks invariably suspected the field investigators of being provincial government agents in disguise, their cooperation was never forthcoming. The investigators constantly had to guard against misinformation given by the clerks.[23]

The county archives, the other important source of information for the project, were not only chaotic, but were extremely incomplete. The archives in five out of the eleven counties had been variously damaged either by natural calamity, such as fire or rain, or by man-made disaster.[24] Some counties did not have a complete file for the years dated as recent as 1928.[25] In the rare case where the files were more abundant, they were extremely difficult to use due to the peculiar filing system the clerks had purposely created in order to protect their trade.[26]

In late spring 1933, the Institute made a decision to shift to the participant-observer approach and keep the quantitative aspect of the project to a minimum.[27] Yet no reduction in the scope of the study was yet contemplated. In fact, the Institute claimed that with the adoption of the participant-observer approach, it could cover a larger field in a shorter span of time.[28] It was not until winter of the same year, upon securing the consent of the Hebei government, that the Institute began to concentrate its work on a whole new field – Jinghai, a county located ten miles southwest of Tianjin.

As an area of investigation, Jinghai was not appreciably better than the eleven counties hitherto surveyed. Its archives, though larger and historically deeper, were likewise full of lacunae and arranged under a

---

23. Yue Yongqing, "Hebei sheng shiyi xian caifu gaikuang" (Hsien Taxes in Hebei Province: A Sample Study), *Jingji tongji jikan* (The Quarterly Journal of Economics and Statistics), II.3 (September 1933), p. 627.
24. Ibid., p. 625.   25. Ibid.
26. Zuo De (Feng Huade), "Hebei sheng xian 'li'zhi de qian shili" (The Evil Force Lurking at the Back of the County Administration in the Hebei Province), "Jingji zhoukan" (Economic Weekly), p. 86, in *Dagong bao*, October 24, 1934.
27. "Report on the Work of the Institute for 1932–1933," May 22, 1933, p. 5, RAC RG 1.1 601.52.432.
28. Ibid., pp. 5–6.

peculiar filing system.[29] What made the Jinghai field attractive was that Nankai could appoint two investigators to the secretariat of the county government. Although referred to hyperbolically by Ho to the Rocke-feller Foundation as the Institute's rural center where the Nankai fellows had "the freedom and privilege to participate in the actual working of the government and administration,"[30] Jinghai offered nothing more than granting Nankai's researchers access to the county files. A year later, in September 1934, the Nankai team was transferred to James Yen's Ding Xian to work on the richer archives there.

The project on county government and administration was on the whole a success. The field work was well-represented by seven major arti-cles, one on the eleven counties in southern Hebei,[31] two on Jinghai,[32] and four on Ding Xian,[33] as well as a few smaller newspaper articles.[34] The field investigators played an unusually large role in the project. There is little indication of the input by the project director, Zhang Chunming, whose contribution to the project consisted of one survey of county government expenditure in Hebei and a historical survey of "model officials" as they were depicted in the Standard Dynastic Histo-ries.[35] Virtually all the articles were written by the field investigators. Of

29. Feng Huade, "Xian difang xingzheng zhi caizheng jichu" (The Financial Basis of County Government), *Zhengzhi jingji xuebao* (The Quarterly Journal of Economics and Political Science), III.4 (July 1935), pp. 697–8. Note that Ho himself made a glowing report about the Jinghai archives in *Shinian lai de Nankai jingji yanjiusuo* (The Nankai Institute of Economics in the Past Ten Years) (Tianjin, 1937), p. 11.

30. Zhang Boling and Franklin Ho to Gunn, December 21, 1933, Appendix A, "Work of the Institute, July 1932 – December 1933," RAC RG 1.1 601.52.433.

31. Yue Yongqing, "Hebei sheng shiyi xian caifu gaikuang."

32. Wang Zhixin, "Hebei sheng zhi baoshui zhidu" (The System of Tax Farming in Hebei Province), in *Zhengzhi jingji xuebao* (The Quarterly Journal of Economics and Polit-ical Science), III.3 (April 1935), pp. 530–89; Feng Huade, "Xian difang xingzheng zhi caizheng jichu" (The Financial Basis of Hsien Government), ibid., III.4 (July 1935), pp. 697–749.

33. Feng Huade and Li Ling, "Hebei sheng Ding Xian zhi tianfu" (Land Taxes in Ding Xian, Hebei), ibid., IV.3 (April 1936), pp. 443–520; Feng Huade and Li Ling, "Hebei sheng Ding Xian zhi tian fang qi shui" (Taxes on Land and House Ownership Regis-tration in Ding Xian, Hebei), ibid., IV.4 (July 1936), pp. 751–800; Feng Huade, "Hebei sheng Ding Xian de yashui" (The Brokerage Taxes in Ding Xian, Hebei), ibid., V.2 (January 1937), pp. 285–322; Wang Weixian, "'Mofan xian' qi yu 'shiyan xian' qi de Ding Xian xianzheng" (County Administration in Ding Xian during Its "Model County" and "Experimental County" Phases), ibid., V.3 (April 1937), pp. 635–93.

34. See especially the "Finance" section in Fang Xianting, ed., *Zhongguo jingji yanjiu.*

35. "Local Government Expenditure in China," *Monthly Bulletin of Economic China* 7.6 (June 1934), pp. 233–47 and "Xunli yu xunli de zhengzhi" ("The Biographies of Model Officials" in Dynastic Histories: A Study), *Zhengzhi jingji xuebao* (The Quarterly Journal of Economics and Political Science), III.2 (January 1935), pp. 225–48.

the seven major articles, six were about taxation and county finance. Only one article touched upon the administrative aspect of the county government. Obviously the training and interest of the investigators determined the subjects to be studied.[36]

As a project that professed to present a comprehensive picture of the local society in North China, the published results left much to be desired. Nevertheless, the published articles were all solid pieces of research based on county archives, supplemented by field investigations. They presented a grim picture of the problems of administration, particularly abuses in taxation at the county level and, to a lesser extent, at the ward and village levels.

Indicative of the value of these articles was the fruitful use of them by Prasenjit Duara in his study of North China villages.[37] What these articles revealed was, first, the failure of the state to bureaucratize the increasingly intensifying local government activity, a phenomenon that Duara characterizes as "state involution."[38] This meant the entrenchment of the clerks in county administration, whom Duara refers to as "entrepreneurial state brokers." These ineluctable clerks caused the greatest harm in county administration not so much because they were unaccountable as because they were indispensable, for they alone knew how county government worked; not only did they appropriate tax registers for their own exclusive use, but they made themselves irreplaceable with their outlandish procedures and byzantine filing system.[39]

The second major problem of county administration that the Nankai researchers uncovered was the failure of the state to rationalize its bureaucratic structure. One problem embedded in the county bureaucratic structure was redundancy. Take the fiscal administration as an example. There were four different offices involved in tax collection in Jinghai: (1) the Land Tax Collection Bureau, which collected the land tax for the province and the land tax surcharge for the county; (2) the Revenue Office, which collected the miscellaneous taxes, both for the province and the county; (3) the Education Section, which collected education funds from the rent from school lands; and (4) the Bureau of

---

36. Wang Weixian, who wrote the only article on county government, was a political science major from Qinghua.
37. Duara, *Culture, Power, and the State: Rural North China, 1900–1942* (Stanford, 1988).
38. Ibid., pp. 73–7.
39. Zuo De, "Hebei sheng xian 'li'zhi de qian shili."

Finance, which disbursed the tax revenue collected by the first two offices to the county government offices.[40]

The redundancy in the county bureaucratic structure pointed to the third major problem of county administration, that is, poor utilization of resources. In addition to redundancy, the proliferation of "modernization" projects stretched the budget so thin that most county services existed in name only. For instance, the budget for roads and bridges was a paltry $240 Chinese dollars in Jinghai in 1932, compared to $67,672 of the total county budget for that year.[41] As anemic as the budget already was, it was all but absorbed by personnel expenses. Consider the police budget, which, together with education, consumed more than three-fifths of the county budgets in Hebei. While the expenditure for police administration constituted 32.95 percent of the budget in Jinghai in 1930, a whopping 94.2 percent of it was for wages.[42]

That bureaucratization and rationalization would become the focal points of the project on county government reflected Nankai's intellectual and ideological orientations. Like the notion of a rational economic organization that had guided its "Tianjin Industrialization Project" a few years earlier, bureaucratization and rationalization constituted Nankai's prescription for putting county administration on a scientific basis.

This institutionally oriented approach was ideologically bound. The attacks on county clerks, on redundant and overlapping bureaucratic structures, and on the irrational utilization of resources were all sanctioned by the rhetoric of the government that sought to bureaucratize county administration. Conspicuously missing in Nankai's analysis of county government were the maneuvers and manipulations of the local elite within the county and subcounty political systems. It was not that the information was not there. Nankai researchers were apparently well aware of the elite abuse of power, judging from the many references they made and, particularly, a revealing article about a village head

---

40. The discussion in the following two paragraphs is based on Feng Huade, "Hebei sheng xian caizheng fenpei shang biaoxian de xingzheng xuruo zheng" (The Administrative Anemic Symptom Manifested in the Fiscal Revenue at both the Provincial and County Levels in Hebei), "Jingji zhoukan" (Economic Weekly), p. 86, *Dagong bao*, October 24, 1934.
41. It is not clear whether this budget for roads and bridges was figured into Feng's total county budget for that year. It appears that this budget came from a revenue generated through a separate surcharge.
42. These figures are not to be taken literally, for they differ from what appear in Feng's "Xian difang xingzheng zhi caizheng jichu," which Duara uses. See Duara, *Culture, Power, and the State*, p. 82.

concealing his and his cronies' landholdings with the use of two separate registers.[43]

It is significant that the few instances of elite abuse of power recorded by Nankai researchers all belonged to what Duara characterized as entrepreneurial brokerage.[44] Like the exorbitant rent and usury, which Nankai occasionally touched upon, abusive and predatory brokerage was a symptom that rational, scientific management could rectify. Herein lay the fundamental difference between the Anglo-American-oriented Yanjing and Nankai social scientists and Chen Hansheng's Marxist group discussed in Chapters 7 and 8. While Chen Hansheng perceived the state as an instrument of the ruling class, the Yanjing and Nankai academics viewed the state as an agent of progress in its efforts to bureaucratize local government and to strip entrepreneurial elites of their powers.

These two contrasting visions of state and society had profound methodological implications for the two competing social science discourses. Chen's Marxist vision led him to question the analytic value of the notion of the community – village or county – and to insist on the need to conduct class analysis. By contrast, not only did the Yanjing and Nankai social scientists never question the notion of the community, but they did not see the need to differentiate its members, particularly given Yanjing's functionalist bias for searching functional harmony or equilibrium. They were favorably inclined toward the elite, that is, a certain *kind* of elite – the protective, community-oriented elite – maybe a figment of their imagination? Their belief in how the flight of the elite rendered the countryside defenseless to rapacious county functionaries or evil bullies was not unlike Duara's argument about the displacement of the protective brokers by entrepreneurial ones. Where Chen Hansheng's analysis – of the lineage managers in Panyu county in Guangdong,[45] for example – may offer some insight to refine this argument is to question how "protective" the elite had ever been and whether the village ever constituted a community of common interest for the peasant as well as the elite.

---

43. Feng Huade, "'Fuxing nongcun' de xianjue wenti: pinjun nongmin de fudan" (A Prerequisite to "the Rehabilitation of the Village:" An Equitable Tax Burden for all Peasants), "Jingji zhoukan" (Economic Weekly), 14, *Dagong bao*, May 24, 1933.
44. In referring to the case, as reported by Feng Huade, of the village head possessing two registers, Duara seems to have suggested that it was protective brokerage, in *Culture, Power, and the State*, p. 233. It seems, however, to have been a clear case of entrepreneurial brokerage.
45. See Chapter 8.

After all, as Duara himself concedes, protective brokerage was always susceptible to domination by entrepreneurial interests.[46]

RURAL INDUSTRIES IN HEBEI

The project on rural industries directed by H. D. Fong presented quite a different pattern from that on county government directed by Zhang Chunming. Here Fong assumed close supervision. He participated in the writing of field reports, often jointly with his field investigators. The approach to field investigation was also different. The field work was intensive in character, concentrating on one single industry in one particular region, that is, the handloom weaving industry in Gaoyang, Hebei.

Field work in Gaoyang began in February 1933. The major investigators consisted of Wu Zhi, Bi Xianghui, and Wang Yaoyu.[47] They studied Gaoyang and part of the four surrounding counties that formed a production and marketing network with Gaoyang at the center. The investigation covered all dimensions of Gaoyang's handloom weaving industry, including its history, organization, financial structure, production, labor, and marketing.[48]

Unlike the project on county government, which was in every respect a pioneering work, the rural industries project by no means sailed in uncharted waters. Statistics were available on the handloom weaving industry in Hebei. Furthermore, Gaoyang was a success case, which enjoyed a phenomenal growth until it peaked in 1929. In 1928, while the handloom weaving industries in Hebei produced 73.9 percent of the total production value of forty-four rural industries in the entire province, Gaoyang alone contributed a stunning 30.5 percent.[49] The second most productive county, Shulu, which specialized in leather clothing, contributed only 6.7 percent of the total production value of the rural industries in Hebei.[50] Thus, far from being representative of either industries

---

46. Duara, *Culture, Power, and the State*, p. 57.
47. Wang Yaoyu was like a jack-of-all-trades, working simultaneously on the county government and rural industries projects.
48. Wu Zhi, *Xiangcun zhibu gongye de yige yanjiu* (A Study of a Village Weaving Industry) (Shanghai, 1936).
49. Fang Xianting and Wu Zhi, "Zhongguo zhi xiangcun gongye" (Rural Industries in China), *Jingji tongji jikan* (The Quarterly Journal of Economics and Statistics), II.3 (September 1933), pp. 599–603.
50. The statistics here are not reliable. For instance, according to Fang, Baodi, another important cotton-weaving center in Hebei, had an output worth $3,000,000 Chinese

of its kind or rural industries in general, the Gaoyang weaving industry was a unique case.

However, whether or not the Gaoyang weaving industry was representative of rural industries in China was not an issue that concerned H. D. Fong. He was not so much interested in presenting Chinese industries, urban or rural, as they were, but rather in making diagnoses and recommendations for their improvement. All of his earlier studies on the Tianjin industries contained a section in which he pinpointed the problems and suggested solutions. This practical approach remained as distinctive when the focus of research was shifted toward rural industries. In fact, Fong's interest in rural industries, if only a passing phase, corresponded to Nankai's increasing participation in the rural reconstruction work envisioned and funded by the Rockefeller Foundation. Underlying his investigation of the Gaoyang weaving industry was his reassessment of the strategies for China's economic modernization.

Prior to their shift toward a rural focus, the Nankai people were fully convinced that large-scale industries would eventually prevail in China and follow the course through which the West had evolved. They perceived their role as providing accurate information from the field so as to hasten the process and, at the same time, mitigating the suffering that had marred the Western industrial revolution. Yet it took the unequivocal verdict to the contrary by some foreign authorities to help them abandon their orthodox views on China's road to industrialization.

As early as 1928, J. B. Tayler, the chemist-turned-economist at Yanjing University, had advocated small-scale industries appropriate to farm scale to absorb surplus farm labor. He proposed that small producers organize themselves, secure expert assistance, standardize their products, and create cooperatives for the supply of their various needs and marketing of their products.[51] While Tayler was not the first to have proposed

dollars in 1928. See ibid., table 16. However, Bi Xianghui, the field worker who worked in Baodi, cited the figure for 1929 as $7,524,795 Chinese dollars. See Bi Xianghui, "Gaoyang, Baodi liangge mianzhi qu zai Hebei sheng xiangcun gongye shang zhi diwei," (The Positions of the Two Cotton Weaving Districts, Gaoyang and Baodi, in Rural Industries in the Hebei Province), in Fang Xianting, *Zhongguo jingji yanjiu*, p. 675. This represents an unlikely increase of 2.5 times in just one year. Nevertheless, there is little doubt that Gaoyang was the most productive county in Hebei. Even if the figure is inaccurate, Gaoyang's reported output of C$31,620,000 in 1928 was several times that of the second most productive county, be it Shulu or Baodi.

51. J. B. Tayler, *Farm and Factory in China: Aspects of the Industrial Revolution* (London, 1928), pp. 91–2.

the idea of cooperatives,[52] he was a most persistent and articulate promoter of rural industry and cooperatives. Yet Tayler's proposals did not seem to have made any impact on the Chinese academic circles. The Nankai group, for instance, began to take notice of his argument only after they had served as Tawney's host in Nankai in December 1930, or perhaps even after Tawney's *Land and Labour in China* had been published in 1932. In this book, among many other things, Tawney strongly endorsed Tayler's proposals and urged that China not ignore its handicraft tradition in its planning for the nation's economic development.[53]

Nankai's decision to take on rural industries indicated its recognition that there was little hope for a speedy transformation of China's economy, which its members constantly referred to as "economic medievalism," that is, a locally based economy characterized by the dominance of agriculture and handicraft industries, and supported by backward transportation and an antiquated credit system.[54] The Gaoyang study, however, represented no changes in the assumption and conceptualization with which Nankai approached rural industries. Like his earlier studies of the Tianjin industries, Fong continued to apply the same yardsticks derived from his study of the Industrial Revolution in England. Thus, according to the scheme that he had worked out in his Ph.D. dissertation, *The Triumph of Factory System in England*,[55] the handloom weaving industry in Gaoyang was at the merchant employer stage – out of the three-stage scheme of craftsman, merchant employer, and factory system. The merchant employer, or, "putting-out," was a system in which the merchant supplied the peasant worker with material and then marketed the product he turned out. This system, which had brought phenomenal success in Gaoyang for two decades since the 1910s, ran out of steam in the early 1930s.

Fong's diagnosis of the Gaoyang weaving industry was similar to what he had reached for the Tianjin industries a few years earlier. Thus, Gaoyang's woes were caused by factors both internal and external to the weaving industry. The external factors were: the declining purchasing power of the people due to the world-wide depression, famines, and civil wars; native and foreign competition; and Japanese economic and military aggression as manifested in predatory pricing by Japanese cotton

---

52. The cooperative movement began in the late Qing and experienced much growth after World War One. See Hayford, *To the People: James Yen and Village China*, p. 170.
53. R. H. Tawney, *Land and Labour in China*, pp. 145–6.
54. He Lian, "Zhonggu shi zhi Zhongguo jingji" (The Medieval Mode of the Chinese Economy), *Duli pinglun* (Independent Review), 93 (March 25, 1934), pp. 2–6.
55. The dissertation was accepted by Yale in 1928 and published in Tianjin in 1930.

mills in China and the loss of the Manchurian market after 1931. While these external factors were formidable and were clearly beyond Gaoyang's ability to redress, Fong nevertheless argued that what really undermined the Gaoyang weaving industry were the internal factors: obsolete equipment and poor product quality as well as antiquated management and marketing.[56]

Not surprisingly, Fong's prescription for treating the ailing Gaoyang weaving industry was rationalization, exactly what he had prescribed for the Tianjin industries. There was a new twist, however. Nankai's rural swing in the 1930s ushered in a passing phase during which they entertained the idea that the Gaoyang weaving industry might not have to evolve from the merchant employer to the factory system. While reconciling themselves to the fact that China could not hope to embark on immediate and large-scale industrialization, they took comfort in pointing out that decentralization of industries might now be developing in the West itself. They referred to the reversed flow of the population back to the countryside during the depression, to the desirability of decentralizing the population and industries in the event of war, and even to Kropotkin's vision of a pastoral style of working conditions.[57] All these remarks suggested that China in fact could benefit from being backward because now it could fit into the latest trend of economic development without having to go through the industrial phase.

This self-congratulatory note was incidentally a startlingly enduring one shared by many modern Chinese intellectuals. The Marxists, Mao Zedong included, were particularly attracted by this belief in backwardness as a blessing for China. For Fong and his colleagues at Nankai, Gaoyang's backwardness would enable it to strike out on a new path, different from either the depression-prone and exploitation-ridden capitalist system or the Marxist world of violence and fantasy.[58] Better still, the road to this new path had been tried and proven effective. All it would take was the organization of cooperatives to handle credit, production, and marketing, in addition to the improvement of techniques.[59] Implausible as it may have been, Nankai's proposal to revive the Gaoyang weaving industry through cooperatives reflected the widespread cooperative movement of the 1930s.

---

56. Wu Zhi, *Xiangcun zhibu gongye de yige yanjiu*, pp. 261–71.
57. See Fang Xianting and Wu Zhi, "Zhongguo zhi xiangcun gongye," pp. 561–4; Wu Zhi, *Xiangcun zhibu gongye de yige yanjiu*, pp. 2–3.
58. Wu Zhi, *Xiangcun zhibu gongye de yige yanjiu*, pp. 274–5.
59. Ibid., pp. 277–85.

Like the project on county government, the published reports on rural industries were all solid pieces of research.[60] One problem was that Nankai seems to have had difficulty in fulfilling the overall goals of its projects. Both the projects on the county government and rural industries were supported by grants from the Institute of Pacific Relations, the former for four years and the latter for three years. Both projects, in their second phase, were supposedly to have begun to cover the provinces of Henan, Shandong, and Shanxi. However, neither project ever extended beyond the original field in Hebei. Japanese control of North China from 1933 onward may have hampered Nankai's research, but Ho never indicated it in his reports to the sponsoring Institute of Pacific Relations, as he had when his Manchurian project was disrupted by the Japanese capture of Manchuria in 1931.

Two professors and eight field investigators hardly constituted adequate manpower for work within Hebei itself. Besides being understaffed, Nankai was overextended. In his 1935 report to the Rockefeller Foundation, Ho reported that the Institute had been engaged in a number of new projects in addition to the existing ones on county government and rural industries. They included: in rural economy – marketing of cotton in Hebei and Shandong, marketing of rice in Sichuan, and pawnshops in Jinghai; in rural sociology – a community study of Gaoyang based upon Robert and Helen Lynd's approach in *Middletown*, an approach that the Institute of Pacific Relations, as discussed in Chapter 9, was actively promoting. As could be anticipated, few reports had been published by 1937 when the war broke out.

ATTEMPTS AT SOCIAL ENGINEERING

Unlike Yanjing, Nankai had no tradition in extension or outreach programs. Whatever social service activities the Nankai students had

---

60. They are Wu Zhi, *Xiangcun zhibu gongye de yige yanjiu*; Fang Xianting and Wu Zhi, "Zhongguo zhi xiangcun gongye"; Wu Zhi, "Cong yiban gongye zhidu de yanjin guancha Gaoyang de zhibu gongye" (Gaoyang Weaving Industry: An Analysis of Its Development), *Zhengzhi jingji xuebao*, III.1 (October 1934), pp. 39–79; Fang Xianting, "Huabei xiangcun zhibu gongye yu shangren guzhu zhidu" (Rural Weaving and the Merchant Employers in a North China District), *Zhengzhi jingji xuebao*, Pt. I, III.4 (July 1935), pp. 750–91, Pt. II, IV.1 (October 1935), pp. 107–38; Fang Xianting and Bi Xianghui, "You Baodi shouzhi gongye guancha gongye zhidu zhi yanbian" (The Evolution of an Industrial System: The Case of the Baodi Handloom Weaving Industry), ibid., IV.2 (January 1936), pp. 261–329.

undertaken were spontaneous and noninstitutionalized. The Nankai Institute of Economics, being primarily a teaching and research institution, would have found it difficult to adapt itself to any existing social service scheme. Yet being acutely aware of Gunn's interest, Nankai must have felt a tremendous pressure to develop some work in rural reconstruction.

As an economist who had perhaps the keenest business sense and strongest ties with the business community among the prominent social scientists during the Republican period, Ho eventually initiated some projects for the Institute, using his long-established ties with Zhou Zuomin of the Tianjin-based Jincheng (Kincheng) Banking Corporation. In September 1933, the Institute offered a one-year training program for thirteen trainees whom the Jincheng Banking Corporation had newly recruited through competitive examinations in Peking and Shanghai.[61] It is noteworthy that in both his reports to the Rockefeller Foundation and his letter to William Holland of the Institute of Pacific Relations, Ho referred to this program as though it were a newly instituted M.A. program of the Institute. The Jincheng Banking Corporation was mentioned only as a benefactor and a cooperating institution that would provide on-job training for those students who specialized in banking.[62] Only in his letter to Holland did he intimate to the latter that the Jincheng Banking Corporation was "subsidizing the Institute ten thousand Chinese dollars for the present year with the understanding that the Bank will have a prior claim to the services of the students after they complete their work in the Institute."[63]

A year later, Ho made real progress in involving Nankai in rural reconstruction. In 1934, Nankai, the Jincheng Banking Corporation, and the Mass Education Movement formed a Joint Research and Extension Committee on Agricultural Products in North China, with Nankai responsible for research, the Mass Education Movement for extension, and the Jincheng Banking Corporation for the administration of agricultural credit and loans. The first venture this organization undertook

---

61. See *Jincheng yinhang shiliao* (Historical Materials on the Jincheng Banking Corporation) (Shanghai, 1983), pp. 269–70.
62. See "Report of the Nankai Institute of Economics, Nankai University, to the Rockefeller Foundation, 1933–1934," p. 5, RAC RG1.1 601.52.433.
63. Ho to Holland, November 16, 1933, IPR Box 287 Franklin Ho 1933–1935 Folder.

was the production and marketing of cotton in Hebei with Ding Xian as its headquarters.[64]

Extension projects thus created could not have avoided the pitfall of being haphazard or unsystematic. The one-year training program in cooperation with the Jincheng Banking Corporation seemed to be a one-time experiment.[65] Nankai, moreover, seemed to have dropped out of the joint venture in cotton production and marketing in Hebei; the participation a year later of the more agronomically oriented Qinghua, Nanking, and Cheeloo universities may have made the whole enterprise too technical to require Nankai's expertise. Eventually it was Gunn who steered Nankai to a rural reconstruction project that was both more institutionalized and more ambitious in its social engineering.

As the earlier discussion on the Yanjing program has made clear, Gunn's China Program was approved by the Rockefeller Foundation at its trustees' meeting in December 1934. Yet it took Gunn and his assistant, John B. Grant, more than a year until April 1936 to cajole six institutions into forming a North China Council for Rural Reconstruction.[66] Nankai's role in Gunn's China Program was at first primarily centered around research and training. This was mainly because of Nankai's reputation in field research and the efforts it had made to relate research to practical applications. At the same time, however, like Yanjing, Nankai was just as eager to appeal to Gunn's interest by restructuring its program so that it would become essentially a training program to prepare the students for rural reconstruction work.

In September 1935, the Nankai Institute of Economics launched a rather unorthodox M.A. program with the specific aim of training rural reconstruction personnel. Eleven students were admitted through a competitive examination and were given the choice of specializing in one of three fields targeted for development at the Institute: cooperatives, land problems, and local government and finance. The curriculum was unique in that it was composed of three parts: one year of seminar work at the Institute, four months of visitation to the nation's major rural recon-

---

64. *Jincheng yinhang shiliao*, pp. 460–5.
65. The Jincheng Banking Corporation established its own training program afterwards. See Ji Xiaochun and Yang Guzhi, "Zhou Zuomin yu Jincheng yinhang" (Zhou Zuomin and the Jincheng Banking Corporation), *Tianjin wenshi ziliao xuanji* (Selected Literary and Historical Sources on Tianjin), No. 13 (January 1981), p. 116.
66. For more discussion of the North China Council for Rural Reconstruction, see Chapter 3.

struction centers, and, finally, eight months of experimental work on a project formulated by each student in a selected rural reconstruction center.[67] Nankai, however, did not have the opportunity to experiment with this post-graduate training program. Hardly had the first class graduated when the war with Japan began.

Of the various activities in which Nankai was involved during these years leading toward the Japanese invasion, the most significant was its leading role in the Rockefeller-financed North China Council for Rural Reconstruction, discussed in Chapter 3. Not only was Ho serving as the chairman of the Committee on Training and Research of the Council, but Nankai had the responsibility of staffing two out of seven departments of the Council: economics and civil administration. The Nankai personnel were mainly those who had participated in the Institute's field investigation: Zhang Chunming, head of the Department of Civil Administration with assistants Zhang Jinjian and Yue Yongqing; H. D. Fong, head of the Department of Economics with assistants Li Rui, Wu Huabao, Feng Huade, and Wang Wenjun.

The significance of these appointments lay in the fact that they were both academic and administrative. In addition to providing in-field training for the students, the faculty assumed an administrative role through their appointment to posts in the Jining county government. For instance, Zhang Jinjian was both Professor of Civil Administration and the head of the First Division (Civil Affairs) of the Jining county government. Feng Huade, in addition to being an assistant at the Department of Economics, served as the assistant director of the Land Registration Section.

We have little information on how the Nankai faculty functioned as administrators at Jining. From Zhang Jinjian's *Reminiscences*, however, we have the impression that they did not function too differently from the ordinary bureaucrats once they were placed in the thinly staffed county government machinery and pressed into routine administrative duties. For instance, the first major task the Council devoted itself at Jining was to launch a land survey and registration campaign in an effort to increase the county revenue. The time limit set for this task was only the fifteen days before the spring planting season, when the work could be done without interfering with the peasants working in the fields.[68]

---

67. "Report of the Nankai Institute of Economics, Nankai University, to the Rockefeller Foundation, July–December, 1935," pp. 5–9, RAC RG1.1 601.52.439.
68. "North China Council for Rural Reconstruction, Minutes of the Meeting of the Committee on Training and Research, 1936," November 15, 1936, 3 RAC RG1.1 601.11.109.

In a county that had a territory of approximately eight hundred square miles and a population of close to half a million, this could have been accomplished only very superficially, even if relying upon the existing official and semiofficial machineries.

What actually happened was a self-reporting campaign.[69] The machinery that was mobilized to accomplish this task was the principals of the peasant schools, who were at the same time the rural township (*xiang*) leaders as the Shandong system was designed by the latter-day Confucian sage, Liang Shuming.[70] The principals of these peasant schools were responsible for distributing and collecting landholding report forms to and from the landowners under their jurisdiction. Upon receiving the completed forms, the county clerks and the students registered with the departments of the Council proceeded to make classification, computation, and analysis. The organization of the residents into *bao* and *jia* units was accomplished in similar fashion, with Zhang Jinjian and the students working in the county seat and the principals of the peasant schools in the countryside.

Nor were the professors any more innovative when they had to take disciplinary actions against obstruction by local elite and procrastination of the subbureaucracy. To the landlords who resisted land registration, the professors had their managers and tenants arrested until the landlords agreed to self-reporting. To the clerks who assumed the role as tax farmers and yet failed to delivered their quotas, the professors had them flogged and, if they still procrastinated, imprisoned.

These sketchy references to the actual problems and difficulties the professors encountered in their attempt to "rationalize" county administration revealed only the tip of the iceberg. Much of their academic discourse and social engineering rhetoric evaporated upon contact with the sheer inertia and quagmire of the county government. Aside from having to placate the outwardly receptive and yet inwardly wary provincial authorities,[71] the North China Council for Rural Reconstruction was plagued by organizational as well as personal feuds. Most serious feuds occurred among the Mass Education Movement, Yanjing, and Nankai. While James Yen had little respect for professors because of their inabil-

---

69. The following discussion is based on Zhang Jinjian, *Mingcheng qishi zishu* (Mingcheng's [Zhang Jinjian's] Reminiscences at Seventy) (Taipei, 1972), pp. 138–42.
70. Guy Alitto, *The Last Confucian: Liang Shu-ming and the Chinese Dilemma of Modernity* (California, 1979), pp. 206–12, 248–53.
71. See the discussion in Chapter 3.

ity and unwillingness to step out of the comfort of their studies and enter the real world, the professors at Yanjing and Nankai viewed Yen as a mere doer without much scholarship.[72]

While mutual distrust characterized the relationship between Yen and the professors, fierce competition and animosity divided the professors themselves between those from Yanjing and those from Nankai. At issue here was the leadership role on the Council that each of these institutions attempted to assume.[73] Exasperated by the constant personnel problems, Gunn made the following critical remark, perhaps his only one of this kind, on these people whom he supported.

> Doctor Grant and myself have had a good deal of difficulty in getting the Chinese in these three institutions to cooperate as closely as we had anticipated. These people are highly individualistic and we found that real cooperation was much more difficult to obtain than the "lip service" which was given to the word "co-operation" prior to our actual grants.[74]

In July 1936, Ho resigned from his position as the Chairman of the Committee on Training and Research of the Council to take up a government position as the Director of the Political Affairs of the Executive Yuan. Ho's departure from the Council disturbed Gunn greatly because he had looked to Ho as the mainstay of his China Program. Nankai for its part suffered as well from Ho's departure, for it deprived Nankai of a powerful leadership role on the Council.[75] Yet in the end, the Japanese invasion in July 1937 put all these to a halt and swept away both the bickering and aspiration for social engineering.

RETURN TO A MACROECONOMIC FOCUS

One of the most ugly episodes in the early phase of the war was the deliberate destruction of Nankai by the Japanese military, a punishment

72. Interview with C. C. Chen (Chen Zhiqian), November 15, 1985, Berkeley, California.
73. For further discussion on competition between Yanjing and Nankai, see Chapter 9.
74. Gunn to Max Mason, July 25, 1935, RAC RG1.1 601.14.144.
75. During the war with Japan, because of the departure of senior personnel from Yanjing and that of James Yen, Nankai dominated the National Council for Rural Reconstruction, the successor organization of the North China Council for Rural Reconstruction. Interview with C. C. Chen, November 15, 1985, Berkeley, California.

inflicted upon Nankai for the leadership role its students often assumed in anti-Japanese demonstrations. After bombing the buildings from the air, the Japanese shelled the campus with artillery at close range and then set fire to whatever would burn by pouring three truckloads of gasoline over the ruins.[76] Fortunately, the Nankai Institute of Economics was able to have its library removed to the French Concession before the bombing began. Nevertheless, the materials and manuscripts of the various field investigation projects were all lost.

As one of the first Chinese universities to be dislocated by the war, Nankai joined many other northern academic institutions in their long and tortuous migration to the southwest. By April 1938, when the initial arrangement for resettlement was made, the staff of the Nankai Institute of Economics found themselves in three scattered locations: in Kunming, where most of the staff became affiliated with the National Southwest Associated University, a newly-amalgamated body formed by Peking, Qinghua, and Nankai universities; in Guiyang, where Fong became the secretary-treasurer of the National Council for Rural Reconstruction, the successor organization of the North China Council for Rural Reconstruction;[77] and in Dingfan, Guizhou, where some of the junior members of the Institute served on the county government as in Jining before the war. In 1939, Nankai resumed its graduate training in Chongqing on the campus of the Nankai Middle School, which Zhang Boling had wisely established in 1935. By 1940, the Nankai Institute of Economics claimed to have revived its teaching and research activities to its prewar standard.

The war wrought many changes at Nankai. In many respects, the Institute in Chongqing differed significantly from its Tianjin phase. First, wartime conditions and the resultant economic hardship worked against Nankai's attempt to restore itself to its prewar strength as government service and employment in business remained the two most attractive career alternatives to many economists. Ho himself went on an extended leave to serve as director of the Agricultural Credit Administration until early 1941 when he was forced to resign and the organization was dissolved.[78] Fong, acting director of the Institute,

76. Holland to Alsberg, September 7, 1937, IPR Box 7 Holland Folder.
77. The Guiyang office was abolished in April 1939. Thereafter Fong moved his office to Chongqing, where the Nankai Institute of Economics was located.
78. For Ho's own account of his experience with the administration and events leading to its dissolution, see his "Reminiscences," pp. 194–284.

was simultaneously holding four positions.[79] Zhang Chunming, the third most senior member of the Institute, practically left the Institute for government service in 1937.[80] When the Institute presented a five-year proposal to the Rockefeller Foundation in early 1940, the Foundation's field officer found it necessary to raise a series of questions. Among them was whether the staff, Ho and Fong in particular, would commit themselves full-time to the Institute.[81] As the war drew to a close, the situation worsened. As postwar reconstruction became an item on the agenda and technical missions began to be sent abroad, the Nankai personnel were often drafted. In 1944, for instance, eleven out of the nineteen full-time staff were either in the United States on official missions or transferred to participate in government planning work for postwar reconstruction.[82]

Nevertheless, of the many changes that had manifested themselves in the activities of the Nankai Institute of Economics during the war, the most significant was its reversion to a research focus in macroeconomics and away from field studies. When research was resumed at the Institute after the disruption and confusion caused by the war had subsided, there was neither a central focus nor coordination. For a while, Ho considered organizing research around the central theme of the social and economic history of the Sino-Japanese war.[83] Yet the topic areas that eventually came to define the Institute's research program were economic development in the southwest, wartime inflation, and postwar economic reconstruction. Reverting to the earliest phase of Nankai's research, field investigation was primarily connected with the Institute's work on index numbers. A feeble attempt to conduct field investigations on certain agricultural products yielded few published results and was eventually discontinued upon the departure of the personnel from the

---

79. The four institutions Fong was affiliated with were: the Nankai Institute of Economics, the National Council for Rural Reconstruction, the Institute of Southwest Economic Development, and the National Central University.
80. He was first with the Executive Yuan and later the Henan provincial government.
81. I have not seen Balfour's letter to Fong about this matter, dated February 13, 1940. But I have seen Ho's, Fong's, and Zhang Boling's responses to it, dated respectively March 14, February 29, and February 29, RAC RG1.1 601.52.434.
82. "Nankai Institute of Economics, Nankai University: Twelfth Annual Report to the Rockefeller Foundation, July 1, 1943 to June 30, 1944," pp. 8–9, 11, RAC RG1.1 601.53.440.
83. "Semi-annual Report of Work of the Nankai Institute of Economics to the Rockefeller Foundation, July 1 to December 31, 1940," p. 3, RAC RG1.1 601.52.439. This title was misleading because it was in the impact rather than the war itself that the Institute was interested.

Institute.[84] Initially, economic development in the southwest received the most attention. Then it was wartime inflation. However, toward the end of the war, postwar economic reconstruction came to dominate the Institute's work.

Nankai's departure from its prewar emphasis on microeconomics manifested itself in its graduate training program as well. While the prewar program centered around cooperatives, land problems, and local government and finance, the majority of the students during the war years specialized in money and banking and international economics. As was the case with the prewar emphasis on rural reconstruction, the new focus on postwar economic reconstruction was portrayed by Nankai as serving the most urgent national needs. The wartime situation forced Nankai to redefine its development strategies, and thus its research agenda. However, its shift from a microeconomic focus to one in macro-economics also reflected changes that had occurred both within the Institute and outside it.

First was the attenuated influence of the Rockefeller Foundation. The war practically put an end to the Foundation's active role in rural reconstruction in China. The effort to continue the work in the southwest met with little success and was virtually suspended in early 1941. Gunn, who was much chagrined by the war that interrupted his program, was back at his Paris office. John B. Grant, Gunn's assistant and the real engineer of the China Program, was transferred to India. The supervision of the China Program and the entire social science program in China was devolved upon a reluctant Marshall Balfour, who would rather have concentrated on his duties as the field representative of the Foundation's International Health Division.

While the officers who were deeply committed to a social vision as it was embodied in the China Program were far removed from the scene, the Foundation furthermore adopted a policy of retrenchment, committing itself only to the "conservation" of key personnel in cooperating institutions and the consideration of grants on a yearly basis. These changes in the Foundation's funding policy and the personality of the officers had a significant impact on Nankai's development during the war. It is true that the stringent financial situation required Ho to seek additional support from other sources, such as government and business.

---

84. In 1944, while the project director, Ye Qianji, was in the United States on a government mission, the field investigators were transferred to work in government planning on postwar economic reconstruction.

At the same time, Ho was left alone to develop a research program as he pleased. No longer was there a force, whether emanating from New York or from Rockefeller field officers in China, that would pressure him into conforming to a particular social vision, research agenda, or methodology.

The new research focus reflected a reorganized Nankai faculty as well. Before the war, Nankai functioned basically with a two-tier system. As shown earlier, the majority of the senior faculty was never involved in field investigation. It was the junior researchers, the lower tier of the system, who went into the field. Fong and Zhang Chunming, as project supervisors, were the only members from the upper tier who had some contact with the Institute's field investigation. In a small and yet no less significant way, the Rockefeller policy during the war destroyed the lower tier within the Nankai system. The Foundation's "conservation" policy was designed to preserve only senior personnel. It is noteworthy that none of the seven junior researchers who formed the mainstay of the Nankai field investigation team before the war continued his service at the Institute during the war.[85]

Whether or not the Rockefeller policy during the war was in fact responsible for the demise of the lower tier, it is evident that the lower tier constituted an appendage to the Nankai system. The important role it played before the war was disproportionate to the minor status and weak numerical strength it represented within the system. While it played an important role for Nankai in the Rockefeller program, the rural and microeconomic focus it represented never represented the mainstream within the Nankai system.

From the very beginning, the Nankai enterprise had been interested in macroeconomics. Ho's work on index numbers and Fong's study of Tianjin industries were attempts to measure the extent and effect of industrialization in China. This national scope and macroeconomic focus were never abandoned; they were merely overshadowed by the Rockefeller intervention. In fact, toward the end of the period (1932–37) during which Nankai was supposedly turned rural-minded, topics in macroeconomics began to dominate the forum of the Institute. The heightened

---

85. I have not been able to locate their whereabouts during the war. Some of them may have remained in North China and not have moved to the southwest. While there is indication that Li Rui was in government service during the war, I have no information concerning the remaining six. The only other piece of information I have is about Feng Huade. After the war, he again worked for Ho at the latter's China Institute of Economics in Shanghai.

national crisis created by the ever-growing Japanese territorial ambitions in China prompted many Nankai faculty to discuss the national economy in terms of its capacity to withstand the war.

At the same time, Nankai's field investigators were becoming researchers *cum* petty bureaucrats, participating in the Rockefeller-funded social engineering project in Jining, Shandong. With their dislocation by the war of these field investigators, the Nankai forum was completely taken over by macroeconomists. While the Yanjing-trained Fei Xiaotong began to pick up on the theme of rural industries, the Nankai economists began making plans for the entire nation's postwar economic reconstruction.

As the war with Japan drew to a close, Ho was once again looking to the Rockefeller Foundation for support of his enterprise, which now included a new China Institute of Economics in Shanghai and the Nankai Institute of Economics at the nationalized Nankai University in Tianjin. No longer was he content with the tenuous relationship between research and practical application that his enterprise had hitherto assumed. His ambition now was to create a business- and policy-oriented enterprise that would render consultation service to the business community and would at the same time become a think tank – whether officially or not – for the government.

His new ambition was best illustrated by the relative importance that he attached to the China Institute of Economics and the Nankai Institute of Economics. While Ho and Fong continued to hold the positions of Director and Director of Research, respectively, of the Nankai Institute of Economics, both were on leave in Shanghai. The nationalization of Nankai called into question his future relationship with the Nankai Institute of Economics, particularly his freedom to organize the curriculum, to set the developmental plan, and to raise funds as he pleased.

His interest was clearly with the China Institute of Economics. Established in November 1946, the Institute was financed by the Jincheng Banking Corporation. In line with his long and strong ties with the business community, Ho was then serving as the executive director of the Jincheng Banking Corporation, in addition to being outside director of four corporations.[86] Reflecting the business interest in Shanghai, the most

---

86. They were: the Minsheng Industrial Corporation under Lu Zuofu; the Dacheng Cotton Textile, Spinning, and Weaving Corporation under Liu Guojun; the Tongcheng Corporation under Zhou Zuomin; and the Pacific Steamship Corporation under Dai Zimu.

important business metropolis in China, the Institute targeted the following two fields for research: the relation of government to business, as reflected in government policies toward currency, taxation, industry, labor, trade, and transportation; and international economic problems of China.[87]

Ho was ambitious and resourceful as ever, and the Chinese economy as a whole remained his focus. The return to a macroeconomic focus brought Nankai back to where it had started. The research focuses had of course changed. While it was index numbers and industrialization two decades earlier, it was now government regulations and international trade. Gone was the attention to rural industries and local government and finance that had so impressed the Rockefeller officers for their relevance to China's needs. There was no longer a Selskar Gunn or a John B. Grant on the scene to prod Ho with the magnitude of the problems in China's rural sector, which not too long earlier had prompted him to characterize the nation as a "land of economic medievalism."

Nankai's return to its original macroeconomic focus by no means cast doubt on the power of modern philanthropy, however. The opposite is true. That Nankai's empirical focus and its turn toward the countryside appeared spontaneous bears testimony to Ho's keen insight of and swift adjustment to the funding preferences of first the Institute of Pacific Relations and then the Rockefeller Foundation. It was the Rockefeller money that propelled Nankai to become the foremost center of economic research in China. By the same token, it was the Rockefeller officers, Selskar Gunn in particular, who helped determine the methodology and research agenda at Nankai. The retrenchment policy of the Rockefeller Foundation during the war admittedly reduced the Foundation's influence, as evidenced by Nankai's return to macroeconomics. Nankai faculty's role in the government and ties with the business sector – serving as think tank members and consultants – during and after the war indicated an attempt to diversify. These were, however, stopgap measures. As experienced as he was in having been a government official himself and in his long-term association with bankers and industrialists, Ho had no illusions about either the reliability of government funding or the philanthropic spirit and financial strength of the native business community. While relying on the Jincheng Banking Corpora-

---

87. "Application from the China Institute of Economics to the Rockefeller Foundation for an Endowment Fund to Its Building Program during the Year Beginning August 1, 1947," enclosure, Ho to Joseph Willits, June 14, 1947, RAC RG1.1 601.51.428.

tion for the support of his new China Institute of Economics, he was counting on the return of the Rockefeller Foundation and, particularly, on his astute calculation that the Foundation would naturally turn its attention to issues concerning reconstruction and international trade now that the war was over.

If it was a full circle, the two ends were, however, not destined to meet. The Communist victory brought an end to what Ho and his staff had aspired to achieve. After having served for two months as the president of the nationalized Nankai University, Ho left Tianjin in late November 1948 on the eve of the Communist takeover and sailed with his family for the United States, where he would teach at Columbia University until his retirement in 1961. H. D. Fong, the second in the Nankai duo, too, left China and joined the United Nations' Economic Commission for Asia and the Far East. Nankai University was to continue to exist, and so was the Nankai Institute of Economics – and a reputable one at that. In China after the Communist victory, however, there was no room for international patronage and no pressure to shape or to adjust to a particular methodology and research agenda. In place of American philanthropy stepped in the state. The pressure to conform increased and the room for maneuver became narrower. The era of international bargaining and enterprising individuals was gone and Franklin Ho's Nankai Institute of Economics was history.

6

Marxism, Revolution, and the Study of Chinese Society

MARXISM embodies an entirely different social vision than mainstream social sciences. While the Yanjing and Nankai social scientists tackled social change – whether effected through social service or social engineering, the Marxists operated with the notion of revolution. Like mainstream social sciences, however, Marxism was an import from the West. Before it could serve as the supreme guide for making revolution, Marxism first had to become a conceptual tool for understanding Chinese society. Parallel to the development of academic social sciences, Marxism in China evolved through stages. From the turn of the twentieth century till the eve of the founding of the Chinese Communist Party in 1921, Marxism was perceived simply as one of the many contending theories of nation-building from the West. The 1920s was a decade of experiment. Shanghai University, with its boldly proclaimed goal to equip its students with Marxist social science knowledge for making revolution, was a fascinating episode of radical infiltration into higher education. Then there was one man in the person of Mao Zedong who made a pioneering, solitary effort to study the Chinese peasants. It was not until the early 1930s, however, that Marxism in China found in Chen Hansheng's agrarian research group a social science enterprise that rivaled Yanjing and Nankai.

QU QIUBAI AND SHANGHAI UNIVERSITY

Shanghai University, founded in fall 1922, owed its origin to a group of student rebels who had taken over the administration of a poorly equipped and profit-oriented establishment.[1] During its brief existence,

---

1. Known as the Southeast Higher Normal School, the predecessor of Shanghai University purported to train students to become middle school teachers in the subjects of

Shanghai University aspired to foment revolution by disseminating social science knowledge. The history of the university epitomized the revolutionary fervor manifested in the first United Front between the Guomindang and Communist parties, with all its promises and contradictions.

For most of its existence, Shanghai University functioned as a "back-alley university," as the locals pejoratively called it. There was no auditorium, not even an entrance gate – an identification mark, as it were, of any respectable institution in China. It was a back-alley university even when it was briefly located in the International Settlement. An American left the following vivid description of the "campus" of Shanghai University:

> It was a jerry-built, two story Chinese house in Sz Ying Li [Shiying li], a lane off Seymour Road, which crossed busy Bubbling Well Road near the fabled well. The buildings and annexes occupied three sides of a paved yard about 25 feet square and accommodated almost a hundred students in packed classrooms and dangerously crowded dormitories.[2]

The situation was worse when the university was forced out of the International Settlement and moved back to an alley near its original location. The surroundings were even less inviting: crowded, dirty, and noisy. In a playful, if self-pitying, stanza, Xiao Chunü,[3] a teacher in the sociology department who was killed during the 1927 anti-Communist purge in Canton, thus described the neighborhood:

> In the morning, we listen to the clinking
> of chamber pots [as they were being emptied by the honey wagon crew];
> In the afternoon, we watch the flies dance.[4]

The university eventually purchased a permanent site and construction was completed in spring 1927. However, only weeks after the university

Chinese, English, and drawing. See Huang Meizhen, et al., eds., *Shanghai daxue shiliao* (Historical Materials on Shanghai University), (Shanghai, 1984), p. 37.
2. Percy Finch, *Shanghai and Beyond* (New York, 1953), p. 112.
3. Donald Klein & Anne Clark, eds., *Biographic Dictionary of Chinese Communism, 1921–1965*, pp. 327–8.
4. [Wang Jiagui], "Yang Hansheng tongzhi tan ershi niandai de Shanghai daxue," (Comrade Yang Hansheng's Reminiscences of Shanghai University during the 1920s), *Shehui* (Society), No. 3 (June 1984), p. 4.

moved to its new campus, a purge occurred and the university was closed down. In January 1932, when the Japanese military attacked Shanghai, the campus was destroyed by aerial bombardment.[5]

Myth shrouds the popular image of Shanghai University, created as much in contemporary accounts as in later reminiscences. It is clear, however, that brief as its institutional life-span was, Shanghai University defies simple characterization. Having been swept into the vortex of revolution, the history of Shanghai University reflected the twists and turns of revolutionary politics of the day. In *Alienated Academy: Culture and Politics in Republican China, 1919–1937*, Wen-hsin Yeh presents a portrayal of Shanghai University that suggests a disjunction between academic objectives and revolutionary passion and a process in which radical students subverted its intellectual agenda to the extent that they hijacked the institution.[6] The discussion below will argue that this picture is flawed in two respects. First, it was not so much a disjunction as a displacement of the intellectual agenda by revolutionary passion, for the framer of this intellectual agenda – Qu Qiubai, future secretary general of the Chinese Communist Party – himself underwent the last phase of his ideological transformation during his tenure at Shanghai University. Qu's intellectual agenda for the university and student political activism were not as inherently contradictory as Yeh's juxtaposition of ideals and reality made them to be. Student activism was not, as Yeh alleges, subversive of Qu's vision and intellectual agenda for the university.[7] Second, the trajectory of Shanghai University's turn toward radicalism represented not so much a subversion as a larger power struggle between the Nationalist and Communist parties whose troubled alliance ruptured right at the time when the university was closed down by the Nationalist Party. That "[d]espite Guomindang connections of the university," radicals and revolutionaries "captured a critical following among the students" and came to "assert a major influence over them all" was no surprise. Nor was it unusual that there should exist a polarity between the official Guomindang papers' "muffled tone and terse treatment of the last days of the university" and the leftist lionization of the University for its contributions to the national salvation movement.[8] The fact

---

5. It is the building in the International Settlement that ironically survived. In 1980, the Shanghai city government proclaimed this building a historical landmark.
6. Wen-hsin Yeh, *The Alienated Academy: Culture and Politics in Republican China* (Harvard, 1990), pp. 129–65.
7. Ibid., pp. 138, 162.   8. Ibid., p. 164.

was that the Guomindang lost out in its struggles against the Communists over the control of Shanghai University that the two parties had collaborated.

Because Shanghai University was founded as the United Front policy began, many Communist Party members and sympathizers joined its administration and faculty. Among them, the most celebrated was Qu Qiubai, who arrived in summer 1923 to organize the sociology department. Qu had a grand vision for Shanghai University and its sociology department, which he spelled out in a prospectus written in July.[9] This prospectus reflected more of the May Fourth spirit than that of a Communist, which Qu had become in 1922 while in Moscow. The departmental formats and the curricula he proposed were fairly standard and were the same as those adopted by other universities in China either at the time or later.[10]

Furthermore, of the two major tasks that he called upon the university to undertake, solid social science research and the creation of new literature and arts, the latter was a familiar battle cry of the May Fourth era. Given Qu's recent conversion to Marxism, it is noteworthy that his point of departure in this respect was none other than the "literary revolution" that Hu Shi and Chen Duxiu had initiated in 1917. Qu attributed the phenomenal success of the "literary revolution" to its role in fulfilling the needs of the modernizing Chinese society, for example, the use of the vernacular, the emancipation of the individual, and making knowledge relevant to the masses. Consistent with the attitude of the May Fourth era, Qu affirmed the beneficial effect of Western influence. Far from portending the eventual demise of China's tradition and culture, he argued that Western influence on modern Chinese literature and arts on the contrary signified the renaissance of the Chinese culture and the birth of China's new cultural life.

Such May Fourth rhetoric shows that Qu had not yet completely converted to Marxism.[11] It appears that Qu began to move toward a

---

9. The following citations in this section, unless otherwise noted, are based on Qu Qiubai, "Xiandai Zhongguo suo dangyou de 'Shanghai daxue'" (A "Shanghai University" that Contemporary China Should Have), *Shanghai daxue shiliao*, pp. 1–13.
10. In Qu's prospectus, all the departments of the full-grown university in the future would be subsumed under two major divisions: the College of the Social Sciences and the College of Literature and Arts.
11. For a study that traces and analyzes the development of Qu's literary thought, see Paul Pickowicz, *Marxist Literary Thought in China: The Influence of Ch'ü Ch'iu-pai* (Berkeley, 1981).

139

Marxist stand only as he began his dual career, simultaneously teaching at Shanghai University and editing journals for the Chinese Communist Party. His prospectus for Shanghai University was thus a vestige of his May Fourth phase.[12] Indeed, so orthodox is this prospectus that one could hardly discern any element in it that could be construed as Marxist. It is true that he mentioned Soviet sociology and proclaimed that it occupied a unique place in world scholarship. Yet this pronouncement was made in the context in which he discussed the coming of age of sociology as a discipline sui generis. Qu viewed the development of a scholarly discipline as a cumulative process toward system-building and scientific refinement. He believed that sociology, as a young science, had won its war of independence from the influence of the organicist school of biology toward the end of the nineteenth century. Then it had to fight against other social sciences, particularly social psychology, in order to carve out a distinct realm of inquiry of its own. The real breakthrough, according to Qu, occurred during the years after the First World War, when Soviet and German scholars, building on the systematic tradition of the continental philosophy, created a scientific system of sociology.

Conspicuously absent in Qu's discussion of the rise of "scientific," that is, Soviet, sociology is any reference to its underlying radical ideology. Nowhere in his terse discussion did he reveal an awareness of the ideological chasm that set the nascent Soviet sociology apart from its Western counterpart. He was, however, not completely oblivious to the differences between these two sociological schools. While in Moscow, he had more than likely read Nikolai Bukharin's 1921 treatise, *Historical Materialism: A System of Sociology*, which expounded a Marxist sociology as opposed to "bourgeois sociology."[13] However profound his understanding of the differences between these two discourses was, he viewed them as two consecutive stages in a lineal development of sociology.

While Qu Qiubai had become a devoted Communist by 1923, he was nonetheless too much a participant as well as a product of the May Fourth New Culture Movement to have forsaken many of the assumptions, aspirations, and, indeed, friendships that he shared with intellectual leaders of his generation. The collapse of the May Fourth consensus

12. As Ellen Widmer has pointed out, Qu had never completely shed his May Fourth beliefs. See her "Qu Qiubai and Russian literature," in Merle Goldman, ed., *Modern Chinese Literature in the May Fourth Era* (Harvard, 1977), pp. 103–25.
13. Stephen Cohen, *Bukharin and the Bolshevik Revolution: A Political Biography, 1888–1938* (New York, 1974), pp. 107–22.

and the resultant split among its major leaders had yet to become irreparable.[14] For the time being, neither Qu's new political belief nor the larger societal events had forced his two worlds to collide with each other.

He continued to be friendly with Hu Shi, the then undisputed leader of the May Fourth New Culture Movement, seeking his advice and, perhaps, even approval. In fact, prior to his arrival at Shanghai University, he had followed Hu's advice and applied for a job with the Commercial Press. And he found it necessary to explain to Hu his reason for turning down the Commercial Press's offer to hire him as a translator and editor.[15] Indeed, there was little in Qu's vision of Shanghai University of which Hu would not have approved. In his discussion of both the sociology department and the literature department, Qu stressed the necessity of employing modern scholarship to study the national legacy, a crusade Hu Shi personally began in 1919, which not only was to become his life-long obsession, but to spawn a viable movement during the 1920s.[16] Despite his new political faith, Qu found himself much in agreement with Hu Shi. As he put it to Hu in 1923, he hoped Shanghai University would become "the center of the New Culture Movement in the South,"[17] a clear homage to Peking University as the citadel of the New Culture Movement and a tribute to Hu for his leadership role in the latter.

Friendship or shared aspiration notwithstanding, radical ideology and political activism soon steered both Qu Qiubai and Shanghai University away from the liberal model of the May Fourth era. A case in point here was their choice of texts. Qu Qiubai, for example, chose to rely upon Soviet writings for his lectures on "Sociology" and "Social Philosophy," a radical departure from the common practice of using American textbooks in other universities in China at the time. His *Modern Sociology* (*Xiandai shehuixue*) and *Introduction to the Social Sciences* (*Shehui kexue gailun*), both published in 1924 and presumably representing his class lectures, were based on Bukharin's *Historical Materialism: A System of Sociology*.

14. Although Chow Tse-tsung traces the split to the debate on "Problems and Isms" between Hu Shi and Li Dazhao in 1919, he also points out that the real challenge, that is, from Marxism to the basic May Fourth assumptions, did not come until the middle of the 1920s. See his *The May Fourth Movement*, pp. 215–313.

15. Qu Qiubai to Hu Shi, July 30, 1923, in *Hu Shi laiwang shuxin xuan*, Vol. 1, p. 214.

16. Chow, *The May Fourth Movement*, pp. 314–20. See also Laurence Schneider, *Ku Chieh-kang and China's New History* (Berkeley, 1971).

17. Qu to Hu, July 30, 1923, *Hu Shi laiwang shuxin xuan*, Vol. 1, p. 214.

A pattern emerged. Qu's use of Marxist texts in classroom instruction represented the norm at the sociology department, which became the largest and most popular at Shanghai University.[18] The orthodox curriculum that Qu had designed belied an unorthodox education. Among the founding members of the department, Cai Hesen, for example, made his course on "History of Social Evolution" a forum on Friedrich Engels's *The Origin of the Family, Private Property, and the State* (1884) and *Socialism: Utopian and Scientific* (1880). Later arrivals to the faculty continued this trend. Thus, Zhang Tailei expounded Lenin's *Imperialism: The Highest Stage of Capitalism* (1917) in his course on political science.

The most sophisticated among these later arrivals was Li Ji. After his graduation from Peking University in 1918, Li Ji moved from one temporary job to another, including a one-semester stint teaching English at the preparatory section of Peking University, manager of a cram school for English in Peking, and English secretary at the Zhongxing Coal Mine Co. in Shandong.[19] He left China in 1921, intending to study in England, but ended up studying political economy at the University of Frankfurt in 1922.[20] A year later, after having decided that his professors were all biased toward a bourgeois viewpoint, he withdrew from the university and studied on his own. During the remainder of his sojourn in Germany, he completed an intellectual biography of Marx, entitled *A Biography of Marx* (*Makesi zhuan*). In addition, he translated the popular edition of *Das Kapital* edited and arranged by Julian Borchardt, which he published as *Das Kapital: An Easy Reader* (*Tongsu ziben lun*).[21] After his return from Germany in 1925, he reportedly became the chair of the sociology department.[22] Li Ji used both books in his teaching.

---

18. The discussion in this and the following paragraph is based on *Shanghai daxue shiliao*, pp. 88–92, and [Wang Jiagui], "Yang Hansheng tongzhi tan ershi niandai de Shanghai daxue," p. 1.
19. Li Ji, *Wo de shengping* (My Life) (Shanghai 1932), pp. 165–316.
20. Like many other Chinese at the time, Li Ji was stretching his Chinese dollars by taking advantage of the low Deutsche mark, which hit its all time low in early 1923.
21. The Borchardt edition is entitled *Das Kapital: Kritik der politischen Oekonomie; Gemeinverstandliche Ausgabe*, published in 1919 and appearing in English in 1921 as *The People's Marx*. Both *A Biography of Marx* and *Das Kapital: An Easy Reader* were published in 1926 and reissued later in 1929 and 1930, respectively.
22. Ikeda Kō, tr., Li Ji, "Shina shakai no hatten dankai, I," *Tōa* (East Asia), 7.1–3 (January–March, 1934), quoted in Tai Kuo-hui, "Chūgoku 'shakaishi ronsen' shōkai ni miraleru jakkan no mondai" (Some Problems Embedded in [Japanese] Surveys of "the Social History Debate" in China), *Ajia Keizai*, 13.1 (January 1972), p. 61.

Every student of the department is said to have had a copy of both books.[23]

Their practice of adhering exclusively to Marxist texts and ideology in classroom instruction went beyond the core curriculum of the department. "Philosophy," for example, was devoted to elucidating dialectical materialism. Even "English" was devoted to solidifying students' appreciation of Marxism; the course was reportedly to have used a text entitled *Evolution and Revolution: Darwin and Marx.*[24]

The systematic dissemination of Marxist ideology could not have failed to attract the attention of the authorities of the International Settlement, where the university was relocated in February 1924, after it had outgrown its original premises. Before long, Shanghai University was regarded by the police authorities at the Shanghai International Municipal Council as the headquarters of the Chinese Bolsheviks. The police gathered intelligence reports and compiled dossiers on the faculty, whom they believed to be mostly Communists.[25]

Shanghai University's difficulties with the authorities of the International Settlement were compounded by the "extracurricular" political activities engaged by its students. Nevertheless, students' involvement in street demonstrations and organization among workers and the urban poor, though irksome in the eyes of the authorities, was in itself not perceived as particularly dangerous. After all, during those years of heightened tension and growing politicization, it was common for students in major coastal cities to set up free night schools for workers, launch welfare programs for the urban poor, and take to the street to protest imperialism as well as warlordism.

Yet the authorities of the Shanghai International Municipal Council reacted in a particularly brutal and intolerant way against Shanghai University. On December 9, 1924, police raided the university and seized books, magazines, and various other publications. And on June 4, 1925, as demonstrations and general strikes were spreading in the wake of the May Thirtieth Incident, the authorities once again raided the university premises. This time, British and American marines evicted by force students and faculty as well as furniture and all personal belongings.[26]

The authorities were determined to push Shanghai University out of

---

23. *Shanghai daxue shiliao*, p. 90.
24. I have not been able to identify this title or its author.
25. Chen Tiejian, *Qu Qiubai zhuan* (A Biography of Qu Qiubai) (Shanghai, 1986), p. 212.
26. *Shanghai daxue shiliao*, pp. 22–8.

the International Settlement. Student activism was bad enough, but worse was its "Bolshevik" faculty; the combination of the two was deadly in the eyes of the authorities. They were convinced that the majority of some three hundred students were true believers of communism. The scenario, if allowed to unfold by itself, would be the creation of a large corps of well-trained propagandists for communism.[27] The decision was therefore to clear Shanghai University out of the International Settlement.

The authorities of the International Settlement were not alone in perceiving Shanghai University as a Bolshevik haven. Many within the Guomindang concurred. Because the university was an experiment under the United Front policy marred with tensions and conflicts,[28] the university became a major arena of the power struggle between the Guomindang and the Communist parties. At the reorganization of the university in fall 1922, Yu Youren, the veteran and left-wing Guomindang member, was chosen as president. His role, however, was largely ceremonial. University affairs were conducted by an administrative committee.[29] Both Communists and Guomindang members were represented on this committee.[30] Polarization developed primarily between the chair of the sociology department, Qu Qiubai, and that of the English department, He Shizhen (J.D., Michigan, 1923).

The political situation at Shanghai University was merely a microcosm of the larger power struggle in the city of Shanghai. He Shizhen, in addition to being the chair of the English department and the academic dean of the university, was at the same time secretary of the Guomindang's youth and women's department in Shanghai.[31] Staunchly anti-Communist, He struggled against the Communists at the Guomindang's Shanghai bureau. Among the latter were Mao Zedong, secretary of the organization department, Yun Daiying,[32] secretary of the propa-

27. Chen Tiejian, *Qu Qiubai zhuan*, p. 212.
28. Li Yun-han, *Cong ronggong dao qingdang* (From Admitting the Communists to the Purification of the Guomindang) (Taipei, 1966), 2 vols.
29. It consisted of the president, the academic dean, the administrative dean, department chairs, and four elected members from the faculty and the administrative staff. *Shanghai daxue shiliao*, pp. 48–50.
30. Among those elected to the Committee in late 1923, Yu Youren and He Shizhen were Guomindang members, while Deng Zhongxia, Qu Qiubai, and Shao Lizi, Communists.
31. The discussion in this and the following three paragraphs is based on Li Yun-han, *Cong rongGong dao qingdang*, Ch. 5; Chen Tiejian, *Qu Qiubai zhuan*, pp. 210–11; and [Wang Jiagui], "Yang Hansheng tongzhi tan ershi niandai de Shanghai daxue," p. 3.
32. Klein & Clark, eds., *Biographic Dictionary of Chinese Communism, 1921–1965* (Harvard, 1971), pp. 1026–9.

ganda department, and Shao Lizi,[33] secretary of the workers and farmers department. The disputes and conflicts became so acrimonious that in early August 1924 for two days in a row, militant anti-Communist members twice physically assaulted Communist members. In the second incident, they soundly beat Shao Lizi at the party's Shanghai bureau.

The violent struggle for control was amply displayed on the Shanghai University campus as well. As Qu Qiubai and He Shizhen came to personify the two factions on campus, the struggle took on the appearance of collective confrontations between the sociology department and the English department. The esprit de corps of the sociology department, as manifested in its faculty composition and Marxist teaching, of course, fit in perfectly with this perception. The English department, on the other hand, did not constitute a solid ideological block comparable to that of the sociology department. He Shizhen aside, Zhou Songxi, who taught English to non-majors, seems to have been the only other active member of the anti-Communist faction from the English department. In fact, membership cut across departmental lines for either faction.[34]

Nor was the conflict confined to the faculty and the administration. One former student recalled frequent clashes on campus. Violence escalated until it culminated in a tragic event at the Double Ten celebration on October 10, 1924. The organizer of the festivity was the anti-Communist faction, who reportedly had anticipated problems with the Communists and had swelled their ranks with thugs. When it appeared that the Communists were trying to turn the event into a rally for anti-warlord and anti-imperialist agitation, the thugs struck. In the melee, two students were thrown off the platform seven feet above the ground.

Violence intensified antagonism and hatred on both sides. Perhaps as an effort to reduce tension, both Qu Qiubai and He Shizhen resigned from the university. But judging from the unabated student activism and raids of the campus by the police and marines of the International Settlement, the Guomindang had clearly lost its battle over the control of

---

33. He was to revert to the Guomindang side in a year or two and eventually to become a trusted man of Chiang Kai-shek. Howard Boorman, ed., *Biographic Dictionary of Republican China* (Columbia, 1970), III, pp. 91–3. Note that the entry dates his reversion earlier than my estimate here.

34. For instance, among the anticommunists, Chen Dezheng was director of the high school division. Cheng Yongyan, one of the student rebels who helped bring about the founding of the university in 1922, was on the administrative staff.

the university. In April 1927, in the midst of the bloody purge of the Communists, Shanghai University was occupied and shut down by the Guomindang forces.

Thus was the end of the institutional life of Shanghai University, four and a half years after its founding. Not only was the life-span of the university short, but there were few legacies of it to speak of. Among them, the most celebrated was undoubtedly student activism, which was most tellingly attested to by police suppression. Equally significant was that of the organizational work of the Communist Party. More difficult to gauge was the extent to which student activism was driven by Marxist ideology, to which contemporary accounts, police reports included, and later reminiscences provided suggestive information but little concrete proof. While Marxist ideology provided students with arguments to explain China's problems, the highly charged political environment and the organizational power of the Communist Party may have been the more potent factors that roused students to activism.

What then was the legacy of the sociology department? Although social science research was one of the two major goals that Qu Qiubai envisioned for the university, he never elaborated on the methodology or research programs that the sociology department might have adopted. Nor is there any information concerning how his notion of social science research changed once he came to embrace Soviet sociology.

What little is known about the activities of the department consists of visits to factories and villages.[35] These visits in themselves were not at all extraordinary; both government and Christian colleges practiced these both earlier and more systematically.[36] Even the department's extension work, such as a free evening school for workers,[37] differed not much from those provided by Christian colleges and could only have been less stable owing to its meager resources. There was nevertheless one significant difference: the special messages the department wished to impart to the workers in its evening school. Whereas the Christian colleges envisioned nothing more than social service of an ameliorative nature, the department wanted nothing less than to rouse the workers to take part in revolution.

This picture of the sociology department is admittedly skewed; later

---

35. *Shanghai daxue shiliao*, p. 94.
36. Hayford, *To the People*, pp. 35–9.
37. [Wang Jiagui], "Yang Hansheng tongzhi tan ershi niandai de Shanghai daxue," p. 2.

reminiscences on Shanghai University focused on its contribution to revolutionary struggles. It does appear, however, that the department was so preoccupied by attempts to raise the consciousness of workers and students, to organize the urban masses, and to make revolution that social science research was all but forgotten.

There is, however, no reason to believe that making revolution and advancing science had to be mutually exclusive, especially considering the Marxist claims that revolution is a science, and science an agent for revolution. Shanghai University failed to engage in social science research because it had no clear notion of what social science research was. It is significant that neither in Qu Qiubai's prospectus nor in the department's slightly expanded version of the curriculum was "Social Survey" or "Field Work" listed as either a required or elective course.[38] In other words, there was nothing on the curriculum that would require students to apply in real social situations the theories they had learned in the classroom. Even "Institutional Visitation" was not listed as a course. The visits to factories and villages reported by former students were thus "extracurricular" activities organized on the personal initiative of individual faculty.

The theoretical orientation of the sociology department is not at all surprising; empirical social research, Marxist or otherwise, had not yet become an established or respected line of academic pursuit in any Chinese institution at the time. What was surprising was that there was no influence on the sociology department from Qu Qiubai's one-year stint with the YMCA-sponsored Peking Students' Social Service Club from 1919 to 1920.[39] Granted that the Club's social vision would have seemed conservative, if not downright reactionary, to Qu after his conversion to Marxism, but the Club's goal to gather data from the field should have remained relevant and valid for him.

One important reason has to do with Qu Qiubai's role at the Club. As an editor for the Club's magazine, the *New Society*, he must have had only limited exposure to and, possibly, no involvement at all in the Club's activities in community services and social surveys. As a quick perusal of its content would readily indicate, the magazine served more as a platform for philosophical expositions on social reforms than as an outlet for survey results. His essays in the magazine were all written in the same spirit that permeated the May Fourth literature in their call for enlight-

---

38. *Shanghai daxue shiliao*, pp. 5–7, 59–60.
39. Qu Qiubai's involvement with the Club is discussed in Chapter 2.

enment, humanitarianism, and the liberation of the individual from the fetters of tradition.[40] His association with the Club was his participation in the May Fourth Movement and not in the least in empirical social research.

Equally important was the notion of Marxism as *the* science of society; it was supposed to have unraveled the logic behind the past history of mankind and to have predicted the future course of all societies. As such, Marxism was a supreme guide for making revolution. The curriculum at Shanghai University represented an attempt to transmit the universal truth of Marxism without making a corresponding effort to study Chinese conditions. The whole episode epitomized the major thrust of the early Chinese Communist movement in its preoccupation with organization and mobilization work while all but ignoring the need to gain a thorough understanding of the situation in China. There was as yet no awareness of how a correct understanding of society was a prerequisite for making revolution.

This theoretical tendency aside, the politically-repressive environment of the Republican period was not conducive to the rise of empirical Marxist social sciences. Many Chinese Marxists during the 1920s operated clandestinely on the fringes of academia, eking out a living on honoraria for essays or books they managed to publish and on incomes from unstable teaching positions at financially-precarious institutions. The genesis of a Marxist social science enterprise in the early 1930s, the focus of the next chapter, represented a breakthrough by a group of Marxists in gaining access to an institutional base and funding. Before this extraordinary chapter of the development of Marxist social sciences unfolded itself, one man with no academic social science training launched a solitary effort to understand the surging revolutionary forces in rural China.

MAO ZEDONG AND HIS AGRARIAN SURVEYS

Mao Zedong's much celebrated 1927 "Report on an Investigation of the Peasant Movement in Hunan" grew out of one of the first attempts ever made by Chinese Communists to collect information about the social environment of their organization and mobilization work.[41] Mao's crude

40. For a brief summary of the articles he published during this period, see Chen Tiejian, *Qu Qiubai zhuan*, pp. 72–91.
41. Peng Pai was the pioneer in this respect, as was he in the peasant movement. The Guangdong Provincial Peasant Association that he organized from his Haifeng core established a research department in 1923.

attempt at fact-finding would continue to absorb his interest until the 1960s. Most significant, the style that Mao had developed from his survey work would become the model for social inquiries in the People's Republic of China.

Mao did not intuitively grasp the revolutionary potential of the peasants. Like many of his contemporaries who were profoundly influenced by the May Fourth Movement, he began his work in disseminating new culture among the educated in the capital city of his native Hunan province. After his conversion to Marxism around 1920 and especially after the founding of the Communist Party, organization work among urban labor consumed his time and energy until an arrest warrant forced him to flee Hunan in 1923. As the United Front policy commenced the same year, he worked as secretary of the organization department at the Guomindang Party's Shanghai bureau.[42]

Mao discovered the peasants during more than half a year of extended "sick" leave spent in his home village in Shaoshan in 1925.[43] While there, he noticed the burgeoning peasant movement in Hunan. Its impetus came from neighboring Guangdong province; Peng Pai had organized a peasant movement there that was sanctioned by the Guomindang government in Canton.[44] Hunan peasants' struggles for rent and interest reductions were further roused by the widespread nationalistic agitations in the wake of the May Thirtieth Incident of 1925. The astute Mao quickly set out to help organize peasant associations until an arrest warrant forced him to Canton in June 1925.

In Canton, Mao served in the propaganda department of the Guomindang and as an editor of the party's *Political Weekly*. Most significant was his role in the Peasant Movement Training Institute; he served as principal for its sixth session from May to October 1926. He introduced two innovations to the Institute's curriculum. The first was a two-week field trip in September, Mao's version of "Institutional Visitation," to Haifeng to observe Peng Pai's peasant movement. The second innovation was to use students as informants-*cum*-researchers.[45] He had the

---

42. Stuart Schram, *Mao Tse-tung*, pp. 41–62; see also Ross Terrill, *Mao: A Biography* (New York, 1980), pp. 59–68.

43. Schram, *Mao Tse-tung*, pp. 69–74.

44. Fernando Galbiati, *P'eng P'ai and the Hai-Lu-Feng Soviet* (Stanford, 1985), pp. 173–202.

45. Mao Zedong, "Guomin geming yu nongmin yundong: Nongmin wenti congkan xu" (National Revolution and the Peasant Movement: A Preface to the *Series of Peasant Problems*), Takeuchi Minoru, ed., *Mao Zedong ji* (The Collected Works of Mao

three hundred-odd students organize themselves according to their places of origin into thirteen separate peasant question study groups. Each of these study groups was instructed to discuss and present on the basis of the members' personal knowledge the agrarian conditions in the province under its charge. The information collected was published by Mao in his *Series of Peasant Problems* in fall 1926. Crude as this method was, the use of students as informants as well as researchers was a practice commonly utilized by both Chinese and Western researchers in the late 1910s and early 1920s. J. Lossing Buck justified this practice by pleading that the field was vast and trained researchers nonexistent. But Mao singularly remained unapologetic about the fact that he never attempted to corroborate his data by field work.

Mao returned to Hunan in late November 1926,[46] after concluding the sixth session of the Peasant Institute over a month earlier. In December, he addressed the First Peasant Congress of Hunan in Changsha. The peasant movement had flourished in Hunan after the Northern Expedition army took the province in August. In eastern Hunan, particularly Changsha and its neighboring counties, newly organized peasant associations virtually ruled the countryside. On January 4, 1927, Mao embarked on his thirty-two-day tour of the five counties in this region. Out of this tour came his much celebrated report on the peasant movement in Hunan.[47]

The document was above all a status report, a buoyant portrayal of the revolutionary fervor of the peasants who in Mao's view had achieved in months what the revolutionaries could not in "forty years,"[48] and who would soon "break all trammels that now bind them and rush forward along the road to liberation."[49] It was a passionate plea on behalf of the peasants for complete freedom of action.[50]

Zedong) (Tokyo, 1972), I, pp. 177–8; and "Diliu jie nongmin yundong jiangxisuo banli jingguo" (The Sixth Session of the Peasant Movement Training Institute), *Diyi ci guonei geming zhanzheng shiqi de nongmin yundong ziliao* (Source Materials on the Peasant Movement during the Period of the First Revolutionary Civil War) (Beijing, 1983), pp. 67–74.

46. His article, "Hunan de nongmin" (The Peasants in Hunan), *Mao Zedong ji*, I, pp. 187–200, was dated November 30 from Changsha.
47. These five counties are: Xiangtan, Xiangxiang, Hengshan, Liling, and Changsha.
48. A phrase taken from Sun Yat-sen's "Testimony" that claimed that he had devoted himself to the cause of revolution for forty years.
49. Mao Zedong, "Report of an Investigation into the Peasant Movement in Hunan," *Selected Works of Mao Tse-tung* (New York, 1954), Vol. 1, p. 22.
50. Benjamin Schwartz, *Chinese Communism and the Rise of Mao*, p. 74.

Mao's Hunan report was not a field report. He never had the opportunity to work on his data. Shortly after his return from the field, he became involved in the committee work on the sticky issue of land reform for the left-wing Wuhan government. Chiang Kai-shek's rupture with the Wuhan government in July ushered in a period of conspiracies in armed revolts, which ended in defeat and in Mao's retreat to the Jinggang mountains on the border between Hunan and Jiangxi in fall 1927.[51] His field data were left behind at home with his wife, Yang Kaihui, and presumed lost when she was arrested and executed in 1930.

It is thus impossible to find out what kind of data Mao had collected from his first field work (might the data remain locked up somewhere at the Bureau of Investigation and Bureau of Intelligence in Taipei?). Fortunately, the period from his retreat to the Jinggang mountains and the subsequent move to southern Jiangxi witnessed a spurt of survey activities by Mao. Of these surveys, the Jinggang mountains data, on the Ninggang and Yongxin counties, were lost when the base fell in early 1929. But the rest survive and were later put together and distributed to the cadres by Mao himself.[52] Though much has been lost, thanks to the reflective bent and prolific pen of Mao, enough has been salvaged to reveal his survey style and philosophy.

Mao believed that he knew the field. His approach to field work was to organize multisession group interviews, or what he called "investigation meetings" (*diaocha hui*). Depending on the ability of the interviewer to lead the session discussions, he recommended that the minimum of three or five to the maximum of a dozen or two informants be recruited for the interviews. Only persons with thorough knowledge about the social and economic conditions of the locality were qualified to be informants. Old informants were the best because, as Mao pointed out, they had seen it all – the past as well as the present. But young men with experience in class struggle were needed as well because they were progressive and observant. They could be workers, peasants, merchants, intellectuals, soldiers, or even thugs. The group interviews, Mao insisted, had to be personally presided over by the "field worker" who should

---

51. Schram, *Mao Tse-tung*, pp. 89–113.
52. The collection was published in 1937 and again in 1941 under the title, *Nongcun diaocha* (Agrarian Surveys). The edition I use here has a new title and includes some essays that had not been published before: *Mao Zedong nongcun diaocha wenji* (A Collection of Mao Zedong's Agrarian Investigation Essays) (Beijing, 1982).

solicit answers, through debate when in doubt, to the questions he had previously prepared.[53]

Here Mao was speaking from his experience. The only deviation was that his informant pools were much narrower than his recommendations suggested; he seems to have relied heavily on local cadres as his informants. For example, the informants who participated in the group fact-finding sessions for his Hunan and Jinggang mountains surveys were all middle-ranking cadres in the counties involved.[54] He never made much effort to reach beyond cadres for informants. One notable exception was his 1930 Xunwu survey, the most comprehensive he had ever taken.[55] Located in the southeastern corner of Jiangxi, Xunwu was the only county seat in which Mao had the opportunity to try his hands. As he was not familiar with the ways business operated, Mao was eager for knowledgeable informants. But even so, only one merchant was present in his interview sessions out of his eleven predominantly cadre informants.[56]

The Xunwu survey represented the best of Mao's efforts.[57] It was, as with all his other surveys, descriptive. The main body of the survey consisted of three major sections: the business community (at the county seat), previous land relations, and land reform.[58] The business section began with a nice summary description of the flow of goods between Xunwu and its neighboring counties. It then gave a useful list of major market places in the county and their main trading items. The bulk of the section was an inventory of the business community by trade, often with bits of biographical data on the shopkeepers. It was here that Mao made good use of his merchant informant, whose line of business, grocery, was the dominant trade at the county seats. As the survey cen-

---

53. Ibid., pp. 9–10.   54. Ibid., p. 16.
55. Another exception was his Xingguo survey, which was taken about half a year later than the Xunwu survey. All eight informants in this case were poor peasants, though some among them were party members. But this represented an extreme case. Ibid., pp. 182–98.
56. The eleven informants included one former president of local Chamber of Commerce, three middle-ranking cadres – one of whom had been a county clerk in charge of land tax collection, five low-ranking cadres, and two former elementary school teachers. See ibid., pp. 41–2.
57. Roger Thompson has translated the Xunwu survey with a perceptive, if also somewhat glowing, account of its significance as an ethnography and revolution text. See his *Report from Xunwu* (Stanford, 1990).
58. The discussion in this and the following two paragraphs is based on Mao Zedong, "Xunwu diaocha" (The Xunwu investigation), ibid., pp. 41– 181.

tered around the county seats, this section ended with a population profile as well as short profiles of major landlords in the town.

The section on old land relations provided detailed descriptions of landholding patterns. It separated landlords into two distinct categories: corporate landlords (*gonggong dizhu*) and individual landlords (*geren dizhu*). The corporate landlords owned 40% of the land: lineages (24%), temples (8%), education (4%) or public works (4%). The individual landlords – big, middle, and small – owned 30% of the land. The survey provided miniprofiles of the big and middle landlords by regions. Then after a cursory discussion of the rich and the poor peasants, the survey resumed with detailed descriptions of exploitations through rent, usury, taxes, and various contributions.

The last section on land reform was the weakest of the survey. Mao made no attempt to evaluate the implementation and impact of the land reform. It contained in effect his random notes on local problems and their resolution as well as local variations or approaches to land reform policies.

This brief spurt of survey activities was a testimony to Mao's willpower and sense of purpose, particularly considering the adverse conditions under which he conducted his group fact-finding sessions. As an extreme example, the Xingguo survey was taken in late October 1930 while Mao was in retreat from Changsha in the wake of the disastrous multicity attack strategy and was abruptly concluded when the pursuing enemy caught up with him.[59] Equally impressive was his ability to organize and improvise, considering the fact that he had no training in survey techniques. Whether or not he had read any handbooks or published survey results is not known. But the fact remains that he was a versatile survey worker; in addition to his larger surveys, he attempted some in-depth analyses as well, such as the budget analysis in his 1926 "The Livelihood of a Typical Chinese Tenant" and a quasi life-history method, crude as his was, in his profiles of eight tenant families in his Xingguo survey.[60]

Despite his exhortation to the cadres to analyze the field from the Marxist viewpoint, Mao's own surveys lacked a clearly articulated Marxist framework. Like other early researchers, he had to stumble along, improvise, and learn from mistakes. For many years, his class analysis of Chinese society was based on the same conventional cate-

---

59. Ibid., pp. 182–3. For a discussion of the development that led to the adoption of this adventurous strategy, see Schram, *Mao Tse-tung*, pp. 129–31.
60. *Mao Zedong nongcun diaocha wenji*, pp. 28–34; 182–251.

gories used by most rural researchers at the time, Marxist or otherwise. He classified the agrarian population into landlords, owner-cultivators (*zigengnong*), half-owners (*ban zigengnong*), tenants, and agricultural laborers. The categories of the rich peasant and the middle peasant had indeed appeared as early as 1927 in his Hunan report. But they remained descriptive rather than analytic categories. Even in his Xunwu survey, where he included the rich and the middle peasants in a crude break-down of the population, he made no attempt to study the middle peas-ants and a bare minimum the rich peasants. It was not until the Xingguo survey that he finally analyzed the rich and the middle peasants as distinct classes.[61]

Mao was remarkably free of perplexity; he never agonized over the theoretical or methodological issues related to social surveys. He never considered the issue of bias. It may be argued that Mao's conception of social reality was inherently partisan, that is, there were several social constructions of reality,[62] but only the poor peasants represented the true "reality."[63] The fact that none of his informants was from the landlord category seemed to support this argument. Mao probably believed that there was only *one* social "reality" or there was only *one* way to approach it; all others were falsifications, by landlords, the bourgeoisie, or any class enemies. It is conceivable that Mao would have interviewed a landlord or a class enemy who had chosen to stay, recant, and join the revolution. For example, Mao spoke amiably on more than one occasion about the merchant informant for his Xunwu survey.[64] As "president of the chamber of commerce," though allegedly bankrupt by then, he could have been a much-hated class enemy. But he had stayed and, obviously, recanted. As a result, he was eagerly sought after to participate in Mao's efforts at illuminating social reality.

If "reality" in Mao's conception was not socially constructed but existed out there objectively, biases or falsifications could only deny us a true understanding of reality, but could never put in doubt its existence. Group fact-finding sessions to him provided a mechanism of checks and balances to insure that reality would be accurately represented. So

---

61. "Xingguo diaocha" (Xingguo Survey), *Mao Zedong nongcun diaocha wenji*, pp. 213–18.
62. The concept is borrowed from Peter Berger and Thomas Luckmann, *The Social Con-struction of Reality: A Treatise in the Sociology of Knowledge* (New York, 1967).
63. For a discussion along this line of argument, especially as it applies to social research in the People's Republic of China, see Siu-lun Wong, *Sociology and Socialism in Con-temporary China* (London, 1979), pp. 67–8.
64. *Mao Zedong nongcun diaocha wenji*, pp. 16, 56.

sanguine was he about the effectiveness of the group interview format that he was completely oblivious to a host of methodological issues involved.

His informants were chosen without consideration for their representativeness. The fact that they were mostly cadres bespoke his criteria: assured cooperation and access to information. Even his noncadre informants were secured through the cadres. Nowhere in his survey writings did he even hint an awareness that bias could creep into his group sessions. His pristine naivete, or to borrow the castigation leveled against him by his own comrades, "rigid empiricism,"[65] as regard to the way we understand the world manifested most clearly in his "tunnel vision"-like approach to glean information from his informants: "Naturally, people who have nothing to do with the questions under investigation need not be present. For example, when the subject concerns the business, no members from the labor, peasant, and intellectual communities need to be present."[66] He would have interviewed as many informants as possible if it had been manageable. His crude empiricism suggested that the more the informants were, the easier it would be to compile accurate statistics (such as the percentage of poor peasants) as well as to reach better policy suggestions (such as the best way to redistribute land). Mao was here counting on the hazards of human memory or perception to do his field work. His approach to the field was information-gathering in its crudest sense; he asked questions and he got answers. In one essay, he derided some cadres for producing survey results that read like "dog meat ledgers" (*gourou zhang*).[67] The irony is that he himself had churned out a few results that were quite worthy of this epithet.[68]

Even more astounding was the fact that the group fact-finding sessions constituted Mao's notion of what "field work" was all about. There was to be no further tedious checking in the field itself; the group fact-finding sessions had happily substituted for the back-breaking field work. In fact, Mao believed that it was not even necessary to actually visit the field itself; one could stay home and conduct "field work" by summoning the people who were acquainted with the field to attend the group fact-finding sessions.[69] His Xingguo survey could easily qualify as a candidate for notorious scandals in the world sociological community. The survey

---

65. Ibid., p. 17. I have yet to identify his critics.   66. Ibid., p. 9.
67. Ibid., p. 5.
68. This is especially true of the minisurveys that constitute the last quarter of the collection.   69. Ibid., pp. 2–3.

was in fact not conducted in Xingguo but in Ji'an, which is about one hundred miles away. Furthermore, he made do with what informants he could get; they were eight Red Army peasant recruits who had newly arrived from Xingguo.[70]

Mao never intended to subscribe to academic and, worse, Western bourgeois standards; the one and the only goal of his surveys was to further the revolution. Indeed, he would have scoffed at any suggestions to safeguard academic objectivity. Furthermore, it may also be argued that Mao had no leisure nor freedom to be concerned with the academic merit of his surveys. Thus even though his 1927 survey of the peasant movement in Hunan was indeed flawed in that it was conducted in eastern Hunan, where the movement was the strongest, it could be excused because it was after all his first attempt. And all his subsequent surveys were inevitably dictated and affected by military exigencies.

Nevertheless, the fact remains that Mao was extremely self-assured. There is no doubt that his surveys were conducted primarily with the goal to devise better strategies to further the cause of revolution. At the same time, he was equally convinced that his surveys "objectively" reflected the situations in the field. After all, his advocacy of the Marxist approach was based on its revolutionary vision and its claim to be scientific. He had a definite vision as to how social surveys ought to be conducted. It matters not that he did few or no social surveys after the spurt of activities in the late 1920s and early 1930s. The power and prestige of Mao were such that his vision and approach dictated the way social investigations were conducted in the People's Republic until the 1970s.

Mao was unique in that among the early Chinese Communists he alone perceived the need to gain a thorough understanding of the field in order to make revolution. He had learned the hard and bitter lessons from the party's many disastrous defeats, many of which were through his as well as the party's miscalculations and ignorance of the situation. As he became more involved in survey work, he came to be more convinced of the absolute need to gather information from the field. "No investigations, no right to speak!" was his rather stern phrase in 1930 chiding some comrades for their dogmatic adherence to theory and total ignorance of the field, a thinly veiled attack on the Central Committee then still operating in its Shanghai refuge.[71] While affirming the need to

---

70. Ibid., p. 182.
71. Mao Zedong, "Fandui benben zhuyi" (Against everything-according-to-the-book-ism), in ibid., pp. 1–11. The original title of this essay was "Diaocha gongzuo" (Investigation

study Marxism, Mao was quick to add that it had to be a Marxism that was not detached from the Chinese reality.[72] A decade later in Yan'an, Mao handed down his most scathing remarks about how the party had suffered immeasurably at the hands of many "imperial commissioners," an obvious reference to the Comintern agents and possibly the Russian-trained Chinese Communists such as the "28 Bolsheviks" as well, who puffed away with their theories yet knew nothing about the field.[73]

There are two important legacies of Mao's surveys. The first concerns the purpose of social investigations. Mao's slogan, "No investigations, no right to speak," epitomized his vision that social investigations served the need to help the party devise better mobilization strategies. Translated to the post-1949 situation, policy formulation, implementation, and evaluation have come to define the role of social investigations. Being so sensitively linked to the mobilization of the masses and the implementation and evaluation of policies, social investigations came to be jealously guarded by the state as solely within its purview. As early as 1931, Mao had already required the Red Army and local government agencies to report in specifically prescribed forms detailed statistics concerning the population and land in southern Jiangxi.[74] In 1941, the party took a further step to establish research bureaus in central and regional party organs to engage in "systematic and comprehensive social surveys as the basis for decision-making."[75] The party and the government continued to play the dominant role in carrying out social investigations after 1949.[76] Indeed, the whole issue of the abolition of sociology in 1952 can only be properly understood in the context of the state's determination to control this sensitive field of information-gathering.[77]

The second major legacy of Mao's agrarian surveys is the particular style of field work that he had developed. His group fact-finding sessions became the ubiquitous format according to which all social investigations

Work). According to Mao, the term *"benben zhuyi"* was used then to mean "dogmatism" before the term *"jiaotiao zhuyi"* came into vogue. See Mao's note quoted in the endnote on p. 355, ibid.
72. Ibid., p. 4.
73. "Preface" to the 1941 edition; ibid., p. 17.
74. Ibid., pp. 12–13.
75. "The resolution of the Central Committee of the Communist Party on Investigation and Research," quoted in Siu-lun Wong, *Sociology and Socialism in Contemporary China*, p. 65.
76. Ibid., p. 71.
77. For more discussion on the abolition of sociology and the subsequent rehabilitation of the discipline, see Chapters 3 and 10.

have been conducted in China. No longer was there any need to agonize over the thorny issues concerning the choice of informants, their representativeness, and their cooperation; the field work, which would have been a crucial germinating point or testing ground for theories or models in sociological practice in the Western bourgeois tradition, has become an exercise in mobilization as well as of policy evaluation and recommendation.

In fact, Mao's impact goes beyond the format of the group fact-finding sessions. His vision of ideal social survey work has become that of the nation. As early as 1941 in Yan'an, he had already laid out the basic features of ideal social surveys. He exhorted the cadres to launch long-term case studies. The cases were to be selected according to their representativeness in their class (*dianxing*), that is, the most advanced, the average, and the least developed.[78] Although it appears that case studies of representative types have not been systematically carried out, the chairman's vision has defined the norm according to which social investigations ought to be conducted.[79]

Such was the profound impact of Mao Zedong's agrarian surveys. But in the late 1920s and early 1930s, his agrarian surveys were all but unknown. His solitary style and patently anti-intellectualistic approach, furthermore, were never conducive to concerted efforts in advancing Marxist social science research, let alone the emergence of a research enterprise. In this respect, the impetus came from a young academic Marxist by the name of Chen Hansheng, who, through his vision, knowledge, leadership, as well as organizational and entrepreneurial skills, created a Marxist social science enterprise.

---

78. *Mao Zedong nongcun diaocha wenji*, pp. 15, 21.
79. For a summary of the "model" method that is almost word by word Mao's, see Wong, *Sociology and Socialism in Contemporary China*, p. 74. Wong points out it is cases that belong to the most advanced types that have received most attention.

Leonard Hsu, circa 1936. Courtesy of Special Collections, Yale Divinity School Library, Record Group No. 11.

Wu Wenzao, circa 1930s. Courtesy of Special Collections, Yale Divinity School Library, Record Group No. 11.

Franklin Ho, New Haven 1947. Courtesy of the Ho Family.

H. D. Fong, circa 1950. Courtesy of Samuel Ho.

Pomona Chinese Students' Club, 1918. From left to right: Chen Hansheng, M. Y. Dziao, Li Jinghan, Eliot F. Ho, P. T. Chang *Chinese Students' Monthly*, XIV. 4 (February 1919) 256.

7

Genesis of a Marxist Social Science Enterprise in the Early 1930s

A S a system of theories, Marxist social science embodies a vision of society radically different from mainstream Anglo-American social sciences. The two traditions share few common characteristics; each contains its own separate, and often starkly incompatible, set of assumptions, vocabulary, research agenda, and conceptual framework. Yet as an enterprise, Marxist social science in China during the 1930s shared strikingly similar attributes with its Anglo-American counterparts. The rise of the Marxist social science enterprise in the 1930s paralleled that of the only other two social science enterprises during the Republican period: the Yanjing Sociology Department and the Nankai Institute of Economics. Not only was the Marxist social science enterprise no less committed to the notion of social engineering, but it flourished as Yanjing and Nankai did by developing a research field, seeking political patronage, and reaching out to American philanthropies. This Marxist enterprise owed its origins and success to the pivotal figure of Chen Hansheng (Chen Han-seng; Chen Shu; Geoffrey Chen), whose extraordinary political, organizational, and entrepreneurial skills created an agrarian research enterprise that rivaled Yanjing and Nankai both in terms of its scale of operation and its contribution to social science research.

CHEN HANSHENG AND HIS DISCOVERY OF THE FIELD

Chen Hansheng was born in Wuxi in Jiangsu province in 1897.[1] His mother came from a wealthy family that owned a distillery. Though

---

1. Unless otherwise noted, the discussion in this section on Chen's early life is based on his reminiscences as told to Ren Xuefang and entitled *Sige shidai de wo* (My Life across Four Epochs) (Beijing, 1989).

illiterate, she had a strong influence on Chen, who, like many famous modern Chinese, remembers his mother with deep affection.[2] His father was a licentiate (*xiucai*) who made a dramatic career change by enrolling in the Jiangnan Army Academy, which was founded in 1896.

In 1909, the family moved to Changsha, where Chen enrolled in the well-known Mingde Middle School. Two years later, his father sent him to Peking to sit on the third examination for selecting students to study in the United States on the funds from the American remission of the Boxer Indemnity. Chen failed the test owing to his then low level of proficiency in English.[3] Smarting from the failure, he transferred to the English-speaking Yale-in-China Academy, an expensive institution whose annual cost in tuition and room and board was over one hundred dollars, more than four times as expensive as the average Chinese schools in Hunan.[4] Upon his graduation in 1915, Chen wanted to study in the United States. When it became clear that his father did not approve of his plan, he resorted to a hunger strike. It was the mother who came to his rescue. She sold all her dowry and obtained a loan from her parents to put together $2,000 Mexican dollars, a significant amount that at the then prevailing rate could be exchanged for over US$2,000.[5]

Following the recommendation of his teachers at the Yale-in-China Academy, Chen went to Mount Hermon School for Boys, a secondary school in Massachusetts founded in 1881 by the famous revivalist, Dwight Moody, to train evangelists to spread the gospel. Whether or not Chen was a Christian, Mount Hermon was an attractive choice for him because it had a work program for its students to keep the costs of the school at a minimum.[6] A year later, in 1916, he entered Pomona College. His search for a suitable major followed a familiar pattern set by many among his generation: They began by choosing a major that they believed would enable them to serve China better regardless of their own interest or ability. Recalling a lecture he had heard in Changsha on the cross-

---

2. Mao Zedong, Chiang Kai-shek, and Hu Shi are examples that come to mind.
3. In his reminiscences, Chen related his disastrous interpretation of the question for English composition, "On Currency Reforms," which he took as meaning: "On Diverting a River Current."
4. The figure and comparison were provided by Franklin Ho, who was Chen Hansheng's classmate at the Yale-in-China Academy. See his, "Reminiscences," p. 25.
5. The nearly 1:1 exchange rate was reported by Franklin Ho in his "Reminiscences." See ibid., p. 31.
6. I am indebted to Clifton Phillips, professor emeritus at DePauw, for helping me identify Mount Hermon School for Boys.

fertilization process in plants, including the use of Sichuan mandarin oranges to produce the juicy seedless California oranges, he decided to major in botany.[7] His bad eyesight, however, made it difficult for him to observe the specimens under his microscope. He then tried geology, having in mind China's proverbial mineral resources, but finally settled on history. It is in history that he graduated Phi Beta Kappa from Pomona in 1920.

In addition to being academically excellent, Chen was politically active. He was active in Chinese students' circles in the San Francisco Bay area, attending meetings and contributing articles for publication.[8] He became even more active after he moved from Pomona to the University of Chicago, where he enrolled in the M.A. program in history. He was elected secretary for the Chinese Students' Alliance in the United States of America for 1921–2 and simultaneously served as one of the associate editors for the Alliance's publication, *The Chinese Students' Monthly*.

Despite his busy extracurricular activities, Chen finished his M.A. degree in history in 1921 with a thesis, "The Conference of Ambassadors in London, 1912–1913, and the Creation of the Albanian State: A Diplomatic Study."[9] In winter, just a few days after his marriage in Seattle to Susie Ku (Gu Shuxing), a fellow Wuxi native whom he had met in San Francisco in 1919, he set out for Washington, D.C. Chen went as an observer sent by the Chinese Students' Alliance to monitor the Chinese delegation to the Washington Conference.[10] In spring 1922, Susie joined him in Cambridge, where she enrolled at Radcliffe College while he studied at Harvard. He apparently did well at Harvard, where he assisted Charles Haskins, a medievalist and then dean of the Graduate School of Arts and Sciences, in the latter's seminar on "Historiography." A year

---

7. Chen recalled that the lecture was delivered by Luo-bo-te (C. H. Robertson?), famous in China for his science lectures.
8. Franklin Ho of Nankai remembered that while fresh off the boat and staying with Chen Hansheng in Berkeley, where the latter was taking a summer course, the latter took him to hear Wu Chaoshu (C. C. Wu), who had represented Sun Yat-sen's Canton government at the Versailles Conference. See Franklin Ho, "Reminiscences," p. 35.
9. Note that Chen was mistaken in his reminiscences – and so are all who have quoted him – about the title of his M.A. thesis. The correct title here is ascertained by checking with the record at the University of Chicago.
10. For an account of their monitoring activities, see Tsiang T'ing-fu, "The Reminiscences of Tsiang T'ing-fu (1895–1965)," pp. 80–4; for an account from the perspective of the government delegates being monitored, see Mary Thayer, *Hui-lan Koo [Madame Wellington Koo]: An Autobiography as Told to Mary Van Rensselaer Thayer* (New York, 1943), p. 146.

later, however, he decided to go to Germany to take advantage of the low Deutsche mark, which by November 1923 had fallen to 4.2 trillion to the dollar. He reportedly received a Ph.D. degree from the University of Berlin in 1924.[11]

Following the completion of his study in Berlin, Chen returned to China for a position in history at the National Peking University. After nearly ten years abroad, he returned as a well-groomed young man and an accomplished scholar; his portrait in *The Chinese Students' Monthly* that identified him as secretary-elect for 1921–2 of the Chinese Students' Alliance showed him in a handsomely tailored suit, a pair of glasses with a thin and elegant metal frame, and with his hair cut *en brosse*.[12] In addition to being flawless and eloquent in both spoken and written English, he read German and French, as well as some Russian. He shared a common intellectual outlook and networks of friendship with other Chinese returned from the West, and contributed to Hu Shi's and Wang Shijie's *Contemporary Review*. As he testified years later, he did not have the slightest idea about Marxism when he started teaching at Peking University.[13]

The process of intellectual conversion to Marxism began slowly. Pyotr Grinevich, a young sinologue at the Russian Language College, introduced him to *Das Kapital*. Similar in age and obviously attracted by each other's intellectual caliber, the two often discussed current events and economic issues till late at night.[14] Through Grinevich, Chen became acquainted with Anatoly Kantorovich, a Dickens enthusiast and legal attaché at the Soviet embassy.[15] In spring 1925, through the introduction of Li Dazhao, his colleague at Peking University, Chen joined the Guomindang, which was then pursuing the United Front policy with the Communists.

The May Thirtieth Incident of 1925 was the turning point. In the wake

11. I have not been able to verify Chen's Ph.D. degree and his dissertation title. Bettina Gransow, who is located in Berlin and who reported, though mistakenly, about the title of Chen's M.A. thesis, indicated only that Chen graduated but she was silent on the title of his Ph.D. dissertation in her *Geschichte der chinesischen Soziologie*, p. 91.
12. *The Chinese Students' Monthly*, 16.8 (June 1921).
13. See his "Jiechu de gongchan zhuyi zhanshi" (An Outstanding Communist Fighter) in Wang Xi and Yang Xiaofo, eds., *Chen Hansheng wenji* (A Collection of Chen Hansheng's Essays) (Shanghai, 1985), p. 455.
14. The discussion in this and the following paragraph is based on Chen Hansheng's reminiscences in *Sige shidai de wo*, pp. 34–5.
15. Vera Vladimirovna Vishnyakova-Akimova, *Two Years in Revolutionary China, 1925–1927* (Harvard, 1971), pp. 41–3.

of the massacre, he was sent by Li Dazhao to Shanghai to instigate a strike among the Indian Sikh policemen at the International Settlement, presumably because of his proficiency in English. Little is known about how the history professor functioned as a strike instigator, but the scheme may never have gone beyond the planning stage. His talent was better utilized upon his return to Peking. Through Kantorovich, he began contributing articles to the Comintern's *International Press Correspondence*.[16] Soon afterward, Li Dazhao and the Soviet ambassador Karakhan recruited him to work for the Comintern. Though he operated only in the background, his work for the Comintern was dangerous. On April 6, 1927, warlord Zhang Zuolin raided the Soviet embassy, seized and later executed Li Dazhao and nineteen other Chinese Communists hiding there. Susie and Chen were forced to seek safe haven in Moscow.

The exile, though lasting only a little more than a year, had such a profound impact on Chen that it was to reorient him to focus on the agrarian problems in China and thereby determine his career until 1949. His Moscow sojourn coincided with the final stage of Stalin's destruction of the Trotsky opposition and the beginning of a systematic elimination of the various doctrinal "deviations." Stalin's need to suppress Trotsky was accelerated by his own debacle in directing the Chinese Communist revolution that had suffered disastrous defeat in Chiang Kai-shek's bloody purge of the Communists in Shanghai on April 12, 1927.

In Moscow, Susie and Chen worked at the International Agrarian Institute,[17] collecting and translating into English materials on the peasant movement in China. Chen reportedly had a number of sharp exchanges at the Institute with Liudvig Mad'iar, the author of *A Study of the Rural Economy in China* and the head of the Oriental department of the Institute. The exchanges were on the latter's depiction of China as belonging to the Asiatic Mode of Production and his belief in the predominance of the capitalist relations of production in contemporary China.[18] The debates in the Soviet Union on the nature of Chinese

16. Chen recalled that he published a dozen articles in the *Inprecor*, on subjects such as the May Thirtieth Incident, the Northern Expedition, and Chiang Kai-shek's purge of the Communists in 1927. *Sige shidai de wo*, p. 35.
17. "Krestintern," in *The Modern Encyclopedia of Russian and Soviet History* (New York, 1982), 18.63–4; and "Peasant International," *Great Soviet Encyclopedia* (New York, 1976), 13.600.
18. *Sige shidai de wo*, p. 40. This may not have been accurate because the concept of the Asiatic Mode of Production in general and Mad'iar and his followers in particular would not succumb to Stalin's ideological axes until the 1931 Leningrad meeting. See

society had made him acutely aware of his ignorance of China and prompted him to resolve to study Chinese society upon his return. Susie and he may have left Moscow and embarked on their journey back to China via Europe before the sessions of the Sixth Congress of the Chinese Communist Party and the Sixth Congress of the Communist International began in July 1928.[19] He was nonetheless fully cognizant of the new Comintern line, for he returned with a sense of mission to engage in research in order to illuminate the semifeudal and semi-colonial nature of agrarian China – the Stalinist thesis that was made supreme at the two Congresses.

THE INSTITUTIONAL BASE

Resolved to venture into his newly discovered field, agrarian China, Chen Hansheng did not resume his earlier career as a college professor. He was fortunate to have had help from Cai Yuanpei, the venerated former president of Peking University and the president of the newly founded Academia Sinica. Because of opposition,[20] due to Chen's ideological leaning, Cai had to place him temporarily as an editor at the Commercial Press before he could appoint Chen to head the sociology section of the Institute of the Social Sciences of the Academia Sinica in March 1929.

Until its relocation to Nanjing in early 1932, the Institute of the Social Sciences was located in the French Concession in Shanghai: first on Avenue du Roi Albert, and then Rue Ferguson from February 1929. The Institute consisted of four sections: law, ethnology, economics, and sociology. As testimony to Chen's leadership role, it was the sociology section alone that experienced phenomenal growth in its early years.[21]

Three characteristics marked Chen Hansheng's research enterprise. The first was its ambition to cover the entire nation, urban as well as

Anne Bailey and Josep Llobera, eds., *The Asiatic Mode of Production: Science and Politics* (London, 1981), pp. 49–106.

19. For an analysis of these two congresses and their resolutions on China, see Benjamin Schwartz, *Chinese Communism and the Rise of Mao*, pp. 109–26.
20. Chen identified the opposition as Wang Shijie. See his "Zhuinian Cai Jiemin xiansheng" (Remembering Mr. Cai Yuanpei), in *Chen Hansheng wenji*, p. 452.
21. The law section, plagued by a high turnover rate of its staff, ceased to function in 1932. The ethnology section was transferred to the Institute of History and Philology in 1934. The economics section only began to flourish after the Institute was merged with the Institute of Social Research of the China Foundation in 1934.

agrarian.[22] The second was its attempt to study the deepening agrarian crisis symptomatic of China's semifeudal and semicolonial status. The final characteristic was the magnitude of its organization. He went into the field in a big way; his survey teams, recruited locally for specific projects, were perhaps the largest ever assembled during the Republican period.

The sociology section launched a two-pronged research program, attacking the agrarian and urban sectors simultaneously.[23] The urban component focused on Shanghai, which started as a library research project on the history of the city, under the direction of Wang Jichang (Wang Tsi Chang, M.A., 1922, Oberlin; Ph.D., 1925, Chicago). However, the Shanghai project dramatically turned empirical and radical. In September 1929, a large research team with seventy-three members at its peak, began a five-month survey of the lives of workers in Yangshupu (Yangtzepoo), a cotton mill district located in the eastern section of the International Settlement.[24] The team interviewed nearly two thousand workers, surveyed 474 of its 530 factories and workshops,[25] and visited over one thousand shanties, several hundred terrace apartment buildings, one hundred pawn shops, scores of workers' dormitories, and half a dozen or so each of godowns, union headquarters, and tea houses.

That the survey exposed the miserable existence of the workers in

22. "Zhongguo nongcun jingji diaochatuan jinkuang" (The Latest Activities of the Research Team on China's Agrarian Economy), *Nongye zhoubao* (Farmers' Weekly), 35 (June 15, 1930), p. 954.
23. Chen recalled in his reminiscences that he began his work with an investigation of the contract labor system in Japanese cotton mills in Shanghai and that it was only under political pressure that he took up Cai Yuanpei's advice to shift to the study of the agrarian economy. However, a careful reading of contemporary Academia Sinica reports suggests a more complicated story discussed below.
24. Chen Hansheng, *Zhongguo nongcun jingji yanjiu zhi faren* (Genesis of Research on China's Agrarian Economy) (Shanghai, 1930[?]), pp. 2–5. It should be pointed out that Yangshupu was an area where Shanghai Baptist College had operated a Yangshupu Social Center since 1917.
25. The following table gives the breakdown of the number of factories, arranged according to ownership by nationality, that participated in or refused the survey. See ibid., p. 2.

Ownership	Surveyed	Not surveyed
Chinese	433	23
Japanese	21	10
Western	20	23
Total	474	56

Yangshupu was no surprise. More significant was the finding that set the plight of urban workers, particularly that associated with the notorious contract labor system among women workers in cotton mills, against the background of the crisis situation in the surrounding countryside.[26] The exposure of the contract labor system and, with it, the magnitude of the agrarian crisis was as significant as it was sensational, particularly in a city with a history of Communist-led strikes and union activities that had only been shattered by Chiang Kai-shek's coup three years earlier. It was natural that the Yangshupu survey was perceived as being instigated by the Communist Party.

Perhaps because of its shocking findings, the project was suspended abruptly. The intense political pressure led Cai Yuanpei to advise Chen to abandon the urban field and to concentrate on the agrarian economy. Although the details remain obscure, the outline of the episode can be reconstructed. While the sociology section requested as late as April 1930 an appropriation to engage five more staff members to work on the Yangshupu data, the Institute announced suddenly in June that the sociology section would henceforward concentrate exclusively on the agrarian economy and that the Yangshupu data were to be transferred to the economics section. Major personnel changes followed; Wang Jichang, the project director, resigned. Meanwhile, the transplanted project mutated and took on an innocuous nature in the economics section, having being transformed into an inquiry into the housing problems of the workers.[27] The sociology section did not let the episode end with a bland finale, however; it resurrected the contract labor project in spring 1932 with the rationale that, mindful of its newly designated field of research, it constituted a follow-up study of the lives of women who had left the villages.[28] Although the project was short-lived, the staff produced a pamphlet to publicize the evils of the system.[29]

---

26. Chen Hansheng, *Zhongguo nongcun jingji yanjiu zhi faren*, pp. 2–5. For a description of the contract labor system in Shanghai cotton mills, see Emily Honig, *Sisters and Strangers: Women in the Shanghai Cotton Mills, 1919–1949* (Stanford, 1986), pp. 94–131.

27. See the progress report in *Guoli Zhongyang yanjiuyuan yuanwu yuebao* (Monthly Bulletin of Academia Sinica), II.7 (January 1931), p. 31.

28. *Guoli Zhongyang yanjiuyuan ershi niandu zong baogao* (Fourth Annual Report, Academia Sinica, 1931–1932), p. 312.

29. I have not been able to locate this report. An article was produced by Sun Yefang, one important member on Chen's research team. See Sun Baoshan [Sun Yefang], "Shanghai fangzhichang zhong de baoshenzhi gongren" (Contract Laborers in Shanghai's Cotton Mills), originally published in *Huanian* (Huanian Weekly), I.22 (September 10, 1932), pp. 430–2; I.24 (September 24, 1932), pp. 467–72.

Fascinating as the Shanghai project could have become, it had never been one in which Chen Hansheng was involved, save possibly for that aborted effort to revive it in spring 1932. Furthermore, there is no information on how Wang Jichang envisioned and designed the survey or whether he shared Chen's ideological and methodological positions. However, this does not make the withdrawal from the urban field any less significant. Political pressure aside, the shift toward an agrarian focus reflected also a conviction held all along by Chen that it was in the agrarian sector that China's problems most clearly manifested themselves. Before it became necessary to abandon the urban field, the sociology section had pronounced that "[i]t is not the factory . . . but the farm, that is the social and economic foundation of China."[30]

DIAGNOSIS OF THE AGRARIAN CRISIS THROUGH RESEARCH

Chen Hansheng brought to the sociology section his social vision and ideological conviction, which completely redefined its research agenda and style, as illustrated by the fate of the section's first rural project undertaken before Chen joined the Institute. Launched in fall 1928, it was a survey of the agricultural economy in northwestern Zhejiang conducted under the direction of Tao Menghe, a research associate of the Institute and the head of the Department of Social Research of the China Foundation for the Promotion of Culture and Education in Peking. The project was shelved soon after the field work was completed in spring 1929, about the time when Chen joined the Institute. Eventually the section abandoned the project and transferred the data to Tao's department in Peking. The reason Chen disassociated himself from the project was that he disagreed with its methodology – one pioneered in China by J. Lossing Buck of the University of Nanking, which, as discussed in Chapter 8, was an anathema to Chen.[31]

Chen Hansheng's own first project at the Institute was not a field

---

30. *Academia Sinica with Its Research Institutes* (Nanjing, 1929), p. 51.
31. The field data from the project were written up by Han Dezhang and published in *Shehui kexue zazhi* (Quarterly Review of Social Sciences): "Zhexi nongcun zhi jiedai zhidu" (The Credit Systems in West Zhejiang), III.2 (June 1932), pp. 139–85; (co-authored with Qu Zhisheng), "Zhexi nongchang maoyi de jige shili" (Some Important Markets of Agricultural Products in West Zhejiang), III.4 (December 1932), pp. 444–78; and "Zhexi nongcun zhi zudian zhidu" (Farm Tenancy in West Zhejiang), IV.1 (March 1933), pp. 34–53.

research. *The Peasant and Landlords in the Amur Region*, published in 1929, was a library research based primarily on data collected by the Economic Bureau of the Chinese Eastern Railway in 1922–3. Herein lay the crux of his diagnosis of the problems besetting Chinese society that he was to devote his entire social science enterprise to refining and confirming.

His diagnosis rested on four key observations. The first concerned the worsening of the already impoverished state of the peasants in the face of ruthless accumulation of land by the landlords. The second pertained to the various factors contributing to the crisis. The most conspicuous of these was the sharp rise in farm rent. In Hulan county, for example, cash rent had increased more than ten times during the period from 1905 to 1915.[32] The speed with which farm rent rose outpaced that of the land price by four times during the same period,[33] implying that landlords had exacted from their tenants far more than the purchasing cost of their land would warrant. While poor peasants were made to pay more for the use of the land, they received less in return. Agricultural wages fell by 58.6 percent for day laborers and 70.8 percent for year laborers during the period from 1910 to 1923, when measured in terms of their real purchasing power against the principal grains, sorghum and millet, consumed by the peasants.[34] The excessive taxation and usury furthermore hastened the downward mobility of the already hard-pressed peasants.

The plight of the peasants, whom Chen still referred to in the then widely used (non-Marxist) classification scheme as owner-cultivators, tenants, and agricultural laborers, led him to his third observation. This was what he would first refer to as the precapitalistic and, eventually, as the semifeudal and semicolonial nature of the Chinese society. He was unequivocal about what he viewed as the root causes of the suffering, particularly when farm rent was not farm rent pure and simple, but included the landlords' profit, tax obligations, and what should have been considered the tenants' wages.[35] To compound the problem, capitalistic forces from abroad wrought just as much havoc to their semifeudal society. That most of the grains they produced were shipped to Japan,

---

32. Chen Hansheng and Wang Yinsheng, *Heilongjiang liuyu de nongmin yu dizhu* (The Peasant and Landlords in the Amur Region), pp. 7–8. There is an English summary of this report: "Tendencies of farm economics in northeastern China," Institute of Pacific Relations [Chen Hansheng], comp. & trans., *Agrarian China: Selected Source Materials from Chinese Authors* (Chicago, 1939), pp. 136–44.
33. Ibid.   34. Ibid., pp. 8–9.   35. Ibid., p. 7.

England, the United States, and Denmark, put them at the mercy of fluctuations in the international grain markets.[36]

Chen's final observation was a prognosis. The more the peasants were victimized by high land and grain prices as well as excessive taxation and usury, the less they would be able to accumulate capital for agricultural production. Thus, unless China could break out of this contradiction between the productive forces and the production relations, it would never be able to solve its acute agrarian crisis.[37]

Although Chen was convinced that his diagnosis was true for both northern Manchuria and the rest of China, he realized that the data he needed to support his case were nonexistent. His Manchurian data were flawed in that they were totally silent on issues he deemed crucial for an understanding of the production relations, such as the conditions of the poor peasants, the differential rates of investment and returns between owner-cultivators and other peasants, and the credit system.[38] Nevertheless, if the Manchurian data were flawed, other data available were useless. While the statistics published by the Ministry of Agriculture and Commerce of the Peking government in 1919 were laughable, J. Lossing Buck's analyses were simply off the mark, for not only did he fail to address the issues of landownership and tenancy, but he also dealt inadequately with such crucial questions as rural employment, prices of agricultural products, incomes from side-line activities, and the credit system.[39]

Believing that misinformation was worse than not having any data, he decided to start out afresh with his research. Library research, which characterized Chen's Manchurian project, remained an important component of his enterprise. With a cataloging system with fifty-two headings, he employed four full-time staff members to canvass over twenty major newspapers for information on taxation, usury, military requisitions, famines, and bandits.[40] In addition, he utilized extensively published and unpublished materials, including personal correspondence

---

36. Ibid., p. 10.
37. Ibid., p. 15. See also *Academia Sinica with its Research Institutes*, p. 51.
38. *Zhongguo nongcun jingji yanjiu zhi faren*, pp. 5–6.
39. Ibid. Chen had most likely not yet seen Buck's *Chinese Farm Economy: A Study of 2866 Farms in Seventeen Localities and Seven Provinces in China*, which was published in 1930. His criticisms here were, therefore, directed at Buck's earlier surveys, most likely his *An Economic and Social Survey of 102 Farms near Wuhu, Anhwei, China*, Nanking, Pt. I (December 1923), Pt. II (July 1924) and *An Economic and Social Survey of 150 Farms, Yenshan County, Chihli Province, China* (Nanjing, 1926).
40. *Guoli Zhongyang yanjiuyuan yuanwu yuebao*, I.3 (September 1929), p. 7.

and government archives. However, it was field work that was the mainstay of his research enterprise. His field work represented an attempt to address the limitations of earlier surveys by Westerners. It would not be concerned narrowly with farm management, as Buck's had been; nor would its purpose be a call for ameliorative actions, as were surveys made by Westerners associated with Christian colleges.

Chen set out to analyze the structure of Chinese society in order to determine its stage of development according to the universal pattern of development. If the semifeudal forces became more deeply entrenched when impinged upon by the capitalistic forces from abroad, as suggested by his Manchurian data, did this process also characterize the rest of Chinese society? Indeed, determining the stage in which Chinese society belonged would be more than half accomplished if cross-sectional surveys of China would confirm that the northern Manchurian situations typified the nation as a whole.

Field work in Chen's enterprise was at the same time polemical; it represented a direct challenge to what he considered Buck's gross misrepresentations of China's agrarian sector. Although he never specified how Buck misconstrued China, he must have reacted strongly against the following statement with which Buck opened his report on a survey of Wuhu in Anhui by one of his students in 1922:

What would you think of an investment which only gave you 2.5% interest per year? Or of working a whole year on a farm and paying out $1.25 a month for the privilege? And having the tenant on your farm make by comparison $105 a year? . . . One is startled into the realization that perhaps the landlords of China have a 'case' as well as the 'poor' tenants! Moreover the tenants' profits per year were $105 as compared with minus $15 for the farmers who own and work their own farms, and this groups of farmers, who were losing money at the rate of $15 a year, constituted 55% of all the farmers.[41]

There was as yet no frontal attack on Buck. In fact, Buck's name rarely appeared in Chen's writings, even though Buck and the conclusions he drew from his farm surveys had loomed large in his thought and had pricked his sense of social justice and truth. Chen was not ready, however; he had yet to learn the ropes in the field. The challenge would

41. Buck, *An Economic and Social Survey of 102 Farms near Wuhu*, Pt. I, p. 1.

come, as discussed in Chapter 8, but not until he had plunged into the field, confronted with a reality more complicated than he had anticipated, and had successfully resolved a conceptualization crisis in the process.

Chen's first field work took place in his native Wuxi, a common practice among contemporary field workers – much as Fei Xiaotong and Lin Yaohua did in their respective native places. In Chen's case, it was not just his familiarity with the dialect and presence of local connections. Wuxi was chosen for its illustrative value in gauging the extent of the modern transformation of the Chinese economy.[42] Unlike Shanghai, Tianjin, or Canton, where foreign capital dominated, Wuxi thrived on native industrial and finance capital. A survey of the agrarian economy in Wuxi provided a case study to measure the extent and pattern of development of capitalism in China's most advanced region.[43]

The Wuxi survey was commenced in July 1929 and completed in three months. The forty-five member team was recruited locally. Among them, one-third were college students or graduates, another third, high school students, and the final third, elementary school teachers. While everyone participated in the survey work, college students and elementary school teachers assumed additional administrative duties, with the former serving as team leaders and the latter, liaison officers. Members received training on basic survey techniques and the use of schedules prior to their departure for the field.

The survey work fell into four categories: first, a house-to-house survey of twenty-two representative villages, nine of which were selected as typical villages and the remaining thirteen, atypical villages; second, a survey of the general conditions of fifty-five villages; third, a survey of industries and commerce in eight market towns; and lastly, a detailed study of 1,207 peasant households.

Neat and tidy as the survey was envisioned, the reality in the field, however, turned out to be extremely complicated and defied simple

---

42. Liao Kaisheng, "Shehui kexue yanjiusuo Wuxi nongcun diaocha jilüe" (A Brief Account of the Wuxi Survey Conducted by the Institute of the Social Sciences), *Guoli Zhongyang yanjiuyuan yuanwu yuebao*, I.8 (February 1930), pp. 9–15.
43. *Guoli Zhongyang yanjiuyuan shijiu niandu zong baogao* (Third Annual Report, Academia Sinica, 1930–1931) (Nanjing, 1931), p. 358.

analysis. Much of the earlier optimism about obtaining quick survey results evaporated. As an example, the land tenure system was so complex that mere exposure of the distribution of land ownership scratched only the surface of the production relations in the villages. Much to the consternation of the field workers, land ownership in Wuxi did not express itself neatly in the usual three-tiered landlord, owner-cultivator, and tenant categories. To the extent that property rights crisscrossed among these different strata in the villages, it rendered meaningless the entire scheme of classifying farm population in terms of the then widely used definition of land ownership. Instead of the conventional three-tiered strata, the research team discovered that there were in Wuxi no less than fourteen different categories of farm households: four kinds of landlords, five kinds of tenants, and five kinds of owner-cultivators.[44]

Technical problems also encumbered the progress of the survey. Most thorny of all was that there was no standard measurement of *mu* (*mow*) in Wuxi, not even in the same village. In fact, the research team discovered that there were altogether 173 different sizes of *mu* in the twenty-two villages surveyed, the largest among them being equivalent to nearly nine *are* (100 square meters) and the smallest, to less than three *are*.[45] There was no standard measurement even within the same village, where the variations ranged from five to twenty. Given that most peasants in Wuxi cultivated patches scattered in four or five different places, it was no surprise that "[e]ven among the *mows* cultivated by one family, two or three different sizes are to be found."[46] Painstaking efforts had to be made to convert all these 173 different sizes of *mu* into a standard unit, which in this case was *are*, before the research team could proceed to compile useful and reliable statistics.

Furthermore, once the field work was completed, the team was scaled down to seven, who were confronted with the task of sorting through the immense and inchoate data collected. By June 1930, they had only completed work on the statistics for the distribution of farm land and crop area, for the relation of amount of farm land to size of household, and a census of the 1,207 households on which they had conducted a detailed survey.[47] Work became bogged down when they began to attempt income–expenditure analyses for each category of farm households.

44. *The Academia Sinica and Its National Research Institutes* (Nanjing, 1931), pp. 110–11.
45. Ibid., p. 110.   46. Ibid.
47. *Guoli Zhongyang yanjiuyuan yuanwu yuebao*, II.1 (July 1930), p. 55.

Price figures from the field, they discovered, had been collected in such a way that no adjustment was made to take into account differences caused by market conditions. Their solution was to use an average. In addition to sampling errors, they found data lacking on a variety of agricultural outlays, including wages for yearly and seasonal laborers. As a result, they had to conduct supplementary field work in early 1931.[48]

Another factor that delayed progress was that Chen had overextended himself. No sooner had the field work in Wuxi been completed than planning for the second project began. It was Chen's intention that the survey of Wuxi was to be followed by a survey of an underdeveloped hinterland case. His choice for this second field project was Datong in Shanxi. However, as the Shanxi warlord Yan Xishan allied with warlord Feng Yuxiang to struggle against Chiang Kai-shek in early 1930,[49] Datong, being located in the potential war zone, was deemed too dangerous. As a result, Chen chose Baoding county in Hebei (about one hundred miles from Ding Xian, the headquarters of James Yen's Mass Education Movement), thus making his second field research also a case that illustrated littoral, albeit relatively poor, rather than hinterland China.

Field work in Baoding began in May and concluded in August 1930. Like the Wuxi survey before it, the sixty-six members on the team, except for team leaders, were recruited locally. Research design too was patterned after that of the Wuxi survey. Thus, the team conducted surveys of eleven typical villages and of the general conditions of seventy-eight villages and six market towns. There was one difference; instead of conducting house-to-house surveys in typical villages, as was done in Wuxi, the Baoding team conducted in-depth studies of 1,773 selected households.[50]

Although the Baoding survey was in collaboration with the Department of Social Research of the China Foundation, it was practically Chen Hansheng's project. Not only was the research design Chen's, but the execution of the project was in the hands of Chen's group. The field director, Wang Yinsheng, was Chen's student at Peking University and had been his chief lieutenant since his Manchurian project. Furthermore, three out of the four team leaders were Chen's members from the

---

48. *Guoli Zhongyang yanjiuyuan yuanwu yuebao*, II.9 (March 1931), p. 33.
49. James Sheridan, *Chinese Warlord: The Career of Feng Yü-hsiang* (Stanford, 1966), pp. 255–67.
50. *Guoli Zhongyang yanjiuyuan yuanwu yuebao* II.5 (November 1930), p. 39.

Academia Sinica: Zhang Jiafu, Qian Junrui, and Zhang Xichang. The latter two were to become the mainstay of Chen's agrarian research enterprise.[51] The only team leader from the Department of Social Research was Han Dezhang (B.S., 1928, Yanjing), who subscribed to Buck's methodology and assumptions.[52]

The Baoding survey illustrated even more clearly Chen's view on China's agrarian crisis than the Wuxi survey. The issues for which data were collected were exactly what he had found lacking in the Manchurian data and what he had criticized Buck for having failed to address adequately. Thus, the field work concentrated on the issues of tenancy, rural employment, income from side-line activities, the credit system, and the differential rates of investment and return for each stratum of the peasantry.[53]

Work on the data collected from the Baoding field progressed even slower than the Wuxi project. The project was in fact put on hold for two years. Nothing came out of Chen's celebrated Wuxi survey, save for some statistics that he cited in an article.[54] The Baoding project fared hardly any better. Although his team published *Military Requisitions and Peasants in North China* in 1931, much of it came from news reports and questionnaire responses.

A CONCEPTUALIZATION CRISIS

There was an important factor that may have contributed to the lack of progress in Chen Hansheng's first two surveys. It involved a crisis in conceptualization that he was going through at the stage when the field data were being processed. It is probable that the methodological and philosophical foundation of his agrarian research enterprise was Karl

51. Contrary to the accounts given in memoir literature and current scholarship on which it is based, none of Chen's important future lieutenants participated in his first field project in Wuxi. All three team leaders referred to here did not join the Academia Sinica until the fall of 1929, after the field work for the Wuxi survey had been completed.
52. This observation is confirmed by Qian Jiaju. Interview with Qian in Hacienda Heights, California, October 20, 1990.
53. See Zhang Peigang, "Qingyuan de nongjia jingji" (Farm Economy in Tsing Yuen, Hebei), *Shehui kexue zazhi* (Quarterly Review of Social Sciences), Pt. I, VII.1 (March 1936), pp. 1–65; Pt. II, VII.2 (June 1936), pp. 187–266; and Pt. III, VIII.1 (March 1937), pp. 53–120.
54. See his "The Agrarian Problem of China," presented at the biennial conference of the Institute of Pacific Relations at Banff in 1933 and published in Bruno Lasker and W. L. Holland, eds., *Problems of the Pacific, 1933* (Chicago, 1934), pp. 271–98.

Kautsky's *The Agrarian Question* (*Die Agrarfrage*).[55] In a letter from the field in 1930, he mentioned Kautsky and praised his study of the agrarian economy in Western Europe as a most valuable reference work.[56] Memoir literature provides another piece of evidence. Qian Junrui, for example, reported that they studied Kautsky's *The Agrarian Question* while they were conducting field research.[57]

Chen's research agenda and the major thrust of his argument provided the most compelling evidence of Kautsky's influence. First was the very notion of the "agrarian crisis" itself. Like Kautsky, Chen viewed the crisis as growing both in intensity and scope. Furthermore, the crisis was wrought by factors that defied the remedial measures that directed at symptoms rather than root causes. Most important for Chen was Kautsky's analysis of the increasing misery and suffering of the peasant, or what Kautsky characterized as the proletarianization of the peasantry. According to Kautsky, this process began with the incorporation of the peasantry into the market economy. Having been swept into the market economy, the peasants became commodity-producers. Gone was the "well-being, independence, and security of the free peasant,"[58] a romanticized picture of the peasant before he was robbed of his innocence by the market force. In addition to the vicissitudes of the market, the peasants became the victims of exploitation in the forms of merchant manipulation, usury, and high taxation. Peasant indebtedness increased, which often resulted in the loss of their land, and ultimately in "their transformation into *proletarians*."[59] While minuscule farms persisted, the meager income they generated drove peasants to seek supplementary agricultural as well as nonagricultural forms of employment, with not only a detrimental effect on their own farms, but with the consequence of bringing new and more intense forms of exploitation onto themselves.

Kautsky's influence was manifested in Chen's research agenda as well. In both the Wuxi and Baoding surveys, Chen's attempt to calculate the differential rates of investment and return for each stratum of the peasantry was an effort to prove, with Chinese data, Kautsky's observation

---

55. Pete Burgess, tr., *The Agrarian Question* (London, 1988), 2 vols.
56. "Guanyu Baoding nongcun diaocha de yixie renshi" (On the Baoding Survey), *Nongye zhoubao* (Farmers' Weekly), No. 41 (July 27, 1930), pp. 1120–1.
57. Lin Shuiyuan, "Zhuming de shijie jingjixuejia Qian Junrui" (The Famous Economist on the World Economy: Qian Junrui), in Sun Liancheng and Lin Pu, eds., *Zhongguo dangdai zhuming jingjixuejia* (Noted Economists in Contemporary China) (Chengdu, 1985), Vol. I, p. 389.
58. Kautsky, *The Agrarian Question*, p. 17.   59. Ibid.

concerning the superiority of the larger farm.[60] In compiling the statistics, he followed Kautsky's method in arranging the figures in blocks according to size, that is, *mu* in Chen's cases, as opposed to the less precise terms of small, medium, and large used by Buck. The credit system, another important item on Chen's research agenda, echoed Kautsky's observation on the effect of credit, and its pernicious variant, usury, on helpless peasants.

Kautsky's analysis of the proletarianization of the peasantry was invaluable for Chen, but some of his observations threatened to undermine Chen's own analysis of the Chinese case. The notion of the agrarian crisis itself posed one conceptual problem. While Chen adopted this Kautskyian notion, the agrarian crisis that he perceived in China in fact took place in a completely different context from what Kautsky had in mind. Chen was convinced that China's agrarian economy remained precapitalistic in nature, as evidenced by Wuxi's byzantine tenure system, fragmentation of cultivated land, and its complete lack of standard land measurements. It was in terms of this precapitalistic economy of China that Chen analyzed its agrarian crisis. However, the agrarian crisis Kautsky referred to belonged to an entirely different order; it was a crisis that was peculiar to the capitalistic mode of production. In Kautsky's own words: "Capitalist farming has now reached the stage which feudal agriculture arrived at in the late eighteenth century – a dead end, from which it cannot emerge by virtue of its own forces on the given social foundation."[61]

Even more difficult for Chen to reconcile was Kautsky's analysis of mortgage indebtedness and tenant farming. Kautsky argued that the increase in mortgage indebtedness, far from being a sign of agrarian distress, reflected instead progress and prosperity. This was so "first because such progress generates a growing need for capital, and secondly because the extension of agricultural credit allows ground-rents to rise."[62] Tenant farming similarly received high praise as "the classical manifestation of capitalist agriculture."[63] The logic was simple. According to Kautsky, the price of the land typically constituted from two-thirds to three-quarters of the farmer's capital if he chose to own it. This would leave only about a quarter of his capital for actual operation of his farm. It therefore made sense that farmers should prefer renting to owning the

60. The progress reports for the Wuxi survey cited earlier gave the gist of the team's findings. For similar effort with the Baoding survey, see Zhang Peigang, "Qingyuan de nongjia jingji." For Kautsky's analysis, see "chapter 6:" "Large and Small Farms," in *The Agrarian Question*.
61. Ibid., p. 231.   62. Ibid., p. 89.   63. Ibid., p. 200.

Table 7.1. *Percent of Distribution of Peasant Households by Management Mode*

Capitalistic	7.10
Partly capitalistic	24.20
Pre-capitalistic	68.70
Total	100.00

Source: *Guoli Zhongyang yanjiuyuan yuanwu yuebao* (November 1930), II.5, 40. See also *The Academia Sinica and its National Research Institutes* (1931), p. 111.

land. By leasing rather than owning the land, tenants – the agricultural entrepreneurs – could apply all their money to farming and achieve the highest possible yield.

These arguments ran counter to what Chen had believed; he had held that increasing mortgage indebtedness forced peasants into tenancy and contributed to their misery. It must have been a shock for Chen that what he had believed to have oppressed the peasants were taken by Kautsky to be the manifestations of the capitalistic mode of production. To make matters worse, Kautsky was not the only source that had provoked a crisis in conceptualization for Chen. Sometime in the middle of 1930, the work of another authority in Marxism that Chen had only then discovered, delivered a second and more shattering blow. This was Lenin's *The Development of Capitalism in Russia*. It appears that despite his knowledge of Russian and earlier sojourn in Moscow, Chen came across this work of Lenin's through Shiratori Keisuke's Japanese translation in summer 1930 when his team began to compile reference materials on the different social structures of the precapitalistic, capitalistic, and modern colonial societies.[64]

The evidence of influence from Lenin first appeared in a brief progress report published in November 1930, in which Chen presented in Table 7.1 the breakdown by percentage to indicate the predominance of the pre-capitalistic mode in the agrarian economy in Wuxi.

It is no surprise that there was no definition nor reference to the ter-

64. His first reference to this work of Lenin's appeared in "The Agrarian Problem of China," p. 289. The reference was to Shiratori Keisuke, tr., *Rōshia ni okeru shihon shūgi no hattatsu* (Tokyo: Hakuyō sha, 1930), vol. I.

minology used, considering the practice among contemporary leftist Chinese writers to refer to Marx by "Karl" and Lenin by "Ilyich" to elude censorship.

The intellectual indebtedness to Lenin is unmistakable. The inspiration behind this tripartite tabulation clearly came from Lenin's analysis of the Russian economy after the abolition of serfdom in 1861. According to Lenin, the Russian economy during this transitional stage consisted of the capitalistic mode based on wage labor on the one end, the remnant of the natural economy based on labor service on the other, and a mixed system in between.[65] The difference is that whereas Lenin demonstrated the predominance of the capitalistic economy in European Russia, Chen stressed the precapitalistic nature of the agrarian economy in Wuxi.

In the same report on the predominance of the precapitalistic economy in Wuxi, Chen still used the non-Marxist classification to refer to the peasants as owner-cultivators and tenant peasants.[66] However, he soon became aware of the need to differentiate the peasantry. In a progress report published in summer 1931, the peasants in Wuxi were for the first time broken down according to the Leninist categories of the "rich peasant," the "middle peasant," and the "poor peasant."[67]

Like Kautsky's, Lenin's discussion of the development of capitalism in Russia contradicted Chen's own agrarian analysis. The intensification of land concentration, of tenancy, and of peasant impoverishment, though in themselves ruthless and sources of untold suffering, nevertheless were historically progressive in that they were harbingers of change toward capitalism, as Lenin had demonstrated in his analysis of the Russian case. In fact, the issue of tenancy assumed just the opposite significance in Russia; the tenancy rate was an index to measure the inception of agricultural capitalism in Russia because it was the rich peasants, rather than the poor peasants, as was the case in China, who rented the land. Because land tenure, whatever the form it took, would not pose an insurmountable obstacle to capitalism, Lenin categorically dismissed it as an unimportant question.[68]

While Chen was by no means a Narodnik, who, as noted contemptuously by Lenin, longed for a return to an idealized peasant community, he viewed the unabated trend toward land concentration by the land-

---

65. Lenin, "The Development of Capitalism in Russia," in *V. I. Lenin: Collected Works* (Moscow, 1960), Vol. 3, pp. 193–7.
66. *Guoli Zhongyang yanjiuyuan yuanwu yuebao*, II.5, p. 40.
67. *Guoli Zhongyang yanjiuyuan shijiu niandu zong baogao*, p. 358.
68. Lenin, "The Development of Capitalism in Russia," pp. 323–4.

lord and impoverishment of the peasant as indices of a deepening agrarian crisis in China. Yet, the same indices acquired exactly the opposite significance in Lenin's analysis. According to Lenin, the differentiation of the peasantry – the polarization of the agricultural sector into a rural bourgeoisie on the one hand and a rural proletariat on the other – was precisely what signaled the transition, whether in the more backward Russia or the more advanced western Europe, to a capitalist economy. It must have been devastating to Chen to have discovered that the powerful analytic categories he had acquired threatened to invalidate the assumptions upon which his agrarian research enterprise rested.[69]

CLANDESTINE ACTIVITIES

There is one more factor that led to the disappointing outcome of the two well-designed and well-executed surveys of Wuxi and Baoding. For a person with a keen interest in politics dating from his student days in the United States and a background as a Comintern member, the revolutionary passion and intrigues of Shanghai, the crucible of the Chinese revolution, proved too powerful and tempting to resist. He was distracted from his agrarian research activities by the pull of politics.

Like his earlier work for the Comintern during his days in Peking, Chen's "extracurricular" activities in Shanghai remained largely in the background. In 1929, through Song Qingling's (Madam Sun Yat-sen) introduction, he met Agnes Smedley, who had just arrived in Shanghai as a correspondent for the *Frankfurter Zeitung*.[70] Intellectually inquisitive and passionately sympathetic to the down-trodden, Smedley accompanied Chen on one of his field trips to villages in Wuxi. In an autobiographical account written nearly fifteen years later, she painted an abhorrent picture of the wealth and rapaciousness of a landlord, Zhu (Chu), contrasted with the poverty and helplessness of his tenants. Even if she had dramatized the situation, her account, exemplified by the following conversation with Chen, underscores how ideology conditions one's perception of society.

As soon as we were alone I exclaimed: "An army ought to march in, imprison the Chu family, and free the peasant!"

---

69. See the discussion in Chapter 8 concerning Chen's resolution of this conceptual crisis caused by his encounter with Kautsky's and Lenin's analysis.
70. For a study of Smedley and her life, see Janice and Stephen MacKinnon, *Agnes Smedley: The Life and Times of an American Radical* (Berkeley, 1988).

"Which army?" my friend asked.

I met the scholar in Shanghai a week later and said: "Last night I dined with some German business men and told them of the Chu family and the peasants. They criticized my attitude furiously. To hear them talk, you would think such an attitude as mine was their funeral!"

"It is!" my friend answered dryly.[71]

These two like-minded friends soon began to collaborate on clandestine rescue missions, though not for peasants but for political fugitives fleeing from Guomindang police. The routine they worked out was like this: Chen would take a cab to pick up the fugitive at Smedley's apartment on Rue Joffre in the French concession, which, with more than twenty entrances and exits, was an ideal sanctuary.[72] The cab would then continue on to the Huangpu wharf, with no words exchanged nor the identity of the person revealed.[73]

Their clandestine activities went beyond simple rescue missions and took on a new dimension to include intelligence gathering in early 1930, when they befriended Richard Sorge. A Comintern agent who later operated a famous spy ring in Tokyo in the 1930s and 1940s and was arrested and executed in 1944, Sorge had arrived in Shanghai in January 1930 with an assignment to collect intelligence in China for the Soviet Red Army.[74] Through Smedley, Chen Hansheng became Sorge's chief Chinese collaborator. Chen was identified only as "Wang" and praised for his competency by Sorge in his prison "memoirs."[75] Susie, Chen's wife, became the second member of Sorge's group in China. In addition to introducing informants and arranging contact persons in various places, Chen brought in data and helped Sorge with translation and analysis.

One day in February 1932, Smedley requested that Chen leave from Nanjing for Xuzhou in order to accompany someone there to Xi'an. He only found out in Xuzhou that the person he was supposed to meet with was none other than Sorge, who had come up from Shanghai. The two were picked up at the Xi'an train station and entertained by Yang

---

71. Agnes Smedley, *Battle Hymn of China* (New York, 1943), pp. 68–9.
72. MacKinnon, *Agnes Smedley*, p. 166.
73. Chen Hansheng, *Sige shidai de wo*, pp. 53–4.
74. For Sorge and his espionage activities, see Chalmers Johnson, *An Instance of Treason: Ozaki Hotsumi and the Sorge Spy Ring* (Stanford, 1964).
75. Charles Willoughby, *Shanghai Conspiracy: The Sorge Spy Ring* (New York, 1952), pp. 176–8. See also Chen Hansheng, *Sige shidai de wo*, p. 54.

Hucheng, who, together with Zhang Xueliang, was to kidnap Chiang Kai-shek in the same city in 1936. Upon completing the mission, the purpose of which Chen never inquired, they discovered that the eastbound trains were cancelled due to plague in the region. Sorge then arranged to have the two of them flown to Loyang on a German plane. From there, Sorge returned to Shanghai and Chen journeyed on to Taiyuan, where he saw Feng Yuxiang who had been in "forced" retirement after his defeat by Chiang Kai-shek a year earlier.[76]

Less dramatic, but equally clandestine, was the courier role that he played for Song Qingling in the latter's civil rights campaigns. Following Song's advice to remain in the background, he did not become a member of the Chinese League for the Protection of Civil Rights organized in December 1932 by Song and his senior colleagues at the Academia Sinica, Cai Yuanpei and Yang Quan. He nonetheless performed the important task of delivering press releases to newspaper offices in an effort to break government censorship. When the Noulens (whose real names were Paul and Gertrude Ruegg) were arrested in June 1931 on the charge of being Comintern agents,[77] Song and others organized a Noulens Defense Committee. It was Chen's courier service that kept the communication functioning smoothly between the committee and the Swiss attorney it had engaged.[78] That Chen's courier role was clandestine can be seen from the fact that the Nanjing government viewed the actions of both the league and the committee as seditious. The assassination of Yang Quan, secretary-general of the league, on June 18, 1933 underscored the danger involved in trying to publicize political persecutions.

Although Chen covered well his clandestine activities, his ideological position was public knowledge. One telling episode occurred not long after the Institute of the Social Sciences was relocated to Nanjing in early 1932. Chen Lifu, then head of the organization department of the Guomindang Party, invited him to give a talk. The topic was to be Chen's own choosing. Fully aware that this was a security test that was not meant to be declined, Chen decided on the topic "The Relation between Land Tax and Land Rent." In his lecture he discoursed on how the landlords had

---

76. Here I follow the story given in Chen Hansheng, *Sige shidai de wo*, pp. 54–5, instead of the slightly different version in Stephen MacKinnon, "The Life and Times of Chen Han-sheng (1897–)," *Selected Papers in Asian Studies, Paper No. 35* (Western Conference of the Association for Asian Studies, 1990), p. 4.
77. MacKinnon, *Agnes Smedley*, pp. 148–9.
78. Chen Hansheng, *Sige shidai de wo*, pp. 51–2.

historically gained at the expense of the state, a brilliant coup which enabled Chen to pass the judgement of the Guomindang propaganda boss without having to compromise his own ideological convictions.[79]

The crackdown came in spring 1933. Not surprisingly, Chen's colleagues at the Academia Sinica knew best his ideological position. He apparently made no attempt to hide it. It is said that he had hanging in his office a huge framed picture with four big characters, "*jimin zhi shi*" (food of famine victims), made of grass roots, wild leaves, and tree bark.[80] Memoir literature put the blame on Fu Sinian, the staunchly anti-Communist head of the Institute of History and Philology, who allegedly was the one agitated for action against Chen and his team.[81] The crackdown in fact reflected a systematic effort by the Guomindang Party to control an insubordinate Academia Sinica, considering the fact that Cai Yuanpei and Yang Quan, its president and secretary-general, were on the governing board of the antigovernment Chinese League for the Protection of Civil Rights discussed above. In April 1933, Fu Sinian became the head of the Institute of the Social Sciences. In late May, the Academia Sinica was ordered to set up a secret party branch.[82] The axe fell first on Chen's assistants at the sociology section; they were dismissed one by one. One of them was arrested as a Communist a few months after he had been dismissed.[83] Then Yang Quan was assassinated on June 18. Feeling the threat of the juggernaut, Chen resigned.

With the head of its only active Section gone and the research staff decimated, the Institute of the Social Sciences existed in name only. At

79. During the Cultural Revolution, this talk was used as evidence to accuse him of being a C.C. member and caused him nine months of confinement. *Sige shidai de wo*, p. 57.
80. Ren Xuefang, "Makesi zhuyi nongcun jingjixue de xianqu: Chen Hansheng Shilüe" (A Pioneer in Marxist Agrarian Economy: A Biographical Sketch of Chen Hansheng), in *Economics Daily* ed., *Zhongguo dangdai jingjixuejia zhuanlüe* (Biographical Sketches of Contemporary Chinese Economists) (Liaoning, 1986), p. 100.
81. See, for example, *Sige shidai de wo*, p. 57; Qian Junrui, "Zhongguo nongcun jingji yanjiuhui chengli qianhou" (Events Surrounding the Founding of the Society for the Study of China's Agrarian Economy), *Wenshi ziliao xuanji* (Selections of Materials on History and Literature), No. 84 (December 1982), p. 21; and Sun Xiaocun, "Zhongguo nongcun jingji yanjiuhui yu Nongcun fuxing weiyuanhui" (The Society for the Study of China's Agrarian Economy and the Rural Rehabilitation Commission), in ibid, No. 84, p. 32.
82. No. 695 secret order to the Academia Sinica by the Executive Committee of the Nanjing Guomindang Party Bureau (Zhongguo Guomindang Nanjing tebieshi zhixing weiyuanhui), May 23, 1933 the Academia Sinica Archives (*Zhongyang yanjiuyuan dang*) 393.508, deposited at the Second Historical Archives of China in Nanjing.
83. Shi Kaifu was his name. See the Academia Sinica Archives 393.1713.

first, the Academia Sinica contemplated the idea of merging the Institute with that of History and Philology, but a much better option soon emerged. As it happened, the China Foundation was going through its own soul-searching process with regard to its Institute of Social Research.[84] Both sides quickly saw in each other an ideal partner for merger. When the deal was completed in 1934, it was more a takeover by the China Foundation's Institute of Social Research than a merger between equals. As a result, the history of the Institute of Chen's era was all but obliterated. With convenient historical amnesia, the history of the China Foundation's Institute subsumed that of the original Institute.

Also consigned to oblivion were the field data from the unmentionable past. The Wuxi data were left to gather dust on the shelves. The Baoding data fared slightly better.[85] To make use of the data from the Baoding survey, on which the takeover Institute had collaborated, one member in the reorganized Institute of the Social Sciences was assigned to prepare a report.[86] The published report, which appeared in 1936–37, utilized only a small portion of the field data and reflected none of Chen's ideological and methodological convictions, though it retained the original Leninist categories under which data were processed.[87]

Nevertheless, the loss of the institutional base at the Academia Sinica did not spell the end of Chen's research enterprise. It was as if his four years at the Academia Sinica were his apprenticeship in agrarian research. With brilliant maneuvering to create alternative institutional bases, to secure funding, and to deploy his research assistants, he was to enter an intense and productive phase of his agrarian research career in the years ahead.

---

84. For a discussion on this matter within the China Foundation, see Chapter 9.
85. Neither the Wuxi nor the Baoding data are in the Academia Sinica Archives at the Second Historical Archives in Nanjing. The data may have been removed in 1958, when the State Statistical Bureau and the Jiangsu Provincial Statistic Bureau jointly launched a new survey of Wuxi. See Qin Liufang, "Dui 'Jiefang qian lao shehui gongzuozhe de nongcun diaocha' yi wen de yijian" (Some Points of Correction on the Article 'The Agrarian Surveys by Former Social Researchers before the Liberation'), *Shehui* (Society), No. 3 (June 20, 1984), p. 63.
86. This report, entitled "Qingyuan de nongjia jingji" (Farm Economy in Tsing Yuen [Baoding], Hebei), was written by Zhang Peigang and appeared in three parts in the Institute's journal, *Shehui kexue zazhi* (Quarterly Review of Social Sciences), Pt. I, VII.1 (March 1936), pp. 1–65; Pt. II, VII.2 (June 1936), pp. 187–266; and Pt. III, VIII.1 (March 1937), pp. 53–120.
87. Ibid., Pt. I, p. 4.

8

The Social Sciences, Agrarian China, and the Advocacy of Revolution

CHEN Hansheng's four years at the Academia Sinica constituted the germinating period for his agrarian research enterprise. Even though nothing significant came out of the two large-scale surveys of Wuxi and Baoding, the reward was tremendous. Aside from the analytic concepts that he had acquired, the most valuable was perhaps the corps of committed researchers he had recruited and trained. This group had developed such an esprit de corps that not only were they not broken by the loss of the base at the Academia Sinica, but they would regroup, first by using ad hoc bases and then creating an alternative institutional base, and would continue to propagate their diagnosis of and remedies for China's agrarian crisis.

SUSTAINING THE ENTERPRISE ON AD HOC
INSTITUTIONAL BASES

Just as Chen was about to lose his institutional base at the Academia Sinica, the Executive Yuan of the Nanjing government established the Commission for Rural Rehabilitation in April 1933, to which he was appointed a member, a feat that revealed both his connections in high places and the existence of room for maneuver in spite of Nanjing's best efforts. The Commission sponsored studies of such problems as credit, tax burden, marketing of major food grains and cash crops, and irrigation. One quick, tangible result the Commission obtained was the surveys of the four provinces of Jiangsu, Zhejiang, Henan, and Shaanxi.

As a member on the Commission, Chen helped put together the planning committee, which was composed of Sun Xiaocun, Wang Yinsheng, and Zhang Xichang. All three shared his ideological convictions: Sun was an ally whose position on the Commission provided a useful cover for

184

Chen's subversive research activities into the mid-1930s; Wang and Zhang had been members of Chen's team at the Academia Sinica. They were charged to design the schedules, to formulate the research program, and to recruit field workers.[1] In addition to being on the planning committee, Wang and Zhang directed survey work in Shaanxi and Henan respectively. The four survey teams set out to their respective provinces during July and August in 1933 and published their reports in 1934.[2]

By adroit maneuvers and brilliant deployments of his research assistants, Chen thus made the Nanjing government commission him to conduct surveys with an agenda and ideology it deemed subversive. The research design of these four-province surveys bore Chen's hallmarks: a sampling of representative units and a central focus on land distribution. The province was demarcated into three or four of what he referred to as natural economic areas. One county that was deemed representative in each of these economic areas was chosen for general survey. Within each of the counties chosen, a certain number of representative villages was selected for detailed house-to-house surveys.

More significant was the Leninist classification scheme that divided the peasantry into the landlords, the rich peasants, the middle peasants, the poor peasants, and agricultural laborers. This classification scheme was an ideological marker shunned by both establishment social scientists and the authorities. It is astonishing that the Commission went along with the planning committee in adopting this classification scheme.[3] The Commission must have had second thoughts immediately afterward, however, because it reverted back to the conventional classification scheme of landlords, owner-cultivators, half-owners, tenants, and agri-

---

1. "Benhui juxing Su-Zhe-Yu-Shaan sisheng nongcun diaocha zhi choubei jingguo" (The Planning Process of the Surveys of the Four Provinces of Jiangsu, Zhejiang, Henan, and Shaanxi conducted by the Commission), *Nongcun fuxing weiyuanhui huibao*, No. 2 (July 26, 1933), p. 16.
2. *Jiangsu sheng nongcun diaocha* (The Agrarian Survey of the Jiangsu Province), *Zhejiang sheng nongcun diaocha* (The Agrarian Survey of the Zhejiang Province), *Shaanxi sheng nongcun diaocha* (The Agrarian Survey of the Shaanxi Province), and *Henan sheng nongcun diaocha* (The Agrarian Survey of the Henan Province).
3. Sun Xiaocun, "Zhongguo nongcun jingji yanjiuhui yu Nongcun fuxing weiyuanhui" (The Society for the Study of China's Agrarian Economy and the Rural Rehabilitation Commission), in *Wenshi ziliao xuanji* (Selections of Materials on History and Literature), No. 84 (December 1982), p. 33. Note that Sun mistakenly recalled that they were forced to abandon their classification scheme.

cultural laborers for the two surveys of Yunnan and Guangxi conducted only six months later.[4]

The Leninist class analysis of the village used the economic strength of the peasants as the criterion.[5] There were two types of landlords: rent-collecting and managerial. The former collected rents on most or all the land they owned; the latter, by contrast, hired laborers to work on most or all of their land. The rich peasants engaged in farming themselves, while hiring a long-term laborer or day laborers for more than one-hundred days, and had the potential to expand their holding. The middle peasants cultivated either their own land or rented land, but did not hire laborers nor hire themselves out, and could only manage to hold on to what they had. Finally were the poor peasants, who either cultivated tiny plots, whether owned or rented, or had to hire out all or most of the time and saw their already minuscule holdings ever-diminishing.[6]

The survey workers nonetheless had to tread a fine line between exposing corruption and exploitation on the one hand, and staying within the ideological parameter that the Commission would sanction on the other. Land tenure and taxes, including miscellaneous surtaxes, were relatively safe issues, given the official rhetoric on the need to lighten the burden of the peasants.[7] Less clear, however, was the issue of corrupt rural administration, be it the result of collusion between the landlords and rural authorities or of rapacious extractions by the latter as military requisitions. It is not accidental that the field reports published contained disproportionately little information about rural administration. Obviously alarmed by the radical bent of the drafts, the Commission imposed a heavy censorship, citing concerns that the field data may not have accurately reflected local situations.[8] One clever device the drafters of the reports resorted to was the "Diary from the Field," which appeared in the appendix of each volume and contained gists of information about some of the particularly blatant cases of political corruption.

4. See *Yunan sheng nongcun diaocha* (The Agrarian Survey of Yunnan Province) (Shanghai, 1935) and *Guangxi sheng nongcun diaocha* (The Agrarian Survey of Guangxi Province) (Shanghai, 1935).
5. Lenin, "The Development of Capitalism in Russia," p. 102.
6. See the general "Explanatory Notes" of the surveys.
7. Philip Kuhn has convincingly demonstrated that this rhetoric should be understood as an attempt by the state to rebureaucratize the process of taxation at the local level. See his "Local Taxation and Finance in Republican China," in Susan Mann Jones, ed., *Select Papers from the Center for Far Eastern Studies* (University of Chicago), No. 3, 1978–79, p. 124.
8. See the general preface written by Peng Xuepei, secretary general of the Commission.

The conclusion of the four-province surveys is, in a nutshell, that China's agrarian economy by itself would not move toward capitalism. All the villages surveyed had very few resident landlords, ranging from less than 1 percent to slightly over 2 percent. The rich peasants likewise were in the minority.[9] The middle peasants varied from the 6 and 7 percent range to the 20 and 30 percent range. The largest in number were the poor peasants and agricultural laborers, ranging from the lowest of 37.6 percent in Yancheng in Jiangsu, through the majority of 60 percent range, to the highest of 87.32 percent in Fengxiang in Shaanxi.

These social stratification patterns had an inverse relationship to the landholding patterns in the villages. It is no surprise that landlord holdings in the villages were insignificant, given the fact that the surveys covered only the holdings of resident landlords. Rich peasants in Jiangsu, except in Pi Xian, led all other provinces in holding the largest percentage of the land in the villages, with Yancheng registering 61.4 percent. In all other areas, it was the middle and poor peasants whose combined holdings constituted the majority, with Fengxiang registered at 90.87 percent. The pattern was clear: Inequality was the common feature in all four provinces. In Shaanxi and Henan, the upper strata held holdings many times larger than those of the bottom stratum. The ratio was in the sixty- and seventy-fold range in Zhejiang and Jiangsu, with Qidong reaching the horrific hundred and sixty-fold ratio.[10]

The minuscule holdings of poor peasants created pressure on them to augment their income from supplementary employment and resulted in irrational use of their labor and draft animal power – a Kautskyian thesis. It is, however, precisely here that Chen parted with Kautsky. The misery and drudgery of the bottom stratum did not help bolster an economically vital upper stratum in China, as had happened in both Europe and European Russia. In the villages where rich peasants dominated, these Kautskyian and Leninist carriers of seeds of agricultural capitalism had been in decline both in terms of their number and size of their holdings. The two Jiangsu samples of Yancheng and Qidong, where a rich peasant economy might have had the best chance to emerge, witnessed a sharp reduction in the holdings of the rich peasants from 1928 to 1933: 10 percent for Yancheng and 5.4 percent for Qidong. The decline of the rich

---

9. This was particularly true in Zhejiang and the two hinterland provinces of Henan and Shaanxi, where the percentage ranged from less than 1%, through the 2% range, to the highest of 8.08% in Hui Xian in northern Henan.
10. *Jiangsu sheng nongcun diaocha*, p. 11.

peasants, in contradistinction to the fate of their counterparts in Lenin's analysis, provided Chen Hansheng with a most persuasive argument to both depart from Lenin's analysis and to prognosticate that China's agrarian economy would not by itself move toward capitalism.

Landlords, by contrast, fared rather well. And it was here that lay the crux of China's agrarian problem. As a rentier class, landlords were no harbingers of agricultural capitalism. Like Kautsky, Chen saw the landlords as parasites who extracted the resources that could have been put to more productive use by the tenants. The reclamation companies in Jiangsu were cases in point here. In the four coastal counties that form a north-south axis with Yancheng in the middle, there were forty-one reclamation companies. Together they had reclaimed nearly five million *mu* of land that had previously been used to produce salt by evaporation. None, however, was engaged in modern, large-scale production and management. After having reclaimed the land, they rented it in parcels to tenants, thereby assuming the traditional role of landlords rather than that of modern enterprises.[11] The concentration of the land at the top of the upper stratum, instead of giving impetus to bring agriculture into a higher level of production, perpetuated precapitalistic production relations in the villages. To prop up this *ancien régime* was the large reservoir of poor peasants, who, without an industrialization to absorb them, were condemned to their pitifully minuscule plots.

Powerful and provocative as the central argument and prognosis of these four-province surveys were, they contained some serious defects. They were hastily planned, executed, and written: two weeks for planning and two months each for field work and writing. There were no reasons why these provinces were chosen other than not to duplicate a separate four-province surveys of Anhui, Jiangxi, Hunan, and Hubei sponsored around the same time by the Sun Yat-sen Institute for the Advancement of Culture and Education.[12] More serious was the small data base: four counties in each province and four to eight villages in each county. The choice of actual field sites furthermore was often dictated as much by favorably inclined local authorities and the availability of local contacts as by transportation difficulties and banditry.[13]

Most serious defects stemmed from the two research designs that

11. *Jiangsu sheng nongcun diaocha*, pp. 4–5.
12. These surveys were never published.
13. For information on how many of the field sites were chosen, see "Diary from the Field," in each volume.

Chen adhered to throughout his entire agrarian research career. Because the goal was to discern broad trends, he studied the village as an aggregate, but not its individual components – the families. This concern with broad trends was reflected also in his decision to combine the statistics from the villages as representing the county in which they belonged, thus obscuring the differences that existed among individual villages.[14] The other serious flaw in research design concerned the study of land distribution. In calculating land distribution in the villages, the surveys left out the land owned by absentee landlords – a research design that characterized all of Chen's agrarian surveys, perhaps because the survey teams had no way to find out who they were and how much they owned.

If the first research design limited the usefulness of the survey data, the second misled future researchers who utilized the survey data. Because the reports made no clear indication that the figures did not include the holdings of absentee landlords, unwary researchers took the statistics as representing the total acreage of the villages and drew conclusions on the basis of this mistaken assumption.[15] By excluding the holdings of absentee landlords, these surveys failed to reveal not only the true magnitude of the concentration of the land in the hands of the few, but the exploitative relations between the market towns and county seats on the one hand and the villages on the other – perfect themes for Chen on the agrarian crisis in China.

These four-province surveys marked Chen's return to his original diagnosis of China's agrarian crisis. He never rejected the Kautskyian or the Leninist analysis, however. In returning to his original agrarian analysis, Chen applied the arguments of these two Marxist authorities, but by turning them around; whereas Kautsky and Lenin associated the concentration of the land and exploitation of the peasants with agricultural capitalism, Chen saw in these phenomena root causes for China's deepening agrarian crisis.

14. Fortunately, the aggregate statistics of individual villages were available in the text in the Shaanxi survey and in the appendices of other volumes.
15. David Faure, for example, thought the four-province reports understated the number of landlords and wondered whether the survey workers could have been more successful than government attempts to register land. See his *The Rural Economy of Pre-Liberation China: Trade Expansion and Peasant Livelihood in Jiangsu and Guangdong, 1870 to 1937* (Oxford, 1989), p. 172. Kawachi Jūzō discusses how an earlier article of his erred in not having noticed these two unfortunate research designs. See his "1930 nendai Chūgoku no nōminsō bunka no haaku no tame ni" (Understanding Social Stratification among the Chinese Peasantry in the 1930s), *Rekishigaku kenkyū* (Historical Studies), 290 (July 1964), pp. 27–41.

Something important was lost in the process, however. One unfortunate result of his successful resolution of this conceptual crisis was a much narrower focus in his agrarian research. He became preoccupied with the issues of the unequal distribution of the land and the exploitation of the peasants. Gone was the effort, as in his earlier Wuxi and Baoding surveys, to calculate income from sideline activities, the credit system, and the differential rates of investment and return for each stratum of the peasantry.[16]

Perhaps because Chen was not personally involved either in their planning or execution, he never claimed these four-province surveys as his. The same was not true with his survey of Guangdong province, his second survey using an ad hoc institutional base. In 1933, through Madam Sun Yat-sen's help, he brought together the Sun Yat-sen Institute for the Advancement of Culture and Education and Lingnan University in Canton to sponsor jointly a survey of the Guangdong province. The two field directors were his former assistants at the Academia Sinica: Wang Yinsheng and Sun Yefang. These two field directors led four team leaders and eight survey workers, all of whom were recruited locally.

The research design was patterned after the four-province surveys. The sixteen counties selected for general surveys represented different economic zones of the province, including the more prosperous Han river region in the east and the Canton delta region in the south, the hilly northern regions, and the more backward southwest. Unlike his previous surveys, however, Chen did not identify representative villages in these sixteen counties for intensive house-to-house surveys. In the Guangdong survey, the representative village study took place instead in one single county in Panyu, where 1,209 households in ten villages were chosen for in-depth study.[17]

Entitled *The Production Relations and Productive Forces in Guangdong*,[18] the Guangdong survey was the finest of Chen's agrarian research and his most eloquent account of China's agrarian crisis. It comple-

16. His *Industrial Capital and Chinese Peasants* (Shanghai, 1939) is the major exception to this statement.
17. The survey team also made use of correspondence to gather information from 335 villages in fifty counties.
18. There are two separate English editions of the survey: *Agrarian Problems in Southernmost China* (Shanghai, 1936) and *Landlord and Peasant in China: A Study of the Agrarian Crisis in South China* (New York, 1936). The New York edition has an expanded version of the "Introduction." The Chinese version is entitled *Guangdong de nongcun shengchan guanxi yu nongcun shengchanli* (The Production Relations and the Productive Forces in Guangdong), which was published in Shanghai in 1934.

Table 8.1. *Land Owned by the Landlords and Peasants (ten representative villages in Panyu county, 1933)*

	Number of families	Percent of families	*Mu* owned	Percent of *mu* owned
Landlords	35	2.9	583.6	18.6
Rich peasants	107	8.8	1212.0	38.5
Middle peasants	193	16.0	689.8	21.9
Poor peasants	540	44.7	540.5	17.2
Agricultural laborers	83	6.9	0	0
Others	251	20.7	118.4	3.8
Total	1209	100	3144.3	100

Source: Adapted from tables 9, 18, and 20 in Chapter 1 of Guangdong *de nongcun shengchan guanxi yu nongcun shengchanli.*

mented his earlier Wuxi and Baoding surveys in providing a basis to examine the production relations in the three economically most advanced coastal provinces of China: Jiangsu, Hebei, and Guangdong.

The significance of the Guangdong survey lay in that it "shows most clearly the effects of imperialist economic penetration on rural life and the growth of class antagonisms in China itself."[19] It was, however, class antagonisms but not imperialism that were the subject of this survey. As will be discussed later, Chen was to have an opportunity to analyze the semicolonial nature of the Chinese society in a separate survey in the future. The Guangdong survey was essentially a treatise on the Comintern's and the Chinese Communist Party's thesis on the semifeudal character of the Chinese society.

The semifeudal production relations in Guangdong manifested themselves in the concentration of land and exploitation of the peasants either by the landlords alone or in collusion with state agents. Table 8.1 gives a breakdown of the number of households, their holdings, and the respective percentage in terms of the number of households and size of holdings in Panyu county.

The statistics in Table 8.1 in fact understate the degree to which the land was unequally distributed in Guangdong villages. In addition to the

19. Chen Hansheng, *Landlord and Peasant in China: A Study of the Agrarian Crisis in South China* (New York, 1936), vii.

Table 8.2. *The Distribution of Land Ownership*
(ten representative villages in Panyu county,
1933)

	Mu Owned and % of *mu* owned
Landlords[a]	5,742.5 (71.3)
Rich peasants	1,115.5 (13.8)
Middle peasants	673.0 (8.4)
Poor peasants	525.0 (6.5)
Total	8,056.0 (100.0)

[a] Including collective and absentee landlords.

Sources: adapted from table 6 and an unnumbered table in Chapter 1 of *Guangdong de nongcun shengchan guanxi yu nongcun shengchanli*.

factor of absentee landlords, over 35 percent of the cultivated land in the province belonged to corporate landlords, which were predominantly represented by lineages and, to a much lesser extent, by "education land" trusts, temples, and merchant organizations.[20] In Panyu, for example, lineage land constituted about 30 percent of the cultivated land in the county. This figure, according to Chen, could have been conservatively raised to over 50 percent if one were to include lineage holdings in the "*shatian*" (polder fields) area, where about 80 percent was reportedly lineage land.[21] Because of the dominance of collective landlordism and the widespread practice of leasing, Chen compiled statistics on the land leased by the peasants in Panyu, thus making it possible for us to reconstitute a statistical breakdown in Table 8.2 to reflect more accurately the distribution of the land in Guangdong villages.

No matter how imprecise these statistics were,[22] they indicated an extraordinary degree of concentration of the land. After having been sensitized by Kautsky and Lenin, however, Chen could no longer attribute the concentration of the land as the principal cause of China's

20. Ibid., pp. 24–5.
21. *Guangdong de nongcun shengchan guanxi yu nongcun shengchanli*.
22. Note that the two tables do not agree on the figures concerning the holdings of the different classes of the peasants.

agrarian crisis. Aside from the link between the concentration of the land and agricultural capitalism, there was the argument that entrepreneurial peasants would profit more through leasing. His own statistics that showed the rich peasants leased more land than the poor were consistent with what Kautsky and Lenin had observed and would seem to have indicated trends toward a higher level of agricultural development rather than agricultural retrogression that he so adamantly insisted on.

Chen rested his case with the Guangdong data. His argument was closely linked to what he viewed as another manifestation of the semi-feudal production relations in China, that is, the exploitation of the peasants either by the landlords alone or in collusion with state agents. On this point Chen, too, followed Kautsky and Lenin only to break away from them. Although both Kautsky and Lenin described the various forms of exploitation the peasantry experienced with the rise of agricultural capitalism, it was Kautsky who inspired Chen. In his euphoria over the rising tide of agricultural capitalism in Russia, Lenin predicted the inevitable triumph of capitalism. Kautsky, by contrast, believed that capitalism would perpetuate and intensify the misery, drudgery, and barbarism of the proletarianized peasants without breaking their ties to the land, dwarf as it was. He argued that the agrarian distress would remain permanent for as long as capitalism itself would last.

In Kautsky's analysis, the first stage of the "proletarianization" of the peasantry began with the incorporation of the peasants into a market economy, whose fluctuations, together with a rising tax burden, generated pressures that increased peasant indebtedness and resulted in the loss of most or all of their land. During the next stage, peasants, due to their dwarf holdings, were forced to seek supplementary forms of employment, whether serving as agricultural laborers for larger farms or as workers in the merchant-employer or putting-out system. While the former made it impossible for the rational operation of the peasants' farms, the latter brought them "the longest, most exhausting working time, the meanest payment, the most children's and women's labor, and the most appalling living and working conditions."[23] Once the process reached this stage, the exploitative relations took on a systemic character and expressed themselves in relentless extractions of agrarian resources by the urban sector. The ever-widening gap between the industrializing towns and backward countryside gave rise to a tributary relationship between the two, wherein the resources from the countryside

---

23. Kautsky, *The Agrarian Question*, p. 185.

flowed into the towns in the forms of taxes, debt interest, and rent. The flight of rural population into the towns further depleted the labor power the countryside needed for rational operation of its farms.[24]

Chen's analysis of the exploitation of the peasantry in Guangdong followed Kautsky's. The Guangdong survey was, in a nutshell, about exploitation. In addition to high rents, up to 78 percent of the estimated annual rice harvest for sugarcane fields in the *Shatian* area,[25] he reported various forms of exactions, such as rent deposits, customary fees,[26] and labor obligations. High rents begot indebtedness, which, under varied but invariably usurious terms, contributed to the loss of the land by the peasants. Tax burdens likewise victimized the peasants, but with a different twist because of the role played by state agents and their collusion with the landlords. He reported the proliferation of the miscellaneous taxes and the land tax itself under the names of local self-government or modernization. Whether these taxes were under direct government control or farmed out to individuals, the burden was always borne by the tenants.[27]

It was collective landlordism that provided Chen with a most poignant context in which to dwell on the exploitation issue. In a province where four out of every five peasants lived with their lineages, corporate ownership supposedly benefited all members, poor or rich. The reality proved otherwise, however. He argued that the collective landlords behaved no differently from private landlords. Although members of a lineage sometimes had a prior right to lineage land or enjoyed a 20 percent reduction as compared to the rent charged to nonlineage tenants, in most districts "no such priority is recognized nor any rent reduction granted."[28] There were places where the tenants had to offer bribery to lineage managers in order to get tenancy contracts.[29]

The collective landlords were no more charitable than nonkin creditors in extending loans to their needy members. The annual interest charged by lineages ranged from the lower end of 18.5 to 24 percent in Hua county near Canton to the higher end of 30 to 50 percent in one area in Maoming

24. Ibid., pp. 212–24.
25. Chen Hansheng, *Landlord and Peasant in China*, p. 48.
26. Contrary to Faure's contention that Chen "seems to have counted as rent deposits all customary dues required at the time the tenancy contract was entered into," Chen was in fact quite specific in distinguishing the two, whether in the Chinese version or the English version (pp. 45–7) – which Faure used – of the survey report. See *Faure's The Rural Economy of Pre-Liberation China*, p. 231 n.47.
27. Chen Hansheng, *Landlord and Peasant in China*, pp. 73–83.
28. Ibid., p. 42.   29. Ibid.

county. Nor were lineages any more lenient with loan defaults. In Hua county, for example, the defaulter would have to forfeit his property and even that of his nearest relatives, if it did not suffice to pay his debt.[30]

What transpired here was the working of class differentiation within the lineage itself – the creation of an exploiting class as embodied in the person of the lineage manager, namely the treasurer, on the one hand, and the tenant peasant class on the other. The treasurer, who invariably came from the strongest branch, often succeeded in so manipulating the common property of the lineage as to treat it as his private property.[31] The power of the lineage manager tended to grow and his functions multiplied. Chen stated that it was not unusual for a lineage manager to act as the chief tax collector on behalf of the provincial government for both lineage and private land in the whole village. This merger of economic and political controls strengthened the power of the few who had already dominated the life of the community. As Chen sarcastically put it, these lineage managers "have assumed all the honours previously reserved for the dead: they have virtually made themselves over into 'living ancestors.' "[32]

Exploitation as a manifestation of agrarian distress was a prominent theme in both Chen's and Kautsky's analyses. There is, however, a difference between the two. Kautsky's was a tough-minded analysis of phenomena of agrarian distress, which were inevitable events accompanying the evolution of a given historical stage. His conviction that agriculture under capitalism was incapable of resolving the agrarian crisis on its own and could only look to urban industry as a motive force to transform its mode of production underscored his belief that it was the impersonal engine of history that moved society.

The same was not true with Chen Hansheng. Underlying his analysis of exploitation of the peasantry was a belief that the agrarian crisis in

30. Ibid., p. 36. 31. Ibid., pp. 37–9.
32. Ibid., p. 41 Chen may have exaggerated the use and misuse of power by lineage managers, as suggested by David Faure in his *The Rural Economy of Pre-Liberation China*, p. 176. However, Faure himself never addressed the various issues raised by Chen. His remark that "lineage land was sometimes rented exclusively to lineage members" misses the point. The point is not access to lineage land, but under what terms and conditions. Equally irrelevant is his remark that tenants benefited from the rent they paid because it underwrote activities important to "the villagers' communal life," such as "temple expenses, . . . with very rich implications." However valid this point is by itself, it does not negate Chen's argument about the exploitation and appropriation of power and wealth by the powerful within the lineage. Rubie Watson's study of the Teng lineage in the New Territories in Hong Kong in fact confirms Chen's argument. See her *Inequality Among Brothers: Class and Kinship in South China* (Cambridge, 1985), pp. 70–2, 88–9.

China was a man-made disaster. His analysis of collective landlordism is a case in point. Collective landlordism exemplified the concentration of resources in the hands of a few. Since the collective landlords owned 14,700,000 of the estimated 42,000,000 *mu* of cultivated land in Guang-dong, assuming an average rent of ten Chinese dollars per *mu*, these lands would yield $147,000,000, of which $126,000,000 was collected by the lineages. The annual land tax of Guangdong was reportedly $5,400,000 and the combined provincial and national revenues, $70,000,000. In other words, lineages in Guangdong collected an annual rent that was almost thirty times the revenue from the annual land tax and more than twice the total collected by all taxes together.[33]

This is the context in which to understand Chen's analysis of the tenancy issue. That the same piece of land could be subject to multiple claims of ownership and, on top of that, separate and, likewise, multiple claims of tenancy rights called into question the use of ownership or tenancy as an index with which to classify the peasants. Moreover, tenants were not necessarily worse off than owners with dwarf holdings, as is evidenced by Chen's data from Panyu where 17.8 percent of those he classified as the rich peasants were landless tenants.[34] The situation was so complex that Chen rejected all the conventional indices for clas-sifying the peasants, whether by the size of the property or size of the farm, by ownership, or in terms of tenancy.[35]

The classification scheme he advocated remained the same as what he had adopted from Lenin since 1931. The two deciding factors in Chen's own words were: "land and labor, and this in quite specific aspects: the land is that which the family uses, and our concern is with the amount of that land and the conditions under which the family may use it; the labour is that which the family puts into the land or hires to use on the land."[36] These were the same criteria he used in the four-province surveys, only that the focus now shifted to exploitation. The middle peas-ants were those who were barely capable of supporting their families

---

33. Chen Hansheng, *Landlord and Peasant in China*, p. 35.
34. Ibid., table 4, p. 123.
35. Ibid., pp. 4–8. It is noteworthy how these keen observations made by Chen Hansheng half a century earlier are recapitulated in Western scholarship. The two prime examples here are Philip Huang and David Faure, coming as they are from the opposite poles of the ideological spectrum. See Huang, "Analyzing the Twentieth-century Chinese Countryside: Revolutionaries Versus Western Scholarship," *Modern China*, I. 2 (April 1975), pp. 132–160, and Faure, *The Rural Economy of Pre-Liberation China*, pp. 164–8.
36. Chen Hansheng, *Landlord and Peasant in China*, p. 8.

from the land and who were neither exploited by, nor exploiting, others with regard to labor. The rich peasants exceeded the middle peasants in the land they cultivated and the labor power they consumed, that is, by hiring one or more long-term laborers or day laborers. Those who cultivated less land than the middle peasants and had to hire themselves out were the poor peasants.

Because Chen's classification scheme focused on the production relations as they were manifested in tenancy and labor exploitation, it was not based on the income level, as alleged by David Faure.[37] Nor was it derived, as Philip Huang asserted, from data on land owned, land rented, and farm size.[38] Chen's scheme was as much an academic analysis as it was a guide to revolutionary action, to borrow Huang's dichotomy. This classification scheme and its focus on exploitation were similar to Mao Zedong's "How to Differentiate the Classes in the Rural Areas," written in October 1933, two months before the Guangdong survey.[39] While this raises the question of ideological conformance, given Chen's Comintern background and clandestine links with the Communist underground in Shanghai, it is important to bear in mind that he had been using this same scheme since 1931, more than two years predated Mao's writing.

Chen's emphasis on exploitation – in tenancy as well as in labor – reflected not just his compassion for the downcast, but also his belief in its detrimental impact on society. Undue concentration of the land occurred at the privation of the majority and the resources thus accumulated were wasted on unproductive activities – another Kautskyian thesis. Its most pernicious effect was the obstruction of the productive forces in society; those who tilled did not have enough land on which to live and the few who owned most of the land did not cultivate. The contradiction between land ownership and land use severely hindered agricultural production. While the landlords wasted away the fruit produced by others in their parasitic existence, the poor peasants subsisted on dwarf holdings that prevented rational use of their labor. In an inversion of the Leninist and Kautskyian analyses, Chen argued that the more concentrated land ownership had become, the more resources would be wasted and labor power lost, and, consequently, the more intensified the agrarian crisis would have become.

37. Faure, *The Rural Economy of Pre-Liberation China*, 168.
38. Huang, "Analyzing the Twentieth-century Chinese Countryside," 144.
39. Mao Zedong, "How to Differentiate the Classes in the Rural Areas," *Selected Works of Mao Tse-tung*, I (Beijing, 1965), pp. 137–9.

While Kautsky could put his faith in industry to deliver European agriculture and its proletarianized peasantry out of the crisis wrought by capitalism, Chen had no grounds for hoping for a similar scenario for China, where the semi-feudal production relations had yet to give way to capitalism. For him, revolution was the only option:

> The essence of the agrarian problem and of the agrarian crisis in China, is how a national liberation movement can be successfully conducted to abolish the basis of all colonial and feudalistic exploitations. For these exploitations prove to be the fundamental obstacle in developing agriculture in China to a higher level, and to raising the living of 400 million people to a higher standard.[40]

CREATION OF AN ALTERNATIVE INSTITUTIONAL BASE

The loss of their base at the Academia Sinica did not cripple Chen Hansheng and his followers, as evidenced by their ingenious use of host institutions. It can be argued that the finest of Chen's agrarian research was produced while he had no institutional base of his own. However, for a group that had a definite agrarian view, and a keen sense of mission to promote it, the use of ad hoc institutional bases was cumbersome and restrictive at best. In late 1933, they organized the Society for the Study of China's Agrarian Economy (Zhongguo nongcun jingji yanjiuhui) to regroup and to recruit like-minded individuals.[41]

The Society for the Study of China's Agrarian Economy (henceforth the Agrarian China Society) was located in the French concession in Shanghai. Because of Chen's various activities, including his work in Richard Sorge's espionage network, his role was primarily a tutelary one. To manage the affairs of the Society, there was a five-member board of directors, with Chen as its permanent chair.[42] At its peak, the Agrarian China Society had more than five hundred members.

40. Chen Hansheng, *Landlord and Peasant in China*, xvii.
41. Chen Hansheng would consider it ideologically and methodologically repulsive if he knew that Sun Chung-hsing and Leo Douw use "rural" – instead of "agrarian" – to refer to the name of this Society, its publication, and its – ultimately his – field of research, as can be clearly seen from the analyses in this and the previous chapters as well as the titles of Chen's publications in English referred to later in this chapter. See Sun Chung-hsing, "The Development of the Social Sciences in China before 1949," pp. 267–69 and Leo Douw, "The Representation of China's Rural Backwardness, 1932–1937," pp. 143–99.
42. The following discussion on the organization and activities of the Agrarian China Society, unless otherwise noted, is based on Feng Hefa, "Zhongguo nongcun jingji yan-

The core of the Agrarian China Society was the half a dozen or so committed researchers whom Chen had recruited and trained at the Academia Sinica. Among them, three were its leading theoreticians. Like Chen himself, all three were from Wuxi, not surprisingly given the fact that they were recruited for the Wuxi project. The first was Qian Junrui, who was born into an upwardly mobile poor peasant family in 1908.[43] He had been a graduate of a junior normal school, elementary school-teacher, and a student of a normal college before he joined Chen's team in fall 1929. After his dismissal from the Academia Sinica, Chen placed him at the Shanghai office of Tass (the Soviet News Agency). He became a Communist Party member in 1935.

Next was Xue Muqiao, who was born into a bankrupt landlord-*cum*-merchant family in 1904.[44] He worked his way up from a railway apprentice to a station master in Hangzhou. When Chiang Kai-shek launched the coup in April 1927, he was imprisoned for his role in the Communist Party's labor organization work. After a brief stint as an elementary schoolteacher following his release in late 1930, he joined Chen's enterprise at the Academia Sinica. When they lost that base, he went to teach in Guangxi. However, his radical teaching and research activities soon made the Guangxi authorities pronounce him persona non grata and necessitated his return to Shanghai in 1934.

The last of the trio was Sun Yefang.[45] Born in 1908, he became a member of the Communist Party and the secretary of the Wuxi party branch in 1923. Two years later, he was sent to Sun Yat-sen University in Moscow, where he first enrolled as a student and then, after his graduation in 1927, served as a classroom interpreter. He returned to

jiuhui manyi" (Random Memories of the Society for the Study of China's Agrarian Economy), *Wenshi ziliao xuanji* (Selected Source Materials on History and Literature), (Beijing, December 1982), No. 84, pp. 43–75.

43. Lin Shuiyuan, "Zhuming de shijie jingjixuejia Qian Junrui" (The Famous Economist on World Economy: Qian Junrui) in Sun Liancheng and Lin Pu, eds., *Zhongguo dangdai zhuming jingjixuejia* (Noted Economists in Contemporary China) (Chengdu, 1985), Vol. I, pp. 388–484.

44. Xue Muqiao, *Xue Muqiao huiyilu* (The Memoirs of Xue Muqiao) (Tianjin, 1996), pp. 1–105. Wu Kaitai, "Qiushi he yanjin de Makesi zhuyi jingjixuejia: Xue Muqiao zhuan-lue" (A Truth-Seeking and Rigorous Marxist Economist: a Biographical Sketch of Xue Muqiao), *Economics Daily* ed., *Zhongguo dangdai jingjixuejia zhuanlue* (Biographical Sketches of Contemporary Chinese Economists) (Liaoning, 1986), pp. 231–265.

45. Deng Jiarong, *Sun Yefang zhuan* (A Biography of Sun Yefang) (Taiyuan, 1998) and Mao Tianqi, "Wei zhenli er xiansheng de guanghui bangyang: Sun Yefang zhuanlue" (A Glorious Model of Sacrificing Oneself for Truth: A Biographical Sketch of Sun Yefang), in ibid., pp. 365–412.

Shanghai in fall 1930 to work among rickshaw pullers and factory workers until his arrest late that year. Sometime after his release for lack of evidence to indict him as a Communist, he joined Chen's research team.

The Agrarian China Society was not a front organization of the Chinese Communist Party. Despite claims in memoir literature to the contrary,[46] the Society's relationship to the Communist Party was a tenuous one. In a 1942 letter to Liu Shaoqi, then secretary of the party's East China bureau, Xue Muqiao acknowledged that although the Agrarian China Society could claim to have been under the party's leadership through individual party members who were members of the Society, there were few organizational links with the party in Yan'an. Aside from the fact that the party's Shanghai branches were all but destroyed, he confessed that not only did they not realize the importance of party linkages, but they also believed it would better facilitate their work to remain independent of the party.[47]

Nevertheless, "being able to grasp correctly the party's theories and political platforms,"[48] the Agrarian China Society endeavored to promote the cause of the Chinese Communist Party. For example, the Agrarian China Society had always been critical of the rural reconstruction movement. However, when the Communist Party began promoting the second United Front, as signaled by Mao's speech in December 1935,[49] the Society modified its position. In July 1936 the Society began advocating "solidarity," its euphemism for "united front," among all rural reconstruction workers.[50] Even more significant were the ideological battles the Agrarian China Society waged on behalf of the Communist Party on two separate fronts: against the Trotskyite inter-

46. Qian Junrui, "Zhongguo nongcun jingji yanjiuhui chengli qianhou" (Events Surrounding the Founding of the Society for the Study of China's Agrarian Economy), *Wenshi ziliao xuanji*, No. 84, pp. 19–26.
47. Xue Muqiao, "Gei Liu Shaoqi tongzhi xie de baogao – guanyu baiqu xiangcun he Zhongguo nongcun jingji yanjiuhui de gongzuo wenti" (A Report to Comrade Liu Shaoqi Concerning Villages in the White Area and the Activities of the Society for the Study of China's Agrarian Economy), *Wenshi ziliao xuanji*, No. 84, p. 16.
48. Ibid.
49. Mao, "On Tactics Against Japanese Imperialism," *Selected Works of Mao Tse-tung*, I, pp. 153–78.
50. This abrupt change of position was signaled by Sun Yefang's article, "Minzu wenti he nongmin wenti" (The National Problem and the Peasant Question), *Zhongguo nongcun*, 2.7 (July 1936). Barry Naughton was therefore mistaken in believing that Sun "consistently advocated cooperation with bourgeois intellectuals." See his "Sun Yefang: Toward a Reconstruction of Socialist Economics," in Carol Hamrin and Timothy Cheek, eds., *China's Establishment Intellectuals* (M. E. Sharpe, 1986), pp. 129, 130.

pretation of China as well as against the Anglo-American oriented analyses of China's agrarian sector.

The battles against the Anglo-American camp were aimed at Buck, who espoused an entirely different approach to the study of China's agrarian sector. Even the words they used to characterize their subject matter were different: the peasant and the agrarian economy for the Agrarian China Society versus the farmer and the farm economy for Buck. To Chen Hansheng, Buck's fundamental mistake was to treat the Chinese peasant as a farmer engaging in business: "The Chinese peasant is comparable, not with the *Bauer* of modern Europe or the 'farmer' of English-speaking countries; but he resembles in status the peasant of other pre-capitalistic countries. He is farming for subsistence and not for profit."[51]

Chen's preference of "peasant" over "farmer" reflected a conscious and deliberate choice, particularly because there are no equivalent terms with comparable ideological connotations in Chinese to distinguish these two English terms. It is perhaps to be expected that the Yanjing and Nankai social scientists, together with Buck, used instead the word "farmer." While they may have used the term with full intention to refer to the Chinese farmers as profit maximizers who made rational decisions based on market conditions, they may not have been aware of the ideological implications of the choice of the word.[52]

If the toilers of the land in China were peasants, who remained fettered by feudal production relations, an approach that focused on farm management simply missed the mark. The Agrarian China Society conceded that Buck had collected some useful data, but challenged his methodology and interpretations. In a review of Buck's 1930 publication of *Chinese Farm Economy*,[53] Qian Junrui made a number of perceptive observations, some of which were echoed in a recent critique of Buck's surveys.[54] He faulted Buck for his haphazard sampling method. In Anhui province, for example, the survey included as many as fifty-three villages in Su county, but only one in Huaiyuan county. Sampling at the village level was equally haphazard. Although only one village in Huaiyuan

---

51. Chen Hansheng, *Landlord and Peasant in China*, p. 4.
52. There is of course no reason why they should prefer "peasant" to "farmer" or to distinguish the two terms when they did not subscribe to the Marxist conceptual framework.
53. The following discussion is based on Qian Junrui's review in *Zhongguo nongcun*, I.1 (October 1934), pp. 114–28; I.2 (November 1934), pp. 89–106.
54. Randall Stross, *The Stubborn Earth: American Agriculturalists on Chinese Soils 1898–1937* (Berkeley, 1986), pp. 161–87.

county was surveyed, the worker canvassed 124 out of its 150 households. By contrast, the survey worker in Wutai county in Shanxi province sampled only 5 of the 50 households in one village and his counterpart in Yanshan (Yenshan) county in Hebei, only 2 out of a total of 84 households in another.

This haphazard sampling method called into question the representativeness of Buck's data in two important respects. About half of his survey workers were his students at the University of Nanking, the rest being paid assistants. All of them conducted surveys in their native places. The fortuitous factor of their native origins thus determined where the surveys took place. Furthermore, because students at the University of Nanking were likely to have come from affluent family backgrounds, their data were probably biased toward more prosperous households and regions.

More serious was Buck's tendency to present arithmetic averages, which, when in aggregate and averaged the second time, becomes average of averages. Average of averages obscures rather than illuminates. As an extreme example, although his percentage figures of tenants from his north China samples varied widely, ranging from the lowest .7%, to 20%, to the highest 60.2%, Buck nonchalantly derived the average figure for north China as 10.1%.[55]

Qian Junrui's critique in this regard echoed that of Lenin's of the Narodniks. The "averages," according to Lenin, in addition to being purely fictitious, served to obscure the differentiation of the peasantry.[56] Buck's analysis assumed that China's rural sector was composed of farm business operators, some of whom were better off than others, but all were basically profit maximizers. As such, farm economy was a study of how such factors as population, farm size, labor input, livestock, and fertilizers determined the performance of the individual farms. By contrast, land tenure, which though was subject to abuse by the landlord (as well as by the tenant as Buck would hasten to add), was relevant for farm management study only in so far as rent payment affected the farm operator's balance sheet.

The Agrarian China Society never questioned the importance of technical factors in farm management. What they objected to was Buck's approach that analyzed farm management without any reference to the social matrix, very much like what Philip Huang refers to as a substan-

---

55. Buck, *Chinese Farm Economy*, table 1, p. 146.
56. Lenin, "The Development of Capitalism in Russia," pp. 70–187.

tivist critique of a formalist approach.[57] The most serious flaw in this approach lay not so much in its narrow technical focus but in its misrepresentations of social reality. In short, Buck failed to differentiate properly the peasantry. His categories of owner, part-owner and tenant obscured the true economic status of different peasant groups in the countryside. As Qian Junrui pointed out, a peasant who owned very little and had to lease most of the land he cultivated was a part-owner. Was his economic status any better than a tenant? Conversely, was a part-owner who owned most of the land under cultivation and leased only very little really much worse off than an owner-cultivator?

What is at issue here involves not just methodology, but also fundamental differences in setting the agenda for addressing the agrarian crisis. While Buck and the Anglo-American oriented Chinese social scientists recognized the existence of poverty and that of exploitation in the forms of tenancy, heavy tax burden, and usury, they did not view these as serious structural or class-based problems. Their diagnosis of the Chinese countryside was that it was poor, backward, and ignorant. And their prescription was rational and scientific social planning.

This prescription called for the injection of knowledge and techniques developed by modern agronomy to boost the productivity. In other words, the key to eradicate rural poverty was scientific farm management. Exploitation that had victimized poor farmers would be equally amenable to scientific management. Take for example the thorny question of the rent. Through careful study and fair-minded calculation, as Buck and the Nationalist government's rural policy planners contended, a fair rent could be determined to guarantee a fair return to the landlord's investment and at the same time allow the tenant a reasonable share to meet his basic needs. Usury and exploitation by the middlemen would pose no problem either. Cooperatives organized to provide technical assistance, direct sales and marketing, and render credit to farmers in need would force usurers and exploitative middlemen out of business.

From Chen Hansheng's perspective, this whole conceptual scheme simply missed the mark. It is true enough that agrarian China was poor and backward. But these were symptoms of deeper structural problems. He believed that there were fundamentally irreconcilable differences that separated the landlords from the tenants. The notion of scientific

---

57. Huang, *The Peasant Economy and Social Change in North China* (Stanford, 1985), pp. 3–6.

management prescribed by the Anglo-American oriented social scientists was not as innocuous as it appeared. If the landlords dominated the agrarian sector, whose interests would this scientific management serve?

Buck's failure to differentiate properly the Chinese peasantry was symptomatic of his indifference to the social and economic conditions that determined their existence. The correct approach, they argued, was to examine farm management in the larger context of China's agrarian economy, that is, to study "the direct and indirect dominance of China's agrarian sector by imperialist capital, the intensification of the feudal nature of the Chinese society, the differentiation of the peasantry, and the predominance of small scale peasant economy."[58]

Although the critique of Buck was unsparing, it never consumed as much of the energy of the Agrarian China Society as did its battles against the Trotskyites. In 1934, the Agrarian China Society waged a debate with a number of individuals, whose views earned them the epithet of Trotskyites in later official historiography of the Chinese Communist Party. This debate, known as the Debate on the Nature of Agrarian China, constituted the second phase of the larger debate on the nature of Chinese society that emerged as an internal debate within the Chinese Communist Party in search of a new revolutionary strategy in the aftermath of Chiang Kai-shek's coup in 1927. What began as an attempt to determine the developmental stage of Chinese society in terms of the Marxist scheme took on a historical character during the first phase of the debate in the late 1920s and early 1930s.[59] Known as the Social History Debate, its participants – defenders of the party's Stalinist line, the Trotskyites, and the left-wing members of the Guomindang Party – subjected the whole span of Chinese history to their divergent Marxist analyses.[60] Not until 1934 did the debate shift to a contem-porary focus.

There was little overlap in the participants on the two Debates. The sole exception was Wang Yichang, who played a leading role in both Debates. Other Trotskyites who participated in this second Debate

---

58. Qian Junrui's review of Buck in *Zhongguo nongcun*, I.1, p. 117.
59. He Ganzhi is the first to have viewed the Debate on the nature of agrarian China and the social history Debate as constituting the two phases of the Debate on the nature of Chinese society. See his *Zhongguo shehui xingzhi wenti lunzhan* (The Debate on the Problems Concerning the Nature of Chinese Society) (Shanghai, 1937).
60. Arif Dirlik, *Revolution and History: The Origins of Marxist Historiography in China, 1919–1937* (Berkeley, 1978).

included: Wang Yuquan, Zhang Zhicheng, and Wang Jingbo.[61] While the Trotskyites argued, as had their kindred souls in the Social History Debate, that Chinese society had entered the capitalist stage, the Agrarian China Society defended the party's Stalinist line, that is, the semifeudal and semicolonial nature of Chinese society. These irreconcilable positions reflected their conflicting views on what constituted the proper subject matter of agrarian economics: While the Trotskyites insisted that it was the productive forces and the Agrarian China Society, the production relations. Capitalism had long become the dominant mode in China's productive forces, proclaimed the Trotskyites. To this the Agrarian China Society retorted that feudal remnants continued to dominate the production relations.

The Debate was touched off by Wang Yichang's article that articulated a set of agendas for agrarian research in China. He charged researchers to go beyond what he considered a narrow concern with the production relations to deal with issues related to agronomy; to analyze agricultural production in terms of technology used and to differentiate the peasantry according to the employment of agricultural laborers; and to engage in budget analyses.[62] The Agrarian China Society was quick to respond to Wang Yichang's article, which they understood as a direct attack on their position. Wang's call for budget analyses and detailed agronomic studies – the soil, fertilizer, use of draft animals, and technology input – read too much like an endorsement of Buck's farm management approach.

Far more ominous and insidious for the Agrarian China Society was the insinuation by the Trotskyites that it was the former who had deviated from true Marxism. Because both sides cited Marx and Lenin, particularly the latter's *The Development of Capitalism in Russia*, the Debate became a contest on the correct exegesis of the doctrine. Their debate on whether it was the production relations or the productive forces that should constitute the central focus of agrarian economy reflected their different views on how the contradiction between this pair came to be the motor of history, an issue to which Marx himself provides no unequivocal answer. Both sides supported their arguments with quo-

---

61. Wang Yuquan, as discussed in Chapter 9, had just graduated from Peking University when the Debate began. According to Qian Jiaju, in an interview with him on October 20, 1990, Wang Yichang was still a college student at the time.

62. Wang Yichang, "Nongcun jingji tongji yingyou de fangxiang zhuanbian" (The Need to Reorient Our Approach to Agrarian Statistics), reprinted in *Zhongguo nongcun*, I.6 (March 1935), pp. 107–11.

tations from the same paragraph in Marx's preface to *A Contribution to the Critique of Political Economy*.

The Agrarian China Society never disputed the primacy of the productive forces, familiar as they were with one argument of Marx's that their opponents never failed to quote, that is, "No social order ever perishes before all the productive forces for which there is room in it have developed."[63] They, however, rested their case on the following pronouncement by Marx: "[T]he sum total of [the] relations of production constitutes the economic structure ... [Once] the material productive forces of society come in conflict with the existing relations of production, ... these relations turn into their fetters."[64]

By focusing on the productive forces, the Trotskyites believed they had pinpointed, *à la* Lenin, the historically progressive capitalistic elements in China's agrarian economy. This argument cut right into the Agrarian China Society's most vulnerable spot. The battle that ensued became a reenactment of the conceptual crisis the Agrarian China Society had previously experienced: that the high tenancy rate and peasant impoverishment, which they had condemned as symptoms of the agrarian crisis, were lauded instead by Lenin and Kautsky as harbingers of capitalism.[65]

Mimicking Lenin's sharp language against the Narodniks and using this term as a code name for deviates from true Marxism, the Trotskyites accused the Agrarian China Society as their Chinese counterparts, who, due to their obsession with the production relations, could detect only the feudal remnants in China's agrarian sector. They ridiculed the Agrarian China Society for their preoccupation with the increase in the tenancy rate and the impoverishment of the peasantry. To the Trotskyites, this reflected at best their opponents' predisposition to look for feudal, backward elements in an economy that had become predominantly capitalistic and at worst their warped understanding of both the social reality and Marxism. Citing Lenin, they argued: "No peculiarities in the system of land tenure can serve as an insurmountable obstacle to capitalism."[66] Equally mistaken, contended the Trotskyites, was the Agrarian China Society's interpretation of the impoverishment of the peasants. The displacement of the peasants from the land, far from signifying the entrenchment of the feudal production relations, reflected instead, again

---

63. Marx, *A Contribution to the Critique of Political Economy* (1859), "Preface."
64. Ibid.   65. See Chapter 7.
66. Lenin, "The Development of Capitalism in Russia," *V. I. Lenin: Collected Works* (Moscow, 1960), III, p. 324.

evoking Lenin, their reincarnation in "agricultural and industrial wage-workers."[67]

The Agrarian China Society was not as vulnerable as the Trotskyites had thought. Instead of getting lost in the theoretical quagmire that would have opened them to heterodoxy charges, they criticized the Trotskyites for quoting Lenin out of context and losing sight of the fact that contemporary China was not as developed as European Russia analyzed by Lenin. Their critique centered on the two key concepts that constituted the cornerstone of the Trotskyite argument: the emergence of a rural bourgeoisie on the one hand and a rural proletariat on the other. While they agreed that such a polarization of the peasantry was an indicator of capitalist development, they contended that it did not occur in China. There was no bourgeoisie nor a proletariat in China's agrarian sector. Most of the rich peasants in China slid down the social ladders and became the middle peasants or even the poor peasants. Those who held on joined the ranks with the landlords and lived off on rents,[68] a far cry from the rural bourgeoisie in Western Europe and European Russia who rented and managed lands. With no large-scale agricultural enterprises to turn to, the poor peasants in China had no chance to become the proletariat. With an argument that was clearly Kautsky's, they maintained that no matter how many the poor peasants there were and how fast their number would grow, as long as most of them remained tenants working on dwarf holdings and under semi-feudal production relations, they were not likely to become a rural proletariat; instead, they would merely serve as "props" of the semifeudal landlord economy.[69]

Despite its scholastic air, it was patently clear that this was a debate on the correct revolutionary strategy for China. At stake in the debate on whether China's economy was capitalist or semifeudal was the strategic correctness and, ultimately, the authority of the Comintern. Much of the contention was created by the Stalin-Trotsky power struggles and the resultant twists and turns of Comintern policies. However, Moscow, though the nerve center of International Communism, was by no means the only source of inspiration for Chinese Marxists. Although Tokyo no

---

67. Lenin, "The Development of Capitalism in Russia," p. 179.
68. Qian Junrui, "Zhongguo nongcun shehui xingzhi yu nongye gaizao wenti," *Zhongguo nongcun*, I.11 (August 1935), p. 11.
69. Yu Lin [Xue Muqiao], "Jieshao bing piping Wang Yichang xiansheng guanyu Zhongguo nongcun jingji de lunzhu" (A Summary and Critique of Mr. Wang Yichang's Writings on China's Agrarian Economy), *Zhongguo nongcun*, I.8 (May 1935), p. 111.

longer served as the conduit for Anglo-American ideas by the 1920s as the increasing number of Chinese students returned from the West began to act as agents of transmission, Japanese continued to be a major medium through which Marxist ideas were introduced to the Chinese reading public.[70] The Debate on the Nature of Agrarian China, as the Social History Debate before it, can only be properly understood when set against the intellectual and ideological universe that stretched from Moscow in the west and Tokyo in the east.

Illustrative of this Moscow-Shanghai-Tokyo axial of International Communism were the striking similarities between the Chinese debates and the Japanese Marxist debate on Japanese capitalism between the Kōza-ha (the Lecture faction) and the Rōnō-ha (Labor-Farmer faction) from 1927 to 1937. The Kōza-Rōnō debate centered around the issue of whether it was capitalist or semifeudal that characterized contemporary Japanese society.[71] Upholding the semifeudal thesis was the Kōza faction, the counterpart of the Agrarian China Society in the Chinese debate, which represented the position of the Comintern and the Japanese Communist Party. The Rōnō faction, on the other hand, echoing the position of the Chinese Trotskyites, articulated the capitalist thesis. Both the Chinese and Japanese debates were intricately tied to Comintern politics and policy debates; if contemporary China and Japan remained semifeudal in character, it would call for a two-stage strategy, a "bourgeois-democratic" phase followed by the final proletarian revolution. By contrast, if both societies had become capitalist, a single proletarian revolution would accomplish the task. A deadly struggle indeed, on which dangled the legitimacy of the Party, of the Comintern, and the fate of the Revolution.

The similarities between and contemporaneousness of the two debates raises an intriguing question about influence. While most contemporary Japanese scholars tend to see the two debates as independent of each other,[72] there is enough evidence to indicate that both sides were in fact

---

70. A systematic study is needed to bear out this important intellectual phenomenon.
71. Germaine Hoston, *Marxism and the Crisis of Development in Prewar Japan* (Princeton, 1986).
72. The Japanese Mantetsu researchers who were in China in the 1930s took this position in their reminiscences. See "'Chūgoku shakaishi Ronsen' ni kansuru chōsa" (Research Works related to "the Social History Debate in China"), *Ajia Keizai* (Monthly Journal of the Institute of Developing Economies), 28.4 (April 1987), pp. 76–7. Tai Kuo-hui argues that modern Japanese scholars have dismissed too easily any influence from China on the Japanese debate. See his "Chūgoku 'shakaishi ronsen' shōkai ni miraleru

well aware of the parallel debate being waged in the neighboring country. Wang Yichang, for example, had once argued, without offering any supporting evidence, that it was the Japanese who were influenced by the Chinese debate.[73] That Japanese neologisms abounded in the writings of the Chinese participants was another evidence that suggests familiarity with the Japanese debate and thus its influence. More interesting perhaps was the evidence on the Japan side, for it hinted at interfertilization. Not only did Hani Gorō and Hirano Yoshitarō of the Kōza faction cite Guo Moruo's pieces written during the Social History Debate,[74] but Hirano himself had many publications on studies of Chinese history.

Most illustrative of the Shanghai-Tokyo axial of International Communism was the participation in the Debate by Japanese Marxists in China. With the exception of one lone figure who took the Trotskyite position,[75] they were all of Kōza persuasion and were thus sympathetic to the Agrarian China Society. These were researchers at the Research Department of the Mantetsu: Amano Motonosuke, Nakanishi Tsutomu, and Ozaki Shōtarō. Among them, Ozaki Shōtarō was the most active supporter of the Agrarian China Society. The first person to have remarked on the parallels between the Chinese and Japanese debates, Ozaki, in addition to contributing a piece himself,[76] befriended members of the Agrarian China Society. In his reminiscences, he gave vivid accounts on how he frequented the premises of the Agrarian China Society and how he arranged a dinner gathering at a Chinese restaurant for the core members of the Agrarian China Society and his fellow Mantetsu researchers.[77]

Fascinating was the word to describe the history of the Agrarian China Society. Its journal, *Agrarian China*, inaugurated in 1934, was a forum for polemics, field notes, and political commentaries. It weathered cen-

jakkan no mondai" (Some Problems Embedded in [Japanese] Surveys of the "Social History Debate" in China), *Ajia Keizai*, 13.1 (January 1972), pp. 64–5.

73. "He Riben de Zhongguo yanjiuzhe lun nongcun jingji" (Discussing Agrarian Economy with a Japanese China Scholar), *Zhongguo jingji*, IV.5 (May 15, 1936), p. 97.

74. Hoston, *Marxism and the Crisis of Development in Prewar Japan*, p. 176.

75. His name was Hara Masaru. I have not seen his article, which was published in the Japanese language weekly, *Shanhai*, in either late 1935 or early 1936.

76. Tamaki Hideo [Ozaki Shōtarō], "Chūgoku nōson shakai keizai no gendankai narabini sono kenkyū hōhōron jo no ronsō o miru" (On the Debate on the Present Stage of China's Agrarian Economy and its Methodology), *Keizai hyōron* (Economic Review), III, p. 4 (April 1936), pp. 130–46; III. 5 (May 1936), pp. 102–21; III. 6 (June 1936), pp. 74–90.

77. *Haikai: ichi Chūgoku kenkyūka no kaisō* (Wandering: the Reminiscences of a China Scholar) (Tokyo, 1981), pp. 85–6.

sorship and several suspension orders until its permit was revoked in 1943. The Agrarian China Society itself survived government persecution, the war with Japan, and the civil war until 1951 when its board of directors, citing the fulfillment of its historical role, voted for its dissolution.[78] During the institutional life span of the Society, with his lieutenants in charge, Chen Hansheng played a nominal role. However, it was through him the Society was incorporated into the patronage network of social science research with monies appropriated by the Rockefeller Foundation and funneled through the Institute of Pacific Relations.

AGRARIAN RESEARCH, POLITICAL INTELLIGENCE, AND TRANSPACIFIC PUBLICITY WORK FOR THE CAUSE OF REVOLUTION

Despite his American education, his excellent command of English, and his great entrepreneurial instinct, Chen Hansheng did not take part in the great frenzy among Chinese academics in campaigns for support from the Rockefeller Foundation, which was set off by the visit of Selskar Gunn in 1931 discussed earlier in this book. Even had he tried, he would have had no chance of getting Rockefeller support. In fact, as late as 1934, Gunn viewed the Institute of the Social Sciences, from which Chen had just severed his relations, as being "not impressive."[79]

The fact is that by 1934 Chen had compiled a solid publication record, albeit only in Chinese,[80] and had become a recognized agrarian economist in China. While the vice-president of the Foundation remained unimpressed, the same was not true with keen Japanese China watchers at the Mantetsu, who soon took notice of Chen and his group. The Mantetsu researchers took the initiative and became acquainted with members of his Agrarian China Society. Their respect for him is well illustrated by Amano Motonosuke's words:

> With his linguistic talent (English, German, French, Russian, Japanese, and Latin), he has devoted himself to a newly emerging

78. During the Cultural Revolution the Agrarian China Society was falsely charged as Liu Shaoqi's organization. See Qian Jiaju, *Qishi nian de jingli* (A Career of Seventy Years) (Hong Kong, 1986), pp. 111–12.
79. See his "China and the Rockefeller Foundation," January 23, 1934, p. 21, RAC RG1.1 601.12.130.
80. His "The Agrarian Problem of China," presented at the biennial conference of the Institute of Pacific Relations at Banff in 1933, was not published until 1934.

field of scientific research. By employing correct methodology, and combining agrarian field research experience with meticulous combing and digesting of bits and pieces of information from newspapers and magazines, he truly has published some remarkably unique works.[81]

The unfavorable verdict uttered by Gunn on Chen's enterprise no doubt demonstrated the limit of his understanding of the academic scene in China. More important, however, was what it revealed about modern philanthropies and their patronage of the social sciences across national boundaries.

A more complete analysis of modern philanthropies and Chinese social scientists will be the subject of the next chapter. Suffice it here to point out that the patronage by philanthropies of social science research across national boundaries has to begin with an effort to identify a native elite who are capable of doing the research as envisioned. Once the foundation has determined the membership of this elite, admission of new members into this patronage network will take place only under extraordinary circumstances.

Chen Hansheng never had a chance to join this network. When foundation officers talent scouted Chinese social scientists, he was abroad in Moscow. The Academia Sinica, which he became affiliated with in early 1929, had just started functioning at the time of Condliffe's visit discussed in Chapter 4. The implications of not being included on Condliffe's list of promising grantees are serious. Neither in his 1931 visit nor his subsequent residence assignment in China from 1932 to 1938, did Gunn ever express any interest in Chen's research.

Fortunately for Chen, the Rockefeller Foundation was not the only institution that supported social science research in China. The Institute of Pacific Relations, the first to have entered the field, continued its programs after the giant Rockefeller philanthropy had adopted the same line of work in China. Even so, there was little prospect initially for Chen to hope for support; he was not included in the map of prominent Chinese social scientists compiled by Condliffe. In fact, membership of the Rockefeller patronage network was essentially concentric to that of

---

81. Amano Motonosuke, "Shina no tochi mondai ni kansuru bunken" (A Bibliographical Essay on Works Dealing with China's Land Problems), *Shanhai Mantetsu kikan* (Quarterly Journal of the Shanghai Office of the South Manchurian Railway company), I. 1 (April 1937), pp. 215–16.

the Institute of Pacific Relations. Franklin Ho and Buck, for example, figured prominently in both circles.

That this clublike patronage network was difficult to crack is well illustrated by Chen's first try with the Institute of Pacific Relations. In 1933, he attended the Institute's fifth biennial conference at Banff in Canada. In addition to presenting a paper, entitled "The Agrarian Problem of China," he attended the meeting of the International Research Committee on behalf of the China Council. And yet, his own proposal for a study of large-scale farming in China was not adopted. The Chinese grantees, not surprisingly, were Buck and Franklin Ho.

However, one decision made at Banff created a situation that opened an avenue for Chen to join the philanthropy's exclusive club that had hitherto denied his entry. The Institute adopted a new agenda, with standards of living as one of the two major subjects for research. This change in agenda created a problem in China, for few of the social scientists with whom the Institute had been cooperating were capable of taking on the new assignment.

All of a sudden, the Institute discovered Chen Hansheng. The paper he delivered at the Banff conference that expounded on the theme of a deepening agrarian crisis caused by the twin evils of landlordism and the rapacious state provided one avenue to approach the question of standards of living in China's agrarian sector. Upon his return from Banff, Chen found himself catapulted into the inner circle of the China Council of the Institute of Pacific Relations, becoming a member of its newly created research committee with power to screen and recommend projects to New York for funding. The endorsement for his entry into the network came from Edward Carter, secretary of the American Council and the most powerful man of the Institute, and William Holland, research secretary of the Institute. Even more astounding was that Carter and Holland pushed the idea of requesting Chen to undertake simultaneously two studies, that is, in addition to a study on a tobacco growing region that Chen himself had proposed, he be asked to take on another one on a silk producing region.[82]

This sudden turn of events could not have occurred at a more opportune time for Chen. His position at the China Council brought prestige for himself and legitimacy to his research, while the commissioned projects provided funds that helped sustain the work of his Agrarian China

---

82. "Minutes of Discussion Meeting, Peiping, Wednesday, May 2nd, 1934," p. 1, IPR Box 285, China Institute of Pacific Relations, 1933–1934 Folder 2.

Society. The work pattern he had established, which allowed him to assume the overall administrative role and left the actual field work to his assistants, served him well now that his work with Richard Sorge's spy ring required his being stationed in Tokyo. To direct the field work were three members of the Agrarian China Society: Wang Yinsheng, Zhang Xichang, and Huang Guogao, of whom the first two were his loyal assistants of longstanding. By now field work had become a routine operation for these veteran agrarian researchers; the analytic categories, survey techniques, and interpretative framework had all been standardized.

Field work for the project on the tobacco-growing regions took place from late 1934 to early 1935, covering the provinces of Shandong, Henan, and Anhui where the American seeds were sown. It used the same format as all of Chen's earlier projects: a survey of general conditions in 127 villages, followed by a more intensive study of six representative villages, two in each of the three provinces, which accounted for 429 peasant families. The underlying theme, likewise, remained that of the exploitation of the peasants. Because a large number of peasants in these regions entered into production agreements with the British-American Tobacco Company, this project offered a unique avenue to assess the impact of international trade and the penetration of foreign capital in a peasant economy.

This project was written up in English by Chen and published in 1939 under the title, *Industrial Capital and Chinese Peasants*. There are two main arguments. Through the analyses of promotional practices, credit extension, and leaf collecting networks, Chen argued that it was the compradores, bureaucrats, and local gentry who facilitated the entry and dominance of the British-American Tobacco Company.[83] Such an alliance with the semifeudal forces reached all the way to the national government, best illustrated by the preferential tax rates it gave the company.[84] The corollary was the demise of the native cigarette industry.

If the semifeudal forces helped prop up the British-American Tobacco Company, it in return helped ensure the entrenchment of these semifeudal forces themselves. The procurement process provided landlords and local gentry acting as collecting agents with ample opportunities for exploitation: through "false grading, arbitrary deduction of weight, taking of commission, currency manipulation, and the shifting of tax

---

83. See especially chapter 4 of *Industrial Capital and Chinese Peasants* (Shanghai, 1939).
84. Ibid., pp. 39–44.

burden."[85] More devastating, however, was exploitation associated with production. In Chinese agriculture where, Chen contended, the peasants in general did not receive the wage that was due them, tobacco peasants faced an even gloomier prospect. While tobacco leaves commanded higher prices than food crops, its production cost was also higher – three to five times more than wheat or sorghum (*gaoliang*).[86] According to Chen's calculation, the tobacco peasants in the three regions surveyed generally operated with a loss, which generated pressure for loans and which, in turn, fed into the vicious cycle that led to further exploitation. Not only were interest rates higher in tobacco regions than non-tobacco regions, but rent for tobacco land was higher than for non-tobacco land.[87]

The peasants thus engaged in a losing business endeavor. The extremely unequal distribution of the land led to a great surplus of labor in the villages, with nowhere else to turn for employment. Gone were domestic handicraft industries, which had traditionally absorbed the surplus labor but had been wiped out by modern factories. Worst of all, there was little prospect that these modern factories would absorb the unemployed labor in the agrarian sector and transform them into a reserve army of labor.

That peasants cultivated tobacco out of desperation can be seen from the fact that "as much as 80 percent of the tobacco fields are cultivated by the middle and poor peasants."[88] Furthermore, while the middle and poor peasants derived over 80 percent of their cash income from tobacco, the figure for the rich peasants was 64.7 percent.[89] In an argument that is similar to what Philip Huang would put forward nearly half a century later, Chen pointed out that the rich peasants who, to borrow Huang's expression, adopted diversified cropping portfolios that spread their risk,[90] did not plant too much tobacco; it was the poor peasants who, compelled by circumstances, "like to gamble on tobacco cultivation, believing that one tobacco harvest may perhaps bring an income equal to two wheat harvests."[91]

85. Ibid., p. 52.
86. Ibid., p. 73. As Sherman Cochran points out, contrary to Myers' allegation, Chen did compare tobacco profits with those of other crops. See his *Big Business in China: Sino-Foreign Rivalry in the Cigarette Industry, 1890–1930* (Harvard, 1980), pp. 142–3 and Myers, *The Chinese Peasant Economy*, p. 16.
87. Chen Hansheng, *Industrial Capital and Chinese Peasants*, pp. 55–85.
88. Ibid., p. 73.
89. Ibid., p. 23.
90. Huang, *The Peasant Economy and Social Change in North China*, p. 162.
91. Chen Hansheng, *Industrial Capital and Chinese Peasants*, p. 73.

Commercialization of the Chinese agriculture thus did not benefit the poor peasants. Discoursing in the same vein as Kautsky, Chen argued how the intensive nature of tobacco farming dragged women, the elderly, and children into the production process. And allowing himself to indulge in sentimentality, he added: "In every piece of the beautifully finished tobacco leaf we can see the images of those frail and foot-bound women, those thin and grey-haired elders, and those pale and somewhat dwarfed children, all of them incessantly at work."[92]

The exploitation issue here was clearly set against a different background than what it had been in Chen's earlier surveys. While the peasants in his earlier surveys were victims of the landlords, merchants, and usurers – the infamous triad in Communist Party ideology, now they had to face also the compradores and foreign capitalists. This tobacco study thus nicely complemented his earlier Guangdong survey in that they covered both the external and internal factors. Together these two studies illustrated the Comintern's as well as the Chinese Communist Party's thesis on China as a semifeudal and semicolonial society.

Before his assistants began work on the tobacco project, Chen and his wife, Susie, went to Tokyo in summer 1934 to join the Sorge spy ring. As a cover, he claimed to be doing research on China's agrarian problems and early Chinese trade with the West at the *Tōyō Bunko* (the Oriental Library).[93] Because Sorge proceeded cautiously, Chen received no assignment and was virtually free. It was his standing within the Institute of Pacific Relations that became solidified during his ten-month sojourn in Japan. He had so impressed the Institute that as early as February 1935, Edward Carter began thinking of bringing him to the United States to work for the American Council of the Institute.[94] He attended the Institute's special conference in Tokyo in April 1935 to evaluate past research and to chart a future course. During the conference, he was awarded a new project on "the cotton-producing areas in north China."

No sooner had the conference ended than events took a sharp turn. One day he read in a newspaper about the arrest in Shanghai of Joseph Walden, a Comintern agent whom he was instructed to meet in Tokyo.[95] Without returning home where he feared the Japanese police would have been waiting, he boarded a ship bound for Shanghai. As soon as he

---

92. Ibid., p. 65.   93. "IPR Notes," No. 1 (October 1934), p. 5.
94. Carter to Frederick Field, February 18, 1935, IPR Box 1, F.V. Field (1935) folder.
95. *Sige shidai de wo*, pp. 61–2. See also MacKinnon, *Agnes Smedley*, p. 166.

arrived, he proceeded to Smedley's apartment. A day later, Smedley transferred Chen to Rewi Alley's house.[96] Meanwhile, Chen dispatched his loyal assistant, Wang Yinsheng, to Tokyo to escort Susie back to Shanghai, where she was put up in the house of a German engineer. Two weeks later, after Smedley had secured for them their visas to the Soviet Union, they made their venture to the Huangpu wharf to board the Russian freighter Smedley had booked for them. What follows is Alley's vivid account of the day of the dramatic getaway:

> They were to carry two bunches of red gladiola as though seeing someone off. And to disguise him better, [Smedley] had him wear white clothing, shorts, long stockings, a Palm Beach coat and a pith helmet. Above all, he was not to wear his spectacles, for that would certainly be in his descriptions, and it was truly something to see the gallant professor trying to look nonchalant under his unaccustomed headgear, peering myopically through the red flowers, and hoping he wouldn't trip up. We passed the plainclothes detectives grouped at the bottom of the gangway, but they hardly bothered to give more than a glance at what seemed obviously wealthy Shanghai types.[97]

Once aboard, the captain locked them in his toilet, where they remained until the freighter had entered the open sea.

Arriving in Moscow, they were placed as researchers at the University of the Toilers of the East.[98] Their second Moscow sojourn lasted for about a year. Although life was more comfortable, thanks to the success of the five-year plans, they found Moscow stifling. Stalin's Great Purge had begun and the chilling effect was noticeable. He later would recall that some of the Russian researchers they knew committed suicide and others disappeared mysteriously.[99]

Chen himself had some explaining to do about his own sudden disappearance. In a letter to William Holland dated June 1935 and supposedly to have been mailed from Nanjing, he informed the latter that, on advice of Susie's doctor, they would leave immediately for an unspecified sanatorium in Geneva. Expressing his regret that his absence prevented him

---

96. Alley was a New Zealander who was to play an important role in the Industrial Co-operative Movement during the war with Japan.
97. Rewi Alley, *At 90: Memoirs of My China Years: An Autobiography of Rewi Alley* (Beijing, 1986), p. 81.
98. It was in Moscow that he, through Wang Ming and Kang Sheng, became a member of the Chinese Communist Party.
99. *Sige shidai de wo*, p. 64.

from undertaking the cotton project, he requested that the Institute appoint a substitute – possibly Ho's right-hand man, H. D. Fong, he added. The letter ended with a forwarding address in Geneva.[100] Needless to say, Holland was greatly mystified by Chen's disappearance. He was willing to believe that Susie's medical condition was a factor behind their unannounced departure. However, knowing well as he did Chen's political connections, though not his Comintern agent status, he speculated that Chen must have been "entrusted to go on a mission for some politician or political group other than the Nanking crowd."[101]

Chen must have so impressed the Institute of Pacific Relations that as much as Holland was mystified by his behavior, when he got the chance to respond, he made Chen an offer to come to New York to work as a staff member of the Institute's International Secretariat.[102] Chen's response did not come until April of the following year. And when it did, his address said Paris. Lest Holland should have accurately deduced his whereabouts, he claimed that he had in fact been in China. His roundabout explanation ran as follows: Because Geneva was both too expensive and too cold for them, after having made the arrangement for Susie to stay in Montone near Nice, he had departed for Hong Kong, then traveled extensively in China, and had only just returned to Paris. He made no commitment to Holland's offer, but indicated that he was to take up the matter with Edward Carter, who was on his way from Moscow to Paris.[103]

Shortly after his meeting with Carter, Chen and Susie arrived in New York. During the following three years, he demonstrated thoroughly his multifaceted talent in research, organization, and political instinct. In New York, he provided bibliographical and editorial support for the Institute's research programs and conference series. Not only did he accomplish his tasks well, but he proved to be imaginative and resourceful. He was an avid memorandum writer, through which he provided information, offered recommendations, and participated in policy debates.

This was the most prolific period in his life. New York, while a hustle-bustle metropolis, provided him with a peaceful environment, away from espionage, persecution, and, after July 1937, when the war with Japan

100. Chen to Holland, June 14, 1935, IPR Box 348, China Institute of Pacific Relations folder.
101. Extracts of letter from Holland to Carl Alsberg, July 22, 1935, IPR Box 356, Holland, William L. – Corresp. (4) folder.
102. Holland to Chen, September 26, 1935, IPR Box 348, China Institute of Pacific Relations folder.
103. Chen to Holland, April 27 [1936], IPR Box 347, Chen, Han-seng folder.

began, carnage and death. Through the help of Frederick Field, secretary of the American Council, the International Publishers put out in 1936 the English version of his Guangdong survey, which he had all but completed in Japan with the help of Bruno Lasker, a staff member of the Institute. His tobacco study came out in 1939.

As a Chinese Research Fellow attached to the International Secretariat, Chen had the advantage of being on the payroll while enjoying a high degree of independence that a regular employee might not have. As a researcher, he was entitled to his own view, to which the Institute could at best edit or insert a disclaimer, short of not publishing it. That Chen had much freedom to pursue his own agenda, which was to propagate the Chinese Communist Party's call for revolution, can be illustrated by the book, *Agrarian China: Selected Source Materials from Chinese Authors*, which he began as a project in early 1937 and published in 1938. It unmistakably represented his view on the agrarian crisis in China. Although it was "staff," but not his name, that appeared on the title page, contemporary Japanese observers knew better. Sugimoto Shūrō, the Japanese translator of the volume, pointed out that more than one-third of the entries were written by members of the Agrarian China Society. The percentage becomes overwhelming if one includes those written by authors who were their allies.[104] Knowing that Chen was then working at the Institute's New York office, Sugimoto correctly inferred that the editor was Chen himself.

Chen disclosed in his reminiscences that his covert assignment in New York was to help operate the party's newspaper.[105] He attended regularly the party's monthly cell meetings. As a competent covert agent, he mingled widely with Chinese sojourners in and visitors to New York from all social circles. So well did he cover himself that not even Hu Shi or Leonard Hsu knew of his agent status, judging from the kind of information they intimated to him. If he could deceive his Chinese acquaintances, so much the easier to deceive Carter and Holland.

What made Chen so impressive to the Institute was not just his ability to deliver research results, but his ability to provide, as no one else could, inside political information as well as keen and studied observations.

---

104. Sugimoto Shūrō, *Chūgoku nōson mondai* (China's Agrarian Problems) (Tokyo, 1940), which for obvious reasons, does not contain "The Chinese Peasantry Under the Puppet Regime of Manchoukuo."
105. *Huaqiao ribao* (Overseas Chinese Daily), which succeeded the *Jiuguo ribao* (Salvation Daily) that the Party had published in Paris. *Sige shidai de wo*, p. 65.

Knowing his ideological position, however, neither Carter nor Holland accepted uncritically whatever he said. For example, Holland rejected Chen's report on the working of the United Front policy in China during the war, which was Chen's contribution to the China section of the Inquiry Series – Carter's controversial pet project during the war.[106] Holland's friendship with and respect for Chen were such that he could take Chen to task in strong words: "We want to give you every opportunity in your report to express your own views on the political situation in China, but there is a corresponding obligation on your part to present a balanced picture of the actual working of the governmental machine in China to-day."[107]

That the Institute of Pacific Relations for seventeen years supported Chen Hansheng, a Comintern agent and Chinese Communist Party member, does not vindicate the false accusation McCarthy and the McCarran Committee later made against the Institute as a Communist front organization. Whether or not the Institute had any knowledge, which it did not, of Chen's agent status is beside the question. The Institute worked with establishment elite and mainstream scholars. The key figures of the China Council of the Institute were closely linked to Chiang Kai-shek either personally or indirectly through his inner power circle. A case can be made that the Institute brought in few "radicals" to counterbalance the establishment viewpoint.

In March 1939, Chen and Susie traveled to Hong Kong. Officially he was to engage in a new project on the land system in China's southwest or, in Carter's astonishing hyperbole, "under an assignment from the International Research Committee to develop a sound agrarian policy for China."[108] With the help of a member of his Agrarian China Society, Chen Hongjin, he conducted the field work in 1940 in southern Yunnan and northern Xikang, where the economy was backward and the Han ethnic group formed the minority. This project, published in 1949 under the title, *Frontier Land System in Southernmost China*, together with his earlier Guangdong and tobacco studies, completed his study of the three major types of agrarian economy in China.

In his reminiscences, however, Chen revealed that his trip to and

---

106. John Thomas, *The Institute of Pacific Relations: Asian Scholars and American Politics* (Seattle, 1974), p. 25.
107. Holland to Chen Hansheng, November 6, 1939, IPR Box 25 Chen Hansheng folder.
108. Carter to Liu Yuwan, March 14, 1939, IPR Box 25 China Council – Hu Shi and Liu Yuwan folder.

sojourn in Hong Kong was an assignment from the party to assist the Chinese Industrial Co-operatives. Here Chen may well have given an interpretation of a past action of his that is ultimately true and ideologically correct, but historically false – a perfectly understandable but hazardous element not uncommonly found in the memoir literature published in China since 1949. In a sense, both versions of the story are equally true; each describes one aspect of the dual roles – an agrarian researcher and a Comintern agent – that he had been playing since the late 1920s. During the war, the balance between this two roles began to tip more toward the covert one, which, though fascinating, is beyond the scope of the present study. Suffice it here to state that his multifarious activities during the war converged on one single aim of promoting the cause of the Chinese Communist Party.

Upon his return to Asia from New York, he first made Hong Kong his base of operation and, when the colony fell to the Japanese in December 1941, moved to Guilin in Guangxi province. In 1943, upon being alerted by a friendly warning about a warrant for his arrest, he sought refuge in India. Three years later, he was back in the United States, again sponsored by the Institute of Pacific Relations. After a one-semester teaching stint at the University of Washington in Seattle, he moved to the East Coast, again, with short-term appointments arranged by the Institute. He remained in the United States until 1950 when, with his keen political instinct, he sensed the danger looming with Joseph McCarthy's investigations of un-American activities at the Senate and decided that it was time to return to China.[109]

It is ironic that while the legacy of Chen's agrarian research lives on in the Chinese studies communities in the United States, as illustrated in the conclusion chapter of this book, it was all but obliterated in China after the revolution. There are no indications that the new regime utilized the data from his research of the 1930s in the postrevolution land reform.[110] Whether by choice or by circumstances, he was kept out of the limelight, holding scholarly and decorative positions.[111] The three theo-

---

109. Chen confirmed this observation in an interview with him in Beijing on June 9, 1991.
110. Only once in 1958, when the State Statistical Bureau and the Jiangsu Statistical Bureau conducted a rural survey in Wuxi, did they consult the Wuxi material that Chen's group had collected in 1929. Qin Liufang, "Dui 'Jiefang qian lao shehui gongzuozhe de nongcun diaocha' yi wen de yijian," *Shehui*, No. 3 (1984), p. 63.
111. The more substantive positions he held were: associate director of the editorial committee of *China Reconstructs* and head of the Institute of World History of the Chinese Academy of Sciences.

reticians in his Agrarian China Society – Xue Muqiao, Qian Junrui, and Sun Yefang – became powerful economic planners and bureaucrats in the new regime, though none had anything to do with the agrarian sector.[112] Whatever the reasons were and whoever was at fault, bitter resentment came to characterize Chen's relationship with his former lieutenants and this may have colored their memories of their shard past and made it difficult to reconstruct this history solely on their memories. All of them suffered during the Cultural Revolution. Susie died alone at home in late 1968 while Chen was in confinement and was going through struggle sessions.

The reform decade of the 1980s saw the publication of both selected essays from the *Agrarian China* and the Chinese translations of all of Chen's agrarian research that appeared originally in English. This is, however, a commemoration of a legacy, which served to bear testimony not so much to the achievements of an agrarian research enterprise, as to the "correctness" of the Communist Revolution. Not only do the translations vary in quality and accuracy, but chapters and tables of statistics are deleted, either because they contain information deemed "commonsense" to the Chinese readers or presumably no longer reflecting the reality and thus become irrelevant.[113]

As for Chen Hansheng, as late as June 1991 when he was interviewed in his Peking apartment, though at ninety-five and totally blind yet lucid and alert and ever-uncompromising on sloppy thinking, he remained a believer in Communism as he knew it during the 1920s, as opposed to what was practiced in the Soviet Union after Stalin and in China after the founding of the People's Republic of China.

112. For their exact titles and positions, see Nina Halpern, "Economic Specialists and the Making of Chinese Economic Policy, 1955–1983," Ph.D. dissertation, University of Michigan, 1985. See also Xue Muqiao, *Xue Muqiao huiyilu*, pp. 200–91.
113. Most surprising is the translation of the Guangdong survey, *Jiefang qian de dizhu yu nongmin* (Landlord and Peasant before Liberation) (Beijing, 1984), when there exists a Chinese version of the survey that Chen published in 1934. The two other translations are: *Diguozhuyi gongyeziben yu Zhongguo nongmin* (Industrial Capital and Chinese Peasants) (Shanghai, 1984) and *Jiefang qian Xishuangbanna tudi zhidu* (Frontier Land Systems in Southernmost China) (Beijing, 1984).

9

The Rockefeller Foundation and Chinese Academic Enterprise

IT is impossible to overstate the crucial role American largess played in the three social science enterprises analyzed in this book. The story of Yanjing and Nankai as reconstructed here would have been utterly inconceivable, and that of Chen Hansheng's categorically less exciting without the resources and opportunities provided by the Rockefeller Foundation and the Institute of Pacific Relations. What transpired from the analyses in this book is not just a fascinating story of the efforts on the part of these three enterprises to transfer and indigenize the social science disciplines they promoted. It is also an extraordinary drama of international bargaining between them and American philanthropies using the social sciences as the medium.

The cross-cultural nature of this drama provides a rich and poignant context to address some of the most contested issues in the literature on modern philanthropies. Aside from offering case analyses touching upon the issue of the perpetuation of a conservative ideology, it bears testimony to the power of modern philanthropies to determine not only methodology and research agenda, but also the configuration of the social science community. Foundation support tends to go to people who are more adept and in the right disciplines and belong to the right networks. Once the methodology and research agenda are set, they in turn shape the hierarchy in the social science community. While the grant getters thrive and receive further support, the losers can anticipate defeat and even atrophy.

Conspicuously absent in this competition for the Rockefeller largess were the elite institutions within the Chinese university system, particularly the National Peking and Qinghua universities. It is not that Peking and Qinghua were oblivious to the importance of funding, but rather that they had under their control a funding agency, in addition to the regular appropriations from the government. The brilliant maneuvers by Yanjing and Nankai for Rockefeller support thus illustrated efforts by institutions that were not in the mainstream and had to seek funding from without. International patronage was, however, subversive of its counterpart system on the receiving end, as reflected in the endemic factionalism in Chinese academia. As epitomized by what transpired at the Yanjing Sociology Department, factionalism is not simply a symptom of personality clashes. Rather, it involves disputes over resource allocation and, ultimately, a symptom of a crisis that I characterize as an academic patricide – a sad case of how foreign education and networking, together with international patronage, erode and break up the normal patronage networks within China.

PATRONIZING SOCIAL SCIENCE RESEARCH
IN CHINA FROM NEW YORK

The Rockefeller Foundation's support of social science research in China began with the seven-year grant totaling $140,000 that the Laura Spelman Rockefeller Memorial appropriated to Yanjing University in 1928. The Memorial's contribution to the development of the social sciences in China was in fact more profound than this grant to Yanjing suggests. This is because the Memorial also made appropriations to organizations such as the Social Science Research Council and the Institute of Pacific Relations, which in turn distributed funds for social science research. These agencies provided the institutional framework for the rise of academic and organizational entrepreneurs acting as managers of research funds.

One of these entrepreneurial managers of Rockefeller funds was Edward Carter of the Institute of Pacific Relations. Carter was a promoter and organizer. For more than twenty years, he was a YMCA foreign secretary in India, France, and England. In 1923, he returned to the United States and became an executive secretary of The Inquiry, an organization set up in 1922 by the Federal Council of Churches. The original purpose of The Inquiry was "to promote the serious study and full discussion of industrial, racial and international problems in the light of the spirit and teaching of Jesus."[1] Under Carter's leadership, it became involved in the development of a technique, pioneered by William Kilpatrick and Harrison Elliot of Teachers College at Columbia

1. Robert MacIver, "Report on The Inquiry," (n.p., n.d.), pp. 5–6.

University, of group discussion and diagnosis of the causes of social conflict.

This conference method found its application at the international level with the Institute of Pacific Relations through Carter's affiliation with both organizations. The roundtable format with detailed discussion outlines constituted the core of the biennial conference of the Institute of Pacific Relations. Yet the Institute soon outgrew this preoccupation with conference techniques as it realized that discussion without information is barren.

Carter steered the Institute of Pacific Relations away from its mission to solve cultural and racial conflict in the Pacific region through discussions among its leaders. Merle Davis, general secretary of the Institute, resigned in protest and charged that "[t]he direction and control of the policies of the I.P.R. are in the hands of the men who are raising the funds in New York" and that "[t]hey are making the I.P.R. a society for the study of Pacific questions, not an Institute of Pacific Relations."[2]

Davis' misgivings represented perhaps the sentiment of one who had lost out in a power struggle. However, his resentment against fundraisers in New York touched upon a genuinely new phenomenon associated with the advent of modern philanthropy, that is, the rise of professional managers of research funds. Carter's rise within the Institute of Pacific Relations was due to his ability to solicit support from the Rockefeller Foundation. From 1928 to 1933, the Rockefeller Foundation contributed nearly half of the total expenditure – one million dollars – of the American and Pacific Councils.[3] About a quarter of this expenditure was for research.

Although the Institute had engaged John B. Condliffe to become the research secretary in early 1927, no research program had crystallized before its biennial conference in Honolulu in the summer of that year. Condliffe favored a more patient approach, especially because he had not made a reconnaissance trip to East Asia. However, pressure for projects from New York was mounting. Carter had funds from the Laura Spelman Rockefeller Memorial and was eager to prove to the latter the efficiency of the Institute as an agency for social science research on East Asia.[4] There was pressure from academic entrepreneurs as well. James

---

2. Merle Davis to Ray Lyman Wilbur, January 23, 1930, Ray Lyman Wilbur Papers, Box 133, 1930 Folder, deposited at the Hoover Institution.
3. Carter to Gunn, October 7, 1932, IPR Box 112 Gunn Folder, "Finance," pp. 2, 3.
4. Roger Greene to George Vincent, January 24, 1928, RAC RG4 53.1243.

Shotwell, professor of history at Columbia University and chairman of the International Research Committee of the Institute, was eager to have projects that he could present to the Social Science Research Council.

This pressure turned the Institute's Research Committee meetings at the 1927 Honolulu conference into a desperate search for projects. The meetings were attended by a motley group with diverse backgrounds and interests. While some were more interested in "political intelligence" than in long-term social science research, Carter and Shotwell were handicapped by not having operated in their respective fields of specialization.[5] The meetings were chaotic and futile. Condliffe was soundly reproached by Carter and Shotwell for failing to come up with projects in advance. The exasperated Shotwell went so far as telling Condliffe that "the tail was going to wag the dog" and that there was no future for him in the Institute.[6] A fiasco was narrowly avoided only at the last minute. Carl Alsberg, director of the Food Research Institute at Stanford, took a few research-oriented delegates to a sukiyaki lunch. Sitting over the lunch all afternoon, they turned out five projects on food and population in the Pacific countries.[7] With the help of other conference participants, Condliffe eventually came up with an assortment of a dozen projects for Shotwell to take to the Social Science Research Council.

The need to justify their existence generated a pressure for projects within these subsidiary fund-distributing agencies. Most illustrative of this pressure for projects was the anomalous relationship between the Institute of Pacific Relations and the Social Science Research Council, which supposedly operated only within the United States and Canada. In fact, the Social Science Research Council formed its first Committee on International Relations in 1927 solely for the purpose of functioning as a vehicle for administrating the projects that Shotwell had brought back from the Honolulu conference.[8]

As for the Institute of Pacific Relations, before the Rockefeller Foundation made the annual grant of $50,000 toward the Institute's research program, this arrangement with the Social Science Research Council had contributed to a substantially larger program than its budget could have allowed. In 1927, for instance, while the Institute's budget for research

---

5. Condliffe, "Travel notes," p. 3, October 1927–February 1928 Folder, Condliffe papers, Carton 36.
6. Ibid., p. 132.
7. Ibid., p. 3; Condliffe, "Reminiscences of the Institute of Pacific Relations," p. 15.
8. James Shotwell, "Report of the Director of the Program of Research in International Relations for the year 1931," Pt. IV, 1.

was only about $10,000, the projects that went to the Social Science Research Council amounted to $40,600. The Social Science Research Council too benefited from its collaboration with the Institute of Pacific Relations. It was an efficient way of expanding its own program and thus expending the funds that had been appropriated to it by the Rockefeller Foundation. This was attested by Condliffe: "[T]he Social Science Research Council is itself experimental and I had not realized that for its sake even more than for ours it was advisable and even necessary to send up some projects which could be put under way at once."[9]

Regular Rockefeller appropriation of research funds beginning from 1929 stabilized the program of the Institute of Pacific Relations. The anomalous relationship between the Institute and the Social Science Research Council also ceased, as each had become capable of expending funds with projects. The patronage of social science research by the Institute of Pacific Relations became routinized, with the new research secretary, William Holland, working amicably with the different national groups in East Asia. If expenditure on research can be taken as an indicator, the figures in Table 9.1, which show China with more than all others combined, clearly demonstrate the Institute's contribution to social science research in China.

Although the Institute continued to support social science research in China until 1949, its importance was outshone in the early 1930s by the entry of the Rockefeller Foundation into the social science field.

The Rockefeller patronage of the social sciences in China had been sporadic, represented by a grant to Yanjing in 1928 and another to Nankai in 1932. Both were block grants to be expended entirely at the discretion of the beneficiaries, a practice Ruml pioneered at the Laura Spelman Rockefeller Memorial.[10] When the Foundation entered the social science field in China in the early 1930s, its China Program departed in two important aspects from its established practices. First, in bringing together social scientists, public health experts, engineers, and agronomists for a concerted attack on China's rural problems, the China Program cut across several divisional lines within the Foundation – the Division of the Social Sciences, the China Medical Board, and the Inter-

9. Condliffe, "Travel notes," p. 3.
10. In 1934, the Foundation changed its funding policy. Instead of making block grants, it began to award grants for specific projects. See Raymond Fosdick, *The Story of the Rockefeller Foundation* (New York, 1952), pp. 207–8.

Table 9.1. *Institute of Pacific Relations Expenditure on Research, 1931–1934, in U.S. dollars*

China	164,912.58
United States	66,418.52
Japan	36,199.43
Great Britain	25,527.61
Pacific Council	21,921.65
Canada	4,155.38
Australia	1,238.00
Philippines	742.94
Total	316,953.73[a]

[a] Note that the sum total above, which does not add up, is in the original. The correct total should be $321,116.11.
Source: Edward Carter to Max Mason, November 11, 1935, p. 7, IPR Box 292, letter to Dr. Max Mason from Edward Carter Folder.

national Education Board. Second, the China Program articulated an ambitious goal in social engineering, which the Foundation had eschewed. This program owed its tenacity to its creator, Selskar Gunn, vice-president of the Foundation.[11]

Graduated from the Massachusetts Institute of Technology in 1905, Gunn had been a public health official and teacher before he joined the Rockefeller Foundation's International Health Division in Europe in 1917. For more than a decade, Gunn had had extensive experience in public health work in Czechoslovakia, Yugoslavia, and Poland. He arrived at the conviction that public health had to be coordinated with a simultaneous attack on social, economic, and political problems in the community if it is to be successful. In 1930, he presented a memorandum at a meeting of the Foundation at Princeton, in which he proposed a

11. Gunn was the Foundation's vice-president in Europe from April 1, 1927 to April 1932 and vice-president of the New York office from April 1932 to April 1, 1942, RAC Gunn Personnel File.

cooperative public welfare program between the International Health Division and the Division of the Social Sciences.[12]

The proposed program was experimental and modest. It involved only the provision of foreign fellowships in rural economics, rural sociology, and public finance, as well as support for studies of communities chosen for experiment by the fellowship recipients upon their return.[13] This proposal caused some consternation among some of the senior trustees who, mindful of the controversies and bad publicity in which the Foundation had found itself in the 1910s,[14] feared that the officers were steering the Foundation into controversial and potentially explosive activities – meddling in affairs in foreign countries.[15] This fear was finally dispelled with the help of sympathetic and powerful trustees and senior officers – Raymond Fosdick (the most trusted lieutenant to John D. Rockefeller, Jr.), Jerome Greene, Max Mason (president of the Foundation), and Ruml.

Gunn, however, was soon to envision an even more ambitious program. His trip to China in 1931 brought him into contact with James Yen's Mass Education Movement, which contained all the elements that he had conceived for his eastern Europe project – a multifaceted approach and implications for nationwide application. Moreover, he found in the Mass Education Movement an unequivocally articulated goal in social engineering, which was only latent in his own proposal. His fascination with Yen's movement turned him into an ardent advocate of social engineering.

Although the China Program Gunn recommended deviated from the course the Foundation had consistently pursued, it did not generate the kind of fear that his earlier much more modest Eastern Europe proposal had. One major reason was that the Foundation had by the early 1930s recovered from its earlier paranoid avoidance of sensitive issues. The

12. "Memorandum by Selskar M. Gunn on Proposed Cooperative International Health Division, Social Science Public Welfare Program," in "A Brief Summary of the Conference of the Trustees and Officers," October 1930, "Appendices," RAC RG3 900 22.166.

13. Ibid., p. 2.

14. The trustees had in mind especially the strike at the Colorado Fuel and Iron Company in 1914 that culminated in the infamous "Ludlow massacre," the Walsh Commission investigation on the Foundation after the massacre, and the Foundation's ill-timed move to appoint Mckenzie King to study industrial relations. See Fosdick, *The Story of the Rockefeller Foundation*.

15. "Verbatim Notes on Princeton Conference of Trustees and Officers," October 29, 1930, especially pp. 150–164, RAC RG3 900 22.167.

experience at the Laura Spelman Rockefeller Memorial had demonstrated that the Foundation could patronize social science research without suffering the much feared repercussions. As an indication of this new attitude, the Foundation in 1928 decided that "[s]ubjects of a controversial nature cannot be avoided if the program is to concern itself with the more important aspects of modern social life."[16] In 1933, the trustees even decided to concentrate on the fields that had been considered controversial: economic planning and control, international relations, community organization and planning.[17]

By the mid-1930s, when Gunn presented his China Program proposal, neither its ideological implications nor political repercussions concerned the trustees. If they did, they were overshadowed by the concern over the best strategy to utilize the Foundation's investment. The special committee appointed to study Gunn's proposal, with statistics reproduced in Table 9.2, commented on China's unusually large share of the Foundation support:

> The question that confronts us . . . is whether China's needs and opportunities are so great as to justify us in expending in that country still further amounts. Or to put the matter in another way, is the welfare of mankind best served by enlarging our investment in China? Is China the outstanding strategic point in which we ought to push our attack? Is there no other sector of the world where we can hope to obtain as large as a return in human happiness and welfare as we can in China?[18]

No difficulties arose at the trustees' meeting, nonetheless. Gunn's China Program was approved. As vice-president, he operated at the highest level of the Foundation hierarchy. Gunn's ability to secure the approval of the China Program was translated into a persuasive power over Chinese social scientists to apply their expertise to rural reconstruction.

COMPETITION FOR RESEARCH FUNDS

The patronage of social science research in China by the Rockefeller Foundation and its subsidiary fund-distributing agencies was a mixed blessing to many a Chinese social scientist. The provision of funds for

16. "Report of the Committee on Appraisal and Plan," December 11, 1934, RAC RG3 22.170.
17. Ibid., pp. 24–5.   18. Ibid.

Table 9.2. *The Rockefeller Contribution to the Fifteen Largest Recipient Countries, 1913–1934*

United States	$117,208,233
China	37,481,104
Great Britain	14,346,068
Canada	7,375,807
Belgium	5,724,828
Brazil	5,499,634
France	5,128,162
Germany	2,701,600
Italy	1,510,336
Syria	1,367,872
Czechoslovakia	1,330,798
Poland	1,306,266
Turkey	1,143,192
Japan	1,109,197
Denmark	996,328

Source: "Report of the Committee on Appraisal and Plan," submitted at the trustees meeting, December 21, 1934, p. 107, RAC RG3 900.22.170.

research conforms nicely with the traditional ideal of patronage of scholars. Chinese social scientists certainly appreciated the offer of assistance that would enable them to engage in research at a time when the teaching load was heavy, salaries were in arrears, and funding for research was virtually non-existent. However, the modern ways of patronizing scholarship involves practices that were not entirely congenial to the Chinese. Particularly difficult for them was the practice of presenting themselves to patrons in language that amounted to self-praise.

Writing proposals and soliciting research funds were alien to Chinese tradition. A true scholar never promoted nor advertised himself; he was to be discovered and appreciated. He could subject himself to a test of excellence such as the examination system. Yet he found it beneath his dignity to partake in a form of competition that required personal initiative such as writing grant proposals. Few Chinese academics during the Republican period acquired the necessary skills in this modern academic salesmanship and even fewer mastered the art.

A sense of pride inhibited Chinese academics from seeking funding from abroad even though chronic financial crisis had characterized the Chinese educational system during the Republican period. This quixotic pride clearly manifested itself in the disparaging views about Yanjing and Nankai expressed by the dominant Peking-Qinghua clique. From their vantage point, Yanjing and Nankai would naturally have excelled in begging money from the Rockefeller Foundation; after all, they felt, Yanjing was merely a missionary college and Nankai a "petty" private Chinese university founded by an ex-naval officer.

The Peking-Qinghua clique never disguised their contempt for Yanjing and Nankai. As Qian Duansheng, the well-known political scientist at Qinghua, once commented:

> In my opinion, national universities in the North will not have an opportunity to make any progress in the coming two or three years. As for missionary colleges, being what they are, they are not where one should be teaching. Private [Chinese] universities are after all petty and cannot be expected to establish themselves. Therefore, Qinghua is the last hope for endangered college education in the North.[19]

Gu Jiegang, the famous historian and folklorist, had the following statement: "My decision to go to Yanjing should not be interpreted as a sign of my favor toward foreigners; I know very well that one could not hope to work without any constraints under foreigners."[20]

Chinese academics were not oblivious to the importance of funding, as was illustrated by the debates they generated when the Powers, following the action of the United States, agreed to return the as yet unremitted portion of the Boxer Indemnity.[21] Not only did they lobby for the return of these funds, but they competed unabashedly for a share of them.[22] There was nothing undignified about their behavior; since the Boxer Indemnity funds were paid by China, they must have felt that they

---

19. Qian Duansheng to Hu Shi, November 14, 1926, in *Hu Shi laiwang shuxin xuan* (A Selection of Hu Shi's Correspondence) (Beijing, 1982), I.408.
20. Gu Jiegang to Hu Shi, August 20, 1929, ibid., I.539.
21. Wang Shu-huai, *Gengzi peikuan* (The Boxer indemnity) (Taipei, 1974), pp. 269–558.
22. For instance, the Science Society of China, with its highly placed and well-connected members, such as Hu Shi, Ren Hongjun, and Yang Quan, aggressively devised plans to assure a share for the Society. See the following letters in Hu Shi, *Hu Shi laiwang shuxin xuan*, I: Ren Hongjun to Hu, May 25, 1924, pp. 250–252; Yang Quan to Hu, May 26, 1924, p. 252; Ren to Hu, July 9, 1924, pp. 255–6.

were merely claiming what was rightfully theirs. However, as demonstrated by the Indemnity fund that the United States returned, it was earmarked for educational and cultural purposes whether with or without the appeal by Chinese academics. The China Foundation for the Promotion of Education and Culture established in 1924 to administer the American Indemnity funds, became an important funding agency in Republican China. Because its administrative body was composed of members of the Science Society of China, such as Ding Wenjiang (V. K. Ting), Fan Yuanlian, Hu Shi, and Ren Hongjun (Zen Hung-chün), the resources of the China Foundation were devoted to teaching and research in the natural sciences.[23] One clear indication of this preferential treatment is in the number of fellowships the China Foundation gave to junior scholars in the natural sciences relative to those in the social sciences. From 1928 to 1945, out of the 735 fellowships given, only seven were in economics and six in sociology, and all these were given only after 1937.[24]

The negligible status accorded the social sciences within the China Foundation is best illustrated by the crisis-ridden history of its Institute of Social Research. Established in 1926 as a department, the Institute of Social Research never received wholehearted support from the leadership of the China Foundation. It owed its origin to a three-year grant from the Institute of Social and Religious Research in New York. A crisis emerged in 1928 when the grant expired and the director, Tao Menghe, threatened to resign and join the Institute of the Social Sciences at the Academia Sinica if the China Foundation did not assume the entire financial responsibility.

The whole situation was a classic case of dispute over funding priority. Ren Hongjun, the director, believed that the Foundation should concentrate on "hard" sciences. An explosive situation occurred in 1934 when the Academia Sinica proposed a merger of its Institute of the Social Sciences and the China Foundation's Institute of Social Research.[25] Ren seized this opportunity to propose a plan for the abro-

23. Peter Buck, *American Science and Modern China, 1876–1936* (Cambridge, 1980), pp. 216–26. See also Yang Ts'ui-hua, *Zhongjihui dui kexue de zanzhu* (Patronage of the Sciences: the China Foundation for the Promotion of Education and Culture) (Nankang, Taipei, 1991).
24. E-tu Zen Sun, "The Growth of the Academic Community 1912–1949," John K. Fairbank and Albert Feuerwerker, eds., *The Cambridge History of China*, Vol. 13, p. 404, table 8.
25. See also the discussion in Chapter 7.

gation of the China Foundation's financial obligation to the joint enterprise. As expected, Ren's plan drew protest from Tao Menghe, who attributed Ren's action correctly to a lack of appreciation for the social sciences. The merger plan was eventually carried out, but only after Ding Wenjiang and Hu Shi had prevailed upon Ren to maintain the level of annual subsidy and leave unspecified the date for the reduction or termination of the subsidy.[26]

The whole episode illustrates a dilemma in which the leadership of the China Foundation found themselves. As leaders of the May Fourth Movement, they were mesmerized by the idea of being patrons of scientific research. Yet at the same time, they felt compelled to set aside some funds for Tao Menghe, even though the scientific status of his field remained dubious to them. The net result was a less than generous budget for Tao that in turn produced a less than impressive record.

If leaders of the May Fourth Movement failed in their half-hearted support of social science research, the implications went beyond the China Foundation. Since the Foundation made no appropriation to outside institutions for social science research,[27] the social science programs at the universities controlled by the May Fourth group, such as Peking and Qinghua, suffered as a result. Despite their reputation for being the best universities in China, neither Peking nor Qinghua was known for empirical social science research.

Although the Peking-Qinghua clique viewed Yanjing and Nankai as either quasi-Chinese or intellectually inferior, it was the latter two that produced entrepreneurial social scientists. Perhaps precisely because they were not in the mainstream and hence not in a position to compete for resources within the system that Yanjing and Nankai were less averse to resort to seeking alternative funding from without the system. Among the contenders for funding from foreign sources, the most brilliant was Franklin Ho. Beginning with a meager budget of $4,500 Mexican dollars in 1927, he transformed the Nankai Institute of Economics into a thriving enterprise with an annual budget of well over one hundred thousand Mexican dollars in five years.

This impressive achievement incurred jealousy. In 1933, Liu Yuwan (Wellington Liu), secretary of the China Council of the Institute of

---

26. Tao Menghe to Hu, July 20, 1934, July 21, 1934, and V. K. Ting to Hu, July 24, 1934, in Hu Shi, *Hu Shi laiwang shuxin xuan*, II, pp. 249–55.
27. The only exception is the $4,000 Mexican dollars grant that the Nankai Institute of Economics received in 1927 from the Institute of Social Research. See Chapter 4.

Pacific Relations, questioned in a memorandum the wisdom of concentrating the Institute's research funds in the hands of a few researchers, namely Ho, J. Lossing Buck, and Liu Dajun.[28] As the research secretary of the China Council, Ho must have felt this was a charge directed against him since it was through his office that research proposals from China were submitted and authorization of grants from New York was given. Ho's first reaction was to avoid confrontation. He chose not to attend the Institute's conference at Banff late that year. Because as the research secretary of the China Council he would have to evaluate the Chinese research proposals, which in his opinion were mostly in poor shape.[29] Eventually, however, he chose to compromise. In a China Council meeting on research held in Peking in 1934, he declared that the China Council should endeavor to groom young research workers and to develop new research centers.[30] A year later, he offered to transfer one Nankai project to Lingnan University.[31]

This action of Ho's was in fact less altruistic than it appeared. The five-year grant from the Rockefeller Foundation beginning from 1932 had made the Institute of Pacific Relations a much less important source of funding for Nankai. In addition, funding from the Institute of Pacific Relations had the drawback of being tied to specific projects, which was not only restrictive in its use, but was too unpredictable for the recipient institutions to make long term research plans. By contrast, the five-year grant from the Rockefeller Foundation was in the form of block grants to be expended entirely at Nankai's discretion.

After having graduated from the project-to-project appropriations by the Institute of Pacific Relations and having entered the realm of Rockefeller abundance, Ho encountered J. Leighton Stuart of Yanjing, whom, in addition to being a master fundraiser himself, had a promotional office in New York. In fact, long before Nankai completed its preparation for application to the Rockefeller Foundation, Stuart had shrewdly observed that Nankai could pose a threat to Yanjing's interests and had thus alerted the New York office to that effect.[32] Indeed Yanjing

28. Liu Yuwan to Frederick Field, April 19, 1933, IPR Box 290 Research Policy 1929–1933 Folder.
29. Gunn to Edward Carter, November 15, 1933, IPR Box 6 Finance: Foundations: Rockefeller Foundation Folder.
30. "Minutes of Discussion Meeting, Peiping, Wednesday, May 2nd, 1934," IPR Box 285 China Institute of Pacific Relations, 1933–1934 Folder II.
31. Ho to William Holland, July 18, 1935, IPR Box 287 Franklin Ho, 1933–1935 Folder.
32. Stuart to Olin Wannamaker, December 22, 1930, UB RG11 356.5491.

and Nankai were soon drawn into a collision course in their respective bids to take part in the Rockefeller Foundation's new social science program in China then contemplated by Selskar Gunn.

Yanjing and Nankai were forced into a tense yet skillfully maneuvered competition rather unexpectedly by J. B. Tayler, a chemist turned economist on the Yanjing faculty. Tayler had been sent to China by the London Missionary Society. He was among the first in China to advocate the idea of developing rural industries to raise the standard of living for the peasant. In an effort to promote this idea through research and extension, he set up the North China Industrial Service Union in September 1932.

In order to relieve the London Missionary Society of its financial difficulties, Tayler resigned in 1932 from both the London Missionary Society and Yanjing and accepted an offer from Nankai. This innocent move created a dilemma for Yanjing. With resources reduced as a result of the Depression, Stuart felt that Yanjing could "scarcely indulge in the luxury of having a man most of whose time will be spent by his own preference and sense of duty, in research."[33] However, knowing Gunn's interest in Tayler's work, Stuart realized that he would "stand the best chance of help from the Rockefeller Foundation" if Tayler were retained by Yanjing.[34] While Stuart was trying to find funds in the United States to keep Tayler in the Yanjing camp, Gunn intervened, which gave Nankai a victory in the first round. Since Nankai was unable to raise enough local contributions to claim the full amount of the Rockefeller appropriation, Gunn ruled that Tayler should go to Nankai and be supported by the unexpended Rockefeller surplus until his new China Program was approved by the Foundation.

Nankai's victory turned out to be temporary, however. By late 1933, as a result of the sharp rise of the value of the silver dollar, Nankai's income from the Rockefeller Foundation was reduced by almost one half when exchanged for silver dollars. Instead of having the surplus Rockefeller money to pay for Tayler's salary, Ho had to appeal to Gunn for emergency appropriations to offset the loss in exchange.

Stuart seized this opportunity to turn the situation to Yanjing's advantage. Knowing Gunn's preference for coordinated efforts, he proposed that Tayler's North China Industrial Service Union be made into a joint Yanjing-Nankai enterprise. He announced that Yanjing and Nankai

---

33. Stuart to N. Gist Gee, December 5, 1932, UB RG11 361.5564.
34. Ibid. For Gunn's ruling that Tayler should go to Nankai, see Gee to Stuart, June 28, 1933, UB RG11 361.5564.

would jointly provide Tayler's salary and the institutional setting for the execution of his projects, leaving Tayler "free to render his best service in investigation, dreaming, inspiring, and otherwise promoting."[35] By a brilliant manipulation of the situation, Stuart had turned Tayler into an asset in his all-out drive to win Rockefeller support.

Stuart's joint Yanjing-Nankai enterprise never took shape, for Gunn was soon to formulate his bigger and more ambitious China Program in which, not just Yanjing and Nankai, but four other institutions partici- . pated. The Tayler case dramatically illustrates how important continued funding was for the Yanjing and Nankai leaders. While their actions smack of intrigue and manipulation, it is worth remembering that it was they and the funding they thus solicited that brought Yanjing and Nankai into national and international prominence. By contrast, the Peking-Qinghua clique, while watching Yanjing and Nankai with disgust and perhaps not without some admiration, contributed little to empirical social science research in China. By staying high and above the "slavish" submission to foreign foundations – what they disparaged as the "Nankai approach"[36] – they indeed served their institutional pride.

The Peking-Qinghua clique only began to appreciate the Nankai approach in the early 1940s, when they too, upon discovering that wartime situations had wiped out the resources under their control, desired to seek support from American foundations. Qian Duansheng, who had castigated Yanjing and Nankai fifteen years before, found himself making a painful aboutface. In a letter to Hu Shi, then ambassador to the United States, Qian asked Hu to approach the Rockefeller Foundation on his behalf. Even he himself, however, realized that his conversion came too late: "I am anxious to know the attitude of the Rockefeller Foundation. The Foundation's representative in Shanghai is M. C. Balfour. *But no one here knows anything about him.* I assume he is in the same bunch with Gunn. [If it is the case,] how would I, not being a member of Nankai or Yanjing, have any chance?"[37] (emphasis added)

FACTIONALISM AND ACADEMIC PATRICIDE

The competition for funds touches upon the issue of factionalism in academia, an elusive and yet fascinating subject that is often referred to but seldom documented. There is enough information on Yanjing to be

---

35. Stuart to Gee, August 21, 1933, UB RG11 361.5564.
36. See Luo Changpei to Hu Shi, April 24, 1946, *Hu Shi laiwang shuxin xuan*, III, p. 105.
37. Qian to Hu, January 21, 1941, *Hu Shi laiwang shuxin xuan*, II, pp. 508–9.

pieced together to suggest what may have been the contributing factors in that particular institution. Drawn primarily from archival sources, this information reveals a wider and more enduring pattern of factionalism in Yanjing and, I would argue, in Chinese academia in general. The analysis presented below enables us to transcend a mere fixation on personality clashes to see how factional infighting reflected disputes over resource allocation within the department and, ultimately, a symptom of a crisis in which foreign education erodes and breaks up the normal patronage networks within China.

The Yanjing Sociology Department, in the words of Grace Boynton, a veteran English teacher at Yanjing and close friend of the famous woman writer Bingxin, was "a perfect hornets' nest."[38] Boynton did not get into the details except to imply that the main culprit was an outsider, Jane Newell (B.A., Wellesley, 1907; M.A., Wisconsin, 1908; Ph.D., ibid., 1919), who taught sociology at Yanjing from 1927 to 1930 and whom she termed persona non grata to many people. The department was, however, strife-ridden with or without stimulations from visitors. One major contributing factor was the allocation of the resources. One classic example involved Li Anzhai. In 1934, Li applied for a Rockefeller Fellowship to study in the United States. Gunn, who administered the China Program through which Li's fellowship was to come from, received several unsolicited letters from Li's colleagues that urged him to turn down the application.[39] It is to Gunn's credit that he approved Li's application on the basis of his own evaluation of Li and ignored the advice to the contrary in those letters.

Although the content of these attacks is not known, it is possible to surmise what the motivations might have been. Li did not have an advanced degree; all he had was a B.S. degree from Yanjing in 1929. He had just secured a marginal appointment in the department in the year when he applied for a Rockefeller fellowship.[40] Since his graduation from Yanjing, he had been everything but a "respectable" academic – a translator, a columnist, an advocate of Basic English,[41] and even a guerrilla

38. Grace Boynton to Family, April 7, 1929, Grace Boynton Papers, North China 1919–1955, Vol. 3, "Letters to her family: Jan. 6–July 6 1929," Folder 3:7 deposited at the Schlesinger Library at Radcliffe College, Harvard University.
39. Gee to Stuart, June 7, 1934, UB RG11 361.5564.
40. He was appointed associate editor, Committee on Social and Population Studies. RAC Fellowship Cards.
41. B(ritish) A(merican) S(cientific) I(nternational) C(ommercial). It is a copyrighted form of English, originated and developed by C. K. Ogden, with a vocabulary of 850

organizer fighting the Japanese after the Manchurian Incident of 1931.[42] As a nonaligned member, he was protégé of neither the dominant social service wing nor the small yet aggressive sociology wing within the department. The malicious attacks might have come from those who felt he was trying to claim a fellowship that should have been theirs.

Li's difficulties within the department are confirmed by an anonymous report.[43] According to this report, Leonard Hsu blocked Li for a position at the department after his graduation from Yanjing. Allegedly it was why Li went to work on the promotion of Basic English with I. A. Richards of Cambridge University, who visited Qinghua from 1929 to 1930. The report claimed that it was Wu Wenzao who helped Li obtain his Rockefeller fellowship, a dubious claim that attributed to Wu a power he in fact did not possess. It further alleged that when Li returned to China he felt he was treated as an inferior by his age cohorts within the department and he never overcame his resentment.

Although Li Anzhai leaned closer to Wu Wenzao's sociology wing, he was only an ally, but not a protégé. In early 1939, he joined his wife, Yu Shiyu, in Labrang, where they were determined to devote the rest of their lives to serve local Tibetans – through research, service, and training. Li's work in Labrang was supported for three years by Rockefeller funding. However, in 1941 Marshall Balfour, the Foundation's field officer, questioned whether Li's work fell into the category of the social sciences to qualify for the Foundation's funding slated for that purpose.[44] The funds in question were under Wu Wenzao's discretionary management, as discussed in Chapter 3. Not being a protégé of Wu's, Li was dropped from the program. The report alleged that funding for Li was cut because he rejected Wu's ultimatum that ordered him to separate "his reform work from his scientific work." Tension between advocacy and disinterested scholarship may have indeed been a factor in Wu's decision to drop Li Anzhai. What the report failed to reveal, however, was that Wu had to find room in his budget for Lin Yaohua, his protégé who had joined the Yanjing faculty in 1942 after his return from Harvard and a year of teaching at Yunnan University.

English words and a short list of non-English words, intended to provide a basis for an auxiliary language and for the introductory teaching of English.
42. UB RG11 311.4777.
43. This report, probably written by Fei Xiaotong, is filed with the Robert Redfield Papers, 6.23 deposited at the Regenstein Library, University of Chicago.
44. See discussion below.

The best-known case of feuds that involved the products of the Yanjing Sociology Department was between Fei Xiaotong and Lin Yaohua. Much of our perception of their conflict is admittedly shaped by the vicious attacks on Fei by Lin during the Anti-Rightist campaign in 1957.[45] There are nonetheless indications that they were never close. Aside from the competition over who was the heir apparent to Wu Wenzao, there was an element of competition for funding as well. Fei's Yanjing-Yunnan Station had been supported by funds under Wu Wenzao's management since 1939. In 1942, Wu added Lin Yaohua to the budget. The following year, in anticipation of the transfer of the funds under his control to the Yanjing administration, Wu recommended that the Foundation continue its support for Lin and liquidate that for Fei's Yanjing-Yunnan Station. Wu's recommendation to the Foundation seems to have been quite sensible and appropriate. After all, the funding had been intended for Yanjing, with which Lin, but not Fei, was affiliated. When queried by Wilma Fairbank, his confidant who was then an officer at the division of cultural relations at the State Department, about the implications this decision would have for his Yanjing-Yunnan Station, Fei nonetheless exploded:

> Transference of money from Kunming [Yanjing-Yunnan Station] to Chengtu [Chengdu, that is, Yanjing] is monkey business. I accepted this when I left. Yunnan Station can be independent financially by any means. . . . Wu tries to be fair to all his students. So Lin should have his chance to start something like Yunnan Station. I will not interfere [with] him.[46]

Fei in fact suffered no damage. The China Program, from which these research funds were drawn, was scheduled to be liquidated the following year anyway. Neither was Fei concerned about the cut. His State Department-sponsored visit to the United States in 1943 to 1944 had been a phenomenal success.[47] He was working on two translation projects, one at the Harvard Business School and the other at the University of Chicago, based on research from his Yanjing-Yunnan Station. Through his prodding, Robert Redfield was negotiating with the Rockefeller Foundation to bring Redfield to survey the social science scene in China. He had also entered into negotiations with a number of uni-

45. David Arkush, *Fei Xiaotong and Sociology in Revolutionary China*, pp. 264–5.
46. Fei to Wilma Fairbank, April 29, 1944, Wilma Fairbank Papers.
47. Arkush, *Fei Xiaotong and Sociology in Revolutionary China*, pp. 105–12.

versities to obtain graduate school fellowships for his protégés at the
Yanjing-Yunnan Station. He had, in short, become an academic entrepreneur, just like his teacher Wu Wenzao. No longer was Lin Yaohua a
worthy competitor – "I must create my own rivals," he reveled, "[O]ther-
wise I will be dead. It sounds queer, but that is the fun of life. However,
I do not think Lin is in fact my real rival."[48] He felt he had beaten Chen
Da, the Qinghua sociologist, who was his former teacher and competitor at Qinghua's Institute of Census. It would not be long, declared he,
before he would challenge Lin Yutang and Pearl Buck.[49]

Fiercely loyal to his friends and protégés but deadly to his enemies,
Fei was creating, with a vengeance as it were, his own patronage network.
There was little in his network that would suggest his intellectual and
emotional ties with his former mentor, Wu Wenzao, but plenty with
Robert Redfield, Alfred North Whitehead, and Elton Mayo. Here a
pattern emerged. Less than six years earlier, before his return to China,
he had had an exchange of letters with Malinowski. It happened that
Malinowski had lost the notes on what he had agreed to write in the
preface for Fei's *Peasant Life in China*. The master, as he was addressed
by Fei, therefore commanded Fei to draft the preface. Upon concluding
his assignment, Fei reported:

> It will be very helpful in our future work if you would like to
> give your orders to your young children by pointing out the possi-
> ble line of inquiry in the future. Let your preface not confine itself
> only to this book, which hardly deserves anything, but to the future
> development of Chinese sociology in which I am only an insigni-
> ficant banner carrier. A captain will be born in your spiritual
> parenthood.[50]

By 1944, Fei Xiaotong had established himself as an accomplished
scholar and research director. He had published one major book, with
two more nearing completion; he had been a director of a thriving
research station; and he had demonstrated his acumen in getting people
excited about his work and forging ties with American universities. Malinowski had died two years earlier. The filial language remained with Fei,
however. He had persistently pursued possibilities with graduate schools

---

48. Fei to Wilma Fairbank, April 29, 1944.
49. Ibid., and also Arkush, *Fei Xiaotong and Sociology in Revolutionary China*, p. 139.
50. Fei to Malinowski, September 10, 1938, Malinowski Papers 3.182, deposited at Sterling
    Library, Yale University.

to place two of his favorite students: Zhang Ziyi and Shi Guoheng – the "'two sons' in my pocket," as he called them. According to the plan worked out with the Harvard Business School, Mayo was to take in Shi Guoheng, whose study of labor in a Kunming factory was translated into English by Fei as *China Enters the Machine Age.*[51] Projecting unto Mayo and Shi his own relationship with Malinowski, he mused playfully at how Disciple Shi would, in a Zenlike fashion, engage in a total immersion body and soul in Master Mayo's presence: "Mayo is a nice old man and willing to take him as his student and give him Chinese way of training: to follow an [the] old man, sweeping the floor for him and sitting in the corner and listening to the talks of the master, and doing house work for the 'mother' etc."[52]

Much of Fei's use of filial language is admittedly simply Chinese. He was fond of hyperbolic language. But he did not use the same language when referring to his Chinese teachers. Now that he had come to operate at the international level, they appeared to be his equals or, worse, his intellectual inferiors. As mentioned above, he said he had beaten his former Qinghua teacher Chen Da, as if there could only be one socio-logical approach. His mentor Wu Wenzao fared no better. Their rela-tionship had apparently become strained and distant. He revealed far more than what he actually stated when he told Wilma Fairbank: "Our relation, Wu and Fei, continues as before. As real Chinese, personal rela-tion accounts above anything."[53] It does not indicate a warm and respect-ful feeling toward a former mentor when he nonchalantly asked Wilma Fairbank: "How about the IPR conference? Has Wen-tsao Wu done any-thing worthwhile?"[54]

What transpires here is a crisis that may be characterized as an acad-emic patricide, a sad case of how foreign education and networking, together with international patronage, erode and break up the normal patronage networks within China. Its root cause is a belief that the ulti-mate authority lies outside the system. Each generation of aspiring schol-ars learns to idolize great masters in the West through contact with those who have been abroad. Their Chinese teachers act simply as transmit-ters of knowledge from abroad. As such, their mentor role is at best

51. *China Enters the Machine Age: A Study of Labor in Chinese War Industry* (Harvard, 1944).
52. Fei to Wilma Fairbank, March 8, 1944, Wilma Fairbank Papers.
53. Fei to Wilma Fairbank, November 13, 1944, Wilma Fairbank Papers.
54. Fei to Wilma Fairbank, January 29, 1945, Wilma Fairbank Papers.

a temporary one. Once the more fortunate of the younger generation have made their own journey to the West, their former mentors look dated and sterile to them. They believe they have become their former mentors' intellectual superiors. When they return, they will become mentors to yet another new generation of aspiring scholars. And a new cycle begins again.

PHILANTHROPIES AND CHINESE SOCIAL SCIENTISTS

The Peking-Qinghua clique perhaps intuitively understood the unpleasant or even humiliating situations that could occur when the patron is from a dominant foreign culture. Patronage of social science research across national boundaries is a delicate undertaking. The mechanics, such as the setting of the research agenda, the choice of methodology, and the execution and supervision of the project can become a source of tension and conflict.

Tension and conflict occur at the point of contact where the patron meets the native researchers. The relationship between the patron and the researchers has the danger of being overshadowed by that of domination and dependence. A case in point is an episode involving Sidney Gamble, an heir of the founder of Procter & Gamble Co. Known for his several surveys of cities and towns in north China, especially the one on Peking, Gamble was himself a patron of social research in China. In the late 1910s and early 1920s, he was *the* center of social research in Peking, where he supervised his own Gamble Institute, offered fellowships to students at the Yanjing Sociology Department, and financed his own social surveys.

The one assistant who was most loyal and contributed most to his success was Li Jinghan (Franklin Lee, B.A., 1920, Pomona; M.A., 1920, California). Gamble, however, almost did not keep Li. In 1924, Li Jinghan resigned from the department of Chinese at Columbia University to accept Gamble's offer to assist the latter in his social research in Peking. Eager to engage in the work for which he had been trained, Li took the $700 dollar advance from Gamble and sailed for China with his new Swiss wife.

Gamble, however, changed his mind. With the following cable to Lucius Porter, a Yanjing professor and administrator who was then chairman of the Chinese department at Columbia University, Gamble thus announced: "Is there any truth in the rumor Franklin Li is married? Situation very delicate account family affairs. Successful research will be prevented. University opposed to employing if report confirmed. Must cancel."[55]

After having meditated the matter "mightily, " Porter felt that Yanjing should not be too particular about Li's having a foreign wife – a potential cause for demanding a higher salary. What if he did "something desperate, suicide or something like that[?]"[56] He shielded Li from the cruel truth while trying to persuade Gamble to honor the contract. Meanwhile, he personally guaranteed repayment to Gamble of the advance given to Li in the event that he failed to convince Gamble.

The capriciousness of Gamble's action can be explained partly by the fact that the patron in this case was also the supervisor of research and that the patron was not institutionally detached from the routine operation, a stage of development major American philanthropies had by then largely surpassed. However, racial prejudice did not dissipate with the rise of modern philanthropy. Racial prejudice was expressed in modern philanthropic foundations through a number of institutionalized practices, of which the foreign fellowship program was a conspicuous example.

The Rockefeller Foundation's foreign fellowship program was designed to provide further training in the United States for promising young foreign scholars with the understanding that they would return to the institutions where they had been affiliated upon the expiration of their fellowship term. However, the Rockefeller Foundation did not enforce this stipulation for many of its fellowship recipients from Europe, Australia, and New Zealand. A case involved Elton Mayo from Australia. Though not a fellowship recipient himself, the Foundation endeavored to secure for him the status to stay permanently in the United States.[57]

The Rockefeller Foundation's attitude toward Chinese fellowship recipients was different. The Foundation made sure that every one of their Chinese fellows returned home. With the Exclusion Act and the tendency among Chinese to stay on indefinitely in the United States, especially during the Second World War, the Foundation's officers had an understandable concern lest they should inadvertently assist those who tried to escape the military service and economic hardship at home.

---

55. Leslie Moss to Lucius Porter, June 19, 1924, UB RG11 339.5190.
56. Porter to Moss, June 23, 1924, UB RG11 339.5190.
57. Martin Bulmer, "Support for Sociology in the 1920s: the Laura Spelman Rockefeller Memorial and the Beginnings of Modern, Large-Scale, Sociological Research in the University," *The American Sociologist*, Vol. 17 (November 1982), p. 189.

Nevertheless, the Rockefeller officers' reaction was paranoid when cases did occur in which the Chinese fellows seemed to postpone indefinitely their return trips. With insinuation of their being unpatriotic and threat of cutting off funds for their return voyage, the Rockefeller officers turned themselves into prosecutors mercilessly indicting their guilty Chinese fellows.[58]

More striking was the stipend structure for the Chinese fellows. The stipend was smaller for the Chinese fellows, presumably because the living standard was lower in China. Most astounding, however, is that the Rockefeller Foundation applied a one-rate stipend structure to the Chinese fellows. In short, it was $120 a month regardless of the fellow's professional status. In 1943, William Holland of the Institute of Pacific Relations made the following comment on the Rockefeller Foundation's treatment of H. D. Fong, the number two man at the Nankai Institute of Economics: "Fong has a legitimate complaint against the Foundation for having originally put him on such a ridiculously low stipend, particularly when the minimum for western social science married fellows is usually $200 a month and in special cases like [Jan] Broek's [a Dutch geographer] they have practically matched his previous salary."[59] Holland urged the Foundation to increase Fong's stipend to $250 a month and the Institute to contribute another $50.

It is hard to argue that the Chinese fellows could subsist in the United States on a smaller stipend than that given to their European colleagues due to their lower living standard back home. It is even more difficult to justify the one rate stipend structure for all Chinese. Two underlying assumptions are at work here: The Chinese fellows, senior or junior, were Chinese nonetheless; and being Chinese, they were Chinese first and scientists second.

Modern, large-scale research, the spiritual child of modern philanthropy, begot a generation of academic entrepreneurs whose research enterprises provided ample outlets for such a superiority complex. For example, until the middle of the 1930s, J. Lossing Buck's land utilization

---

58. The specific cases referred to here concerned two members of the sociology wing from Yanjing: Huang Di and Xu Yongshun. It would of course be ludicrous to compare these two with a person of Mayo's stature. There is also no doubt that the Rockefeller officers were simply enforcing the fellowship terms when they pressured the two to return. The point here is the ferocity and the insinuating language with which the officers pressured the two.

59. Holland to Condliffe, June 23, 1943, Condliffe Papers, Box 9, American Institute of Pacific Relations Folder.

project claimed the largest share of the research funds allocated to the China Council of the Institute of Pacific Relations. Buck, however, always submitted his requests directly to the Institute's Honolulu office, thus bypassing the Chinese research secretary whose recommendation and authorization he was supposed to secure first.

Another case involves Karl Wittfogel, the author of *Oriental Despotism*. Arriving in summer 1935, Wittfogel began research on the socioeconomic history of China, in which he had established himself as an authority with the publication of his *Wirtschaft und Gesellschaft Chinas* in 1931. An academic entrepreneur, he assembled in Peking a large research team – of seventeen scholars at its peak – who combed through the Standard Dynastic Histories for information according to a master schedule drawn up by Wittfogel himself. This "Big Scheme," as he effervescently called it, was to develop into the Chinese History Project, which he later directed at Columbia University.

Among his collaborators, the one he relied upon most was Wang Yuquan, a graduate of Peking University and a Troskyite polemicists as discussed in Chapter 8. In 1936, Wittfogel began negotiating some form of collaboration with Franklin Ho. As part of the collaboration agreement, Wang was admitted to the graduate program at the Nankai Institute of Economics with the understanding that he would continue to work on the Wittfogel project while at Nankai.

The relationship between Wittfogel and Nankai turned sour, however. As Wang Yuquan had been admitted to Nankai, Wittfogel faced the crisis of losing his most valuable assistant in the fall when the school began. Determined to keep Wang, Wittfogel decided to try gunboat diplomacy. He wrote to Edward Carter, the most powerful man at the Institute of Pacific Relations.

> I beg you very much, dear Mr. Carter, to back my step by writing a little letter to Franklin Ho, supporting my demand. . . . [T]he IPR helped me to get the additional fellowship, which enables me to carry out my bigger research schemes. Franklin Ho, who is a leading member of the IPR himself, should therefore not hamper but help a research work, which is being undertaken under the auspices of the IPR itself. I know your letter would settle the question at once and beyond any wavering.[60]

60. Wittfogel to Carter, May 17, 1936, IPR Box 3, Karl Wittfogel Folder.

While Carter was very much impressed by Wittfogel, he had high respect for Ho as a scholar and administrator as well. He chose to adopt a policy of nonintervention.[61]

Personal interaction between the patron and native researchers touches upon only one dimension of the complex cross-cultural impact of modern philanthropy upon the host society. American patronage of social science research in China reached a stage in which it dictated the research agenda and methodology. Much has been written, inspired by Antonio Gramsci's notion of cultural hegemony, about philanthropies and their role not only in determining research agenda and methodology, but in perpetuating a conservative ideology.[62]

The Gramscian thesis illustrates well the conservative ideology of philanthropies. The tepid response some Rockefeller officers had toward James Yen's Mass Education Movement was a case in point. Despite John D. Rockefeller Jr.'s interest in Yen's Movement, his officers remained skeptical. George Vincent, president of the Foundation, expressed this doubt most succinctly when he said: "To make millions of Chinese literate is releasing a tremendous force. Where is the literature to come from – Moscow or New York, London or Paris? ... [T]his thought of spreading all kinds of suggestions through millions of minds in China gives one pause."[63]

That Moscow was on the mind of Rockefeller officers revealed the ideological nature of their enterprise. The apprehension of Rockefeller officers about making "millions of Chinese literate" belied their real intent when using such terms as "social control," "social technology," "planning," and "demonstration." It demonstrates that these watchwords they tossed around freely since 1930 were primarily heuristic and referred more to the process itself than to its relations to any specific

61. Carter to Wittfogel, June 15, 1936, IPR Box 3, Wittfogel Folder.
62. A handy collection of this view can be found in Robert Arnove, ed., *Philanthropy and Cultural Imperialism: Foundations at Home and Abroad* (Boston, 1980). For more recent discussions and debates on this issue, see the following articles: Donald Fisher, "The Role of Philanthropic Foundations in the Reproduction and Production of Hegemony: Rockefeller Foundation and the Social Sciences," *Sociology*, 17.2 (May 1983), pp. 206–33; Martin Bulmer and Donald Fisher, "Debate," *Sociology*, 18.4 (November 1984), pp. 572–87; and Barry Karl and Stanley Katz, "Foundations and Ruling Class Elites," *Daedalus* (Winter 1987), pp. 1–40. For Gramsci's own view on hegemony, which he never had the chance to develop fully, see Quintin Hoare and Geoffrey Nowell Smith, eds. and trans., *Selections from the Prison Notebooks of Antonio Gramsci* (New York, 1971), pp. 5–16, 147–57, 195–6, 245–70.
63. George Vincent to Roger Greene, October 8, 1928, RAC RG4 57.1411.

social goals. The Soviet experiment deprived these terms of their neutral or innocuous character in the eyes of Rockefeller officers.

The following two episodes illustrated their wary attitude. In late spring of 1935, Gunn sent for comment to the New York office a copy of "Statement of Principle" on rural reconstruction prepared by Leonard Hsu. This statement passed through more than a dozen offices and must have raised quite a furor. Edmund Day, director of the division of the social sciences, suggested some deletions.[64] He crossed out the first section, where Leonard Hsu stated: "Rural reconstruction is one phase of social planning, a correlated attack for the realization of a planned society."[65] Day counseled the wisdom of rhetorical restraint: "In my opinion, it is unwise to put rural reconstruction in China explicitly under the caption of social planning. To do this has no advantages, and some manifest disadvantages."[66] Whether or not it was the Soviet five-year plan that was on his mind when Day made his pronouncement, it was clear that "social planning" had become anathema to the Rockefeller director of the social sciences.[67]

Even more revealing was the ambivalent attitude some Rockefeller officers had toward Gunn's China Program. In 1936, John B. Grant, professor of public health at the Peking Union Medical College (PUMC) and the real architect of the China Program,[68] requested from the New York office materials concerning the Minnesota and Virginia projects in public administration. In his acknowledgement to Stacy May, assistant director of the division of the social sciences, the exuberant Grant went a little too far when he suggested that the China Program approach should be adopted by the Rockefeller Foundation in the public administration projects it supported in the United States:

> Should not Minnesota's "laboratory in government," instead of being only "a room of adequate size," be a community in which the public services are controlled by the academic authorities in order

64. Edmund Day to Gunn and the enclosure, June 25, 1935, RAC RG1.1 601.12.125.
65. Ibid.
66. Ibid.
67. As for Gunn, he seemed to view the whole matter a minor difference in phraseology. He thought Day's surgical action on Leonard Hsu's statement that expunged all references to "social planning" made it, in fact, "a concentrated statement but containing the essence of the rural reconstruction as we see it." See Gunn's handwritten notes on the copy of the statement edited and sent back by Day. Ibid., enclosure.
68. Mary Bullock, *An American Transplant: the Rockefeller Foundation and Peking Union Medical College* (Berkeley, 1980), pp. 134–61.

to permit supervised practice for the students being taught and controlled research conditions in practical fields for the teachers themselves? This concept is at least the one toward which development
in China are [*sic.*] tending.[69]

If the officers in New York disregarded deferentially the vice-president's
reference to social engineering, they were unusually intolerant of such
rhetoric coming from Grant, whose "unorthodox" outlook and activities
had earned him the appellative "medical Bolshevik."[70] May exploded:

> I am not sure whether or not you are urging that a Chiang Kai-shek-
> Kemel Ataturk-Hitler-Mussolini-Stalin procedure be adopted
> generally in America and, unlike some of our Republican critics,
> are convinced that the plague of academicoes who have swarmed
> into public office constitutes the type of procedure that you are
> recommending.[71]

Misgivings of the officers notwithstanding, the vice-president's
program continued and was only disrupted and eventually all but suspended by the Japanese invasion of China. Gunn's China Program
underscores the power of foundation officers in pushing through projects
of their choice. At the same time, May's unusually stern criticism of Grant
revealed the conservative outlook of the foundation officers in a cross-
cultural setting. Grant's problems lay, however, not merely in his radical
viewpoints. In the eyes of Rockefeller officers, the most serious problem
with this China-born officer was, simply put, that he had gone native.

A pioneer in public health education in China, Grant was an inde-
fatigable force who endeavored to develop a native leadership in public
health. He scouted for the best and the brightest from his students at the
PUMC, where, on loan from the international health division, he taught
hygiene and public health from 1921 to 1934. He steered them into public
health, helped the best among them to pursue graduate studies abroad,
and, upon their return, placed them in key positions in public health
administrations he helped develop.[72] His multitudinous efforts in
working with Chinese political leaders to set up public health agencies
drew him increasingly into Chinese politics by the late 1920s and early

---

69. John B. Grant to Stacy May, August 4, 1936, RAC RG1.1 601.14.145.
70. Bullock, *An American Transplant*, p. 134.
71. Stacy May to John B. Grant, October 13, 1936, RAC RG1.1 601.14.145.
72. C. C. Chen, *Medicine in Rural China: A Personal Account* (Berkeley, 1989), pp. 37–9.
    Bullock, *An American Transplant*.

1930s.[73] As early as 1932, Frederick Russell, director of the international health division from 1923 to 1935, had expressed his hope to Gunn that Grant would reduce his involvement in political activities and concentrate on the control of disease.[74]

This innocuous remark by Russell masked in fact an increasingly alarmed perception of Grant in the Rockefeller offices in New York. It appears that Grant was caught in factional fights of international dimensions. In 1931, Victor Heiser, Grant's superior at the international health division, recorded a unflattering remark on Grant made by Ludwig Rajchman, director of the League of Nations' Health Organization, and a friend and supporter of T. V. Soong (Song Ziwen):

> Grant has worn himself into an extremely nervous condition over the many difficult situations he has had to meet, and in Grant's own interest as well as that of health work in China, Rajchman strongly recommends that Grant be withdrawn for a period of about a year; that he could give Grant some work in Europe which would entirely take his mind off China's affairs.[75]

Wu Liande, director of Nanjing government's National Quarantine Service, added a Chinese perspective two years later when he sent a litany of complaints to Russell.[76] Criticisms leveled against Grant had so alarmed the Rockefeller officers in New York that they prompted its president, Max Mason, to consult with Gunn in 1935 about how to "utilize to the full Grant's social outlook and enthusiasm," but at the same time, "to preserve the traditional careful attitude of the Foundation against exerting pressure and becoming arbiters of the institutions which we assist."[77] Gunn, in his response, believed that he could discount most of the criticisms directed against Grant. He assured Mason that he had endeavored to administer control over Grant, who, in his words, "has a mind of considerable brilliance."[78]

Never, however, had Gunn completely grasped the full implications of

---

73. Bullock, *An American Transplant*, p. 157.
74. "Memorandum by Dr. Heiser re: Conference on China and Japan with FFR [Russell] and Mr. Gunn," September 28, 1932, RAC RG1.1 601.12.125.
75. "Excerpt from Memorandum by Dr. Heiser," August 20, 1931, RAC J. B. Grant Personnel File.
76. [Gunn?] to Heiser, April 13, 1934, RAC J. B. Grant Personnel File. I have not seen Wu's letter to Russell.
77. Mason to Gunn, June 27, 1935, RAC J. B. Grant Personnel File.
78. Gunn to Mason, August 19, 1935, RAC J. B. Grant Personnel File.

Grant's "social outlook and enthusiasm." Scarcely had two years passed, when he too wished to see Grant take his leave and, better still, have his mind "occupied during the entire time that he is absent."[79] The straw that broke the camel's back occurred in October 1937, when Peking was already under Japanese occupation. At the request of the Nanjing government, Grant sent a telegram to summon C. C. Chen, his protégé and a professor at PUMC, presumably for a government position there. This action of Grant's antagonized Henry Houghton, director of the PUMC, who viewed Grant as butting in on matters that fell under his purview. Gunn confided to Raymond Fosdick, who became president of the Foundation in 1936, that he was "frankly somewhat annoyed at him in connection with this and other matters outside of his own family complications."[80] In an exacerbated mood, he made the following astounding comment that revealed as much about himself as it did about the unsung hero and architect of his China Program:

Grant, as you know, *is in some respects more Chinese than European,* and I just want to warn you that it may be necessary to check up with me some of the statements which he may make to you. His memory is not always to be depended on.[81] (emphasis added)

Sensitive and generally supportive of the Chinese with whom he cooperated, there were nevertheless limits beyond which Gunn was not prepared to go. As much as he was sympathetic to their needs and sensitivities, the Chinese remained to him a race apart.

Equally compelling is the Gramscian thesis on the power of the philanthropies to determine methodology and research agenda. The first American social science agenda in China was put together in the late 1920s by John Condliffe. As a result of his travel in China in late 1927 and early 1928, a number of individuals and centers were put on the map. More prominent among them were the cluster of economists in Shanghai – Liu Dajun among others – mostly working in government bureaus, Buck of the University of Nanking, Franklin Ho of Nankai, Yanjing social scientists, and James Yen's Ding Xian group. His training and interest as an economist clearly were reflected in the fact that the majority of the Chinese he interviewed were economists. Both Franklin Ho and Buck in

---

79. "Excerpt from Letter from S. M. Gunn to W. A. Sawyer," July 19, 1937 RAC J. B. Grant Personnel File.
80. Gunn to Fosdick, October 27, 1937, RAC J. B. Grant Personnel File.   81. Ibid.

fact owed the initial success of their respective enterprises to Condliffe.[82] Buck in particular benefited from the meetings with Condliffe. It was through Condliffe's help that Buck put together his proposal for the Institute, which was eventually published under the title of *Land Utilization in China* in 1937. Statistical studies, of industries and agricultural economy, thus emerged to become the first American social science research agenda in China. In the early 1930s, William Holland, though himself a statistical economist, began to steer the Institute's research projects away from statistical analysis. The model Holland promoted was Robert and Helen Lynd's *Middletown: A Study in Contemporary American Culture*, an influential study of Muncie, Indiana, published in 1929, using a participant observation approach.[83]

Even though the social science agenda put together by Condliffe was to be modified later, his map of prominent social scientists and centers would serve as a guide for future foundation officers to China. For example, during his 1931 visit to China, Gunn interviewed exactly the same groups of social scientists that Condliffe had identified. It is not accidental that the Rockefeller support went to James Yen's Ding Xian group as well as to the social scientists at Yanjing, Nankai, and Nanking, exactly those deemed promising by Condliffe. Even in the middle of the 1930s, when Gunn was redefining the Foundation's social science agenda in China by focusing on rural reconstruction, he never went beyond his patronage network and sought out other social scientists. Whether by cajolery or threats, he was determined to stick to his club members and make them do the work, rather than bringing in new members.

One of the most critical policy consequences of this philanthropy's exclusive patronage network was the entrenchment of a tiny native elite who were both privileged and Western-oriented. Equally significant was the imposition of a research agenda. Once the research agenda was defined, any departure from it could mean the withdrawal of support. One revealing case in point here involved Li Anzhai. His enthusiasm in

---

82. See Chapter 4 for more detailed discussion on Condliffe's visit to China and his efforts in helping Ho develop his struggling enterprise.
83. Robert and Helen Lynd, *Middletown: A Study in Contemporary American Culture* (New York, 1929). The transition from the statistical approach to observatory and descriptive analysis proved difficult. Despite Holland's best effort, Liu Dajun's Wuxing silk district study, for example, did not turn out as a "Middletown" type of community study but rather as a study on the silk industry, which Holland had repeatedly urged Liu to avoid.

developing a frontier sociology in Labrang that would combine research, service, and training sparked no interest whatsoever in Marshall Balfour, the Rockefeller field officer for China during the war.

By taking a narrow interpretation of the Foundation's China Program, Balfour questioned the use of the China Program's social science funds to support Li's work, which he, following the Foundation's conceptualization, viewed to be in the humanities. Li wrote him and tried to convince him of the importance of his work, but was rebuked:

> Having made four trips to the Interior myself, I have no misunderstanding that your work in Kansu is due to phantasy or pleasure travel. . . . My observation, whether or not critical, has been that *you* decide *what* your work shall be and *where* it shall be, and then from various sources, appeals are made to the Foundation to support it. You were supported by Yanjing's C. P. A. [College of Public Affairs] budget from R. F. funds. When that arrangement was concluded, you became attached to the Rural Institute, financed by the R. F. You have communicated with Dr. [Robert] Redfield of the Carnegie Institution, and he in turn, warmly recommends your work for support by the Foundation, and the matter comes to this office again.[84]

However, feeling himself not competent to judge the matter, Balfour referred the case to Gunn. As a vindication for Li Anzhai, Gunn praised Li as a scholar and affirmed that Li's work "is entirely within the scope of my interpretation of the proper use of research aid funds."[85] Gunn's verdict notwithstanding, Li Anzhai was dropped, not by Balfour, but voluntarily by Wu Wenzao, the research supervisor. Even though Balfour professed that he did not question Li Anzhai's devotion to scholarship, by raising objections to using the Yanjing grant to support Li's work, he effectively punished Li for straying from the Foundation's research agenda.

The fate of individual researchers was only a manifestation of a larger and more critical issue concerning the power of the Foundation officers to set the research agenda for the social science community at large. This study of the Chinese social scientists, particularly those at Yanjing and Nankai, has illustrated how attempts to get Rockefeller money compelled them to turn rural-minded. The case of the Mass Education Move-

84. Balfour to Li, April 22, 1941, RAC RG1.1 601.23.213.
85. Gunn to Balfour, April 30, 1941, RAC RG1.1 601.23.213.

ment is admittedly much less dramatic; after all, it was James Yen who pioneered the concept of rural reconstruction. It is nonetheless clear that even the proud James Yen had to humble himself before the Rockefellers. The need to secure continued funding was so great that he had to swallow his contempt for city-bound intellectuals and work with them on the North China Council for Rural Reconstruction put together by Gunn.

Nor was the compulsion limited to the grant-getters. The losers were under tremendous pressure as well. Once the patrons put rural reconstruction on the agenda, even the losers had to stumble along unless they decided to drop out of the picture completely. In this regard, Cheeloo University offered a pathetic commentary. Cheeloo had been designated to develop a rural program since the 1920s. Even though the so-called correlated program never took shape, there seems to have been a tacit agreement about it among Christian colleges. It is therefore not entirely unjustified for some to view Yanjing's all-out drive to participate in Gunn's rural reconstruction as amounting to an encroachment on Cheeloo's "territory."

Yet for reasons that awaits further research, Cheeloo lost without even putting up a fight. It never developed a rural program. But even if apathy or sheer inertia in the field would continue to hold Cheeloo back, the directors, governors, and the supporting missionary boards in the United States had run out of patience. The word was rural reconstruction and those in New York were determined not to allow Cheeloo to become anachronistic. In 1936, Cheeloo received what amounted to an ultimatum to embark on a rural program or else face the cutoff of financial support from the mission boards. In early August, a missionary board formally announced its withdrawal of support, save for a modest contribution to the School of Theology, to this ever-procrastinating institution.[86]

The Cheeloo case illustrates the power of modern philanthropies to determine not only the methodology and research agenda, but the configuration of the social science community. Foundation support tends to go to people who are more adapt and in the right disciplines and belong to the right networks. And once the methodology and research agenda are set, they in turn shape the power relations in the social science community. While the grant-getters thrive and thus are more likely to receive further support, the losers can anticipate further defeat and even atrophy.

---

86. B. A. Garside to E. H. Cressy, August 7, 1936, UB RG11 5.100.

The Gramscian thesis explains much of the behavior of modern philanthropies – their ideological leaning and their power to construct both learning and the community that produces it. It is a compelling argument that through their participation in the production and reproduction of knowledge, philanthropies construct ideas and values that the society at large comes to internalize as "common sense" – hence the notion of "cultural hegemony."[87]

There are, however, two major flaws in this argument. First, the argument is too simple to explain the contemporary American scene with its proliferation of foundations that serve divergent interests.[88] Second, it is unidirectional. This study of the interactions between the Rockefeller Foundation and Chinese social scientists demonstrates that clients manipulate patrons as much as patrons dominate clients.

Rare as Chen Hansheng's case may have been, it is a striking example of a client – a Comintern agent and a member of the Chinese Communist Party – fashioning the game of patronage to serve his interests as well as those of his patrons. Equally successful were the social scientists at both Yanjing and Nankai. Their turn toward a rural research focus illustrated the power of Gunn in dictating to them a new research agenda. It was no less a triumph for themselves, nevertheless. The social science enterprise at each of these two institutions would not have survived, let alone thrive, without the Rockefeller funding. Chen Hansheng was indeed unique in his uncanny ability to promote his radical ideology and research program by utilizing the resources of the Institute of Pacific Relations, which ultimately came from the Rockefeller Foundation. No such feat admittedly had taken place at either Yanjing or Nankai. Yet Nankai was perhaps the more successful of these two enterprises in tailoring its research program to conform to Gunn's research agenda and funding preference. In a quiet, though also less dramatic fashion, Franklin Ho had astutely steered his research program from urban industries to rural industries and county government. In fact, as a testimony to his leadership and resourcefulness, Nankai's shift toward rural society was much smoother than Yanjing's. It appeared so effortless and spontaneous that it never elicited the kind of suspicion Gunn had about Yanjing, that the rural shift was calculated to get Rockefeller money.

---

87. Donald Fisher, "The Role of Philanthropic Foundations in the Reproduction and Production of Hegemony," p. 206.
88. Barry Karl and Stanley Katz, "Foundations and Ruling Class Elites," p. 38.

Thus, while Chinese social scientists had to accept the research agenda and methodology defined for them by American philanthropies, they were by no means passive partners. The more prominent among them even participated in the formulation of the research agenda and the determination of the methodology. Chen Hansheng, among his compatriots, was the closest to assuming such a role during his years at the New York office of the Institute of Pacific Relations.

Together, Chen Hansheng and the Yanjing-Nankai social scientists were remarkably proficient players in the game of the Rockefeller patronage of the social sciences in China. In this unique chapter of Sino-American cultural interactions, social science became a kind of lingua franca of the cultural frontier. The patron and clients negotiated through the medium of social science agendas and methodologies. While the Chinese social scientists were co-opted into the American academic culture, their American patrons were being manipulated by them. In this "frontier language," social science was the syntax and money the grammar.

10

Conclusion: The Legacy

THE story of the three social science enterprises analyzed in this book constitutes a fascinating chapter of the history in the social sciences in modern China. All three enterprises, each with its unique mix of leadership, financial resources, and an institutional base, endeavored not only to build its respective academic field, but to prove its usefulness to China's modernization. With imagination and hard work, the leaders of these enterprises formulated research projects, obtained financial patronage from abroad, forged political partnerships, and made bold claims linking their disciplines to the ideal of social engineering.

Their success, however, belied the fact that the individuals whose visions and entrepreneurial skills created these enterprises operated in an environment that was debilitated by poverty, paralyzed by domestic strife, and ravaged by Japanese aggression. That these three enterprises emerged in a period of economic scarcity and political instability had profound implications for the under-professionalization of the social sciences in modern China. The Chinese educational system was centralized under the control of the Ministry of Education, much like the case in the French and Japanese systems. This vertical integration worked to hinder horizontal interactions among the faculties at the same level of the educational hierarchy. There was little lateral integration in the Chinese academia. Research projects and journal publications were typically organized and handled by institutions, rather than by professional associations. The state, which had played the pivotal role in establishing and maintaining the monopoly of professions in the Anglo-American settings,[1] in the Chinese case created conditions that

---

1. Eliot Freidson, *Profession of Medicine: A Study of the Sociology of Applied Knowledge* (New York, 1970), p. 23.

contributed to the under-professionalization of the social science disciplines. It was the institutions where they taught, rather than the professional associations of which they were members, that delineated the boundaries, set the reward structure, and controlled the work of Chinese social scientists.

However, the Chinese state, weak and financially strapped, was not able to contribute to the emergence of major social science centers within its vertically integrated educational system – unlike the more commanding and stable French and Japanese systems, where vertical integration gives rise to academic "clusters" organized around central chairs at the Sorbonne or the Collège de France or at the major "schools" centered at the universities of Tokyo and Kyoto in Japan.[2] The low priority given to the social sciences by the Nationalist government rendered social science faculty in Chinese universities powerless with no resources for research, let alone for the creation of a patronage network within their institutions.

That Yanjing, Nankai, and Chen Hansheng all depended on American largess for their success was both a strength and a weakness. Yanjing, being a missionary institution, was the least encumbered among the three by the institutional constraints and budgetary crises endemic to the Chinese system of the period. As a private university, Nankai enjoyed a higher degree of freedom than public institutions that depended entirely on state appropriations. Chen Hansheng's case was unique. As a research team as adaptable and chameleonlike as a guerrilla unit, it carried on its work on the basis of resources Chen brought in through his political skills and connections. All three enterprises succeeded because of their ability to solicit resources outside the system.

American largess thus played the role of sustaining social science centers in China, a role that one might have expected a more stable and wealthy state itself would have played within its vertically integrated system. And herein lay the fundamental weakness of these three enterprises: Their successes were exceptions rather than the rule within the Chinese system and were sustainable only as long as American philanthropies remained committed to the field. The Rockefeller Foundation's retrenchment policy during the war caused all three enterprises to contract. While Nankai succeeded to some extent in drawing resources from the business sector, Yanjing languished. After the war, both Yanjing and

2. For a discussion of the French case, see Terry Clark, *Prophets and Patrons: The French University and the Emergence of the Social Sciences* (Harvard, 1973), pp. 66–92.

Nankai eagerly awaited the return of the Rockefeller Foundation. The civil war that ensued, however, dimmed that prospect. The final blow came with the Communist Revolution in 1949, and with it the era of international patronage and bargaining drew to a close. Nor could Yanjing or Nankai maneuver in the new and more rigid vertically integrated system. Nankai had been nationalized by the Nationalist government in 1946 and Yanjing ceased to exist in 1952 and had its campus taken over by Peking University. There would no longer be social science research independent of the Chinese Communist Party; in its attempt to exercise total control over society, it extinguished all nonparty sponsored activities.

Not only did the Communist Revolution destroy the three social science enterprises analyzed in this book, but the new regime it ushered in reconstituted the social sciences, as is best illustrated by its decision to abolish sociology in 1952. The rupture with the past seemed total; it was as though the histories of these three enterprises were no longer relevant. Yet it is clear, particularly from the vantage point of the 1990s, that these social science enterprises left behind a powerful legacy both in terms of their aspirations for social engineering and in terms of the research data and conceptual categories they had bequeathed.

SOCIAL ENGINEERING

The year of 1979 marked the revival of sociology after its nearly thirty years of suspension since 1952. Because the discipline has developed anew within the Chinese Marxian framework, sociology in China today is problem-oriented and full of policy implications. In many ways, this problem-oriented approach and emphasis on policy implications reflect a continuation of similar attempts by Chinese social scientists before 1949 to relate their disciplines to national needs.

Underneath the unabashed talk about the usefulness of social science disciplines in the nation's modernization lies a quest for a role in the sociopolitical process. In late 1980, sociologists established a number of field stations, including a permanent one at Fei Xiaotong's old village in Kaixiangong. In 1983, three key areas of research during the sixth five-year plan period were decided upon: first, small towns in Jiangsu province; second, the present and future trends of families in five cities; and thirdly, Chinese population, with regard to problems of and trends toward the decline of the birth rate and the analysis and prediction of the population in Peking.[3] Although couched in modest terms (that of fact-finding and of training of personnel),[4] these new developments are reminiscent of the state of sociology in the early 1930s, when it began to exhibit the aspiration for engineering social change through a better understanding of the society.

Similar aspirations have characterized the development of economics as well since 1979. Among the social science disciplines, economics has had the least problem in adjusting itself in the Chinese Marxian framework. Referred to as political economy, economics in China since 1949 has been devoted to the exposition of Marxist economic theory, the critique of capitalism, and the dissemination of ex post facto rationalization of government policies in the form of fact-finding reports. While these same emphases continue to characterize the post-Cultural Revolution development, Western economic techniques and research tools such as linear programming and input-output analysis have increasingly attracted the attention of Chinese economists.[5]

The appeal of statistical models or tools to Chinese economists is that they are ideologically neutral, capable of performing sophisticated analysis without committing the researchers to any ideological positions. More important, however, is their claim of being scientific. Since economists, too, discourse profusely and unabashedly on how to contribute to the "Four Modernizations," the techniques that claim to approximate mathematic accuracy could enable them to aspire to an engineering role in the planning and management of the nation's economy.

In fact, short of assigning the role of "social engineers" to themselves, Chinese economists during the post-Cultural Revolution period have once again begun to toy with the idea of social engineering. In 1979, for example, the magazine, *Economic Management*, carried an article in its first issue titled "The Technology That Organizes and Manages Socialist Reconstruction – Social Engineering."[6] In this article, the authors advocated the application of the concept of systems engineering to the man-

---

3. "Jianxun" (News Summaries), *Shehui* (Society), 1983.3 (6/20/1983), p. 12.
4. In a paper delivered in the United States in 1983, Zhao Baoxu characterizes these field stations as "social laboratories" – a striking resurrection of a popular term used by the Yanjing sociologists in the 1930s and 1940s. See his "Sociology and Population Studies in China," ("Texas Population Research Center Papers," Series 5, 1983), p. 19.
5. See Robert Dernberger, "Economics," Anne Thurston and Jason Parker, eds., *Humanistic and Social Science Research in China: Recent History and Future Prospects* (New York, 1980), p. 111.
6. Qian Xuesen and Wu Jiapei, "Zuzhi guanli shehui zhuyi jianshe de jishu – shehui gongcheng", *Jingji guanli*, 1979.1, pp. 5–9.

agement of society. The development of cybernetics, operations research, and supercomputers have made it possible, the authors argued, to formulate in exact and scientific manner comprehensive plans for China's socialist modernization. This was an article that celebrated the prospect in which the social engineers could present to the leadership for consideration a variety of long-range developmental plans, say, for thirty years, in just six months of time by the use of simulation techniques with computers.[7]

It is too early to foresee whether social scientists in China will reach the position in which they, like their predecessors in the 1930s and 1940s, can aspire to be social engineers, or whether they will prove to be mere social technicians facilitating the implementation of policies from the center. Until the crackdown in June 1989, the decade-long reforms had created an intellectual milieu that was hospitable to the idea of social engineering. This perennial Chinese ideal is once again gaining momentum as China continues to move toward economic as well as political reforms.[8] Most illustrative of the reemergence of this aspiration is the Debate on neoauthoritarianism that began in 1988 until it was cut off following the crackdown in 1989.[9] This Debate occurred in the context of a heightened sense of urgency for China to search for a rapid and proven approach to modernization. The proponents viewed neoauthoritarianism as a means to achieve the ultimate goals of democracy and economic prosperity for China. Their opponents, by contrast, believed that the best way to achieve democracy was through immediate implementation of democratic institutions and procedures. As an intellectual debate, little here was new. Its premise has been enunciated and debated several times in the past hundred years, as in Yan Fu's social Darwinist interpretation of the notion of liberty; Liang Qichao's "enlightened despotism"; and the Debate on Democracy and Autocracy between Hu Shi and Ding Wenjiang and others in the mid-1930s. But as a debate that was powered by a belief that it was possible to steer the course of mod-

---

7. Ibid., p. 8.
8. Social scientists, together with natural scientists and engineers, have played an important role in Taiwan's economic development since the 1960s. The credo of social engineering is so widely accepted that the term "technocrats" has become a favorite label for government officials by both the press and the government in Taiwan since the late 1980s.
9. For a brief survey of this Debate, see Mark Petracca and Mong Xiong, "The Concept of Chinese Neo-Authoritarianism," *Asian Survey*, XXX.11 (November 1990), pp. 1099–117.

ernization, it bespoke the reemergence of the notion of social engineering, particularly in view of the fact that the notion of neoauthoritarianism was closely associated with the then general secretary of the party, Zhao Ziyang, and his brain trust.

The crackdown in 1989 is a setback for aspiring social engineers at least at the Peking level. As long as the social sciences are allowed to continue to develop, however, this aspiration to participate in the nation's modernization efforts will likely be kept alive by their practitioners.

A TRANSPACIFIC TRANSPLANTATION
OF A PARADIGMATIC DEBATE

The rhetoric of social engineering masked sharp ideological differences that divided the Anglo-American and Marxist social science enterprises during the Republican period. Not only did these two social science discourses differ in their respective definition of the goals of social engineering, but they also clashed on the approaches. So powerful and ubiquitous was ideology that not only did it affect the career choice and political actions of the social scientists during the Republican period, but it helped shape their world views and conceptualizations of society.

The ideological chasm in this debate on how to conceptualize China's agrarian sector is another legacy of the social sciences during the Republican period, which ironically is more alive in the Chinese studies community in the United States than in China today. The debate among American China scholars, particularly during the 1980s, on how to interpret economic growth or the lack of it and its respective contributing factors during the Republican period, though much more sophisticated, is no less ideologically bound than what took place in the 1930s. Initiated by Philip Huang and Ramon Myers, the debate has widened to include David Faure and Loren Brandt, who gravitate in varying degrees toward Myers' position.[10] Leaving aside the often unstated contention over whether the Communist Revolution of 1949 was a mistake, this

---

10. I am referring here to the following works: Ramon Myers, *The Chinese Peasant Economy: Agricultural Development in Hopei and Shantung, 1890–1949* (Harvard, 1970); Philip Huang, *The Peasant Economy and Social Change in North China* (Stanford, 1985); David Faure, *The Rural Economy of Pre-Liberation China: Trade Expansion and Peasant Livelihood in Jiangsu and Guangdong, 1870–1937* (Oxford, 1989); and Loren Brandt, *Commercialization and Agricultural Development: Central and Eastern China, 1870–1937* (Cambridge, 1989).

debate has mainly revolved within the same perimeters delineated by the Chinese themselves fifty years ago as analyzed in this book.

With the exception of Myers, participants in the current debate use the word, "peasant" or "farmer," consciously and deliberately.[11] Although none has spelled out the rationale for his choice of the word,[12] it is clear that each has chosen one or the other for a host of ideological considerations. Thus, for Faure and Brandt, the Chinese "farmer" was basically an "economic man" making rational decisions in response to the market. For Philip Huang, however, such characterization is appropriate only for the study of capitalist economies. Calling his an integrated approach, he argues that the Chinese "peasant" can best be understood as an entrepreneur, a subsistence producer-consumer, or an exploited cultivator, depending on his status within the peasantry.[13]

The "farmer" faction takes issue with Chen Hansheng, whom Myers terms a "distributionist" and Faure, a "pessimist."[14] While "distributionist" is an accurate label for a host of agrarian reformers, Sun Yat-sen and Guomindang theorists included, who believed, as Myers put it, that the solution was "to equalize land holdings and lower rents and interest rates,"[15] it is a fundamental misreading of Chen Hansheng's position; it turns him into a petty-bourgeois Narodnik, no more and no less. If Chen believed that at the root of China's agrarian crisis were the semifeudal production relations whose destruction was possible only through revolution, what good would it serve to redistribute land without altering these production relations?

If Chen Hansheng was no "distributionist," neither was he the "pessimist," Faure portrays him to be. While many commentators during the 1930s gave pessimistic accounts about the agrarian distress, few were pessimistic about the prospect for its cure. Much has been written about the optimism shared by many modern Chinese intellectuals – Liang Qichao, Sun Yat-sen, Mao Zedong, to name a few – about the possibility for China to compress the time needed for its quest for modernity. How

11. Myers would have no doubt used the word, "farmer," had his book been published a decade later.
12. Philip Huang, like Chen Hansheng more than half a century earlier, is the most articulate in this regard among the participants of the current debate.
13. Huang, *The Peasant Economy and Social Change in North China*, p. 6.
14. See Myers, *The Chinese Peasant Economy*, pp. 15–17. While Faure does not list any names in his survey of the pessimist literature, he refers in an endnote to Chen as a representative of the pessimist view. See his *The Rural Economy of Pre-Liberation China*, p. 218 n.2.
15. Myers, *The Chinese Peasant Economy*, p. 17.

much less optimistic could a social scientist be when he believed in social engineering, whether through scientific planning or the release of the productive forces through revolution?

It is by no means a trivial question as to how Chen Hansheng is labeled, for along with it comes a serious misrepresentation of his agrarian research. Although Chen stressed the landlord-tenant ratio, he never asserted, as would the "distributionists," that the tenants were necessarily the most destitute in society. Knowing as he did the complicated tenure system in Wuxi, the preponderance of owner-cultivators in north China, and rich tenant farming in the *shatian* areas in Guangdong, Chen would be the last person to be fixated upon the landlord-tenant axis when analyzing China's agrarian economy. If he condemned the high rate of tenancy, his concern was not with distribution per se, but with the obstruction this parasitic landlord economy had on the productive forces.

In labeling Chen a "distributionist" or "pessimist," his critics contend that the lot of the peasant was not as bad as he would like us to believe. They argue that commercialization during the Republican period was beneficial to the rural population in general. Brandt most zealously contends that China's agricultural sector experienced a sustained growth until the 1930s and that the benefits of this growth were evenly distributed in rural society. His is a typical example of an argument that infers how the individual farmers should have fared from how the market in general had performed. Granted that the Shanghai rice market was fully integrated with the international market on the one hand, and the county level markets throughout the Yangtze drainage basin on the other, and even granted that local markets were as competitive as he contends, these conditions offer him little basis to go on to argue that "the prices farmers received were closely tied to those prevailing in large markets and Shanghai."[16] Brandt's book is replete with statements about rational farmers making business decisions, taking advantage of their freedom of entry to and exit from the market, and enjoying the income-equalizing effects the competitive market had created. His analyses completely ignore the political and social factors that would have affected the functioning of the market and the standing of the individuals within it. Chen Hansheng would have countered by arguing that the point is not whether the peasant had equal access to the allegedly free rental markets

16. Brandt, *Commercialization and Agricultural Development*, p. 37. See Joseph Esherick's review of Brandt's book in *The Journal of Economic History*, 51.2 (June 1991), pp. 501–3.

for land and draft animals, but under what terms and for what stratum of the peasantry.

More measured in his presentation of the general views of the "farmer" faction is Faure. Nonetheless, he is no less formalistic in his approach that leads him to believe that a gain for the aggregate must have been a gain for the constituents as well. He argues that everyone must have been better off because while the price of rice had increased by 5.3 times during the period between the mid-1870s and mid-1920s, the grain tax calculated in copper cash during the same period had increased by only 2.9 times. Aware as he is of the extra-legal burdens in the forms of surcharges and impositions that the peasants had to bear, he nonetheless dismisses them as either incalculable or intangible.[17] More serious is how Faure's formalistic bias affects his use of data. Faure quotes Chen Hansheng's Guangdong survey in which the latter "reported that rent on mulberry land had dropped 50 percent from the commonly charged 20 to 50 dollars per *mu*" in the famous silk district of Shunde county.[18] After converting the rent into the median price of local rice and setting it against a ten-year trend, Faure concludes that "rent charged on mulberry land remained remarkably constant."[19] What gets lost in this inference from the aggregate to the constituents is Chen's point that the price of mulberry leaves dropped from 5.00 to 0.60 Chinese dollars per picul – an 88% drop in the income of mulberry peasants.[20] Thus, while the rent may have remained constant, the peasants did not necessarily fare better.

It hardly needs elaborating that Philip Huang has presented an analysis that most likely would have met with Chen Hansheng's approval. He has built on Chen's agrarian analysis and brought it to a new height of sophistication. Instead of trying to gauge how the peasants must have lived from the way the market had performed, their approaches brought the peasants to the foreground. It is beyond the scope of this study to evaluate their claim that their analyses reflect more accurately the situation than that of the "farmer" faction. Huang's critical assessment of the Mantetsu researchers, however, brings up an intriguing question con-

---

17. Faure, *The Rural Economy of Pre-Liberation China*, p. 83.
18. Ibid., p. 79. In fact, Chen did not exactly report that rent had dropped 50 percent. He only said that the landlords could grant rent reductions for as high as 50 percent when the area suffered from a disastrous drop in the purchasing prices for silk and cocoons. See his *Landlord and Peasant in China*, p. 66.
19. Faure, *The Rural Economy of Pre-Liberation China*, p. 80.
20. Chen Hansheng, *Landlord and Peasant in China*, p. 66.

cerning whether Chinese field workers differed in any significant ways from their foreign colleagues.

Did the Mantetsu researchers approach the field differently from their Chinese counterparts simply by virtue of their being agents of a conquering army? Were they alone guilty, as Huang has implied, in gaining access to the field through the military authorities, relying on village elite as informants, or conducting interviews by summoning informants from the field, and even occasionally being escorted by armed guards?[21] Chinese field workers were no less alien in the field than their Mantetsu counterparts. The field diaries kept by Chen Hansheng's teams for his four-province surveys contain many vivid accounts of their adventures in the strange, outlandish place they called the motherland. For example, clothed in Western suits and hats,[22] these field workers reported how they were scandalized by a local practice in the major city of Xuzhou in Jiangsu that tore paper money in half and used it as equivalent to the next smaller denomination.[23] Most members on the Jiangsu and Zhejiang teams were moreover handicapped by their inability to communicate with villagers in local dialects. The Zhejiang team was even temporarily stalled in Dongyang when the uncooperative county government sabotaged its work by not providing it with interpreters.[24]

Nor did Chen's field workers enjoyed rapport with their subjects by virtue of the concern for social justice that emanated from their Marxist worldview. The response they elicited from villagers ranged from mild amazement, to guarded receptivity, to fearful suspicion, and to outright hostility, not much different from what the Mantetsu researchers would meet a few years later. In order to secure the cooperation of the villagers, they were often presented as welfare workers.[25] Rarely, however, did they succeed in dispelling the deep-seated suspicion of the villagers. A most spectacular confrontation is recorded a few years earlier in 1930 by Chen's Wuxi team: "When we conducted fieldwork in Renxiang, women came out to resist, having been egged on by men. They goaded us with all the tricks they could muster. But we remained undisturbed. This made

---

21. Huang, *The Peasant Economy and Social Change in North China*, pp. 39–43.
22. See the photos that appear in each of the four province reports. The Zhejiang team reported that they changed into local clothing. See *Zhejiang sheng nongcun diaocha*, p. 224.
23. *Jiangsu sheng nongcun diaocha*, p. 65; and *Henan sheng nongcun diaocha*, p. 84.
24. *Zhejiang sheng nongcun diaocha*, p. 235.
25. Ibid., p. 224.

them nervous. Later, they took out the brooms they used to scrub their chamber pots and waved them above our heads."[26]

Such open displays of hostility made field work difficult, but rarely posed serious danger to field workers. The same was not true, however, with bandits who plagued the countryside. It is therefore to be expected that field workers welcomed, if they did not request on their own initiative, armed protection. One of Chen's field workers gave the following account about their magnificent parade:

> The Eighth ward is not quite tranquil. Magistrate Wang was leading a score of cavalry and one company of infantry to fight the bandits there. For our safety, we went along with them in our rickshaws. We set out at dawn. After having left the northern gate, we marched on the highway, with the cavalry at the front, the rickshaws in the middle, and the winding infantry at the back. It was quite magnificent![27]

Confronting such an unfamiliar and inhospitable environment on the one hand, and fearful and hostile subjects on the other, researchers not surprisingly sought access to the field through intermediaries. Chen's field workers relied on government functionaries from the county, the ward, to the village level. When this failed, they would solicit help from the Guomindang party members, village elders, and local elite. For convenience, they often summoned the peasants and conducted interviews with them in the houses of government functionaries or in public places, such as lineage halls and local temples. Small wonder that villagers had difficulty not treating them as government agents canvassing the countryside for new taxes or impositions. Finally, like all researchers of all ideological persuasions during the Republican period, Chen's workers also relied upon what may be called surrogate research. In other words, they prepared the schedules or questionnaires for local informants, most of whom were total strangers to them and whose credentials and qualifications as surrogate researchers were beyond their control.

That Chen's researchers could gain access to the field through the rich and powerful – government functionaries, village elders, and local elite – and yet at the same time reach antiestablishment conclusions is impor-

---

26. Liao Kaisheng, "Shehui kexue yanjiusuo Wuxi nongcun diaocha jilue" (A Brief Account of the Wuxi Survey Conducted by the Institute of the Social Sciences), *Guoli Zhongyang yanjiuyuan yuanwu yuebao*, I.8 (February 1930), p. 13.
27. *Jiangsu sheng nongcun diaocha*, p. 67.

tant. It suggests the power of ideology in steering researchers through data made available through intermediaries whose ideological persuasions were not necessarily congenial to them. More important is the simple fact about the elements of scholarship it demonstrates: to sift, to corroborate, and to interpret, granting that one's ideological persuasion would always be in the background.

Aside from this truism about what constitutes research, the not atypical experience and practices reported by Chen's field workers revealed the elite and outsider roles of social scientists and social researchers in China during the Republican period. Whether they were the self-styled social engineers of the Anglo-American type, or rural reform advocates of the low-brow intellectual brand, or Chen and his fellow advocates of revolution, they were all outsiders and elite as far as their subjects were concerned, alien in their world view, vocabulary, mannerism, clothing, and even language. While much of the social distance between the researchers and their subjects has narrowed in China since the Communist Revolution, social researchers remain the outsiders. The highly touted group sessions, à la Mao's style, which supposedly would make investigators more sensitive to the wishes and wants of the people, are nonetheless an avenue through which the investigators as outsiders help facilitate the formulation and implementation of state policies. Investigation as a form of advocacy began to emerge after the rehabilitation of the social sciences in 1979 and especially during the reform decade of the 1980s. It remains to be seen, however, whether the elitist character of the social scientists will become pronounced once again as their disciplines adopt more operational apparatus from the West.

As China once again looks to the West, particularly the United States, for inspiration and assistance for the nation's modernization, the legacy of Sino-American intellectual and cultural exchanges during the Republican period is full of implications for the present. Today, there are more than forty thousand Chinese students studying in the United States, making them the largest group of all foreign nationals in American institutions of higher education. Unlike their predecessors during the Republican period, there is no longer the Exclusion Act, repealed in 1943, to bar them from becoming permanent residents and eventually American citizens. Not many of them would opt to return, at least not until the political and economic conditions in China improve significantly. In fact, only 70,000 students, less than one third of the more than 230,000 who had gone abroad since 1978, had returned home by the middle of the

1990s. The return rate from the United States is even lower, only 5 to 10 percent.[28] The Chinese Student Protection Act of 1992, which was enacted in response to the Tiananmen crackdown, offered permanent resident status to nearly 50,000 who had entered the United States before April 11, 1990.

It appears that China will continue for the foreseeable future to lose a considerable number of its educated elite through studies abroad, much as Taiwan and other developing countries experienced during the 1960s and 1970s. However, as the development patterns of these former developing countries illustrate, a braindrain does not have to be a complete loss for the country on the losing end. Through home visits and academic conferences and exchanges, the expatriates can exert potent influences back home. Nor is a braindrain irreversible. The combination of the prolong recession in the United States and the rapid and sustained growth of the Taiwanese and South Korean economies had by the later half of the 1980s produced what some catchy headlines characterized as a reverse braindrain from American industries of their senior engineers of Taiwanese and South Korean origins.

Although an analogous scenario for China at the scales experienced by Taiwan and South Korea will not likely develop as long as there are doubts about the future of reforms and political stability, it is clear that the pull that draws the expatriates homeward remains in the economy. The dramatic growth of the Chinese economy since 1992 has begun to do just that, as illustrated by the growing number of newspaper articles and anecdotal stories about recent returnees. While it is true that most expatriates will remain abroad and maintain their links to China through home visits, business trips, and academic exchanges, an increasing number of them will return. What will be their impact on the social sciences in China? What about the social scientists who have received their training abroad? Will this new generation of Chinese social scientists, dazzled by the wide spectrum on the American academic scene, together with a certain degree of historical amnesia on their part,[29] repeat the same cycle of wholesale importation and indigenization of foreign social sciences with much the same resourcefulness and, perhaps, the same mistakes?

28. *Los Angeles Times*, January 3, 1995, p. A1.
29. No one who does just a cursory survey of the intellectual debates in China since the 1980s – on science, democracy, and Chinese and Western civilizations – would fail to be impressed by the familiar rings that have resounded many times over since the beginning of the twentieth-century and the May Fourth era.

Much of the same drama is being reenacted in the United States as well. Once again, American universities and foundations are involved in the training of Chinese students in the United States and in educational programs and research projects in China. With good intentions, and not without their own share of historical amnesia, Americans are embarking on a new mission to change China. The old enemy – call it Oriental chaos or medievalism – is gone. Or is it? Its new name is the now seemingly anachronistic Communism. What remains eternally familiar, however, is the American call for Democracy and Science – what the Chinese students themselves say they want – and the temptation to see China and its future in terms of the image of the United States. If the Americans are once again eager to sponsor and direct, the Chinese are more than solicitous in their response. It is fraught with historical irony that the National Beijing and Qinghua universities have jettisoned the official pinyin spelling and resurrected Peking and Tsinghua respectively for their English names. A new cycle of international patronage and bargaining has commenced. Much can be learned, lessons appreciated and pitfalls avoided, by pondering China's earlier experience with Western social science.

Glossary

Amano Motonosuke	天野元之助
Baishu cun ("Village of a Hundred Trees")	百樹村
ban zigengnong (half-owners)	半自耕農
bao jia	保甲
Bao Juemin	鮑覺民
Baoding (Hebei)	保定
Beijing shehui shijinhui (the Peking Students' Social Service Club)	北京社會實進會
Bi Xianghui	畢相輝
Cai Hesen	蔡和森
Cai Yuanpei	蔡元培
Cao Rulin	曹汝霖
Chen Da	陳達
Chen Dezheng	陳德徵
Chen Duxiu	陳獨秀
Chen Guangyuan	陳光遠
Chen Guoping (Rockwood Chin)	陳國平
Chen Hansheng (Chen Shu 陳樞)	陳翰笙
Chen Hongjin	陳洪進
Chen Lifu	陳立夫
Chen Xujing	陳序經
Chen Youren (Eugene Chen)	陳友仁
Chen Zhenhan	陳振漢
Chen Zhiqian (C. C. Chen)	陳志潛
Cheng Yongyan	程永言
Chengzhi hui	成志會
Chiang Kai-shek (Jiang Jieshi)	蔣介石
Chongyi qiao (Chengdu)	崇義橋
Dagong bao (*L'Impartial*)	大公報
Daming (Hebei)	大名
Datong (Shanxi)	大同
Dengshikou (Beijing)	燈市口
Dianxing (representative types)	典型

270

diaocha hui ("investigation meetings")	調查會
Ding Ji (Leonard Ting)	丁佶
Ding Wenjiang (V. K. Ting)	丁文江
Ding Xian (Hebei)	定縣
Dingfan (Guizhou)	定番
Dong Chengxian	董承顯
Dong Wentian	董文田
Dongguang (Hebei)	東光
Dongyang (Zhejiang)	東陽
Fan Yuanlian	范源濂
Fang Xianting (H. D. Fong)	方顯廷
Fei Xiaotong	費孝通
Feng Huade	馮華德
Feng Yuxiang	馮玉祥
Fengxiang (Shaanxi)	鳳翔
Fu Sinian	傅斯年
Gaoyang (Hebei)	高陽
geren dizhu (individual landlords)	個人地主
gonggong dizhu (corporate landlords)	公共地主
gourou zhang ("dog meat ledgers")	狗肉帳
Gu Jiegang	顧頡剛
Gu Shuxing (Susie Ku)	顧淑型
Guo Moruo	郭沫若
Haifeng (Guangdong)	海豐
Han Dezhang	韓德章
Hani Gorō	羽仁五郎
Hara Masaru	原勝
Hirano Yoshitarō	平野義太郎
He Lian (Franklin Ho)	何廉
He Shizhen	何世楨
Hu Shi	胡適
Hua Wuqing	華午晴
Huaiyuan (Anhui)	懷遠
Huang Bangzhen	黃邦楨
Huang Di	黃迪
Huang Guogao	黃國高
Huaqiao ribao (Overseas Chinese Daily)	華僑日報
Hui Xian (Henan)	輝縣
Hulan (Heilongjiang)	呼蘭
Jiang Tingfu (Tsiang T'ing-fu)	蔣廷黻
Jiangyin (Jiangsu)	江陰
jimin zhi shi ("food of famine victims")	饑民之食
Jinan University (Shanghai)	暨南大學
Jincheng yinhang	金城銀行
Jinggang mountains	井崗山
Jinghai (Hebei)	靜海
Jining (Tsining, Shandong)	濟寧

Jiuguo ribao (Salvation Daily)	救國日報
Kaixiangong (Jiangsu)	開弦弓
Kang Nairu	伉乃如
Kang Sheng	康生
Kōza-ha (the Lecture faction)	講座派
Li Anzhai (Li An-che)	李安宅
Li Chun	李純
Li Dazhao	李大釗
Li Ji	李季
Li Ji	李濟
Li Jinghan (Franklin Lee)	李景漢
Li Jitong	李繼侗
Li Qinglin (Shison Li)	李慶麐
Li Quanshi (Li Ch'üan-shih)	李權時
Li Rui	李銳
Li Youyi	李有義
Li Yuanhong	黎元洪
Li Zhuomin (Li Choh-ming)	李卓敏
Li Zushen	李組紳
Liang Qichao	梁啟超
Liang Shiyi	梁士詒
Liang Shuming	梁漱溟
Liang Zhonghua	梁仲華
Liao Taichu	廖泰初
Lin Tongji	林同濟
Lin Weiying	林維英
Lin Yaohua (Lin Yueh-hua)	林耀華
Lin Yutang	林語堂
Ling Bing	凌冰
Liu Dajun (D. K. Lieu)	劉大鈞
Liu Duansheng	劉端生
Liu Huaipu	劉懷溥
Liu Shaoqi	劉少奇
Liu Yuwan (Wellington Liu)	劉馭萬
Longyou (Zhejiang)	龍游
Makesi zhuan (*A Biography of Marx*)	馬克斯傳
Ma Yinchu	馬寅初
Mancheng (Hebei)	滿城
Mantetsu chōsabu	滿鐵調查部
Mao Zedong	毛澤東
Mei Yibao (Mei Yi-pao)	梅貽寶
Meng Qinxiang	孟琴襄
Mingde Middle School (Changsha)	明德中學
Nakanishi Tsutomu	中西功
Nanhe (Hebei)	南和
Nanpi (Hebei)	南皮
Ninggang (Jiangxi)	寧岡

Ozaki Shōtarō	尾崎庄太郎
Panyu (Fanyu, Guangdong)	番禺
Peng Pai	彭湃
Pi Xian (Jiangsu)	邳縣
Qian Duansheng	錢端生
Qian Junrui	錢俊瑞
Qidong (Jiangsu)	啟東
Qing Xian (Hebei)	青縣
Qinghe (Hebei)	清河
Qu (ward)	區
Qu Shiying (Qu Junong 瞿菊農)	瞿世英
Qu Qiubai	瞿秋白
Ren Hongjun (Zen Hung-chün)	任鴻雋
Ren Zongji	任宗濟
Renxiang (Wuxi)	任巷
Rōnō-ha (Labor-Farmer faction)	勞農派
Sang Hengkang	桑恒康
Shao Lizi	邵力子
"*Shatian*" (polder fields)	沙田
Shehui kexue gailun (*Introduction to the Social Sciences*)	社會科學概論
shequ yanjiu ("community studies")	社區研究
Shi Guoheng	史國衡
Shi Kaifu	石凱福
Shiratori Keisuke	白鳥啟介
Shiroshi Nasu	那須皓
Shiying li (Sz Ying Li, in the International Settlement in Shanghai)	時應里
Shou Jingwei (Kinn-Wei Shaw)	壽景偉
Shulu (Hebei)	束鹿
sida jingang ("Four Guardians")	四大金剛
sishu (the "old-fashioned" schools)	私塾
Song Qingling (Madam Sun Yat-sen)	宋慶齡
Su (Anhui)	宿縣
Sugimoto Shūrō	杉本俊朗
Suide (Shaanxi)	綏德
Sun Xiaocun	孫曉村
Sun Yat-sen	孫中山
Sun Yefang	孫冶方
Sung Xia (Sung Zejiu 宋則九)	宋俠
Sung Zuonan	宋作楠
Taiyuan (Shanxi)	太原
Tao Menghe	陶孟和
Tian Rukang (T'ien Ju-k'ang)	田汝康
Tongsu Ziben lun (*Das Kapital: An Easy Reader*)	通俗資本論
Tōyō Bunko (the Oriental Library)	東洋文庫
Wang Ganyu	王贛愚
Wang Guozhong	王國忠

273

Wang Hechen	王賀宸
Wang Jichang (Wang Tsi Chang)	王際昌
Wang Jingbo	王景波
Wang Ming	王明
Wang Shijie	王世杰
Wang Wenjun	王文鈞
Wang Yaoyu	王藥雨
Wang Yichang	王宜昌
Wang Yinsheng	王寅生
Wang Yunwu	王雲五
Wang Yuquan	王毓銓
Wang Zhanyuan	王占元
Wang Zhengting (C. T. Wang)	王正廷
Weinan (Shaanxi)	渭南
Weiting (Yuan Shikai's courtesy name)	慰庭
Wenshang (Shandong)	汶上
Wofosi (Beijing)	臥佛寺
Wu Bannong	吳半農
Wu Baoan	吳保安
Wu Daye	吳大業
Wu Huabao	吳華寶
Wu Jingchao	吳景超
Wu Wenzao	吳文藻
Wu Yuzhen	吳榆珍
Wu Zhi	吳知
Wuhu (Anhui)	蕪湖
Wutai county (Shanxi)	五台
Wuxi (Jiangsu)	無錫
Xian Xian (Hebei)	獻縣
Xiandai shehuixue (*Modern Sociology*)	現代社會學
xiang (rural township)	鄉
Xiao Chunü	蕭楚女
Xiao Gongquan (Hsiao Kung-ch'üan)	蕭公權
Xiao Ju	蕭蘧
Xie Wanying (Bingxin 冰心)	謝婉瑩
Xin shehui (New Society)	新社會
Xingguo (Jiangxi)	興國
Xingtai (Hebei)	邢台
xiucai (Licentiate)	秀才
Xiushan (Li Chun's courtesy name)	秀山
Xu Dishan	許地山
Xu Langguang (Francis Hsu)	許烺光
Xu Shichang	徐世昌
Xu Shilian (Leonard Hsu)	許仕廉
Xu Shuxi	徐淑希
Xu Yongshun	徐雍舜
Xue Muqiao	薛暮橋

Xunwu (Jiangxi)	尋烏
Xuzhou (Jiangsu)	徐州
Yan Fu	嚴復
Yan Jingyao	嚴景耀
Yan Xishan	閻錫山
Yan Yangchu (James Yen)	晏陽初
Yancheng (Jiangsu)	鹽城
Yanshan (Hebei)	鹽山
Yang Hucheng	楊虎城
Yang Jingnian	楊敬年
Yang Kaidao (Cato Young)	楊開道
Yang Kaihui	楊開慧
Yang Maochun (Martin Yang)	楊懋春
Yang Qingkun (C. K. Yang)	楊慶堃
Yang Quan	楊銓
Yangtzepoo (Yangshupu)	楊樹浦
Ye Qianji (Yieh Chien-chih)	葉謙吉
Yongxin (Jiangxi)	永新
Yu Chuanjian	喻傳鑒
Yu Rizhang (Yui, David Z. T.)	余日章
Yu Shiyu	于式玉
Yu Shunzhi (Shwen Dji Yu)	余舜芝
Yu Youren	于右任
Yuan Shikai	袁世凱
Yuan Wenbo	袁文伯
Yue Yongqing	樂永慶
Yun Daiying	惲代英
Zhang Boling	張伯苓
Zhang Chunming	張純明
Zhang Hongjun	張鴻鈞
Zhang Jiafu	張稼夫
Zhang Jinjian	張金鑑
Zhang Mengling	張孟令
Zhang Pengchun	張彭春
Zhang Tailei	張太雷
Zhang Xichang	張錫昌
Zhang Zhicheng	張志澄
Zhang Ziyi	張子毅
Zhang Zuolin	張作霖
Zhao Chengxin	趙承信
Zhao Renjun	趙人儁
Zhao Ziyang	趙紫陽
Zheng Zhenduo	鄭振鐸
Zhongguo nongcun jingji yanjiuhui (the Society for the Study of China's Agrarian Economy)	中國農村經濟研究會
Zhou Songxi	周頌西
Zhou Ziqi	周自齊

Zhou Zuomin (Chow Tso-min)	周作民
Zhuo Xian (Hebei)	涿縣
zigengnong (owner-cultivators)	自耕農
Zouping (Shandong)	鄒平

Bibliography

ARCHIVES AND PERSONAL PAPERS

Academia Sinica Archives (*Zhongyang yanjiuyuan dang*), Second Historical Archives of China (Zhongguo Dier lishi dang'anguan), Nanjing, China.

Grace Boynton Papers, Schlesinger Library at Radcliffe College, Harvard University.

John B. Condliffe Papers, Bancroft Library, University of California, Berkeley.

Wilma Fairbank Papers, Cambridge, Massachusetts.

Institute of Pacific Relations Papers (cited as IPR), Rare Books and Manuscript Division, Butler Library, Columbia University.

Bronislaw Malinowski Papers, Sterling Library, Yale University.

Princeton-in-Asia Files, Seeley G. Mudd Manuscript Library, Princeton University.

Robert Redfield Papers, Department of Special Collections, Regenstein Library, University of Chicago.

Rockefeller Archive Center (cited as RAC), North Tarrytown, New York.

James Shotwell Papers, Rare Books and Manuscript Division, Butler Library, Columbia University.

United Board for Christian Higher Education in Asia Archives (cited as UB), Yale Divinity School.

Ray Lyman Wilbur Papers, Hoover Institution for War and Peace, Stanford University.

YMCA Archives, University of Minnesota.

BOOKS AND ARTICLES CITED

Academia Sinica with Its Research Institutes. Nanjing, 1929.

Academia Sinica and Its National Research Institutes. Nanjing, 1931.

"Activities in America: Organization, Development and Present Status of the Princeton-in-Peking Work in U. S. A.," in C. A. Evans, comp., "Princeton in China: A Resume of Fifty Years of Work by Princeton-in-Peking and Princeton-Yenching Foundation" (unpublished MS), 3–7, Mudd Library, Princeton University.

Akin, William E. *Technocracy and the American Dream: The Technocrat Movement, 1900–1941.* Berkeley: University of California Press, 1977.

Alchon, Guy. *The Invisible Hand of Planning: Capitalism, Social Science, and the State in the 1920s.* Princeton: Princeton University Press, 1985.

Alitto, Guy. *The Last Confucian: Liang Shu-ming and the Chinese Dilemma of Modernity.* Berkeley: University of California Press, 1979.

Alley, Rewi. *At 90: Memoirs of My China Years: An Autobiography of Rewi Alley.* Beijing: New World Press, 1986.

Amano, Motonosuke. "Shina no tochi mondai ni kansuru bunken" (A Bibliographical Essay on Works Dealing with China's Land Problems), *Shanhai Mantetsu kikan* (Quarterly Journal of the Shanghai Office of the South Manchurian Railway company), I. 1 (April 1937), 215–26.

Arkush, David. *Fei Xiaotong and Sociology in Revolutionary China.* Cambridge, MA: Council on East Asian Studies, Harvard University, 1981.

Arnove, Robert, ed., *Philanthropy and Cultural Imperialism: Foundations at Home and Abroad.* Boston: G. K. Hall, 1980.

Bailey, Anne, and Llobera, Josep, eds. *The Asiatic Mode of Production: Science and Politics.* London: Routledge & Kegan Paul, 1981.

"Benhui juxing Su-Zhe-Yu-Shaan sisheng nongcun diaocha zhi choubei jingguo" (The Planning Process of the Surveys of the Four Provinces of Jiangsu, Zhejiang, Henan, and Shaanxi conducted by the Commission for Rural Rehabilitation), *Nongcun fuxing weiyuanhui huibao,* No. 2 (July 26, 1933), 16–33.

Berger, Peter, and Luckmann, Thomas. *The Social Construction of Reality: A Treatise of the Sociology of Knowledge.* New York: Doubleday, 1967.

Bi, Xianghui. "Gaoyang, Baodi liangge mianzhi qu zai Hebei sheng xiangcun gongye shang zhi diwei" (The Positions of the Two Cotton Weaving Districts, Gaoyang and Baodi, in Rural Industries in the Hebei Province), in Fang Xianting, ed., *Zhongguo jingji yanjiu,* Vol. 2, 664–76.

Boorman, Howard, and Howard, Richard, eds. *Biographical Dictionary of Republican China.* 4 vols. New York: Columbia University Press, 1967.

Brandt, Loren. *Commercialization and Agricultural Development: Central and Eastern China, 1870–1937.* New York: Cambridge University Press, 1989.

Buck, J. Lossing. *An Economic and Social Survey of 102 Farms near Wuhu, Anhwei, China.* Nanjing: University of Nanking, Pt. I (December 1923), Pt. II (July 1924).

    An Economic and Social Survey of 150 Farms, Yenshan County, Chihli Province, China. Nanjing: University of Nanking, 1926.

    Chinese Farm Economy: A Study of 2866 Farms in Seventeen Localities and Seven Provinces in China. Chicago: University of Chicago Press, 1930.

Buck, Peter. *American Science and Modern China, 1876–1936.* New York: Cambridge University Press, 1980.

Bullock, Mary. *An American Transplant: The Rockefeller Foundation and Peking Union Medical College.* Berkeley: University of California Press, 1980.

Bulmer, Martin. "Support for Sociology in the 1920s: the Laura Spelman Rockefeller Memorial and the Beginnings of Modern, Large-Scale, Sociological Research in the University," *The American Sociologist,* 1982, Vol. 17 (November), 185–92.

The Chicago School of Sociology: Institutionalization, Diversity, and the Rise of Sociological Research. Chicago: University of Chicago Press, 1984.

Bulmer, Martin and Joan. "Philanthropy and Social Science in the 1920s: Beardsley Ruml and the Laura Spelman Rockefeller Memorial, 1922–1929," *Minerva*, XIX.3 (Autumn 1981), 340–407.

Bulmer, Martin, Bales, Kevin, and Sklar, Kathryn Kish, eds., *The Social Survey in Historical Perspective, 1880–1940*. Cambridge: Cambridge University Press, 1991.

Burgess, J. Stewart. "What Chinese Students Are Reading?" *The Intercollegian* (New York, November 1911), 31–7.

"Princeton's World Outlook: The Achievements and Future of the Princeton Center in China," *The Princeton Alumni Weekly*, XVI.34 (May 31, 1916), Supplement.

"China's Social Challenge: I, An opportunity for American Social Workers," *The Survey* (September 8, 1917), 501–3.

"China's Social Challenge: II, Beginnings of Social Investigation," *The Survey* (October 13, 1917), 41–4.

"Community Organization in the Orient," *The Survey* (June 25, 1921), 434–6.

"Statement Regarding Proposed Princeton School of Political and Social Science in Connection with Yenching University," *The Chinese Journal of Sociology*, II.5–6 (June–August 1925), 42–3.

"Where East Meets West," *The Princeton Alumni Weekly*, XXVIII.12 (December 1927), 338–40.

"Some Recollections of Princeton's Work in China," in C. A. Evans, comp., "Princeton in China: a Resume of Fifty Years of Work by Princeton-in-Peking and Princeton-Yenching Foundation," (unpublished MS), 8–15, Mudd Library, Princeton University.

Carter, Edward. "A Personal View of the Institute of Pacific Relations, 1925–1952," *Hearings on the Institute of Pacific Relations*, 82nd Congress, 2nd session, Pt. 14, 5316–36.

Chen, C. C. [Chen Zhiqian]. *Medicine in Rural China: A Personal Account*. Berkeley: University of California Press, 1989.

Chen, Hansheng. "Guanyu Baoding nongcun diaocha de yixie renshi" (Some Information about the Baoding Survey), *Nongye zhoubao* (Farmers' Weekly), No. 41 (July 27, 1930), 1120–1.

Zhongguo nongcun jingji yanjiu zhi faren (Genesis of Research on China's Agrarian Economy). Shanghai, 1930[?].

"The Agrarian Problem of China," in Bruno Lasker and W. L. Holland, eds., *Problems of the Pacific, 1933* (Chicago, 1934), 271–98.

Guangdong de nongcun shengchan guanxi yu nongcun shengchanli (The Production Relations and the Productive Forces in Guangdong). Shanghai, 1934.

Agrarian Problems in Southernmost China. Shanghai, 1936.

Landlord and Peasant in China: A Study of the Agrarian Crisis in South China. New York: International Publishers, 1936.

ed. *Agrarian China: Selected Source Materials from Chinese Authors*. Chicago: University of Chicago Press, 1939.

Industrial Capital and Chinese Peasants. Shanghai: Kelly and Walsh, Limited, 1939.

"Jiechu de Gongchan zhuyi zhanshi" (An Outstanding Communist Fighter) in Wang Xi and Yang Xiaofo, eds., *Chen Hansheng wenji* (A Collection of Chen Hansheng's Essays). Shanghai, 1985, 455–6.

"Zhuinian Cai Jiemin xiansheng" (Remembering Mr. Cai Yuanpei), in *Chen Hansheng wenji*, 452–4.

[as told to Ren Xuefang]. *Sige shidai de wo* (My Life across Four Epochs). Beijing, 1989.

Chen, Hansheng and Wang Yinsheng. *Heilongjiang liuyu de nongmin yu dizhu* (The Peasants and Landlords in the Amur Region). Shanghai 1929.

Chen, Tiejian. *Qu Qiubai zhuan* (A Biography of Qu Qiubai). Shanghai, 1986.

Chinese Students' Monthly. New Haven: 1906–31.

Chow, Tse-tsung. *The May Fourth Movement: Intellectual Revolution in Modern China.* Cambridge, MA: Harvard University Press, 1960.

Christian Education in China: the Report of the China Education Commission of 1921–1922. Shanghai, 1922.

"'Chūgoku shakaishi Ronsen' ni kansuru chōsa" (Research Works Related to "the Social History Debate in China"), *Ajia Keizai* (Monthly Journal of Institute of Developing Economies), 28.4 (April 1987), 61–82.

Clark, Terry. *Prophets and Patrons: The French University and the Emergence of the Social Sciences.* Cambridge, MA: Harvard University Press, 1973.

Cochran, Sherman. *Big Business in China: Sino-Foreign Rivalry in the Cigarette Industry, 1890–1930.* Cambridge, MA: Harvard University Press, 1980.

Cohen, Stephen. *Bukharin and the Bolshevik Revolution: A Political Biography, 1888–1938.* New York: Alfred A. Knopf, 1974.

Collins, S. B. "A Conference for Government School Students of North China," *The Intercollegian* (New York, November 1912), 31–4.

Commonwealth Fund. *The Commonwealth Fund: Historical Sketch, 1918–1962.* New York: Harkness House, 1963.

Condliffe, John B. "The Industrial Revolution in the Far East," *Economic Record* (Melbourne), II.3 (November 1926), 180–209; II.4 (May 1927), 82–101.

Reminiscences of the Institute of Pacific Relations. Vancouver, B.C.: University of British Columbia, 1981.

Converse, Jean. *Survey Research in the United States: Roots and Emergence 1890–1960.* Berkeley: University of California Press, 1987.

Cressy, Herbert. *Christian Higher Education in China.* Shanghai, 1928.

Davis, Allen. *Spearheads for Reform: The Social Settlements and the Progressive Movement, 1890–1914.* New York: Oxford University Press, 1967.

Deng, Jiarong. *Sun Yefang zhuan* (A Biography of Sun Yefang) (Taiyuan, 1998).

Dernberger, Robert. "Economics," in Anne Thurston and Jason Parker, eds., *Humanistic and Social Science Research in China: Recent History and Future Prospects* (New York: Social Science Research Council, 1980), 107–29.

"Diliu jie Nongmin yundong jiangxisuo banli jinguo" (The Sixth Session of the Peasant Movement Training Institute), *Diyi ci guonei geming zhanzheng shiqi de nongmin yundong ziliao* (Source Materials on the Peasant Movement During the Period of the First Revolutionary Civil War) (Beijing, 1983), 67–74.

Dirlik, Arif. *Revolution and History: the Origins of Marxist Historiography in China, 1919–1937*. Berkeley: University of California Press, 1978.

Dou, Shouyong and Su, Yumei. "Li Chun yisheng de julian" (Li Chun's Lifelong Plunder), *Tianjin wenshi ziliao xuanji* (A Selection of Literary and Historical Materials Related to Tianjin), No. 1 (Tianjin, 1978), 113–23.

Douw, Leo. "The Representation of China's Rural Backwardness, 1932–1937," Ph.D. Dissertation, University of Leiden, 1991.

Duara, Prasenjit. *Culture, Power, and the State: Rural North China, 1900–1942*. Stanford: Stanford University Press, 1988.

Esherick, Joseph. Review of Loren Brandt, *Commercialization and Agricultural Development: Central and Eastern China, 1870–1937, The Journal of Economic History*, 51.2 (June 1991), 501–3.

Evans, C. A. comp., "Princeton in China: a Resume of Fifty Years of Work by Princeton-in-Peking and Princeton-Yenching Foundation" (unpublished MS), deposited at the Mudd Library, Princeton University.

Fang, Xianting [H. D. Fong]. *Hosiery Knitting in Tientsin*. Tianjin, 1930.

ed., *Zhongguo jingji yanjiu* (Studies of Chinese Economy), 2 vols. Changsha, 1938.

Grain Trade and Milling in Tientsin. Tianjin, 1934.

"Huabei xiangcun zhibu gongye yu shangren guzhu zhidu" (Rural Weaving and the Merchant Employers in a North China District), *Zhengzhi jingji xuebao* (The Quarterly Journal of Economics and Political Science), Pt. I, III.4 (July 1935), 750–91; Pt. II, IV.1 (October 1935), 107–38.

Reminiscences of a Chinese Economist at 70. Singapore, 1975.

and Bi Xianghui. "You Baodi shouzhi gongye guancha gongye zhidu zhi yanbian" (The Evolution of An Industrial System: the Case of the Baodi Handloom Weaving Industry), *Zhengzhi jingji xuebao*, IV.2 (January 1936), 261–329.

and Wu Zhi. "Zhongguo zhi xiangcun gongye" (Rural Industries in China), *Jingji tongji jikan* (The Quarterly Journal of Economics and Statistics), II.3 (September 1933), 555–622.

Faure, David. *The Rural Economy of Pre-Liberation China: Trade Expansion and Peasant Livelihood in Jiangsu and Guangdong, 1870 to 1937*. Oxford: Oxford University Press, 1989.

Fei, Xiaotong. "Gui xing tongxun weisheng" (Epilogue to Letters from a Journey to Guangxi), "Shehui yanjiu," *Yishi bao*, n.s., No. 5, June 3, 1936.

"Xie zai 'Wenshang xian de sishu zuzhi' zhi qian" (Preface to "The Old-Fashioned Schools in Wenshang County"), *Yishi bao*, n.s., No. 15, August 12, 1936.

"Lunshi jiyan: i, benkan sannian de huiyi" (The London Letters: 1, Remembering the Three Years of History of this Supplement), "Shehui yanjiu," *Yishi bao*, n.s., No. 30, December 2, 1936.

"Lunshi jiyan: iii, guanyu shidi yanjiu" (The London Letters: 3, On Field Work), "Shehui yanjiu," *Yishi bao*, n.s., No. 44, March 10, 1937.

Peasant Life in China: A Field Study of Country Life in the Yangtze Valley. London: Routledge & Kegan Paul Ltd., 1939.

China Enters the Machine Age: A Study of Labor in Chinese War Industry. Cambridge, MA: Harvard University Press, 1944.

"Liu Ying ji" (Remembering My Journey to England to Study), *Wenshi ziliao xuanji* (Selected Sources on Literature and History), No. 31 (October 1962), 31–65.

Gary Hamilton and Wang Zheng, trs., *From the Soil: The Foundations of Chinese Society.* Berkeley: University of California Press, 1992.

Feng, Hefa. "Zhongguo nongcun jingji yenjiuhui manyi" (Random Memories of the Society for the Study of China's Agrarian Economy), *Wenshi ziliao xuanji*, No. 84, 43–75.

Feng, Huade. " 'Fuxing nongcun' de xianjue wenti: pingjun nongmin de fudan" ("A Prerequisite to 'the Rehabilitation of the Village:' An Equitable Tax Burden for all Peasants), "Jingji zhoukan" (Economic Weekly), 14, *Dagong bao*, May 24, 1933.

"Hebei sheng xian caizheng fenpei shang biaoxian de xingzheng xuruo zheng" (The Administrative Anemic Symptom Manifested in the Fiscal Revenue at both the Provincial and County Levels in Hebei), "Jingji zhoukan" (Economic Weekly), 86, *Dagong bao*, October 24, 1934.

(Zuo De). "Hebei sheng xian 'li' zhi de qian shili" (The Evil Force Lurking at the Back of the County Administration in the Hebei Province), "Jingji zhoukan" (Economic Weekly), 86, *Dagong bao*, October 24, 1934.

"Xian difang xingzheng zhi caizheng jichu" (The Financial Basis of County Government), *Zhengzhi jingji xuebao*, III.4 (July 1935), 697–749.

"Hebei sheng Ding Xian de yashui" (The Brokerage Taxes in Ding Xian, Hebei), *Zhengzhi jingji xuebao*, V.2 (January 1937), 285–322.

and Li Ling. "Hebei sheng Ding Xian zhi tianfu (Land Taxes in Ding Xian, Hebei), *Zhengzhi jingji xuebao*, IV.3 and Li Ling. (April 1936), 443–520.

and Li Ling. "Hebei sheng Ding Xian zhi tian fang qi shui" (Taxes on Land and House Ownership Registration in Ding Xian, Hebei), *Zhengzhi jingji xuebao*, IV.4 (July 1936), 751–800.

Feng, Huanian. "Zhongguo zhi zhishu" (Index Numbers in China), *Jingji tongji jikan*, I.4 (December 1932), 661–717.

Ferguson, Mary. *China Medical Board and Peking Union Medical College.* New York: China Medical Board of New York, Inc., 1970.

Finch, Percy. *Shanghai and Beyond.* New York: Charles Scribner's Sons, 1953.

Fisher, Donald. "The Role of Philanthropic Foundations in the Reproduction of Hegemony: Rockefeller Foundation and the Social Sciences," *Sociology*, 17.2 (May 1983), 206–33.

"Philanthropic Foundations and the Social Sciences: A Response to Martin Bulmer," *Sociology*, 18.4 (November 1984), 580–7.

Fisher, Irving Norton. *My Father Irving Fisher.* New York: Comet Press Books, 1956.

Fosdick, Raymond. *The Story of the Rockefeller Foundation.* New York: Harper, 1952.

Freidson, Eliot. *Profession of Medicine: A Study of the Sociology of Applied Knowledge.* New York: Harper & Row, 1970.

Galbiati, Fernando. *P'eng P'ai and the Hai-Lu-Feng Soviet.* Stanford: Stanford University Press, 1985.

Gamble, Sidney and Burgess, J. Stewart. *Peking: A Social Survey.* New York: Geroge H. Doran, 1921.

Garrett, Shirley. *Social Reformers in Urban China: the Y.M.C.A., 1895–1926.* Cambridge, MA: Harvard University Press, 1970.

Gramsci, Antonio, eds. and trans., Quintin Hoare and Geoffrey Nowell Smith. *Selections from the Prison Notebooks of Antonio Gramsci.* New York: International Publishers, 1971.

Gransow, Bettina. *Geschichte der chinesischen Soziologie.* Frankfurt/Main; New York: Campus Verlag, 1992.

Great Soviet Encyclopedia. New York: MacMillan, Inc., 1976.

Guo, Tingyi (Kuo T'ing-yee). "He Cuilian xiansheng nianbiao" (A Chronological Table of Mr. He Lian's life), (incomplete, n.d.), in Mrs. Franklin Ho's possession, New York City.

Guoli Zhongyang yanjiuyuan shijiu niandu zong baogao (Third Annual Report, Academia Sinica, 1930–1931). Nanjing, 1931.

Guoli Zhongyang yanjiuyuan ershi niandu zong baogao (Fourth Annual Report, Academia Sinica, 1931–1932). Nanjing, 1932.

Guoli Zhongyang yanjiuyuan yuanwu yuebao (Monthly Bulletin of Academia Sinica), I.3. September 1929, I.8. February 1930, II.1. July 1930, II.5. November 1930, II. 7. January 1931, II.9. March 1931.

Haas, William. *China Voyager: Gist Gee's Life in Science.* Armonk, New York: M. E. Sharpe, 1996.

Halpern, Nina. "Economic Specialists and the Making of Chinese Economic Policy, 1955–1983," Ph.D. Dissertation, University of Michigan, 1985.

Han, Dezhang. "Zhexi nongcun zhi jiedai zhidu" (The Credit Systems in West Zhejiang), *Shehui kexue zazhi* (Quarterly Review of the Social Sciences), III.2 (June 1932), 139–85.
"Zhexi nongcun zhi zudian zhidu" (Farm Tenancy in West Chekiang), IV.1 (March 1933), 34–53.

Han, Dezhang, and Qu Zhisheng. "Zhexi nongchan maoyi de jige shili" (Some Important Markets of Agricultural Products in West Chekiang), *Shehui kexue zazhi*, III.4 (December 1932), 444–78.

Han, Minghan [mo]. *Zhongguo shehuixueshi* (A History of Chinese Sociology). Tianjin: Tianjin Renmin chubanshe, 1987.

Hayford, Charles. *To the People: James Yen and Village China.* New York: Columbia University Press, 1990.

He, Ganzhi. *Zhongguo shehui xingzhi wenti lunzhan* (The Debate on the Problems Concerning the Nature of Chinese Society). Shanghai, 1937.

He, Lian (Franklin Ho). *Industrialization in China: A Study of Conditions in Tientsin.* Tianjin, 1929.
"Dong sansheng beibu jianglai yimin kenzhi liang guji" (An Estimate of the Capacity for Colonialization in Northern Manchuria), "Jingji yanjiu zhoukan" (Economic Research Weekly Supplement), *Dagong bao*, No. 15, June 8, 1930.
"Minguo yilai Dong sansheng nongye zhi fazhan" (The Development of Agri-

culture in Manchuria Since the Founding of the Republic), "Jingji yanjiu zhoukan," *Dagong bao*, August 17, 1930.

Population Movement to the Eastern Frontier in China. Tianjin, 1931.

"Zhonggu shi zhi Zhongguo jingji" (The Medieval Mode of Chinese Economy), *Duli pinglun* (Independent Review), 93 (March 25, 1934), 2–6.

"The Reminiscences of Ho Lien ([He Lian] Franklin Ho)." New York: East Asian Institute, Columbia University, 1972.

Henan sheng nongcun diaocha (The Agrarian Survey of the Henan Province). Nanjing, 1934.

Honig, Emily. *Sisters and Strangers: Women in the Shanghai Cotton Mills, 1919–1949*. Stanford: Stanford University Press, 1986.

Hopkins, C. Howard. *History of the Y.M.C.A. in North America*. New York: Association Press, 1951.

Hoston, Germaine. *Marxism and the Crisis of Development in Prewar Japan*. Princeton: Princeton University Press, 1986.

Hu, Shi. *Sishi zishu* (Autobiography at Forty). Shanghai, 1933.

"Chang Po-ling: Educator," *There is Another China* (New York, 1948), 4–14.

Hu Shi laiwang shuxin xuan (A Selection of Hu Shi's Correspondence), 3 vols, Beijing, 1979.

Huabei nongcun jianshe xiejinhui xunlian yanjiu weiyuanhui jilu (Minutes of the Committee on Training and Research of the North China Council for Rural Reconstruction) (n.p., n.d.).

Huang, Meizhen, et. al., eds. *Shanghai daxue shiliao* (Historical Materials on Shanghai University). Shanghai, 1984.

Huang, Philip. "Analyzing the Twentieth-century Chinese Countryside: Revolutionaries versus Western Scholarship," *Modern China*, I.2 (April 1975), 132–60.

The Peasant Economy and Social Change in North China. Stanford: Stanford University Press, 1985.

Ikeda, Kō., tr., Li Ji, "Shina shakai no hatten dankai, I," *Tōa* (East Asia), 7.1 (January 1934).

Ji, Xiaochun and Yang, Guzhi. "Zhou Zuomin yu Jincheng yinhang" (Zhou Zuomin and the Jincheng Banking Corporation), *Tianjin wenshi ziliao xuanji* (Selected Literary and Historical Sources on Tianjin), 13 (January 1981), 100–34.

Jiang, Tingfu. "The Reminiscences of Tsiang T'ing-fu (1895–1965)." New York: East Asian Institute, Columbia University, 1974.

Jiangsu sheng nongcun diaocha (The Agrarian Survey of Jiangsu Province). Nanjing, 1934.

"Jianxun" (News Summaries), *Shehui* (Society), No. 3 (June 20, 1983), 12.

Jincheng yinhang shiliao (Historical Materials on the Jincheng Banking Corporation). Shanghai, 1983.

Johnson, Chalmers. *An Instance of Treason: Ozaki Hotsumi and the Sorge Spy Ring*. Stanford: Stanford University Press, 1964.

Karl, Barry and Katz, Stanley. "Foundations and Ruling Class Elites," *Daedalus* (Winter 1987), 1–40.

284

Kautsky, Karl, tr., Pete Burgess. *The Agrarian Question* (*Die Agrarfrage*, originally published in 1899), two vols. London: Zwan Publications, 1988.

Kawachi, Jūzō. "1930 nendai Chūgoku no nominsō bunkai no haaku no tame ni" (Understanding Social Stratification among the Chinese Peasantry in the 1930s), *Rekishigaku kenkyū* (Historical Studies), 290 (July 1964), 27–41.

Klein, Donald, & Clark, Anne, eds. *Biographic Dictionary of Chinese Communism, 1921–1965*, 2 vols. Cambridge, Mass.: Harvard University Press, 1971.

Kuhn, Philip. "Local Taxation and Finance in Republican China," in Susan Mann Jones, ed., *Select Papers from the Center for Far Eastern Studies*, University of Chicago, No. 3, 1978–9, 100–36.

Kuklick, Henrika. "The Sins of the Fathers: British Anthropology and African Colonial Administration," Rober Jones, ed., *Research in Sociology of Knowledge, Sciences, and Art*. Greenwich, Conn.: JAI Press, Inc., 1978, 93–119.

Latourette, Kenneth. *World Service*. New York: Association Press, 1957.

Lenin, V. I. "The Development of Capitalism in Russia" in *V. I. Lenin: Collected Works*. Moscow, 1960, Vol. 3, 23–607.

Li, Ji. *Makesi zhuan* (A Biography of Marx). Shanghai, 1926.

Tongsu Ziben lun (*Das Kapital: An Easy Reader*). Shanghai, 1930.

Wo de shengping (My Life), 2 vols. Shanghai, 1932.

Li, Jinghan. "Beijing wuchanjieji de shenghuo" (Lives of the Proletariat in Beijing), *Shenghuo* (Life Weekly), I.37 (July 4, 1926), 218.

"Shenru minjian de yixie jingyan yu ganxiang" (Some Experiences and Thoughts from My Efforts to Immerse Myself with the Masses), *Duli pinglun* (Independent Review), 179 (December 1, 1935), 8.

Li, Yunhan. *Cong rongGong dao qingdang* (From Admitting the Communists to the Purification of the Guomindang). Taipei, 1966.

Liao, Kaisheng. "Shehui kexue yanjiusuo Wuxi nongcun diaocha jilue" (A Brief Account of the Wuxi Survey Conducted by the Institute of the Social Sciences), *Guoli Zhongyang yanjiuyuan yuanwu yuebao*, I.8. February, 1930, 9–15.

Liao, Taichu. "Wenshang xian de sishu zuzhi, xu wan" (Old-Fashioned Schools in Wenshang, Continued), "Shehui yanjiu," *Yishi bao*, n.s., No. 19, September 9, 1936.

"Rural Education in Transition: A Study of the Old-Fashioned Chinese Schools (*Ssu-shu*) in Shantung and Szechuan," *The Yenching Journal of Social Studies*, IV.2 (February, 1949), 19–67.

Lilley, Charles. "Tsiang T'ing-fu: Between Two Worlds, 1895–1935," Ph.D. Dissertation, University of Maryland, 1979.

Lin, Shuiyuan. "Zhuming de shijie jingjixuejia Qian Junrui" (The Famous Economist on the World Economy: Qian Junrui) in Sun Liancheng and Lin Pu eds., *Zhongguo dangdai zhuming jingji xuejia* (Noted Economists in Contemporary China) (Chengdu, 1985), Vol. I, 388–483.

Lin, Yaohua. *The Golden Wing: A Sociological Study of Chinese Familism*. London: Kegan Paul, Trench, Trubner & Co., Ltd., 1947.

Lubove, Roy. *The Professional Altruist: The Emergence of Social Work as a Career, 1880–1930*. Cambridge, MA: Harvard University Press, 1965.

MacIver, Robert. "Report on The Inquiry." n.p., n.d.
As a Tale That Is Told. Chicago: University of Chicago Press 1968.

MacKinnon, Janice and Stephen. *Agnes Smedley: The Life and Times of an American Radical*. Berkeley: University of California Press, 1988.

MacKinnon, Stephen. "The Life and Times of Chen Han-sheng (1897–)," *Selected Papers in Asian Studies*, Paper No. 35 (Western Conference of the Association for Asian Studies, 1990).

Mao, Zedong. "Report of an Investigation into the Peasant Movement in Hunan," *Selected Works of Mao Tse-tung*, I. New York: International Publishers, 1954, 21–59.

"How to Differentiate the Classes in the Rural Areas," *Selected Works of Mao Tse-tung*, I. Beijing, 1965, 137–9.

"On Tactics against Japanese Imperialism," *Selected Works of Mao Tse-tung*, I, 153–78.

"Guomin geming yu nongmin yundong: Nongmin wenti congkan xu" (National Revolution and the Peasant Movement: a Preface to the *Series of Peasant Problems*), Takeuchi Minoru, ed., *Mao Zedong ji* (The Collected Works of Mao Zedong) (Tokyo, 1972), I, 177–8.

"Hunan de nongmin" (The Peasants in Hunan), *Mao Zedong ji*, I, 187–200.

Mao Zedong nongcun diaocha wenji (A Collection of Mao Zedong's Agrarian Investigation Essays). Beijing, 1982.

Mao, Tianqi. "Wei zhenli er xiansheng de guanghui bangyang: Sun Yefang zhuan-lue" (A Glorious Model of Sacrificing Oneself for Truth: A Biographical Sketch of Sun Yefang), *Economics Daily*, ed., *Zhongguo dangdai jingjixue-jia zhuanlue* (Biographical Sketches of Contemporary Chinese Economists) (Liaoning, 1986), 365–412.

Marx, Karl. *A Contribution to the Critique of Political Economy*. New York: International Publishers, 1970.

Matthews, Fred. H. *Quest for an American Sociology: Robert E. Park and the Chicago School*. Montreal: McGill-Queen's University Press, 1977.

McClymer, John. *War and Welfare: Social Engineering in America, 1890–1925*. Westport, Ct.: Greenwood Press, 1980.

The Modern Encyclopedia of Russian and Soviet History. New York: Academic International Press, 1982.

Myers, Ramon. *The Chinese Peasant Economy: Agricultural Development in Hopei and Shantung, 1890–1949*. Cambridge, Mass.: Harvard University Press, 1970.

Nankai Institute of Economics: Its History and Work, 1927–1936. Tianjin, 1937.

Nankai daxue xiaoshi: 1919–1949 (A History of Nankai University: 1919–1949). Tianjin, 1989.

Nankai University Committee on Social and Economic Research: Work and Project. November 1928.

The National Cyclopaedia of American Biography. New York, 1954, 39.423–4.

Naughton, Barry. "Sun Yefang: Toward a Reconstruction of Socialist Economics," in Carol Hamrin and Timothy Cheek, eds., *China's Establishment Intellectuals*. Armonk, New York: M. E. Sharpe, 1986, 124–54.

Ozaki, Shōtarō. *Haikai: ichi Chūgoku kenkyūka no kaisō* (Wandering: The Reminiscences of a China Scholar). Tokyo: Ni-Chū Shuppan, 1981.

Palmer, Vivien. *Field Studies in Sociology: A Student's Manual.* Chicago: University of Chicago Press, 1928.

Petracca, Mark and Xiong, Mong. "The Concept of Chinese Neo-Authoritarianism," *Asian Survey*, XXX.11 (November 1990), 1099–117.

Pickowicz, Paul. *Marxist Literary Thought in China: The Influence of Ch'ü Ch'iu-pai.* Berkeley: University of California Press, 1981.

Princeton Peking Gazette, I.1 (February 1925); II.2 (January 1927).

"The Princeton Work in Peking." n.p., n.d.

Qian, Jiaju. *Qishi nian de jingli* (A Career of Seventy Years). Hong Kong, 1986.

Qian, Junrui. "Zhongguo nongcun jingji yanjiuhui chengli qianhou" (Events surrounding the founding of the Society for the Study of China's Agrarian Economy), *Wenshi ziliao xuanji* (Selections of materials on history and literature), No. 84 (December 1982), 19–26.

Qian, Xuesen and Wu Jiapei. "Zuzhi guanli shehui zhuyi jianshe de jishu – shehui gongcheng" (The Technology That Organizes and Manages Socialist Reconstruction – Social Engineering), *Jingji guanli* (Economic Management), 1979.1, 5–9.

Qin, Liufang. "Dui 'Jiefang qian lao shehui gongzuozhe de nongcun diaocha' yi wen de yijian" (Some Points of Correction on the Article "The Agrarian Surveys by Former Social Researchers before Liberation"), *Shehui* (Society), No. 3 (June 20, 1984), 63.

Qinghua daxue xiaoshi gao (A Draft History of Qinghua University). Beijing, 1981.

Qu, Qiubai. "Xiandai Zhongguo suo dangyou de 'Shanghai daxue'" (A "Shanghai University" That Contemporary China Should Have) *Shanghai daxue shiliao*, 1–13.

Ren, Xuefang. "Makesi zhuyi nongcun jingjixue de xianqu: Chen Hansheng shilue" (A Pioneer in Marxist Agrarian Economy: A Biographical Sketch of Chen Hansheng), in *Economics Daily*, ed., *Zhongguo dangdai jingjixuejia zhuanlue* (Biographical Sketches of Contemporary Chinese Economists) (Liaoning, 1986), 78–115.

"Research: Special Research Conference in Tokyo," *I.P.R. Notes*, No. 2 (February 1935), 16–41.

Schmutz, Georges-Marie. *La sociologie de la Chine: Matériaux pour une histoire 1748–1989.* Berne: Peter Lang Sa., 1993.

Schneider, Laurence. *Ku Chieh-kang and China's New History.* Berkeley: University of California Press, 1971.

Schram, Stuart. *Mao Tse-tung.* New York: Simon and Schuster, 1966.

Schwartz, Benjamin. *Chinese Communism and the Rise of Mao.* Cambridge, MA: Harvard University Press, 1951.

Shaanxi sheng nongcun diaocha (The Agrarian Survey of Shaanxi Province). Nanjing, 1934.

Sheridan, James. *Chinese Warlord: The Career of Feng Yü-hsiang.* Stanford: Stanford University Press, 1966.

Shinian lai de Nankai jingji yanjiusuo (The Nankai Institute of Economics in the Past Ten Years). Tianjin, 1937.

Shils, Edward. *The Calling of Sociology and Other Essays on the Pursuit of Learning*. Chicago: University of Chicago Press, 1980.

Shiratori, Keisuke, tr., *Rōshia ni okeru shihon shūgi no hattatsu* (The Development of Capitalism in Russia). Tokyo: Hakuyō sha, 1930.

Shotwell, James. "Report of the Director of the Program of Research in International Relations for the Year 1931, Social Science Research Council" (n.p., n.d.), Pt. IV.

Smedley, Agnes. *Battle Hymn of China*. New York: Alfred A. Knopf, 1943.

Stross, Randall. *The Stubborn Earth: American Agriculturalists on Chinese Soil, 1898–1937*. Berkeley: University of California Press, 1986.

"Suggestions for the Organization of An Institute of Social and Economic Research," prepared by the Commission of Social Research in China, *The Chinese Journal of Sociology*, II.5–6 (June–August 1925), 19–42.

Sugimoto, Shūrō. *Chūgoku nōson mondai* (China's Agrarian Problems). Tokyo: Iwanami Shoten, 1940.

Sun, Baoshan [Sun Yefang]. "Shanghai fangzhichang zhong de baoshenzhi gongren" (Contract Laborers in Shanghai's Cotton Mills), originally published in *Huanian* (Huanian weekly), I. 22 (September 10, 1932), 430–2; I.24 (September 24, 1932), 467–72, and reprinted in *Sun Yefang xuanji* (Selected Works of Sun Yefang) (Shanxi, 1984), 1–10.

Sun, Chung-hsing. "The Development of the Social Sciences in China before 1949," Ph.D. Dissertation, Columbia University, 1987.

Sun, E-tu Zen. "The Growth of the Academic Community 1912–1949," in John K. Fairbank and Albert Feuerwerker, eds., *The Cambridge History of China*, Vol. 13, 361–420.

Sun, Xiaocun. "Zhongguo nongcun jingji yanjiuhui yu Nongcun fuxing weiyuanhui" (The Society for the Study of China's Agrarian Economy and the Rural Rehabilitation Commission), *Wenshi ziliao xuanji*, No. 84 (December 1982), 30–7.

Sun, Yefang. "Minzu wenti he nongmin wenti" (National Problem and the Peasant Question), *Zhongguo nongcun*, 2.7 (July 1936), 23–30.

Tai, Kuo-hui. "Chūgoku 'shakaishi ronsen' shōkai ni miraleru jakkan no mondai" (Some Problems Embedded in [Japanese] Surveys of "the Social History Debate" in China), *Ajia Keizai*, 13.1 (January 1972), 57–72.

Tamaki, Hideo [Ozaki Shōtarō]. "Chūgoku nōson shakai keizai no gendankai narabini sono kenkyū hōhōron jo no ronsō o miru" (On the Debate on the Present Stage of China's Agrarian Economy and its Methodology), *Keizai hyōron* (Economic Review), III, 4 (April 1936), 130–46; III. 5 (May 1936), 102–21; III. 6 (June 1936), 74–90.

Tao, Juyin. *Beiyang junfa tongzhi shiqi shihua* (An Anecdotal History of the Period under the Northern Warlords). Beijing, 1958.

Tao, Menghe. "Beijing renli chefu zhi shenghuo qingxing" (Lives of Rickshaw Pullers in Peking) in *Menghe wencun* (A Collection of Tao Menghe's Essays) (Shanghai, 1926), *juan* II, 101–21.

Tawney, R. H. *Land and Labour in China*. London: Allen and Unwin, 1932; paperback edition, Boston: Beacon Press, 1966.

Tayler, J. B. *Farm and Factory in China: Aspects of the Industrial Revolution*. London: Student Christian Movement, 1928.

Terrill, Ross. *R. H. Tawney and His Times*. Cambridge, MA: Harvard University Press, 1973.

Mao: A Biography. New York: Harper & Row, 1980.

Thayer, Mary. *Hui-lan Koo [Madame Wellington Koo]: An Autobiography as Told to Mary Van Rensselaer Thayer*. New York: Dial Press, 1943.

Thomas, John. *The Institute of Pacific Relations: Asian Scholars and American Politics*. Seattle: University of Washington Press, 1974.

Thompson, Roger, tr. *Report from Xunwu*. Stanford: Stanford University Press, 1990.

Thomson, James. *While China Faced West: American Reformers in Nationalist China, 1928–1937*. Cambridge, Mass.: Harvard University Press, 1969.

Vishnyakova-Akimova, Vera Vladimirovna. *Two Years in Revolutionary China, 1925–1927*. Cambridge, MA: East Asian Research Center, Harvard University, 1971.

[Wang, Jiagui]. "Yang Hansheng tongzhi tan ershi niandai de Shanghai daxue" (Comrade Yang Hansheng's Reminiscences of Shanghai University during the 1920s), *Shehui* (Society), 1984.3 (June 1984), 1–4.

Wang, Shuhuai. *Gengzi peikuan* (The Boxer Indemnity). Taipei, 1974.

Wang, Weixian. "'Mofan xian' qi yu 'shiyan xian' qi de Ding Xian xianzheng" (County Administration in Ding Xian During Its "Model County" and "Experimental County" Phases), *Zhengzhi jingji xuebao*, V.3 (April 1937), 635–93.

Wang, Yaoyu. "Dong sansheng zudian zhidu" (The System of Land Tenure in Manchuria), *Zhengzhi jingji xuebao*, III.1 (October 1934), 80–108.

"Jin ershinian lai Shandong Yidu xian wushi ge nongcun de nonghu he gendi suoyouquan zhi bianqian" (The Changes in Peasant Households and Land Ownership in Fifty Villages in Yidu County in Shandong in the Past Twenty Years), "Jingji yanjiu zhoukan," *Dagong bao*, No. 115 (May 29, 1935).

"Shandong nongmin licun de yige jiantao" (An Analysis of the Reason Why Peasants in Shandong Left Their Villages), in Fang Xianting, ed., *Zhongguo jingji yanjiu*, Vol. 1, 178–87.

"Dongbei nongcun de 'maiqing' zhidu" (The System of 'Sale before the Harvest' in Manchuria), in Fang Xianting, ed., *Zhongguo jingji yanjiu*, Vol. 1, 262–72.

"Dong sansheng 'xiang' de chayi" (The Variation of the 'Hsiang' Size in Manchuria), in Fang Xianting, ed., *Zhongguo jingji yanjiu*, Vol. 1, 406–10.

Wang, Yichang. "Nongcun jingji tongji yingyou de fangxiang zhuanbian" (The Need to Reorient Our Approach to Agrarian Statistics), reprinted in *Zhongguo nongcun*, I.6 (March 1935), 107–11.

"He Riben de Zhongguo yanjiuzhe lun nongcun jingji" (Discussing the Agrarian Economy with a Japanese China Scholar), *Zhongguo jingji*, IV.5 (May 15, 1936), 97–105.

Wang, Zhixin. "Hebei sheng zhi baoshui zhidu" (The System of Tax Farming in Hebei Province), *Zhengzhi jingji xuebao*, III.3 (April 1935), 530–89.

Watson, Rubie. *Inequality Among Brothers: Class and Kinship in South China.* Cambridge: Cambridge University Press, 1985.

Wei, Katherine and Quinn, Terry. *Second Daughter: Growing Up in China, 1930–1949.* Boston: Little, Brown and Company, 1984.

West, Philip. *Yenching University and Sino-Western Relations, 1916–1952.* Cambridge, MA: Harvard University Press, 1976.

Widmer, Ellen. "Qu Qiubai and Russian Literature," Merle Goldman, ed., *Modern Chinese Literature in the May Fourth Era.* Cambridge, MA: Harvard University Press, 1977, 103–25.

Willoughby, Charles. *Shanghai Conspiracy: the Sorge Spy Ring.* New York: E. P. Dutton & Company, 1952.

Wong, Siu-lun. *Sociology and Socialism in Contemporary China.* London: Routledge & Kegan Paul, 1979.

Wu Bannong. "Hebei xiangcun shicha yinxiang ji" (Impressions of a Study Tour of Villages in Hebei), Qian Jiaju ed., *Zhongguo nongcun jingji lunwen ji* (A Collection of Essays on Agrarian Economy in China) (Shanghai, 1936), 390–437.

Wu, Kaitai. "Qiushi he yanjin de Makesi zhuyi jingjixuejia: Xue Muqiao zhuanlue" (A Truth-Seeking and Rigorous Marxist Economist: A Biographical Sketch of Xue Muqiao), *Economics Daily*, ed., *Zhongguo dangdai jingji xuejia zhuanlue* (Biographical Sketches of Contemporary Chinese Economists) (Liaoning, 1986), 231–65.

Wu, Wenzao. "Xiandai shequ shidi yanjiu de yiyi he gongyong" (The Meaning and Function of Modern Community Studies), in *Shehui yanjiu* (Social Research), Nos. 51–100 (bound volume), (No. 66, January 9, 1935), 125–8.

"Wu Wenzao zizhuan" (Wu Wenzao's Autobiography), 20pp, reprint of the article originally published in *Jinyang xuekan* (Jinyang Bi-monthly), No. 6 (1982).

Wu, Xiangxiang. *Yan Yangchu zhuan* (A Biography of Yan Yangchu). Taipei, 1981.

Wu, Zhih. *Xiangcun zhibu gongye de yige yanjiu* (A Study of a Village Weaving Industry). Shanghai, 1936.

"Cong yiban gongye zhidu de yanjin guancha Gaoyang de zhibu gongye" (Gaoyang Weaving Industry: An Analysis of Its Development), *Zhengzhi jingji xuebao*, III.1 (October 1934), 39–79.

Xu, Shilian (Leonard Hsu). "Duiyu shehuixue jiaocheng de yanjiu" (A Study of the Curriculum of Sociology), *Shehuixue zazhi* (The Chinese Journal of Sociology), II.4 (April 1925), 1–11.

"The Teaching of Sociology in China," *Chinese Social and Political Science Review*, 11.3 (July 1927), 11–17.

"A Brief Report of the Extension and Research Work of the Department of Sociology and Social Work, Yenching University," March 17, 1930, *Sociology Fellowship News*, 4 (April 1930), 3–9.

Xu, Yinglian et al. *Quanguo xiangcun jianshe yundong gaikuang* (A General

Account of the Nationwide Rural Reconstruction Movement). Zouping, 1935.

Xue, Muqiao. "Gei Liu Shaoqi tongzhi xie de baogao – guanyu baiqu xiangcun he Zhongguo nongcun jingji yanjiuhui de gongzuo wenti" (A Report to Liu Shaoqi concerning Villages in the White Area and the Activities of the Society for the Study of China's Agrarian Economy), *Wenshi ziliao xuanji*, No. 84, 7–18.

Xue Muqiao huiyilu (The Memoirs of Xue Muqiao). Tianjin: Tianjin renmin chubanshe, 1996.

Yan, Fu. "Yuan qiang" (On Strength), Cuncui xueshe, comp., *Yan Fu sixiang zhitan* (Themes of Yan Fu's Thought). Hong Kong, 1980, 14–50.

Yang, Maochun. *Jindai Zhongguo nongcun shehui zhi yanbian* (The Transformation of Modern Chinese Rural Society). Taipei, 1980.

Yang, Ts'ui-hua. *Zhongjihui dui kexue de zanzhu* (Patronage of Sciences: The China Foundation For the Promotion of Education and Culture). Nankang, Taipei: Institute of Modern History, Academia Sinica, 1991.

Yang, Yabin. *Zhongguo shehuixueshi* (A History of Chinese Sociology). Jinan: Shandong Renmin chubanshe, 1987.

Yeh, Wen-hsin. *The Alienated Academy: Culture and Politics in Republican China*. Cambridge, MA: Council on East Asian Studies, Harvard University, 1990.

Yenching Faculty Bulletin, May 1, 1930.

Yu, Lin [Xue Muqiao]. "Jieshao bing piping Wang Yichang xiansheng guanyu Zhongguo nongcun jingji de lunzhu" (A Summary and Critique of Mr. Wang Yichang's Writings on China's Agrarian Economy), *Zhongguo nongcun*, I.8 (May 1935), 101–22.

Yue, Yongqing. "Hebei sheng shiyi xian caifu gaikuang" (Hsien Taxes in Hebei Province: A Sample Study), *Jingji tongji jikan* (The Quarterly Journal of Economics and Statistics), II.3 (September 1933), 623–92.

Zhang, Chunming. "Local Government Expenditure in China," *Monthly Bulletin of Economic China* 7.6 (June 1934), 233–47.

"Xunli yu xunli de zhengzhi" ("The Biographies of Model Officials" in Dynastic Histories: A Study), *Zhengzhi jingji xuebao* (The Quarterly Journal of Economics and Political Science), III.2 (January 1935), 225–48.

Zhang, Jinjian. *Mingcheng qishi zishu* (Mingcheng's [Zhang Jinjian's]. Reminiscences at Seventy). Taipei, 1972.

Zhang, Peigang. "Qingyuan de nongjia jingji" (Farm Economy in Tsing Yuen, Hebei), *Shehui kexue zazhi* (Quarterly Review of Social Sciences), Pt. I, VII.1 (March 1936), 1–65; Pt. II, VII.2 (June 1936), 187–266; and Pt. III, VIII.1 (March 1937), 53–120.

Zhang, Zhongfu. *Miwang ji* (A Record about Perplexity: An Autobiography). Hong Kong, 1968.

Zhao, Baoxu. "Sociology and Population Studies in China" ("Texas Population Research Center Papers," Series 5, 1983, the University of Texas at Austin.

Zhao, Chengxin. "Shehui diaocha yu shequ yanjiu" (Social Surveys and Community Studies), *Shehuixue jie* (Sociological World), Vol. 9 (August 1936), 151–205.

Zhejiangsheng nongcun diaocha (The Agrarian Survey of the Zhejiang Province). Nanjing, 1934.

[Zheng,] Zhengduo. "Fakan ci" (Inaugural Editorial), *Xin shehui* (The New Society) (November 1, 1919), 1.

"Zhongguo nongcun jingji diaochatuan jinkuang" (The Latest Activities of the Research Team on China's Agrarian Economy), *Nongye zhoubao* (Farmers' Weekly), 35 (June 15, 1930), 953–4.

INTERVIEWS

Chen Hansheng, Beijing, China, June 9, 1991.

Chen Zhiqian (C. C. Chen), Berkeley, CA, November 15, 1985.

Francis Hsu (Xu Langguang), San Francisco, CA, August 1983.

Huang Di, Framingham, MA, May 1982.

Li Shuqing, Arlington, VA, June 23, 1984.

Li Zhuomin (Li Choh-ming), Berkeley, CA, November 1985.

Lin Yaohua, Framingham, MA, May 7 and 8, 1982.

Qian Jiaju, Hacienda Heights, CA, October 20, 1990.

Tian Rukang, Cambridge, MA, January 1982.

Wu Daye, Palo Alto, CA, November 1985.

C. K. Yang (Yang Qingkun), Mars, PA, September 1985.

Shwen Dji Yu (Yu Shunzhi; Mrs. Franklin Ho [He Lian]), New York City, July 1985.

Index

Academia Sinica, 11, 51, 94, 164, 174, 181,
182, 183, 184, 185, 190, 198, 199, 211, 232
Adams, T. S., 87
agrarian crisis, 11, 165, 166, 167, 169, 174,
175, 176, 179, 184, 189, 190, 193, 195, 197,
198, 203, 206, 212, 218, 262; Chen
Hansheng's notion of and departure
from Kautsky's, 174–177, 187–189,
192–198; Kautsky's notion of, 174–177,
193–194
Alley, Rewi, 216
Alsberg, Carl, 93, 225
Amano, Motonosuke, 209, 210

Balfour, Marshall, 131, 236, 238, 252
Berlin, University of, 162
Bi, Xianghui, 119
Blaisdell, Thomas, 32
Blumer, Herbert, 4
Borchardt, Julian, 142
Boxer Indemnity, the, 82, 86, 160, 231
Boynton, Grace, 237
Brandt, Loren, 261, 262, 263
Brinton, Crane, 4
British-American Tobacco Company, 213
Brockman, Fletcher, 32
Buck, J. Lossing, 23, 91, 150, 167, 169, 170,
174, 176, 201–205, 212, 234, 244–245,
250–251
Buck, Pearl, 240
Bucklin, H. S., 23
Bukharin, Nikolai, 140, 141
Bureau of Agriculture and Industry
(Canton), 15
Bureau of Markets (Shanghai), 15
Burgess, John Stewart, 23, 25, 27; arrives in
Peking, 25, 26; returns to the U.S., 45;
and Peking Students' Social Service
Club, 28–31; social service philosophy
of, 34–37; solicitations of foundation

support by, 40–44; student work of,
26–27; and Yanjing Sociology
Department, 32–34, 37–39

Cai, Hesen, 142
Cai, Yuanpei, 164, 166, 181, 182
California, University of (Berkeley), 2, 3,
4, 83
Cambridge University, 5, 238
Cao, Rulin, 81
Carnegie Corporation, 3, 252
Carter, Edward, 90, 91, 95, 104, 212, 215,
217, 218, 219, 223, 224, 225, 245, 246
Cheeloo (Shangtung Christian) University,
52, 67, 68, 125, 253
Chen, C. C., 250
Chen, Da, 55, 240, 241
Chen, Duxiu, 139
Chen, Eugene, 50
Chen, Guangyuan, 80
Chen, Hansheng, 7, 11, 12, 13, 14, 15, 21,
22, 118, 136, 158, 159, 200, 203, 222, 254,
255, 257; and Academia Sinica, 164–166,
182–183; and Agnes Smedley, 179–180,
216; Amano Motonosuke on, 210–211;
Baoding survey of, 173–174, 175, 183,
190; on China's agrarian crisis, 167–169,
187–189, 192–198; clandstine and
Comintern activities of, 179–181,
215–216; conceptualization crisis of,
174–179; conversion to Marxism,
162–163; education in China, 159–160;
education and sojourns in the U.S.,
160–161, 217–220; exile in India, 220;
exiles in Moscow, 163–164, 216;
Guangdong survey of, 190–198, 215, 218,
264; hostility encountered during
fieldwork, 265–266; ignored by
Rockefeller Foundation, 210–211; and
Institute of Pacific Relations, 211–212,

Index

Kōza-ha (Lecture faction), 208, 209
Kōza-Rōnō (Lecture and Labor-Farmer factions) debate, 208
Ku, Susie (Gu Shuxing), Comintern activities with Richard Sorge, 180, 215; death during Cultural Revolution, 221; enrolls at Radcliffe College, 161; exiles in Moscow, 163–164, 216; in Hong Kong, 219; marries Chen Hansheng, 161
Kulp, Daniel, 23, 34
Kuznets, Simon, 4

Lasker, Bruno, 218
Lasswell, Harold, 4
Laura Spelman Rockefeller Memorial, 2, 3, 4, 5, 42, 43, 44, 49, 50, 55, 101, 223, 224, 226, 229
Lee, Franklin. *See* Li Jinghan
Lenin, V. I., 142, 177, 178, 179, 188, 189, 192, 193, 196, 202, 205, 206
Li, Anzhai, 56; caught in Yanjing politics, 237–238; fieldwork at Labrang, 74–75; and Rockefeller Foundation, 251–252
Li, Choh-ming, 83, 112
Li, Chun, 79–80, 82
Li, Dazhao, 162
Li, Ji, 142
Li, Ji (Li Chi), 84
Li, Jinghan, 20–21, 242–243
Li, Jitong, 86
Li, Quanshi, 16
Li, Rui, 20, 112, 126
Li, Youyi, 56, 73
Li, Yuanhong, 81
Liang, Qichao, 27, 260, 262
Liang, Shiyi, 99
Liang, Shuming, 68, 127
Liang, Zhonghua, 68
Liao, Taichu, 61, 74
Lieu, D. K. *See* Liu Dajun
Lin, Yaohua, 74, 171; and Fei Xiaotong, 238–240; functionalism of, 59–60; as member of Sociology Wing, 56
Lin, Yutang, 240
Ling, Bing, 83
Lingnan University, 190, 234
Liu, Dajun, 15, 234, 250
Liu, Shaoqi, 200
Liu, Yuwan, 233
London Missionary Society, 50, 235
London School of Economics, 3, 5, 57, 112
Loomis, Charles, 4
Lynd, Robert and Helen, 123, 251
Lyon, D. W., 32

Ma, Yinchu, 16
MacIver, Robert, 18
Mad'iar, Liudvig, 163
Malinowski, B., 57, 73, 75, 240, 241
Mantetsu (South Manchurian Railway Company), 209, 210, 264, 265
Mao, Zedong, 10, 11, 77, 122, 136, 144, 197, 200, 262, 267; agrarian surveys of, 148–157; agrarian survey legacies of, 157–158; fieldwork style and vision of, 154–157
Marx, Karl, 142, 143, 178, 205–206
Mason, Max, 228, 249
Mass Education Movement, 29, 47, 49, 58, 64, 65, 66, 68, 69, 70, 104, 108, 115, 124, 127, 173, 228, 246, 250, 251, 252–253
May Fourth Movement, 24, 29, 30, 54, 81, 87, 139, 140, 141, 147–148, 149, 233
May, Stacy, 247, 248
Mayo, Elton, 240, 241, 243
McCarran, Senator Pat, 219
McCarthy, Joseph, 219, 220
Mead, Margaret, 4
Mei, Yibao, 73, 74
Michigan, University of, 4
Minnesota, University of, 2, 4, 247
Mitchell, Wesley, 17
Monroe, Paul, 94
Moody, Dwight, 160
Mott, John, 32
Mount Hermon School for Boys, 160
Myers, Ramon, 261, 262

Nakanishi, Tsutomu, 209
Nankai University, financial basis of, 79–82; nationalized, 133, 135, 258; Western-educated faculty of, 82–87; Zhang Boling's vision for and contribution to, 78–79
Nankai University: Nankai Institute of Economics, 7, 8, 9, 11, 21, 66, 78, 85, 87, 102, 103, 104–112, 113, 114, 115, 123, 124, 125, 126, 129, 130, 131, 132, 133, 135, 159, 233, 244, 245
Nanking, University of, 23, 34, 68, 167, 202, 250
National Bureau of Economic Research, 3
National Central University, 52
National Council for Rural Reconstruction. *See* North China Council for Rural Reconstruction
National Research Council of the National Academy of Sciences (US), 3–4

296